Toronto
FOR
DUMMIES®
1ST EDITION

by Michael Kelly

John Wiley & Sons Canada, Ltd

Toronto For Dummies®

Published by
John Wiley & Sons Canada, Ltd
6045 Freemont Boulevard
Mississauga, Ontario, L5R 4J3
www.wiley.ca

National Library of Canada Cataloguing in Publication

Kelly, Michael B.

      Toronto for dummies / Michael B. Kelly.

Includes index.

ISBN - 13 978-0-470-83398-8

ISBN - 10 0-470-83398-X

      1. Toronto (Ont.)—Guidebooks. I. Title.

FC3097.18.K43 2004   917.13'541044   C2003-906729-7

Printed in Canada

1 2 3 4 5 TRI 09 08 07 06 05

Distributed in Canada by John Wiley & Sons Canada, Ltd.

For general information on John Wiley & Sons Canada, Ltd., including all books published by Wiley Publishing, Inc., please call our warehouse, Tel 1-800-567-4797. For reseller information, including discounts and premium sales, please call our sales department, Tel 416-646-7992. For press review copies, author interviews, or other publicity information, please contact our marketing department, Tel 416-646-4584, Fax 416-236-4448.

For authorization to photocopy items for corporate, personal, or educational use, please contact CANCOPY, The Canadian Copyright Licensing Agency, One Yonge Street, Suite 1900, Toronto, ON, M5E 1E5 Tel 416-868-1620 Fax 416-868-1621; www.cancopy.com.

About the Author

Michael Kelly is a freelance editor and writer, focusing on such diverse general interest topics as travel, sports, and religion. A seasoned traveler, he has lived on both U.S. coasts and in the U.S. Midwest before contentedly settling down with his wife and daughter in Toronto. As an editor and writer, Mike has contributed to dozens of . . . For Dummies titles. He can be reached at tofd@sympatico.ca.

Dedication

To Joan and Harper, who make Toronto home.

Author's Acknowledgments

In the odd sort of way that events sometimes progress, I would never have written this book without Diane Steele at Wiley Publishing in Indianapolis, who introduced me to the . . . For Dummies world and experience and who enlisted me to coach the Wiley Publishing team in Toronto through the publication of their first . . . For Dummies books. All that is a roundabout way of thanking Diane for her confidence in me, for her many hours mentoring me, and for our friendship. Thanks also to Robert Harris, the publisher — then and now — of those first . . . For Dummies books, for believing in this project and in me. An extra dose of gratitude goes to Melanie Rutledge for her enthusiasm and passion for this book — and for her faith in me to write it. Many thanks also to the editors who helped bring this book to completion, including Michelle Marchetti, Robert Hickey, Kelli Howey, and Allyson Latta. And finally, much love to Bruce and Judy, for letting me in on the excitement of traveling and living all over the world.

Publisher's Acknowledgments

We're proud of this book; please send us your comments at canadapt@wiley.com. Some of the people who helped bring this book to market include the following:

Editorial

Acquiring Editor: Melanie Rutledge

Associate Editor: Robert Hickey

Developmental Editors:
Kelli Howey, Allyson Latta

Copy Editor: Allyson Latta

Cartographer: Mapping Specialists

Cover Photos:

Front Cover Photo:
Alan Marsh/firstlight.ca

Back Cover Photo:
Corbis Digital Stock

Cartoons: Rich Tennant,
www.the5thwave.com

Production

Publishing Services Director:
Karen Bryan

Publishing Services Manager:
Ian Koo

Project Manager:
Elizabeth McCurdy

Project Coordinator: Pam Vokey

Layout: Pat Loi

Proofreader: Liba Berry

Indexer: Edna Barker

John Wiley & Sons Canada, Ltd.

Bill Zerter, Chief Operating Officer

Robert Harris, General Manager, Professional and Trade Division

Publishing and Editorial for Consumer Dummies

Diane Graves Steele, Vice President and Publisher, Consumer Dummies

Joyce Pepple, Acquisitions Director, Consumer Dummies

Kristin A. Cocks, Product Development Director, Consumer Dummies

Michael Spring, Vice President and Publisher, Travel

Kelly Regan, Editorial Director, Travel

Publishing for Technology Dummies

Andy Cummings, Vice President and Publisher,
Dummies Technology/General User

Composition Services

Gerry Fahey, Vice President of Production Services

Debbie Stailey, Director of Composition Services

Contents at a Glance

Maps at a Glance

Table of Contents

Introduction

• •

*T*oronto is a cosmopolitan city with a small-town feel in a metropolitan setting. All that's missing from anyone's definition of an ideal city are a waterfront locale and an outdoor landscape to rival the garden centers of the world — and Toronto has some of that too.

No Canadian city embraced the loosening of Canadian immigration policies in the 1970s more fervently than Toronto. And nowhere is this ethnic diversity more evident than in Toronto's restaurants — with more than 7,000 of them offering the city's very own gastronomic détente for the world's longest-standing cultural clashes: cuisines ranging from Indian to Pakistani, Croatian to Serbian, Chinese to Tibetan, Greek to Turkish, Canadian to American.

Toronto's cosmopolitan backdrop gives way to a very metropolitan scene when you step into its thriving Financial and Entertainment districts. The Financial District boasts its share of city skyscrapers housing the international headquarters for Canada's largest firms, leaving its lower levels open for occupants to high-step, and visitors to meander, through Toronto's underground — from building to building, subway station to subway station, making multiple stops for reliable, if not necessarily world-class, shopping along the way. (Most of Toronto's world-class shopping — and there is a ton of it — is actually aboveground.) Toronto's theater offerings are on par with (if not as abundant as) those of Broadway and London's West End. And the Toronto International Film Festival (held each September) is *the* symbolic indicator of the city's Hollywood North label.

As a complement to the city's hustle and electricity, at times you may be lucky enough to experience Toronto's small-town-ness. A city defined by its neighborhoods — some ethnic, some most WASP-ish — Toronto features quaint residential streets, with compressed and close-fitting homes and small community schools and parks; individual city blocks of independent businesses cater to the day-to-day needs of their residential neighbors. Of course, you may decide that it's only a small-town *feel,* after you've navigated Toronto's often-nightmarish traffic congestion to reach these charming areas.

About This Book

Toronto For Dummies, 1st Edition, is a travel guide and reference in one. Organized logically so that you can read it from cover to cover as you begin to plan, the book is also designed to be referred to again and again as you build your Toronto trip. When you're ready to book your hotel, and you need to find one that's within walking distance of the CN Tower and the Rogers Centre (formerly known as the SkyDome), turn to Chapter 9 — it offers reviews and locations of hotels, accompanied by a handy map to help you find your way. Then, skip to Chapter 10 to discover your dining-out options around the hotel you've booked.

This dive-in, dive-out design makes the book great for taking along on your trip — it's up to you whether you want to brazenly carry the guide around Toronto, or keep it under wraps in your hotel room. If you're looking for a particular restaurant in The Beaches neighborhood, or just need to know whether you need exact change to hop on the Queen streetcar to get there (you do), dive right in to the appropriate sections of this book (the extensive Table of Contents and Index are great tools for diving excursions), find out what you need to know, and then dive right out again, back to the streets of Toronto.

I've made every effort to provide accurate advice, but remember that travel information is subject to change at any time — and this is especially true of prices. I therefore suggest that you write or call ahead for confirmation when making your travel plans. The author, editors, and publisher cannot be held responsible for the experiences of readers while traveling; your safety is important to us, however, so we encourage you to stay alert and be aware of your surroundings. Keep a close eye on cameras, purses, and wallets, all favorite targets of thieves and pickpockets.

Dummies Post-it® Flags

As you read this book, you may find information that you may want to reference as you plan or enjoy your trip — whether a new hotel, a must-see attraction, or a must-try walking tour. To simplify your trip planning, mark these pages with the handy Post-it® Flags included in this book.

Conventions Used in This Book

I've organized this book so that you can quickly find the information you're looking for and then get back to planning your Toronto trip. It's your book: use Post-it® Flags or those annoying subscription cards that fall out of all your magazines to mark the sections you find yourself going back to again and again. Or just fold over the corners and, while you're at it, use a highlighter (preferably yellow — this is a ...*For Dummies* book, after all) to mark the details that are of greatest interest to you. (If you've borrowed this book from your local library, ignore the preceding sentence.)

In this book, I've included reviews of the hotels, restaurants, and attractions that I highly recommend. Included with each review are the details you'll need to get the most out of your trip planning, such as contact information, prices, opening hours, and so on. These details also include commonly accepted credit cards, using the following abbreviations:

AE	American Express
DC	Diners Club
MC	MasterCard
V	Visa

Hotel and restaurant reviews also include a system of dollar signs that show you what one night in that hotel or one meal at that restaurant is likely to cost you. Hotel prices are the rack rates for a double-occupancy room (see Chapter 9 for more about rack rates), and meal prices are for main courses, not including appetizers, dessert, or alcohol. The following table explains the dollar signs:

Cost	Hotel	Restaurant
$	C$100 (US$82) and under	Under C$10 (US$8.20)
$$	C$100–$175 (US$82–$144)	C$10–$20 (US$8.20–$16)
$$$	C$175–$250 (US$144–$205)	C$20–$30 (US$16–$25)
$$$$	C$250–$325 (US$205–$267)	Over C$30 (US$25)
$$$$$	C$325 (US$267) and above	

Foolish Assumptions

I've taken the liberty of making some assumptions about you and what
kind of information you may be looking for as you plan your trip to
Toronto. Any or all of these assumptions may apply to you and your
traveling companions; if so, I think you've made the right choice in picking
up this book.

- You're an experienced traveler, but you've never been to Toronto.
  Or you don't have a lot of time to devote to planning your trip and
  are looking for a book that offers expert advice and helpful reviews
  that will help you maximize your time when you get here.

- You're looking for a book that focuses on the places that will give
  you the best or most unique experiences that Toronto has to offer —
  not one that provides all the information available about Toronto,
  or one that lists every available hotel, restaurant, or attraction.

Toronto is an especially welcoming destination for families with children
and teens. From festivals and fairs to farms and flower shows, from
towering aboveground views to thriving belowground activities,
from sporting events to sporting goods, Toronto presents seemingly
endless opportunities for entertainment for every family member. If
you're bringing along the kids, this book has you in mind too.

How This Book Is Organized

Toronto For Dummies, 1st Edition, is broken down into informative,
bite-sized chunks of information so that you can review parts and
chapters on their own, focusing on the areas that interest you the most.
Or you can just start with Chapter 1 and read straight through. It's up to
you; either way, here is what you'll find.

Part I: Introducing Toronto

With the help of this part, you'll decide whether Toronto is the next
travel destination for you, and give some thought to the time of year you
plan to visit. I'll share the best of what makes Toronto such an inviting
travel choice; what the changing seasons bring; and a brief background
look at Toronto's history, cuisine, and standing in literature and film.

Part II: Planning Your Trip to Toronto

In Part II, you'll find the tools you need to get down to the nitty-gritty of trip planning. This part covers the variety of options you have for getting to Toronto, what kinds of budgeting questions to consider, and how Toronto stacks up as a destination for visitors with unique travel needs. Finally, this part includes a chapter to help you remember all those last-minute details that we always seem to forget until — well, the last minute.

Part III: Settling into Toronto

Think of this part as a primer for getting acclimated to Toronto after you arrive. With help from the three chapters in this part, you should be able to get a good feel for the city and its neighborhoods, review your options for getting around, and gather tips for choosing an area of town to stay in once you've arrived. You can also find information you'll need to book a room in one of Toronto's best lodging choices. This part also shares the scoop on eating out in Toronto, as well as eating out (of doors) in Toronto and eating out (of a paper bag) in Toronto.

Part IV: Exploring Toronto

You can use this part to plan your itinerary not only for Toronto, but also for some choice areas within a day's drive. In these chapters, you'll discover Toronto's top attractions, find out your best shopping options, discover how to check out Toronto by guided tour, and plan a day trip outside the city. I even offer a few customized itineraries to consider.

Part V: Living It Up after Dark: Toronto Nightlife

From world-class theater to improvisational comedy, from pubs and taverns to hotel bars and classy clubs, Toronto has many nightlife alternatives. This part discusses the best of the best, whether it's high culture that interests you — or the high life.

Part VI: The Part of Tens

A standard feature of every ...*For Dummies* book, this part provides some fun and even slightly irreverent lists to help you make sure your Toronto vacation stands out as one of your best. You'll find suggestions on how to spend some of your free time, recommendations for specific weeks to target for your trip, and tips for some great Toronto bargains.

Finally, after the Part of Tens, the Quick Concierge appendix includes some need-to-know facts about Toronto, as well as a handy list of travel-related phone numbers and Web sites. You can find this appendix pretty easily; it's printed on yellow paper near the back of the book.

Icons Used in This Book

As with any ...*For Dummies* book, the margins are loaded with icons — symbols to help you spot tidbits like useful tips, as well as flags to alert you to noteworthy information. This book includes the following icons.

 This icon points out a wide variety of helpful advice to ensure that your trip (and trip-planning) experience goes smoothly. Follow the Tip icon to find out where to get the best service, how to navigate Toronto's transit system, who dishes up the best ice cream, and many more useful hints.

 Pay special attention to this icon: Whether it's a potential scam or a potential scare, these pieces of advice help you steer clear of possibly dangerous scenarios.

 Planning to tour Toronto on a budget? Or do you just want to save money on your hotel so that you can spend it all in Toronto's shopping districts? Either way, this icon points out ways that you can save a loonie or two (that's a buck or two, for you non-Canadian types).

 Toronto offers wonderful touring opportunities for the entire family — so much so that most of this book could be designated Kid Friendly. Nevertheless, this icon highlights attractions, activities, and other travel options that are especially appealing to kids.

 This icon highlights what I humbly consider the best that Toronto has to offer in accommodations, dining, and things to do. If you can't wait to find out what has made the cut, Chapter 1 offers brief introductions to each of the places and activities in this book that have earned the Best of the Best icon.

Where to Go from Here

To Toronto, of course! Or to your travel agent. Or to your favorite online booking service. Or to your local garage to service your car for the drive to Toronto. You'll want to use this book to map out your plan of attack, taking advantage of the details it offers to help you get the most out of your trip.

Part I
Introducing Toronto

The 5th Wave   By Rich Tennant

"There's so many reasons we wanted to visit Toronto. There's the Film Festival, the Author's Festival, the Discount Drugs Festival..."

In this part...

Want to know quickly what Toronto has to offer? Part I has the goods. Beginning with the best of the best of Toronto travel experiences, this part will confirm that Toronto is an appealing travel destination for you. You also find a brief history of the region, an overview of the city's architectural heritage, and a look at the city's standing in the areas of literature and film. Finally, this part presents the pros and cons of traveling to Toronto during the various seasons and an abbreviated calendar of events, all designed to help you decide when to visit.

Chapter 1

Discovering the Best of Toronto

In This Chapter

▶ Encountering many cultures in one city
▶ Meandering through Toronto's neighborhoods
▶ Enjoying the scenery
▶ Taking in a Broadway-quality play
▶ Filling up on a festival's fries and festivities
▶ Happening upon "Hollywood North"

*T*oronto isn't afraid to go the distance (its Yonge Street is the world's longest street), achieve new heights (the CN Tower is the world's tallest building), or appreciate diverse cultures (with over a million of its residents hailing from dozens of distinct ethnic backgrounds). This adventurous spirit extends to the city's landmarks, restaurants, and attractions as well. While in Toronto, you can browse museums that celebrate Canadian and international heritage, sample a wide variety of cuisines in some of the city's 5,000-plus restaurants, and marvel at the city's commitment to the beauty of its parks and geographic landmarks.

In this chapter, I get to single out the cream of the crop—from the best travel experiences to the best hotels and restaurants to the best places to spot a celebrity. If a hotel, restaurant, or attraction is included in this chapter, you can find more detail about it in a later chapter, next to a Best of the Best icon.

The Best Toronto Travel Experiences

The largest city in Canada offers plenty to see and do and eat and drink for just about every taste. But what makes this great city really stand out? Here are a few of my favorite Toronto experiences.

✔ **Strolling on the boardwalk in The Beaches:** Yes, it's a bit out of the way if you're based in downtown Toronto, but the drive or streetcar or cab ride to this east end neighborhood is definitely worth the trip. The walk is lovely at just about any time of year, whether it's to enjoy the warmth and sunshine of mid-summer, the mist and fog of a cool fall morning, or the build-up of snow and ice in and around Lake Ontario in the winter. Meander along the boardwalk for a few blocks and then head north to Queen Street for a hot coffee or a cold beer, depending on the season.

✔ **Enjoying a night at the theater:** Any time of year, you can find a terrific selection of theatrical productions in and around Toronto. Whether it's the Broadway-quality plays brought to the city by Mirvish Productions (which has a hand in just about all Broadway shows that make it to this city), or the fine productions of local troupes such as CanStage or Soulpepper, or the two excellent repertory companies within a couple of hours of Toronto (the Stratford and Shaw festivals), theater buffs have plenty to look forward to during a Toronto stay. See Chapter 15 for details about Toronto-area stage offerings.

✔ **Navigating the Martin Goodman Trail — with just about any mode of transportation:** For most of the length of its waterfront, Toronto's lakeshore is a highly accessible and quite beautiful area. (A portion of Toronto's waterfront is an industrial area and, therefore, not as accessible or aesthetically pleasing.) Ideal for biking, walking, in-line skating, and lollygagging, the Martin Goodman Trail runs 20km (12.5 miles) along the waterfront from Toronto's east end to west end (or west end to east end, if you prefer). Chapter 11 discusses some other outdoor activities in and around Toronto.

✔ **Marveling at the eighth wonder of the world:** You can't avoid it, even if you cringe at the thought of dozens and dozens of tour buses, too many tourists wearing too-short shorts and too-black socks, and kitschy tourist-trap souvenir stands hawking 25-cent trinkets for way too many loonies. When you're just a two-hour drive from Niagara Falls, and you have a day to spare in your Toronto itinerary, you must make the trip to take in this almost indescribable wonder of nature. See Chapter 14 for more about day trips to the Niagara region.

The Best Toronto Hotels

Toronto has so many top-quality hotels, it's difficult to assign the "best" superlative to just a handful of the great ones that are out there. So this section breaks the Toronto hotel offerings into a few select categories. And in hotly contested categories, don't be afraid to consider the runner-up option. (Yes, runner-up is not "best." Consider this the horseshoe version of superlatives; you know, "Close only counts in horseshoes and hand grenades." And now in Toronto hotels.)

✔ **Best old-school hotel:** The **Fairmont Royal York** definitely qualifies as an old-school hotel. With the highest of kudos for service and opulence — and a fair amount of praise for its magnificent size and ornate accessories — the Royal York is the prototypical big-city, downtown hotel, right down to its smallish rooms and largeish price tag. A close second is the "**King Eddy**" (Le Royal Meridien King Edward), Toronto's oldest hotel — and still one of its most luxurious.

✔ **Best new-school hotel:** At the **Four Seasons,** you find chic accommodations to go with chic surroundings (the trendy Bloor/Yorkville area). The rooms are quite adequate, especially for a downtown hotel, and the spa, fitness, and dining options are over the top. The recently renovated **InterContinental Toronto Centre** (formerly the Crowne Plaza) is catching up quickly, with one of the best and most beautiful hotel spa facilities in the city.

✔ **Best new-new-school hotel:** In the boutique-hotel category, Toronto has welcomed several new entries in the past few years. The best of the newbies to this point is **Hotel Le Germain** in the Entertainment District. Everything is top-of-the-line here, from the high-ceilinged and open-concept rooms to the rain showers standard in each room to the inspiring lobby/library/sitting area that welcomes you. Practically around the corner is the **Soho Metropolitan,** which, in addition to its plush boutique-style accommodations, has the added benefit of Senses Bakery and Restaurant on-site.

✔ **Best for families:** The **Delta Chelsea** has two indoor pools, including one with a giant waterslide that takes swimmers outside the building briefly before returning inside to reach the pool. The second pool is for adults only, for when the kids are in bed or playing at the second-floor Children's Creative Centre, with staff on hand to supervise games, crafts, and other activities. Even the older kids will appreciate this hotel, with a well-stocked game and arcade room, complete with pool and air hockey tables, and of course video games. Finally, parents can take advantage of the hotel's babysitting service to enjoy an evening at the theater.

✔ **Best bargain:** For the comfortable rooms and amenities available at the **Grand Hotel & Suites,** it's easy to overlook its out-of-the-way location in favor of its attractive room rates. Hotel features include not one but two rooftop Jacuzzis, a full-service spa and fitness facility, and VCRs and DVD/CD players in each suite. The guestrooms are a bit on the small side to do justice to the term "suite," but the money you save here relative to what you'd spend at comparable hotel rooms or suites closer to downtown helps make the tight squeeze more bearable.

✔ **Best hotel inside a baseball stadium:** While the novelty has worn off a bit since its opening in the late 1980s, and the room rates may be especially prohibitive for what you get, there's nothing quite like overlooking a big-league baseball game from the comfort of your hotel room. The **Renaissance Toronto Hotel** at the Rogers Centre (formerly known as the SkyDome) became infamous shortly after its opening when a cameraman working a Toronto Blue Jays game spotted a couple, er, appreciating all the benefits of their hotel room — with the curtains open. Rooms not facing the field are available, but why bother? If you want to splurge for this rather ordinary hotel, go all the way and get a field-side room.

The Best Toronto Restaurants

Toronto certainly has plenty of top-notch dining experiences. If your gourmand taste drives you to Toronto to catch the latest menu at Susur or to appreciate first-hand the buzz about Perigee, I offer a brief review of the finest in haute cuisine in Toronto in Chapter 10. (If you need more detail on the finest dining in the city, check out *Frommer's Toronto,* published by Wiley Publishing.) But in this Best-of-the-Best section I offer some quirkier suggestions (also reviewed in detail in Chapter 10).

- **Best view with your meal, overhead version:** The menu is fine, with a strong emphasis on Canadian fare; the service is mostly above par for this kind of touristy establishment; and the prices, well, are as high as you would expect when dining atop the world's tallest structure. Nevertheless, the appeal of the **360 Revolving Restaurant** is, quite simply, the view. At about 360m (1,200 ft.), with the night lights of Toronto illuminating the view, you'd be hard pressed to come up with a more inspiring vantage point for a meal — plus, they throw in the elevator ride for free!

- **Best view with your meal, street-level version:** Warm weather in Toronto is an invitation for restaurants and pubs to throw open the front windows, set up the outdoor furniture, and entice customers to fill up the patios and sidewalks of Toronto. For the best in people-watching, sun-worshiping, and pint-sipping, the **Black Bull** on Queen Street West makes a strong case for best patio in the city. And the standard pub fare of burgers, nachos, and the like are okay as well.

- **Best for families:** Spend a few minutes during an early evening meal rush at **Alice Fazooli's! Italian Crabshack** and you'll quickly appreciate the draw for families to this fun restaurant. Even though parents (presumably) foot the bill (and the tip), the waitstaff clearly has a more enjoyable time seeing to the whims and wishes of the kids in every party. For larger parties of adults and kids, the restaurant actually places kids at their own table separate from the boring adults — and a great time is had by all. The small Toronto chain serves above-average Italian, specializing in seafood and some great starters that are appealing to all ages.

- **Best burger and brew:** Okay, so maybe the draw for locals is the lovely shaded patio out back that easily fits a couple of dozen tables — sturdy wood tables, not the flimsy plastic variety. Or maybe it's the selection of 200-plus single-malt scotches on hand. That's all good and appealing, but for my money, **Allen's** on the Danforth has the best hamburger in Toronto, with a selection of over 100 beers to accompany your burger (including a dozen on tap and a couple of dozen Belgian beers).

✔ **Best buffet:** I'm not talking Ponderosa buffet here. The 50-plus items on the C$10.95 (US$9) buffet at **Dhaba,** an Indian restaurant in the Entertainment District, amount to grand larceny. The menu changes daily, but always includes standards such as tandoori chicken, butter chicken, and a variety of curry dishes, as well as some more proto-typical buffet items (try the rice pudding). If buffet is not your cup of tea, come back in the evening for a pleasant sit-down meal from a menu that boasts "healthwise" Indian fare.

✔ **Best breakfast with a milk shake: Flo's Diner** used to reside in its own '50s-style building on a prime corner spot in plush Bloor/Yorkville. Alas, in the early 1990s, it was razed to accommodate a high-rise condo building. But Flo's returned, albeit in not as pleasing quarters (a second-floor location still in Yorkville), but still with quality comfort food. Breakfasts are among the best in the city, service is always above par (though expect a wait on Sunday morning), and if you ask nicely, you can enjoy a fresh-scooped milk shake with your omelette.

✔ **Best smoked meat:** You're never quite at risk of public humiliation when you recommend the "best" smoked meat in Toronto. At least, not the way you might be in making such a recommendation in Montreal, where smoked meat is legendary. For classically moist and flavorful smoked meat, head for the Entertainment District and a drab little storefront eatery called **Reuben S.** Don't back away when the proprietors welcome you to the place with a hearty "Eat in or carry out!" followed by a command to sit at a particular table, both healthily barked. And when your server recommends the smoked meat platter, don't argue. You won't regret it.

✔ **Best island taste with a view of a strip club:** Not exactly the comeliest of neighborhoods, the area around Queen Street East and Broadview is home to seedy cafes, doughnut shops, and "adult entertainment venues," but also, importantly, **The Real Jerk,** a respectable Caribbean eatery featuring some of the best rotis, jerk, and curry in Toronto. The healthy dose of traditional rice and peas makes the trip to this part of town worth every bite.

✔ **Best greasy spoon:** Farther east on Queen (almost to The Beaches neighborhood), the **Tulip Steak House** has been serving hearty breakfasts and even heartier steak dinners to locals for more than 50 years. Don't be mistaken: this is not your typical Ruth's Chris Steak House kind of establishment. No linen tablecloths on the '50s-vintage furniture. No separate menu for vegetable and potato sides. Just good, hot, greasy-spoon food — and plenty of it.

The Best Ways to Celebrate Toronto's Diversity

With nearly 50 percent of the city's population not born in Canada, Toronto fully embraces Canada's tradition of multiculturalism as envisioned by former prime minister Pierre Trudeau in 1971: "Every ethnic group has the right to preserve and develop its own culture and values within the Canadian context."

As a visitor, you have the opportunity to experience how rewarding Toronto's cultural diversity can be in a variety of entertaining ways:

✔ **Dining:** From the distinct ethnic dining districts of Chinatown, Little Italy, and the Greek establishments on the Danforth (see Chapter 8 for more about these and other Toronto neighborhoods) to the scattered takeaway shops featuring rotis, falafels, and shawarmas (see Chapter 10 for more about Toronto's food-to-go), Toronto offers many samplings of the world's culinary treats.

✔ **Festivals:** Year-round celebrations of cultural heritages take place in Toronto. Ring in the Chinese New Year, experience the Caribbean during the Caribana Festival, or even mix in some international snacking at events such as the Taste of the Danforth. Pick any summer weekend in Toronto, and you're likely to find an outdoor event with an international flavor. Chapter 3 features a calendar of events where you can find more detail on many of these fascinating festivals.

✔ **Film:** The Toronto International Film Festival, held annually for ten days in September, features a selection of new Canadian, American, and international releases, including four of the previous five Academy Award winners for best foreign language film.

✔ **Markets:** Whether it's a local storefront market that caters to the residents of one of Toronto's more distinctly multicultural neighborhoods, or the international flavor of the shops and markets that make up the narrow streets of the Kensington Market area, you can find dozens and dozens of small shops and markets around town that stock the kitchen basics and more from dozens and dozens of countries.

The Best Toronto Neighborhoods

Many Toronto neighborhoods are distinguished by their ethnic heritage. From Little Italy to Chinatown to Indian Bazaar to Koreatown, these neighborhoods have developed over the years to welcome Torontonians and non-Torontonians to their shops and restaurants, while maintaining their charm and character.

Other Toronto neighborhoods are defined more by the activities that take place in them or by their particular way of life. The Financial District and the Entertainment District, for example, are pretty self-explanatory; Cabbagetown — thankfully — is not (though the roots of its name do come from the oft-fragrant vegetable).

Still other neighborhoods are defined more by their residential status. These too, though, have a whole lot more than residing going on in them. Here are the best Toronto neighborhoods for visitors (see Chapter 8 for more about Toronto's neighborhoods).

- ✔ **Bloor/Yorkville:** The trendiest of the trendy areas in Toronto, this neighborhood caters to high-rolling fashionistas, visiting film celebrities in town for a shoot (most likely staying at the Four Seasons here), and downtown condo-dwellers — though not exclusively. Bargains can be had in many of the fashionable shops, and you can find a reasonably priced bite to eat at several places around Cumberland Street and Yorkville Avenue. Visitors are also just a block or two away from the Royal Ontario Museum.

- ✔ **The Beaches and Bloor West Village:** While these two neighborhoods are on opposite ends of Toronto (east end and west end, respectively), they are almost mirror images of each other. Both neighborhoods clearly cater to the needs of their close-by neighbors, as evidenced by the frequent and thriving flower shops, fruit and vegetable markets, corner convenience stores, and meat markets. These same neighborhoods, however, also recognize that such neighborly services also attract non-residents, as do the independent shops (many), chain stores (few, though Bloor West Village includes a good-sized Chapters), and restaurants (choices galore) that crop up around them.

- ✔ **Harbourfront and the Islands:** Toronto's waterfront is not really the place to be for Toronto residents. The area has little going for it that's not tourism-related. But for visitors, it's nearly a must-stop, if for no other reason than the city ferry trip across to the Toronto Islands, a bucolic oasis complete with a small and friendly amusement park, cozy and semi-private beachfront, and several kilometers of quiet walking trails. The Harbourfront itself has a few adequate dining and drinking spots, but you're better off heading back downtown for dinner after an afternoon on the Islands.

- ✔ **Queen Street West:** Start at University Avenue and head west on Queen for some of the most eclectic shopping in the city. You can find high-end brand-name stores (such as Roots, a Canadian staple; Club Monaco; and Kiehl's), as well as plenty of local, but no less interesting, shops (say, Pages Books & Magazines, or Pavilion, a contemporary housewares and furniture store). Queen West is also one of the happening nightspots in the city, complete with classically cool restaurants and many of the hottest of the hot music and dance clubs. And, as of 2004, the area has the über-hip Drake Hotel for trendy overnighters.

The Best Places for Celebrity Spotting

The favorable Canadian dollar and a few well-placed tax breaks have helped to draw enough television and movie productions to Toronto that the city now boasts the generally favorable nickname "Hollywood North."

This kind of production activity is going to produce its share of celebrity spottings, especially with such high-profile films as 2002 Best Picture winner, *Chicago,* and the high-grossing film *My Big Fat Greek Wedding* (ironically, also set in Chicago). If you're into celebrity spotting, remember that there's a fine line between celebrity spotting and celebrity hounding.

- **Four Seasons Hotel:** The hotel of choice for stars in Toronto for extended stays for filming, the Four Seasons is the place to be if you're looking to snag an autograph or some pix. Rather, it's the place to be outside of — hotel staff is pretty diligent about keeping its public areas clear of paparazzi and autograph hounds.

- **Avenue Bar:** Okay, so technically this is part of the Four Seasons, but this street-level bar with large plate-glass window is tailor-made for catching a glimpse of your favorite celeb sipping a cocktail. After all, chances are good that the celeb's room is just upstairs.

- **Windsor Arms Hotel:** During its first heyday ('50s, '60s, and '70s), the Windsor Arms was *the* place for celebrities. Elizabeth Taylor and Richard Burton, for example, regularly took a suite here when in Toronto. Now in the middle of its second heyday period (reopened in the early '90s), it's again become a celebrity magnet.

- **Toronto International Film Festival:** For a more intense celebrity-sighting venue, visit Toronto during the first two weeks in September. The Toronto International Film Festival draws the Richard Geres, the Renée Zellwegers, and even the Nia Vardaloses of the entertainment world to Toronto for ten days of movie showings, press conferences, and red-carpet roll-outs.

Chapter 2

Digging Deeper into Toronto

• •

In This Chapter

▶ Getting the lowdown on Toronto's history

▶ Looking toward the horizon: Toronto's architecture

▶ Sampling Toronto's cuisine

▶ Prepping for your trip to the library or the moviehouse

• •

*T*oronto got its name — which means place of meeting — from the Huron tribe that inhabited the area in the 16th and 17th centuries. Between then and now, the city has changed names twice, withstood an American invasion, and weathered a brief tenure as a national capital. Yet still, the city retains its "place of meeting" status, growing its population from multiple heritages around the world, drawn by the city's — and Canada's — broadminded tolerance of diverse peoples and cultures.

This chapter provides a glimpse into this multicultural city's history, inviting you to visit and discover the uniqueness of Toronto on your own. In preparation for your visit, you can bone up on the city's architectural, culinary, and literary and cinematic heritage as well.

History 101: The Main Events

As with many North American regions, Toronto's non-native history begins with the purchase of land from Native Americans (or First Nations Aboriginals) — in this case, the British governor of Quebec negotiated a deal with the Mississauga tribe. And quite a deal it was — a mere £1,700 for about 1,035 sq. km (just under 400 sq. miles) of land; in today's U.S. dollar, that transaction would work out to just over $8 per 2.5 sq. km (1 sq. mile).

John Graves Simcoe arrived shortly thereafter to oversee the construction of a military garrison and town that he named York, which in 1793 became the capital of what was then called Upper Canada. York became Toronto in 1834 after the city's incorporation (hence the two name changes).

Simcoe's garrison — Fort York — bore the brunt of the Canadian battlefront during the War of 1812, when American forces invaded York, burning the garrison and creating other general mayhem. But the events around Fort York would end up being the height of the war's activity in Canada.

The events at Fort York also played a role in the creation of the U.S. White House — at least, the naming of it. Months after the American troops destroyed Fort York, British troops retaliated by setting fire to the president's residence in Washington, D.C. The residence was covered in whitewash to hide the charred evidence of the fire, thus leading to its being dubbed the White House.

When Canada established its Confederation in 1867 and the country began to break up into provinces and territories, Toronto became the capital of the new province of Ontario, and it remains so today.

Toronto's acceptance of immigration began during the early 1800s, when new residents came primarily from the British Isles, Russia, and Germany. The late 1800s and early 1900s brought waves of European immigrants, as similarly experienced in the United States. But the 1970s and beyond have witnessed the greatest introduction of visible minorities to Toronto, which now welcomes most of its new residents from the Caribbean and Latin America, Asia, and Africa.

Toronto's major industries have been concentrated in service and communications. Canada's major banks, financial services groups, and media and publishing empires have long-established roots in Toronto, and these industries remain among the largest employers in Toronto.

For many years Toronto competed with Montreal for the rights to the "Canada's largest city" designation, but Toronto eventually won out: The latest figures from Statistics Canada show the Toronto metropolitan area with a population of just over 5 million (the Montreal metropolitan area has a population of just over 3.5 million). In Toronto proper, just over half of the city's population (52 percent) was born somewhere outside of Canada.

Significant dates in Toronto's history

From the Huron to hockey, Toronto has quite the story to tell.

- **1615:** Etienne Brûlé establishes an early French settlement to Toronto in the early 1700s. The Huron tribe, already settled in the area, call this location "Toronto," meaning "place of meeting."

- **1787:** For a mere £1,700, the land that now makes up most of Toronto is purchased from the Mississauga tribe.

- **1793:** Toronto is renamed York — and is named capital of Upper Canada — when John Simcoe, governor of Upper Canada, arrives to establish Fort York.

✔ **1812–1814**: Canada is an occasional battlefront during the War of 1812 between the United States and England. Fort York is one casualty, invaded and burned by American forces in 1813. American troops are gone from Canadian territory by 1814.

✔ **1834**: The newly incorporated city is renamed once again. William Lyon Mackenzie becomes the first mayor of Toronto.

✔ **1841**: Toronto is no longer the nation's capital, which has moved temporarily to Kingston, Ontario.

✔ **1848**: Toronto opens its first public school.

✔ **1867**: The province of Ontario is formed under the Confederation of Canada. Toronto is named provincial capital, which it remains today.

✔ **1879**: The Canadian National Exhibition (CNE), better known as The Ex, opens for the first time.

✔ **1900**: The Art Gallery of Toronto (now Art Gallery of Ontario) opens.

✔ **1914**: The Royal Ontario Museum opens. A Toronto hockey club — the Toronto Blueshirts — brings the coveted Stanley Cup to the city for the first time. It would be the first of 14 Stanley Cup championships for Toronto, though there have been none since 1967.

✔ **1922**: University of Toronto researchers Frederick Banting and Charles Best discover insulin. Banting later would be awarded the Nobel Prize in medicine.

✔ **1931**: Maple Leaf Gardens, longtime home of the Toronto Maple Leafs hockey franchise, opens.

✔ **1954**: Toronto's first subway line opens.

✔ **1969**: The Ontario Science Centre opens.

✔ **1975**: The first Toronto International Film Festival is held.

✔ **1976**: The construction of the CN Tower is completed.

✔ **1989**: Another Toronto skyline landmark, the SkyDome (now called the Rogers Centre), opens to mixed reviews.

✔ **1992**: The Toronto Blue Jays win the first of two consecutive World Series.

✔ **1998**: The Toronto "megacity" is born, an amalgamation of the old cities of Toronto, East York, Etobicoke, North York, and Scarborough.

Building Blocks: Local Architecture

As befits a city that developed around diverse neighborhoods and among a variety of cultures, Toronto's architectural style is best labeled eclectic, with striking examples from Victorian, Romanesque, Gothic, and, of course, modern genres. And then there's Casa Loma, an architectural oddity all to itself.

Consider a walk around the University of Toronto campus among its ornate Victorian-style buildings. While in the neighborhood, appreciate the many homes in The Annex neighborhood that retain their Romanesque charm, complete with carved red sandstone, arches, and turrets. And in nearby Queen's Park, the Ontario Legislature building is also a study in Romanesque style.

Ongoing construction will update two existing landmark structures in bold ways. The Royal Ontario Museum (ROM) will unveil a Daniel Libeskind–designed crystal addition in 2006, and a modern glass-and-titanium structure—designed by Toronto native Frank Gehry—will be the highlight of a renovation at the Art Gallery of Ontario, scheduled for completion in 2008.

Casa Loma, which is open to the public, is a medieval-style faux-European castle designed in the early 1900s by E.J. Lennox. Arguably the top Toronto architect in his day, Lennox also designed the old City Hall and the King Eddy, among other landmarks. But Casa Loma was (and is) his pièce de résistance. Borrowing from Gothic, Romanesque, and Norman styles, the castle was inspired by a galaxy of castles that original owner Sir Henry Pellatt had grown to love during his travels in Europe.

For interesting—and free—details about Toronto's architectural heritage, check out ROMwalks, with guides from the Royal Ontario Museum leading walking tours of Toronto landmarks and neighborhoods (see Chapter 11).

Taste of Toronto: Local Cuisine

If there's one thing that Toronto *doesn't* offer, it's a certain type of food that's known for coming from Toronto. New Orleans has its Cajun and beignets; London has its fish and chips and bangers-and-mash; the Pacific Northwest has its coffee and microbrews; Toronto has . . . well, Tim Hortons, I guess.

Actually, what Toronto does have one-ups everyplace else. Toronto doesn't do just one thing very well—Toronto does just about everything very well. Because of the diversity of the city's population and culture, you can find cuisine from all over the world within Toronto's city limits. In fact, if there's one city where you should avoid the best of the traditional North American eateries (and Toronto does have them), this is it. Morton's Steakhouse is just fine (in the Park Hyatt Hotel in the Bloor/Yorkville neighborhood), but the great Indian cuisine at The Host on Prince Arthur Avenue just around the corner is even better.

Toronto has over 7,000 restaurants from which to choose, and many of them set out to establish the latest trend in dining. Naturally, the outcome is that dining trends come and dining trends go. In some cases, keeping up with the trends in Toronto's dining scene means keeping up with the perpetually rotating celebrity chefs (make your mark here . . . then move over there to make another mark with a new twist). In other instances, it's all about the *buzz,* the kind of buzz that emanates from locals who've discovered a place that has an exciting new way of fusing, say, Asian and Caribbean cuisine, and they can't wait to tell all their friends — or, more importantly, their business associates — about it. Sadly, by the time it hits the local press, the buzz has more often than not turned into a small hum.

Another way to keep up with Toronto's dining trends is to look in the city's top dining neighborhoods. While most of the restaurants reviewed in this book (look for them in Chapter 10) can be found at or near the hotels and attractions around which you're likely to spend most of your time, you can also explore a few other neighborhoods with a wide variety of dining options:

- ✔ The fare offered in **Little Italy** (mostly along College Street) has expanded beyond the Italian heritage of its residents to some more diverse and excellent cuisine choices.

- ✔ You can find any number of hip and stylish restaurants in the hip and stylish **Bloor/Yorkville** neighborhood, just waiting for you (and the hottest celebrities) to drop in for a fine meal.

- ✔ What's a night out at the theater without a good meal — either before or after the show. **King Street West** and the blocks surrounding it have plenty of options to choose from.

- ✔ As in similar neighborhoods in many other major cities, diners know what they'll find in **Chinatown** — the best of the best in Chinese and other Asian cuisine.

- ✔ In the **Financial District,** appropriately, you generally find the highest-priced restaurants in the city.

- ✔ **Bloor West Village** features fine and casual dining that caters to local residents and neighborhood visitors alike.

- ✔ Dining in **The Beaches** focuses on light and reasonably quick fare so that you can get back to your window-shopping or boardwalk-ambling.

- ✔ **The Danforth** has a collection of Greek establishments to go along with some of the city's trendier spots.

Background Check: Recommended Movies and Books

Toronto likes to refer to itself as "Hollywood North," and its film production activity justifies that boast. The city ranks right behind Los Angeles and New York in terms of film, television, and video production, with between 18 and 40 productions under way in Toronto on any given day. According to the city's Film and Television Office, filming permits were issued for a cumulative total of 9,049 days of shooting during 2003.

Sadly, few of those productions represent Toronto as Toronto. The city instead sits in for New York or Chicago or other settings in a variety of films and television shows.

- ✔ Curious about Toronto acting as Chicago? Check out *My Big Fat Greek Wedding,* which used, appropriately, the Greektown neighborhood around Danforth for exterior shots. (Don't check out the Academy Award–winning *Chicago,* which was filmed mostly on Toronto sound stages.)

- ✔ Toronto fits in well in the Northeast. Toronto as rural Maine? The largely forgettable comedy *Welcome to Mooseport* was filmed in Toronto. Toronto as urban Boston? Check out the largely unforgettable Matt Damon/Ben Affleck/Robin Williams vehicle *Good Will Hunting.*

- ✔ Toronto has sat in as the Big Apple for many films, including such diverse offerings as *Three Men and a Baby, Finding Forrester,* and *American Psycho.*

For films that are actually set in Toronto — and also released in the U.S. — the numbers dwindle dramatically. Your best bet for finding something worthwhile is the campy but fun flick *Bollywood/Hollywood.*

Book lovers will have a bit more success at finding literature that focuses on Toronto. Ranging from works by well-known Canadian authors such as Margaret Atwood (*The Robber Bride*), Carol Shields (*Unless*), and Michael Ondaatje (*In the Skin of a Lion*), to lesser-known works, including a relatively new series of mysteries by Sylvia Maultash Walsh, novelists find plenty of inspiration among Toronto's streets and residents. *Doors Open Toronto: Illuminating the City's Great Spaces* is a valuable introductory book for visitors interested in the city's architectural heritage.

Chapter 3

Deciding When to Go

. . . .

. . . .

*U*ltimately, of course, you have to make the decision — or, more accurately, decisions. First, whether to visit Toronto for your next family vacation: Chapter 1 has a few ideas that should help you with that one. Second, there's the matter of the best time of year to visit. I can't help you with coordinating your work/school/soccer schedules so that you and your traveling companions can agree on several days in consecutive order. I can, however, offer some advice about the pros and cons of visiting Toronto during each season (there's really no *bad* time to tour Toronto, though January is a bit drab, both in terms of special events and the weather). This chapter also features a listing of some of the biggest annual events on Toronto's calendar.

Looking for Snow or Sun (or Something in Between)

Toronto doesn't enjoy the year-round temperate climate of, say, Vancouver; nor does it struggle through the long, cold winters associated with the more northern Canadian cities. (Needless to say, no city in Canada has the pleasure of year-round sun and warmth.) Instead, Toronto clearly falls into the category of cities that experience the typical highs and lows of every season.

Spring reliably brings the promise of warmth and regrowth to come, with trees starting to bud and restaurants once again opening their patios. Nearly every summer features lots of sunshine and some days of high temperature and high humidity. Fall provides the significant and beautiful color variations that are especially vibrant in northern climates. Typical winters offer several decent snowstorms, a number of days with only flurry activity, and fairly regular, very brisk high winds — especially along the waterfront. But winter days in Toronto can just as often be delightfully bright and sunny.

Table 3–1 shows the specifics of Toronto's temperature and rainfall/snowfall variations.

Table 3–1 Toronto's Average Temperatures and Precipitation

Month	Avg. High (°F/°C)	Avg. Low (°F/°C)	Avg. Rainfall (in./mm)	Avg. Snowfall (in./cm)
January	30/-1	19/-7	1.1/29	15.0/38
February	32/0	21/-6	1.0/26	10.6/27
March	41/5	28/-2	1.7/42	8.7/22
April	52/11	39/4	2.5/63	2.4/6
May	66/19	50/10	2.9/73	0/0
June	75/24	59/15	2.8/72	0/0
July	79/26	64/18	2.7/68	0/0
August	77/25	63/17	3.1/80	0/0
September	70/21	55/13	3.3/83	0/0
October	57/14	45/7	2.6/65	0/0
November	45/7	36/2	2.6/67	3.1/8
December	36/2	25/-4	1.7/42	12.6/32

Toronto in springtime

Torontonians love their gardens. Maybe it's something about how gardens represent emerging life following the melting of mounds of snow that covered them for the preceding several months. Whatever the reason, Toronto in springtime is full of colorful flowers and blossoming trees whose beauty competes with that of the world's most renowned garden centers. Here are some positives about Toronto in spring:

✔ The city's outdoor attractions start to gear up for the high tourist season, opening up for weekend admissions during May.

✔ Festivals and fairs (indoor and out) also are in high gear, starting in March with Canada Blooms, the garden show to end all garden shows (see "Getting the Lowdown on Toronto's Main Events," later in this chapter).

✔ Attractions start to extend their opening hours as the days get longer. And the crowds of summer are still a few weeks away.

TIP

School's out for summer (and for a week in spring)

For the Toronto tourism industry, school breaks can be doubly lucrative as Canadian and U.S. school districts generally have different schedules for spring break and school-end dates.

✔ For U.S. residents, if you're visiting Toronto with your school-aged kids, consider scheduling your trip in the late spring, during the first couple of weeks that your kids are out of school. Most Canadian school districts remain in class until the last week of June, so if you can get in a family vacation during the early to middle weeks of June, you'll miss many of the Canadian family vacationers.

✔ Most U.S. and Canadian school districts also schedule spring breaks for different weeks: Canada's breaks are typically in March; most U.S. schools break during April. In 2005, for example, Toronto's school district has March Break during the week of March 14; New York City public schools break during the week of April 25.

Visiting Toronto during spring also has a few negatives:

✔ School break weeks can fill up Toronto attractions and hotels with families traveling with younger kids — the older kids, of course, are likely off to Florida and other warm spring break destinations.

✔ The weather can be unpredictable, with the occasional snowfall even in April and cold winds throughout the season.

A Toronto summer

Visiting Toronto during the summer months has the usual pros and cons of any summer destination: decent weather and more accessible venues, but also some overbearing temperatures and crowds. And here are a few other things you'll find about Toronto in summer:

✔ You'll have plenty of time to explore the city. Daylight hours are long, more than 15 hours' worth for much of the summer — though you may have to get up at 4:30 a.m. to enjoy them all.

✔ Toronto restaurants *love* all those daylight hours. Take a survey of cities with the highest number of alfresco dining options per capita, and Toronto's likely to be at or near the top of the list.

✔ The Toronto festival season is in full swing, with something going on seemingly every weekend. The smaller neighborhood festivals are especially great summer diversions.

✔ While Toronto does have its share of stiflingly hot and muggy days, most summer days are almost perfect weatherwise. Lots of sunshine (though use your sunscreen generously as UV ratings can be high), low humidity, and mild breezes combine to keep everyone comfortable.

To beat the heat on all but the most torrid days, head to The Beaches neighborhood, especially to the boardwalk along the lakeshore, where temperatures can be a good five degrees lower than those in midtown Toronto.

And here are a few reasons that you may want to avoid Toronto during the summer:

- ✔ Fighting the crowds becomes a bit tiresome, especially around the waterfront when the cruise-tour ships come in, and in the neighborhoods such as Yorkville where tourists, shoppers, office workers, and all those alfresco diners compete for sidewalk space.

- ✔ Rainstorms can be quite vigorous; downpours are common. Make sure to pack a travel umbrella.

- ✔ For such a large urban area (the fifth largest city in North America, behind Mexico City, New York, Los Angeles, and Chicago), Toronto does a fair job of dealing with environmental challenges. However, even with the city's extensive mass transit system, and its growing emphasis on waste-collection management, high smog alerts are common during a particularly hot stretch of days.

Autumn in Toronto

The fall months are a great time to catch Toronto while the city comes down from its summer highs.

- ✔ The city's color rivals the beauty of its spring flowers, with its fall foliage offering the vibrant hues that you can find in other northern climates.

- ✔ Attractions continue to offer more extended opening hours, and the city's outdoor venues remain open for weekend activities.

- ✔ Hotels tend to have less expensive room rates, especially for weekend stays, than during the busy summer season. (That is, unless they're full up with conventioners as the business travel and trade show sectors start to gear up again.)

With the exception of an occasional November snowstorm and some very chilly lake winds, you'll find few disadvantages to being in Toronto in autumn.

Bundling up for a Toronto winter

Toronto generally avoids the bitterly cold winters that afflict other parts of Canada and the upper Midwestern states of the U.S., so visiting the city during winter is an underrated pleasure:

✔ Most attractions remain open, with significantly reduced crowds to contend with, though not necessarily reduced rates.

✔ First-rate theater and Toronto's highly regarded musical performances (such as the Toronto Symphony Orchestra and the Canadian Opera Company) continue throughout the season.

✔ A walk along the lakeshore boasts an unexpected, frosted beauty, with waves frozen upon rocks in mid-crash. Or, a day trip to Niagara Falls (just a two-hour drive from Toronto; see Chapter 14) gives you the chance to see the falls surrounded by a winter landscape.

But it does get cold, so Toronto in winter has its downside:

✔ The wind picks up, especially as you move closer to the waterfront, which can make for some unfortunate, if necessary, fashion trends — like ear-flap hats.

✔ If your transportation of choice is a car, be advised that Toronto's streets and heavily trafficked highways become slightly more treacherous during a snowfall. Snow removal crews generally do a pretty good job of clearing the area's highways, but the clearing of city streets can be hit or miss.

✔ Naturally, outdoor celebrations are somewhat curtailed, though the various holiday festivities in late November to January and Winterfest in February perk up the season a bit.

Getting the Lowdown on Toronto's Main Events

During summer, hardly a week goes by in Toronto without some kind of festival, parade, fair, or other such event. Yet, you can also find a number of special activities during the other months of the year. This section highlights the best of the best. For a more complete listing of Toronto happenings, check out Tourism Toronto's Calendar of Events online at www.torontotourism.com.

January

Though January is a slow month for big-drawing events, you can often catch the tail end of the **Cavalcade of Lights,** Toronto's holiday festival (see the "December" section at the end of this chapter), or the front end of **Winterfest,** which celebrates, of course, winter (see "February" below). Also, the Chinese New Year often falls in January (in 2006, it's on January 29) (see "February" below).

February

In 2005, the **Chinese New Year** is on February 9; Toronto's celebration, however, features participants from other cultures that also celebrate the Lunar New Year (including Korea, Japan, Vietnam, and Thailand). Festival highlights include dance, acrobatic, and martial arts performances, and the Asian Food Court is a perennial favorite. Call ☎ **416-483-8218,** or visit www.torontocelebrates.com for details. Dates vary, but the new year always falls in late January or mid-February.

Two weeks in late January and early February full of events run by the City of Toronto, **Winterfest** in Toronto celebrates the cold, snow, and ice of the season. At a variety of indoor and outdoor venues, the festival features plenty of free (and not free) entertainment for young and old. Call ☎ **416-395-0490** or visit www.city.toronto.on.ca/special_events/winterfest/ for more information. Mostly early February.

March

Not just any garden-variety trade show, **Canada Blooms** attracts gardeners and would-be gardeners from all over Canada and the U.S. to check out the latest gardening designs and accessories, just in time for the planting season. The show, held at the Metro Toronto Convention Centre (near the Rogers Centre [formerly known as the SkyDome] and CN Tower), features 30 landscaped gardens, fully in bloom. Find out more at the Canada Blooms Web site (www.canadablooms.com) or call ☎ **800-730-1020** or 416-447-8655. Early March.

Billed as Canada's Spring Antique Spectacular, **Antiques Canada** takes over the Metro Toronto Convention Centre shortly after the Canada Blooms folks leave. In addition to dealers of every stripe from all over Canada, the show features a popular Antiquarian Bookfair. Call ☎ **800-667-0619** or go to www.antiqueshowscanada.com for more information. Mid- to late March.

April

Listen Up! Er — that's not an order, it's the name of the annual **Toronto Festival of Storytelling.** Offering a lineup of free storytelling events at various locations around Toronto, this weeklong festival draws kids and families. The festival includes The Future Folklore Story Contest for Toronto-area students. For more information, contact the Storytellers School of Toronto at ☎ **416-656-2445,** or check out their Web site at www.storytellingtoronto.org. Early April.

Take a morning tour of the Rogers Centre — the first domed stadium with a retractable roof — and then come back later in the day for a Major League Baseball game with the **Toronto Blue Jays.** Hear the crack of the bat and the bark of the hot dog (and beer) vendors as the new season opens up (but note that the roof probably won't — until later in the spring when the weather warms up a bit). Call ☎ **888-654-6529** or 416-341-1234 for Blue Jays ticket information, or you can order tickets online, and check out the team's home schedule, at `http://toronto.bluejays.mlb.com`. (For more about Rogers Centre tours, see Chapter 11.) Early April through September.

In repertory from April through November, the **Shaw Festival** produces around a dozen plays authored by George Bernard Shaw and his playwriting contemporaries. The Shaw has three theaters in Niagara-on-the-Lake, Ontario, about a two-hour drive from Toronto. For more information about plays, schedules, and tickets, call ☎ **800-511-7429** or 905-468-2172, or go to `www.shawfest.com`. (For more about Niagara-on-the-Lake and Ontario's Niagara region, check out Chapter 14.) Early April through November.

In Stratford, Ontario, about a two-hour drive southwest of Toronto, the repertory theater season of the **Stratford Festival** also opens in April. With about 15 plays performed in four theaters, the festival still celebrates its roots as a Shakespearean festival, with three or four Shakespeare plays typically in production. For more information about plays, schedules, and tickets, call ☎ **800-567-1600,** or go to `www.stratfordfestival.ca`. (For more about Stratford, check out Chapter 14.) Early April through late November.

May

Set in one of Toronto's best neighborhood destinations for food and drink, **Santé: The Bloor–Yorkville Wine Festival** features tastings from Canada and international wine regions. Tastings are held at various locations. Tickets are pricey, but each tasting includes expert narrative from representatives of the wineries whose wines are being sampled. For more information, check out `www.santewinefestival.net`. Early May.

Opening during the Victoria Day weekend, the **Milk International Festival of the Arts** (sponsored by the Dairy Farmers of Ontario, naturally) features a week's worth of music, dance, and theater performances, as well as arts-and-crafts opportunities for kids. For details, check out `www.harbourfrontcentre.com/milk/` or call ☎ **416-973-4000.** Mid- to late May.

Nearly always the Monday before the U.S. Memorial Day holiday, **Victoria Day** features citywide celebrations all weekend long. Victoria Day is one of two great fireworks holidays in Canada (Canada Day on July 1 is the other), and in Toronto, you can catch fireworks displays all over town throughout the weekend, with the best at Ashbridge's Bay Park in The Beaches neighborhood. Stake a claim on a spot along the waterfront boardwalk for the best views. Call ☎ **416-338-0338** for details.

Doors Open Toronto is a free weekend event that welcomes visitors to view and learn about the noteworthy and varied architecture of over 100 of Toronto's buildings, particularly those that aren't generally (or fully) accessible to the public. For more information, call ☎ **416-338-3888,** or go to `www.doorsopen.org`. Late May.

June

Celebrate Toronto's multicultural community at the **Metro Toronto International Caravan**, a weeklong event (self-proclaimed "the largest North American cultural festival") full of international flavor, from traditional music and dance to cuisine. Festivities take place at a variety of venues (international pavilions) around town. For details about performances and pavilion locations, call ☎ **416-977-0466.** Late June.

Highlighted by the colorful Pride Parade, **Pride Week** features concerts, speakers, and events that draw on the diversity of Toronto's gay and lesbian community. Get more details by phone at ☎ **416-927-7433** or online at www.pridetoronto.com. Late June.

With over 2,000 musicians participating, the **Toronto Jazz Festival** is held over 10 days in more than 50 venues, mostly in or around downtown Toronto. For details about locations and dates, call ☎ **416-928-2033** or go to www.torontojazz.com. Late June.

Summer is tasty in Toronto

Toronto is *the* place to be during the summer months if you're into outdoor food festivals. You can sample the fare of some of Toronto's ethnic neighborhoods, or stuff yourself for a good cause at a gourmet fundraiser. Actually, proceeds from all of the following feasts benefit Toronto-area agencies and organizations:

✔ **Toronto Taste:** A one-day fundraising event that benefits Second Harvest, an organization that delivers food to Toronto-area social service agencies, Toronto Taste features samplings from the chefs of many of the city's finest restaurants. Call ☎ **416-408-2594** or visit www.torontotaste.ca. Early June.

✔ **Taste of Little Italy:** Head for College Street to sample selections from the restaurants in Toronto's Little Italy. Relax with a gelato and help the event support Toronto's Hospital for Sick Children. Call ☎ **416-240-9338** or go to www.tasteoflittleitaly.com. Mid-June.

✔ **Taste of the Danforth:** Toronto's Greektown hosts this feast along 1.5km (just under a mile) of the Danforth, a major east-side Toronto thoroughfare. The focus is on the neighborhood's Greek restaurants, but you can find fare from other area establishments. Call ☎ **416-469-5634** or check out www.tasteofthedanforth.com. Mid-August.

July

Toronto's celebration of **Canada Day,** which honors the Confederation of Canada in 1867, includes the typical fireworks displays (the best is in The Beaches; see Victoria Day information in "May" above) and city-sponsored events at Nathan Phillips Square outside City Hall. Call ☎ **416-338-0338** for details.

Looking for "500,000 square feet" of party? That's how big the City of Toronto says its annual **Toronto Street Festival** is. The all-free fun and games take place along Yonge Street, the world's longest street, during the weekend after Canada Day. For details, call ☎ **416-338-0338.** Early July.

Theater-in-the-park offerings in Toronto include **CanStage Dream in High Park,** with productions of Shakespeare in west Toronto's High Park amphitheater. Produced by the Canadian Stage Company (CanStage), minimum donations are accepted, though you won't be turned away if you forget your cash. For more information, call ☎ **416-367-1652** or go to www.canstage.com. July through August.

Another of Toronto's many citywide celebrations, the **Toronto Fringe Festival** is the city's premier theater festival, featuring short, independent plays performed in 20 venues around town. For information, call ☎ **416-966-1062;** the festival Web site, www.fringetoronto.com, also has ticket and schedule information. Early to mid-July.

For race fans, **Molson Indy Toronto** roars through the streets of Toronto around Ontario Place as part of the CART racing circuit. A whole week of preliminary parties and charity sporting events precedes the race, which regularly draws more than 150,000 spectators. For more information, call ☎ **416-872-4639** or go to www.molsonindy.com. Mid-July.

The **Toronto Outdoor Art Exhibition** features the works of more than 550 visual artists, from paintings to drawings to photography to ceramics to jewelry to glassworks and much more. This three-day free event at Nathan Phillips Square outside City Hall ranks as the "largest outdoor art exhibition in North America," according to organizers. For event details, call ☎ **416-408-2754** or check out www.torontooutdoorart.org, which includes a catalog of participating artists. Mid-July.

The two-week **Caribana Festival** features the sights, sounds, and tastes of the Caribbean at multiple venues around Toronto. The highlight of the festival is the Caribana Parade (more like a street party, actually), with 15 to 20 colorfully masqueraded bands competing for the title of Band of the Year. The festival also includes carnivals and parades for kids, as well as opportunities to party and enjoy traditional Caribbean music and food. You won't be alone; the festival historically draws more than 1 million party-goers. For details, call ☎ **647-777-1018** or go to www.caribana.com. Late July to early August.

Wander The Beaches neighborhood (with several hundred thousand others) and enjoy the varied jazz sounds of the **Beaches International Jazz Festival**. From vocalists to big bands, jazz takes over 1.5km (just under 1 mile) of Queen Street East, which is closed to traffic; look for impromptu performances by musicians of all stripes. And when you tire of the music, head one block south to the waterfront boardwalk. For festival details, call ☎ **416-698-2152** or check out www.beachesjazz.com. Late July.

August

The professional women's and men's tennis tours visit Toronto during alternate summers. In 2005, it's the women's turn, with the **Rogers AT&T Cup** on tap at the Rexall Centre at York University. (The men will be in Montreal.) For ticket and schedule information, call ☎ **416-665-9777** or go to www.rogersattcup.com. In alternate years, the men come to town for the **Tennis Masters Canada** tournament. For ticket and schedule information, call ☎ **514-273-1515** or go to http://canada.masters-series.com. Mid-August.

Known to locals simply as "The Ex," the **Canadian National Exhibition** offers 18 days on the midway. With carnival rides, farm and animal exhibits, and, of course, plenty to eat (don't miss the powdered mini-doughnuts, as long as you don't mind holding the greasy bag), The Ex is one of the largest fairs in North America, hosting upwards of 1 million visitors during the two and a half weeks before Labour Day. For details, call ☎ **416-263-3800** or go to www.theex.com. Late August through Labour Day.

September

Hollywood North welcomes Hollywood South (and other film production centers) for the **Toronto International Film Festival.** The festival typically runs nearly 300 films from more than 50 countries. Showings are held at a number of locations in downtown Toronto. For a list of films (which are usually announced in August) go to www.e.bell.ca/filmfest or call ☎ **416-968-3456** for additional information. Early September.

September marks the beginning of a new season of the **Harbourfront Reading Series,** weekly readings featuring Canadian and international authors, held at the Harbourfront Centre on Toronto's waterfront. Authors who have read at recent events include Michael Redhill, Salman Rushdie, Jamaica Kincaid, and Jane Urquhart. For schedule and ticket information, call ☎ **416-973-4000** or go to www.readings.org. September through June.

Celebrating books and reading in four Canadian cities — the others are Calgary, Halifax, and Vancouver — **The Word on the Street** in Toronto covers a seven-block stretch of Queen Street West. In addition to book and magazine sales, the one-day event features book signings, author readings, and a designated area called KidStreet, highlighting children's books and events. For more information, call ☎ **416-504-7241** or check out the national Web site at www.thewordonthestreet.ca. Last Sunday in September.

October

The **International Festival of Authors** is the Harbourfront Reading Series on steroids. Actually the highlight event of the Harbourfront Reading Series (see above, under "September"), the festival invites over 100 authors from all over the world to participate in a variety of readings and literary events. For schedule and ticket information, call ☎ **416-973-4000** or go to www.readings.org. Late October.

Tickets are very hard to come by for the National Hockey League's **Toronto Maple Leafs** (especially when the players are locked out), but if you can score some, you'll share the experience with several thousand famously fanatic Maple Leafs fans. Tickets are not as hard to come by for the National Basketball Association's **Toronto Raptors,** which may be your best bet for a professional sports activity in the fall and winter. Both teams play their home games in the Air Canada Centre. For schedules and other information, check out each team's Web site: www.mapleleafs.com and www.nba.com/raptors.

November

The National Trade Centre (near Toronto's waterfront) hosts the largest combined indoor agricultural, horticultural, canine, and equestrian exhibition in the world (whew!), or so say the event's organizers. The **Royal Agricultural Winter Fair** is one big county fair, with livestock and agriculture exhibits, the annual Royal Horse Show, and a variety of special guests (Martha Stewart filmed a segment for her television show here in 2002). For details, call ☎ **416-263-3400** or take a peek online at www.royalfair.org. Mid-November.

Winding nearly 6km (almost 4 miles) through the streets of downtown Toronto is the annual **Santa Claus Parade,** which kicks off the holiday season. The parade has all the standard amenities: colorful floats, school bands, and red-cheeked kids lined up to see the main man himself. For more information, check out www.thesantaclausparade.com. Mid-November.

Discover Canada's early heritage at the **Canadian Aboriginal Festival,** held over three days at the Rogers Centre. Featured events include a lacrosse competition (the game began among native peoples as *baggat-away*), an art exhibition, and traditional music and dance. Traditional arts and crafts are also for sale. For details, call ☎ **519-751-0040** or go to www.canab.com. Late November.

December

The **Cavalcade of Lights** usually starts around the end of November and can run into January, but you're safe anytime in December. With holiday light displays, Toronto's official Christmas tree, and ice-skating events, you'll find more than enough to get in the spirit of the coming holiday season. Call ☎ **416-395-0490** or visit www.city.toronto.on.ca/special_events/cavalcade_lights/ for more information. Late November through December.

Part II
Planning Your Trip to Toronto

The 5th Wave
By Rich Tennant

"I got one of those last minute airfare deals to Toronto."

In this part...

This part covers the nitty-gritty of trip planning, what you really need to do to prepare after you've decided on Toronto as your destination. Ranging from money concerns, to options for getting to Toronto, to Toronto's offerings for travelers with unique travel interests, to passport issues, the information in this part helps you to get organized, and to avoid bogging down over those myriad trip-planning details. Finally, this part also provides some tips on dealing with last-minute pre-travel considerations.

Chapter 4

Managing Your Money

• •

In This Chapter

▶ Figuring out what it will cost to get to Toronto
▶ Picking up a few money-saving tips
▶ Working with the currency
▶ Going with cash or credit (or a combination of both) and protecting each

• •

*N*o doubt about it: Traveling to Toronto can be an expensive proposition. With the amount of business conducted in the downtown core, hotel room rates can be high, with limited availability. Toronto's most popular attractions garner relatively high admission fees. And the cost of dining out continues to rise as more and more premium restaurants open their doors.

But you can do a few things to help keep your costs in check. And this chapter gets you started, with some idea of what to expect in terms of travel, lodging, dining, and sightseeing costs, including expenses that are easy to overlook. I also provide some tips and tricks for keeping your spending to a minimum.

Planning Your Budget

You may be a strict budgeter (or maybe you prefer the more adventurous term, budgeteer). If so, this section gives you a broad idea of what kind of dent your trip to Toronto will make in the family budget. And even if you don't have (or really need) to keep a tight lid on your family's vacation expenditures, this section helps you count up the costs so that you know what kind of cash (or credit) to plan for.

Costing out your transportation

Getting to Toronto via air is, of course, your best option for quick travel, and you'll pay more for that convenience. But what you'll pay to fly to Toronto — as with flying to any destination — varies quite a bit depending on the circumstances under which you travel (staying over a Saturday night, booking your tickets in advance, and so on). With careful planning

(Chapter 5 has more detail on getting the best airfare for your trip), you should be able to keep your airfare to less than C$600 (or US$492), depending on where you fly from.

Taking the train or bus to Toronto will reduce your transportation costs significantly, but you'll pay by virtue of the inconvenience — it's nearly 14 hours by train from Chicago to Toronto, for example.

After you arrive in Toronto, however, you can keep your transportation costs down by making good use of the city's public transit system — that is, after you make your way from the airport to your hotel via airport shuttle (about C$40/US$33). You don't really need to rent a car to explore most of Toronto's major attractions; besides, parking costs in and around downtown Toronto can be extravagant. For more information about getting around town via public transit, check out Chapter 8; Chapter 13 includes a sample itinerary that relies solely on mass transit.

Estimating your lodging costs

Your accommodations will be your biggest expense while in Toronto — unless you're planning a huge shopping excursion. Depending on your tastes, you can easily spend anywhere from C$100 to C$250 (US$82 to US$205) a night on your room. (You can go even higher at some of the ritzier hotels, such as the Four Seasons or the Windsor Arms.) And these rates can increase if your travel schedule coincides with a major convention or with one of the big Toronto festivals.

Chapter 9 includes information to help you decide where to pitch your tent while in Toronto, factoring in the areas with the highest concentration of attractions, shopping, restaurants, and so on. In that chapter, each review includes a dollar-sign rating so that you can quickly find some hotels in your price range.

You can find less expensive accommodations outside the downtown core, but I've assumed in this book that you'll want to stay closer to most of the activities that you'll enjoy while in Toronto. (I do mention a handful of out-of-the-way places to stay, however, in Chapter 9.) Of course, you'll spend a little more on transportation costs, especially if you end up in a hotel with less than convenient access to mass transit.

Eating up those restaurant costs

Even though Toronto's dining scene is rich with fashionable and expensive choices, you can eat pretty well and still keep a fairly tight rein on your budget. One of the best ways to do so is to take advantage of the range of cultural cuisines that are inspired by Toronto's diverse population. You can plan on reasonably inexpensive meals at the restaurants that proliferate in Toronto's ethnic neighborhoods, such as Little Italy, Greektown, or Indian Bazaar. Or you can catch a quick lunch on the run to your next destination, such as a takeaway roti or slice of pizza, or even a hot dog or sausage from one of Toronto's ubiquitous street vendors. (Chapter 10 has suggestions for both sit-down and on-the-run eating in Toronto.)

If you do plan to take in the food and ambience of Toronto's finest restaurants, count on dishing out at least C$100 (US$82) for a dinner for two, including appetizers and/or dessert — more if you add a bottle of wine. But you can mind your budget and still eat at these establishments if you save your dining splurges for the lunch hour, when many restaurants offer most of the same entree choices as they do for dinner (though perhaps in smaller portions) at lower lunchtime rates.

Ponying up to see the sights

Presumably, you're prepared to pay a little more to visit Toronto's attractions; you're not going to just swim in a hotel pool, are you? Well, at some Toronto destinations, you will have to dig a little deeper than at others. For example, to take in the complete package at the CN Tower, you'll need C$32 (US$26); a day at Ontario Place requires C$29 (US$24) for an adult admission and C$15 (US$12) for kids.

On the other hand, you can see a summer play in High Park for C$15 (US$12), and a walk on the boardwalk in The Beaches neighborhood is free of charge. So, balance out your must-see, more expensive attractions with some equally appealing and lower-priced activities; you'll save some money, and enjoy some other engaging experiences to boot.

Shopping by the loonie

So, you've made the journey from Tallahassee to Toronto to take advantage of the favorable exchange rate and get in some serious shopping. Well, that's fine, but at press time, the exchange rate is getting less and less favorable by the day. Also, if you're like me, all those savings tend to be eaten up when you make that extra purchase or two only *because* the rate is so good. And remember, many items that you can find in both the U.S. and Canada are more expensive here in Canadian dollars, so you may not end up with as much of a saving as you anticipated. Table 4–1 gives you an idea of the cost difference (on par) between the same items (at full retail price) in the U.S. and Canada.

Table 4–1	Saving Money in Toronto?	
Item	*U.S. Cost*	*Toronto Cost (with exchange)*
Men's jeans at Old Navy	$32.50	$44.50 ($36.49)
Fleece sweatshirt at BabyGap	$29.50	$34.50 ($28.29)
Swatch watch (original design)	$40.00	$65.00 ($53.30)
The Da Vinci Code (at Barnes & Noble or Chapters)	$14.97	$22.77 ($18.67)
Shrek 2 DVD (at Tower Records or HMV)	$19.99	$25.99 ($21.31)
New Balance women's running shoes	$149.99	$189.99 ($155.79)

As Table 4–1 shows, in the long run you will save money on some items, but other items may end up costing you more. As you're shopping, try to keep in mind what things cost back in the U.S., and then factor in the exchange rate before you whip out your credit card.

For more ideas about shopping in Toronto, from the hippest to the cheapest, check out Chapter 12.

Loving the nightlife — at a cost

From Broadway-quality theater to comedy clubs, from swanky hotel bars to smoky jazz clubs, Toronto offers plenty of evening entertainment options. Just remember that a pint and a play will set you back a few (dozen) bucks.

Tickets for the Broadway-style productions can run from about C$40 to C$100 (US$33–US$82), depending on the popularity of the show. Shows produced by local and smaller companies cost less, but can still be as high as C$60 (US$49). A few laughs at one of Toronto's comedy clubs come with a cover charge ranging from C$10 to C$25 (US$8.20–US$21), more if you stay for dinner. And jiving to a few tunes at the Top o' the Senator can cost you at least a C$10 (US$8.20) cover.

Chapters 15 and 16 include more complete details about the performing arts and nightlife in Toronto.

Taxing matters

Remember that just about every dollar you spend in Toronto — including shopping purchases, restaurant and bar tabs, and hotel bills — is subject to a goods and services tax (GST) of 7 percent and a provincial retail sales tax (PST) of 8 percent (5 percent for lodging).

The good news about GST

If you're visiting Toronto from outside Canada, you can get a rebate on some of the GST (goods and services tax) that you pay for certain purchases, most notably your lodging and goods that you take out of Canada. However, a few conditions apply:

✔ You have to submit original receipts only from the hotel or store. Your credit card receipts won't work.

✔ You have to spend a little to get a little. Only receipts of C$50 and over are eligible for the rebate, and you have to spend a total of at least C$200 (before taxes) before you can claim your rebate.

✔ You have to claim your rebate within a year.

There are a few other conditions; for details, go to www.ccra-adrc.gc.ca/visitors/, which also has information on how to claim your rebate.

If you're traveling from outside Canada, you may be eligible for a GST rebate on some of your purchases and expenses. See the sidebar "The good news about GST" for more information about applying for the GST rebate.

Cutting Costs — But Not the Fun

Throughout this book — in fact, already in this chapter — I highlight some particularly significant money-saving tips with the Bargain Alert icon. This section offers a few general tips for you to consider as you're planning your vacation budget:

- ✔ **Go off-season.** If you can travel at non-peak times (during January and February, for example), as opposed to during the peak summer months, you'll reduce your costs significantly on hotel prices.

- ✔ **Travel midweek.** If you can travel on a Tuesday, Wednesday, or Thursday, you may find cheaper flights. When asking about airfares, see if you can get a cheaper rate by flying on a different day. For more tips on getting a good fare, see Chapter 5.

- ✔ **Try a package tour.** For many destinations, you can book airfare, hotel, ground transportation, and even some sightseeing just by making one call to a travel agent or packager, for a price much lower than if you put the trip together yourself. (See Chapter 5 for more on package tours.)

- ✔ **Always ask for discount rates.** Membership in AAA or CAA, frequent-flier plans, trade unions, seniors' organizations, or other groups may qualify you for savings on car rentals, plane tickets, hotel rooms, and even meals. It doesn't hurt to ask; you may be pleasantly surprised.

- ✔ **Find out what you save by having your kids stay in the room with you.** A room with two double beds usually doesn't cost any more than one with a queen-size bed. And many hotels won't charge you the additional-person rate if the additional person is pint-size and related to you. Even if you have to pay C$10 or C$15 (US$8.20–US$12) extra for a rollaway bed, you'll save hundreds by not taking two rooms.

Making Sense of the Loonie

The *loonie* is Canada's one-dollar coin. The nickname comes from the image of a loon that's engraved on one side of the gold-toned, multi-edged coin. Not to be outdone, Canada's two-dollar coin is dubbed the *toonie* — though you'll find a polar bear, not a toon, on this coin, easily distinguished from the loonie by its wide silver border surrounding a gold-colored inner circle. (Canada has no paper one- or two-dollar bills.) Other Canadian coins are the familiar quarter, dime, nickel, and penny (25¢, 10¢, 5¢, and 1¢, respectively).

Paper currency starts with the $5 bill, and other bills in standard use are the $100 denominations. Keep in mind that the Bank of Canada has recently issued newly designed $5, $10, and $20 bills, but many of the older, similarly valued bills are still in circulation.

While they may be convenient (offering the option of a smaller wad of dough to carry around), you may want to stay away from using $50 and $100 bills. A rash of counterfeiting has resulted in many stores and restaurants refusing to accept these bills, which kind of eliminates their convenience when you're stuck holding on to them for the balance of your trip.

Exchanging your dollars

As of this writing, the Canadian dollar equals roughly US$.82 (or, looking at it the other way, US$1 equals about C$1.23), so U.S. visitors will find that their dollar goes further for many items. (See Table 4–2, for a handy chart to estimate what a Canadian dollar will cost you in U.S. dollars or British pounds.) Keep in mind, though, that the cost of living in Toronto is a bit higher than most U.S. cities, so some things you want to buy may still cost more, even after factoring in the favorable exchange rate. To find out what the exchange rate is just before you leave for Toronto, check out one of the online currency conversion tools readily available (for example, www.xe.com/ucc).

Your best bet for getting Canadian currency — both for its convenience and for its cost-savings — is at an automated teller machine (ATM; also often called an ABM). As in most other major cities these days, cash machines are just about everywhere. But in case you need a pointer to a specific ATM (say, one that's within two blocks of your hotel, or the one with the least exorbitant service charge), check out the upcoming section, "Accessing ATMs and carrying cash."

If you're from outside Canada and you prefer to get your cash the old-fashioned way — at a foreign currency exchange bureau — you can still find places in Toronto to exchange your U.S. dollars (or British pounds, or whatever currency you may bring into Canada with you) for Canadian dollars. But unless you're particularly ATM-phobic, I wouldn't recommend that you do so.

In addition to their convenience, ATMs have the extra benefit of usually giving you the best (and most current) exchange rate for Canadian dollars. And, except for the bank charges associated with ATM transactions discussed in the next section, you won't be hit with the exchange fees at a foreign exchange bureau or bank that can reduce the value of your own currency.

However, if you prefer a little face-to-face interaction when changing your currency, most major downtown-Toronto banks will buy your U.S. dollars. Or you can try one of the following foreign currency exchange bureaus:

✔ **Thomas Cook:** Multiple locations including 1168 Bay St. (at Bloor St.;
☎ **416-975-9940**) and 10 King St. E. (at Yonge St.; ☎ **416-366-1961**)

✔ **Travel Choice American Express:** Two locations in Toronto:
50 Bloor St. W. (in the Holt Renfrew building; ☎ **416-967-3411**) and
100 Front St. W. (at the Fairmont Royal York Hotel; ☎ **416-363-3883**)

Table 4–2		Estimating the Exchange			
CAD$	US$	UK£	CAD$	US$	UK£
1	0.82	0.42	75	62	31
2	1.64	0.84	100	82	42
3	2.46	1.26	125	103	52
4	3.28	1.68	150	123	63
5	4.10	2.10	175	144	73
6	4.92	2.52	200	164	84
7	5.74	2.94	225	185	94
8	6.56	3.36	250	205	105
9	7.38	3.78	275	226	115
10	8.20	4.20	300	246	126
15	12	6.30	350	287	147
20	16	8.39	400	328	168
25	18	10	500	355	210
50	36	21	1000	710	420

Accessing ATMs and carrying cash

These days far more people use ATMs than traveler's checks. Most
cities have these handy 24-hour cash machines, which are linked to
an international network that almost always includes your bank at
home. **Cirrus** (☎ **800-424-7787**; www.mastercard.com) and **Plus**
(☎ **800-843-7587**; www.visa.com) are the two most popular networks.
Check the back of your ATM card to see which network your bank
belongs to. The toll-free numbers and Web sites give specific locations
of ATMs where you can withdraw money while on vacation. You can use
them to withdraw just the money you need every couple of days, which
eliminates the insecurity (and the pickpocketing threat) of carrying around
a large multicolored stash. Of course, many ATMs are little money
managers (or dictators, depending on how you look at it), imposing
limits on your spending by allowing you to withdraw only a certain
amount of money per day.

One important reminder before you go ATM crazy, however. Many banks now charge a fee ranging from 50¢ to $3 whenever a non-account holder uses their ATMs. Your own bank may also assess a fee for using an ATM that's not one of their branch locations. Thus, in some cases, you get charged twice just for using your bank card when you're on vacation. And if you transact at a private ATM — say, at a convenience store — the fees assessed there are likely to be even higher. Reverting to traveler's checks may be cheaper (although certainly less convenient to obtain and use).

Charging ahead with credit cards

Credit cards can be invaluable when traveling: They're a safe way to carry money and they provide a convenient record of all your travel expenses. Of course, the disadvantage is that they're easy to overuse. Unlike ATM or debit cards, which are directly connected to the money you have in your checking account, credit cards can take you as far as your credit limit — which may not bear much relation to your actual financial resources — can go. Credit cards let you indulge in more impulse buying than any other form of payment.

You can also get cash advances on your credit card at any ATM if you know your *personal identification number* (PIN). If you've forgotten it (or didn't even know you had a PIN), call the phone number on the back of your credit card and ask the bank to send the number to you. You'll receive the number in about five to seven business days. Some banks can give you your PIN over the phone if you provide them with security clearance or a confidential "cue" such as your mother's maiden name.

Only get a cash advance from your credit card in an emergency. Interest rates for cash advances are often significantly higher than rates for credit card purchases. More importantly, you start paying interest on the advance the moment you receive the cash. Also note that on airline-affiliated credit cards a cash advance doesn't earn frequent-flier miles.

Dealing with debit cards

Another way of working with money you have — as opposed to the virtual money of credit cards — is to use a debit card — through the Interac system for Canadian travelers — or check card, as they're sometimes called in the States. In many cases, your debit and ATM card are the same piece of plastic. Instead of getting cash, however, the debit card pays for purchases pretty much anywhere a credit card is accepted. The advantage? The money comes out of your checking account rather than pushing up against your credit card limit. Plus, you're not likely to pay an additional fee to use it (though you may end up with some charge if your bank limits, say, the number of debit transactions in a month), and you have less cash to carry around.

Toting traveler's checks

Traveler's checks are something of an anachronism from the days when people wrote personal checks instead of going to an ATM. However, if traveler's checks make you feel more secure about your funds, by all means buy some. Every institution that offers traveler's checks also offers replacements if they're lost or stolen, and the service charges are fairly low, or even nonexistent if you know where to go.

You can get traveler's checks at almost any bank, most often in denominations of $20, $50, $100, $500, and $1,000. For **American Express** traveler's checks, you pay a service charge ranging from 1 percent to 4 percent (unless you're an Amex gold or platinum cardholder, in which case the fee is waived). You can also get American Express traveler's checks over the phone by calling ☎ **800-221-7282** in the U.S. and Canada. U.S. residents who are AAA members can get checks without a fee at most AAA offices. For details, contact your local office or go online to www.aaa.com.

Visa (☎ **800-732-1322** in the U.S. and Canada) also offers traveler's checks, available across the country at Citibank locations and at several other banks. The service charge ranges between 1.5 percent and 2 percent. **MasterCard** has its hand in the traveler's check market, too; call ☎ **800-223-9920** in the U.S. and Canada for details.

Dealing with a Lost or Stolen Wallet

Be sure to contact all of your credit card companies the minute you discover your wallet has been lost or stolen. You'll also want to file a report at the nearest police station; your credit card company or insurer may require a police report number or record of the loss. Most credit card companies have an emergency toll-free number to call if your card is lost or stolen; they may be able to wire you a cash advance immediately or deliver an emergency credit card in a day or two. Call the following emergency numbers in Canada:

- ✔ **American Express:** ☎ **800-268-9824** (for cardholders and traveler's check holders)

- ✔ **MasterCard:** ☎ **800-622-7747**

- ✔ **Visa:** ☎ **800-847-2911**

For other credit cards, call the toll-free number directory at ☎ **800-555-1212.**

If you're using traveler's checks, make sure that you record their serial numbers in a secure place and keep track of where and when you use each check. If your traveler's checks are lost or stolen, you can tell the provider exactly which ones had been legitimately used by you and which are now missing.

If you need emergency cash when you have no access to an ATM or at a time when all banks and American Express offices are closed, you can have money wired to you via **Western Union** (☎ **800-325-6000;** www.westernunion.com).

Identity theft or fraud are potential complications of losing your wallet, especially if your driver's license has gone missing along with your cash and credit cards. Notify the major credit-reporting bureaus immediately; placing a fraud alert on your records may protect you against liability for criminal activity. The three major U.S. credit-reporting agencies are **Equifax** (☎ **800-766-0008;** www.equifax.com), **Experian** (☎ **888-397-3742;** www.experian.com), and **TransUnion** (☎ **800-680-7289;** www.trans union.com). Finally, if you've lost all forms of photo ID, call your airline and explain the situation; they may allow you to board the plane if you have a copy of your passport or birth certificate and a copy of the police report you've filed. (Which, of course, raises the question as to whether you should travel with a photocopy of your passport. In a word, yes; keep a copy of the most critical pages — that is, with your passport number and photo — in a conspicuous, and separate, place.)

Chapter 5

Getting to Toronto

● ●

In This Chapter

▶ Getting to Toronto by air
▶ Making air travel plans online
▶ Going the road-trip route
▶ Joining a tour

● ●

So you've decided to head to Toronto for a little R&R. What's the best way to get your vacation off to a less than restful or relaxing start? To actually plan your trip — not always an easy thing to do when the number of airlines and fare rules and regulations and border crossings and customs requirements just want to make you hole up in your bedroom closet and refuse to take visitors.

This chapter comes to the rescue — though you still have to do some of the legwork, whether you decide to drive to town, sign up with a tour group, or book your airline tickets yourself.

Flying to Toronto

If you're not the ride-along-with-the-crowd kind of traveler, or you simply enjoy the freedom and flexibility that goes along with making your own plans, Toronto is a great destination. With attractions inside and outside the downtown core — and even some great ones an hour or two away, such as Niagara Falls or the Stratford Festival — you can enhance your Toronto experience by making sure that you give yourself the flexibility and the means to enjoy the city and its surroundings.

Finding out which airlines fly there

Each of Canada's three major airlines has a number of nonstops into Toronto, with the country's only national airline (Air Canada) leading the way:

▶ **Air Canada** (☎ **888-247-2262;** www.aircanada.com) has nonstop flights to more than 40 U.S. airports and 25 Canadian cities, as well as several daily nonstop flights from London's Heathrow Airport.

✔ **Jetsgo** (☎ 866-440-0441; www.jetsgo.net) flies to Toronto from ten U.S. airports — Las Vegas, Los Angeles, New York, Newark, and six cities in Florida — and a dozen Canadian cities.

✔ **WestJet** (☎ 888-WESTJET [937-8538]; www.westjet.com) offers nonstop flights to Toronto from five U.S. cities — Los Angeles; New York; and Fort Lauderdale, Orlando, and Tampa, Florida — and ten Canadian cities.

If you're traveling from the United States, you have a number of nonstop options:

✔ **America West Airlines** (☎ 800-235-9292; www.americawest.com) has daily nonstop flights from Phoenix and Las Vegas.

✔ **American Airlines** (☎ 800-433-7300; www.aa.com) has daily nonstops from six U.S. cities (Boston, Chicago, Dallas/Fort Worth, Los Angeles, Miami, and New York).

✔ **Continental Airlines** (☎ 800-231-0856; www.continental.com) has daily nonstops from Cleveland, Houston, and Newark.

✔ **Delta Airlines** (☎ 800-221-1212; www.delta.com) flies nonstop to Toronto daily from Atlanta and Cincinnati.

✔ **Northwest Airlines** (☎ 800-225-2525; www.nwa.com) flies nonstop to Toronto daily from Detroit, Memphis, and Minneapolis.

✔ **United Airlines** (☎ 800-241-6522; www.united.com) has daily nonstop flights from Chicago and Washington Dulles (VA).

✔ **US Airways** (☎ 800-943-5436; www.usairways.com) flies nonstop to Toronto from four locations: Charlotte (NC), Philadelphia, Pittsburgh, and Washington National (DC).

If you're traveling from outside North America, your nonstop options include several daily flights on Air Canada from London's Heathrow Airport, as well as the following:

✔ **Air New Zealand** (☎ 0800 737 000; www.airnewzealand.co.nz) flies nonstop to Los Angeles from Auckland and Christchurch with connections on to Toronto.

✔ **British Airways** (☎ 0870 850 9850; www.britishairways.com) has two nonstop flights daily from London's Heathrow Airport.

✔ **Qantas Airlines** (☎ 13 13 13; www.qantas.com.au) flies from Auckland, Melbourne, and Sydney to Los Angeles, from which you can connect to Toronto.

Getting the best deal on your airfare

Competition among the major airlines is unlike that of any other industry. Every airline offers virtually the same product (basically, a coach seat is a coach seat is a . . .), yet prices can vary by hundreds of dollars.

Business travelers who need the flexibility to buy their tickets at the last minute and change their itineraries at a moment's notice — and who want to get home before the weekend — pay (or at least their companies pay) the premium rate, known as the *full fare*. But if you can book your ticket far in advance, stay over Saturday night, and are willing to travel midweek (Tuesday, Wednesday, or Thursday), you can qualify for the least expensive price — usually a fraction of the full fare. On most flights, the full fare is close to $1,000 or more, but a 7- or 14-day advance purchase ticket may cost less than half of that amount. Obviously, planning ahead pays.

The airlines also periodically hold sales, in which they lower the prices on their most popular routes. These fares have advance purchase requirements and date-of-travel restrictions, but you can't beat the prices. As you plan your vacation, keep your eyes open for these sales, which tend to take place in seasons of low travel volume — such as January and February in Toronto. You almost never see a sale around the peak summer-vacation months of July and August, or around Thanksgiving or Christmas, when many people fly regardless of the fare they have to pay.

Cutting ticket costs by using consolidators

Consolidators, also known as *bucket shops,* are great sources for international tickets, although they usually can't beat the Internet on fares within North America. Start by looking in Sunday-newspaper travel sections; U.S. travelers should focus on the *New York Times, Los Angeles Times,* and *Miami Herald.*

Bucket shop tickets are usually nonrefundable or rigged with stiff cancellation penalties, often as high as 50 percent to 75 percent of the ticket price, and some put you on charter airlines with questionable safety records.

Several reliable consolidators are worldwide and available on the Net. **STA Travel** (☎ 800-781-4040; www.statravel.com), the world's leader in student travel, offers good fares for travelers of all ages. **Flights.com** (☎ 800-TRAV-800; www.flights.com) started in Europe and has excellent fares worldwide, but particularly to that continent. Flights.com also has "local" Web sites in 12 countries. **FlyCheap** (☎ 800-FLY-CHEAP; www.1800flycheap.com) is owned by package-holiday megalith MyTravel and so has especially good access to fares for sunny destinations. **Air Tickets Direct** (☎ 800-778-3447; www.airticketsdirect.com) is based in Montreal and leverages the currently weaker Canadian dollar for low fares; it'll also book trips to places that U.S. travel agents won't touch, such as Cuba.

Booking your travel online

The "big three" online travel agencies, **Expedia** (www.expedia.com), **Travelocity** (www.travelocity.com), and **Orbitz** (www.orbitz.com) sell most of the air tickets bought on the Internet. (Canadian travelers should try www.expedia.ca and www.travelocity.ca; U.K. residents can go for expedia.co.uk and opodo.co.uk.) Each has different business deals with the airlines and may offer different fares on the same flights, so shopping around is wise. Expedia and Travelocity will also send you an *E-mail notification* when a cheap fare becomes available to your favorite destination. Of the smaller travel agency Web sites, **SideStep** (www.sidestep.com) receives good reviews from users. It's a browser add-on that purports to "search 140 sites at once," but in reality beats competitors' fares only as often as other sites do.

Great **last-minute deals** are available through free weekly E-mail services provided directly by the airlines. Most of these deals are announced on Tuesday or Wednesday and must be purchased online. Most are valid for travel only that weekend, but some (such as Southwest's) can be booked weeks or months in advance. Sign up for weekly E-mail alerts at airline Web sites or check mega-sites that compile comprehensive lists of last-minute specials, such as **Smarter Living** (smarterliving.com). For last-minute trips, www.site59.com in the U.S. and in Europe often have better deals than the major-label sites.

If you're willing to give up some control over your flight details, use an *opaque fare service* such as **Priceline** (www.priceline.com) or **Hotwire** (www.hotwire.com). Both offer rock-bottom prices in exchange for travel on a "mystery airline" at a mysterious time of day, often with a mysterious change of planes en route. The mystery airlines are all major, well-known carriers — and the possibility of being sent from Philadelphia to Toronto via Tampa is remote. On the other hand, your chances of getting a 6 a.m. or 11 p.m. flight are pretty high. Hotwire tells you flight prices before you buy; Priceline usually has better deals than Hotwire, but you have to play their "name our price" game.

Great last-minute deals are also available directly from the airlines themselves through a free E-mail service called *E-savers*. Each week, the airline sends you a list of discounted flights, usually leaving the upcoming Friday or Saturday and returning the following Monday or Tuesday. You can sign up for all the major airlines at one time by logging on to **Smarter Living** (www.smarterliving.com), or you can go to each individual airline's Web site. Airline sites also offer schedules, flight booking, and information on late-breaking bargains.

Driving to Toronto

Taking the family minivan to Toronto is an easy and convenient solution for many travelers, particularly if you are traveling from the eastern half of the continent. The Ontario/U.S. border has ten easy-to-access crossings; the major points of entry are around Detroit and Buffalo. From east of Toronto, Highway 20 in Quebec becomes Highway 401 in Ontario; the 401 is the primary east–west highway through the north part of the greater Toronto area. From west of Toronto, you're probably better off (timewise) zipping down to the U.S. and reentering Canada through Michigan.

Riding the rails to Toronto

You can get to Toronto by train, but be prepared for a long trip. From Chicago to Toronto, for example, is a journey of over 13 hours; from New York, it's just over 12 hours. Within Canada, the train from Halifax will take over 24 hours; from Montreal, count on around 5 hours.

All trains arrive at Union Station in downtown Toronto (just across from the Fairmont Royal York). Union is also a TTC subway station, so you can easily board this to reach your accommodation.

For more information on train travel from the U.S., contact Amtrak (☎ **800-872-7245**; www.amtrak.com); within Canada, contact VIA Rail (☎ **888-842-7245**; www.viarail.ca).

Driving *to* Toronto is a pretty easy exercise. Driving *around* Toronto is more like the proverbial exercise in futility. Before you decide to bring the family car with you, review Chapter 8 to find out what kind of traffic you'll likely run into, and how much extra time and money you should allot for using your own transportation to navigate Toronto.

Crossing the border from the U.S. into Canada has become more complex in the wake of the September 11, 2001, terrorist attacks. Be prepared for long waits at border crossings and customs stations, particularly at entry points that see a lot of commercial traffic. Here are a few tips for getting to Toronto from the U.S. by car:

✔ **From Michigan:** Entering Ontario from Michigan, you're usually better off avoiding the Detroit–Windsor crossing, which is almost always encumbered by a heavy amount of commercial traffic — trucks hauling commercial goods and parts back and forth between Canada and the U.S. Plus, with Detroit being a major metropolitan area (of which Windsor, Ontario, is a part), you also run into a lot of cross-border traffic from residents in the area.

If you can, avoid the Detroit area altogether and head north on Interstate 69, which originates in Indianapolis and runs north through Michigan, but west of Detroit. At the crossing in Port Huron, Michigan, and Sarnia, Ontario, Interstate 69 becomes Highway 402 in Ontario. Of course, this crossing can also be busy at times, but the overall volume of traffic is significantly lower than that of its Detroit cousin.

✔ **From New York:** The Buffalo–Niagara Falls area has three major border crossings into Canada: the Queenston–Lewiston Bridge, north of Niagara Falls; the Rainbow Bridge in Niagara Falls; and the Peace Bridge, just west of the city of Buffalo. All crossings have their share of delays, but the Queenston–Lewiston Bridge is generally the least trafficked; from there, you'll find easy access to the Queen Elizabeth Way (QEW), which will take you to the Toronto metropolitan area.

It's a good idea to bring along your car's registration information; you may be asked to show proof at the border that you and your car are together. And if you're driving a fairly new car, a bill of sale may not hurt either.

Choosing an Escorted or Package Tour

Say the words "escorted tour" or "package tour" and you may automatically feel as though you're being forced to choose: your money or your lifestyle. Think again. Times — and tours — have changed.

An escorted tour does, in fact, involve an escort, but that doesn't mean it has to be dull — or even tame. Escorted tours range from cushy bus trips, where you sit back and let the driver worry about the traffic, to adventures that include river rafting or trekking in the Grand Canyon — activities with which most of us can use a bit of guidance. You do, however, travel with a group, which may be just the thing if you're single and want company. In general, your costs are taken care of after you arrive at your destination, but you will have had to cover the airfare.

Which brings us to package tours. Unlike escorted tours, these generally package costs rather than people. Some companies bundle every aspect of your trip, including tours to various sights, but most deal just with selected aspects, allowing you to get good deals by putting together an airfare and hotel arrangement, say, or an airfare and greens fee package. Most packages leave you a lot of leeway, while saving you money.

How do you find these deals? Well, I suggest some strategies in the next two sections, but every city is different; the tour operators I mention may not offer deals convenient to your city. If that's the case, check with a local travel agent: They generally know the most options close to home, and how best to put together components such as escorted tours and airline packages.

Joining an escorted tour

You may be one of the many people who love escorted tours. The tour company takes care of all the details, and tells you what to expect at each leg of your journey. You know your costs up front and, in the case of the tame ones, you don't get many surprises. Escorted tours can take you to the maximum number of sights in the minimum amount of time with the least amount of hassle.

If you decide to go with an escorted tour, I strongly recommend purchasing travel insurance, especially if the tour operator asks you to pay up front. But don't buy insurance from the tour operator! If the tour operator doesn't fulfill its obligation to provide you with the vacation you paid for, there's no reason to think that they'll fulfill their insurance obligations either. Get travel insurance through an independent agency. (I tell you more about the ins and outs of travel insurance in Chapter 7.)

Before you choose an escorted tour, along with finding out whether you have to put down a deposit and when final payment is due, ask a few simple questions:

- ✔ **What is the cancellation policy?** Can they cancel the trip if they don't get enough people? How late can you cancel if you are unable to go? Do you get a refund if you cancel? If they cancel?

- ✔ **How jam-packed is the schedule?** Does the tour schedule try to fit 25 hours into a 24-hour day, or does it give you ample time to relax by the pool or shop? If getting up at 7 a.m. every day and not returning to your hotel until 6 or 7 p.m. that night sounds like a grind, certain escorted tours may not be for you.

- ✔ **How large is the group?** The smaller the group, the less time you spend waiting for people to get on and off the bus. Tour operators may be evasive about this, because they may not know the exact size of the group until everybody has made reservations, but they should be able to give you a rough estimate.

- ✔ **Is there a minimum group size?** Some tours have a minimum group size, and may cancel the tour if they don't book enough people. If a quota exists, find out what it is and how close they are to reaching it. Again, tour operators may be evasive in their answers, but the information may help you select a tour that's sure to happen.

- ✔ **What exactly is included?** Don't assume anything. You may have to pay to get yourself to and from the airport. A box lunch may be included in an excursion but drinks may be extra. Beer may be included but not wine. How much flexibility do you have? Can you opt out of certain activities, or does the bus leave once a day, with no exceptions? Are all your meals planned in advance? Can you choose your entree at dinner, or does everybody get the same chicken cutlet?

Just about all your escorted-tour options for Toronto involve only two or three days in the city before you're off to other Ontario and/or Quebec destinations. So if you want to spend more than a couple of days exploring Toronto, but still want to do the escorted-tour thing, your best bet is to book a tour that starts (or ends) in Toronto and make sure you arrive a few days early (or leave a few days after the tour ends). Here are a couple of reputable tour companies that offer extra nights before or after a tour:

✔ **Collette Vacations** (☎ 800-468-5955; www.collettevacations.ca) offers 9-day escorted tours that include 2 to 3 days in Toronto, as well as stops in Ottawa, Quebec City, Montreal, and other destinations. Rates range from C$1,639 to C$1,799 (US$1,344 to US$1,475) per person based on double occupancy. Collette also offers Toronto package tours.

✔ **Brewster** (☎ 877-791-5500; www.brewster.ca) has a number of tours of varying lengths that run from Toronto. The tours — some with train transportation, others with motorcoach — generally include 1 or 2 days in Toronto before heading off to other Canadian stops. Rates range from C$778 (US$638) for a 6-day tour to C$1,404 (US$1,151) for a 9-day tour.

Choosing a package tour

For lots of destinations, package tours can be a smart way to go. In many cases, a package tour that includes airfare, hotel, and transportation to and from the airport costs less than the hotel alone on a tour you book yourself. That's because packages are sold in bulk to tour operators, who resell them to the public. It's kind of like buying your vacation at a buy-in-bulk store — except the tour operator is the one who buys the 1,000-count box of garbage bags and resells them 10 at a time at a cost that undercuts the local supermarket.

Package tours can vary as much as those garbage bags, too. Some offer a better class of hotels than others; others provide the same hotels for lower prices. Some book flights on scheduled airlines; others sell charters. In some packages, your choice of accommodations and travel days may be limited. Some let you choose between escorted vacations and independent vacations; others allow you to add on just a few excursions or escorted day trips (also at discounted prices) without booking an entirely escorted tour.

✔ To find package tours, check out the travel section of your local Sunday newspaper or the ads in the back of national travel magazines such as *Travel & Leisure, National Geographic Traveler,* and *Condé Nast Traveler*. **Liberty Travel** (call ☎ 888-271-1584 to find the store nearest you; www.libertytravel.com) is one of the biggest packagers, and usually boasts a full-page ad in Sunday papers.

If you're unsure about the pedigree of a smaller packager, check with the Better Business Bureau in the city where the company is based, or go online at www.bbb.org. If a packager won't tell you where it's based, don't fly with them.

✔ Another good source of package deals is the airlines themselves. Most major airlines offer air/land packages, including **Air Canada Vacations** (☎ 877-752-7710; www.aircanadavacations.com), **American Airlines Vacations** (☎ 800-321-2121;

www.aavacations.com), **Delta Vacations** (☎ 800-221-6666; www.deltavacations.com), **Continental Airlines Vacations** (☎ 800-301-3800; www.coolvacations.com), and **United Vacations** (☎ 888-854-3899; www.unitedvacations.com).

✔ Several big **online travel agencies** — Expedia, Travelocity, Orbitz, Site59, and Lastminute.com — also do a brisk business in packages.

✔ **Resorts Ontario** (☎ 800-363-7227; www.resortsontario.com), an association of more than 200 resort facilities (mostly inns and B&Bs) around Ontario, offers an attractive selection of seasonal travel packages that combine accommodations with indoor and outdoor activities, including golf, winter sports, theater, and shopping.

✔ The **Ontario Tourism Marketing Partnership** (☎ 800-263-7836; www.ontariotravel.net) partners with other travel associations in Ontario to provide a one-stop-shopping resource for travelers interested in visiting the province. Check out the main Web site, or one of their seasonal Web sites (for example, www.fallinontario.com or www.winterinontario.com) if you know when you're visiting Toronto, for a listing of getaway packages that include many to Toronto and surrounding areas.

Chapter 6

Catering to Special Travel Needs or Interests

• •

In This Chapter

▶ Exploring family-friendly Toronto

▶ Traveling on the senior circuit

▶ Discovering accessible Toronto

▶ Finding gay and lesbian resources

• •

*O*pportunities and experiences in Toronto are readily available and accessible for travelers with any kind of special travel need. This chapter offers information about distinct resources available to families traveling with kids, seniors, people with disabilities, and gay and lesbian travelers.

Traveling with the Brood: Advice for Families

If you have enough trouble getting your kids out of the house in the morning, dragging them thousands of miles away may seem like an insurmountable challenge. But family travel can be immensely rewarding, giving you new ways of seeing the world through younger pairs of eyes.

Throughout this book, you can find the Kid Friendly icon highlighting hotels, restaurants, and attractions that are particularly kid-friendly. The following list highlights a few other worthy family-friendly tips and resources that can help you plan and complete your Toronto family vacation:

✔ **Mine the Internet.** You can find good family-oriented vacation advice on the Internet from sites like the **Family Travel Network** (www.familytravelnetwork.com); **Traveling Internationally with Your Kids** (www.travelwithyourkids.com), a comprehensive site offering sound advice for long-distance and international travel with children; and **Family Travel Files** (www.thefamilytravelfiles.com), which offers an online magazine and a directory of off-the-beaten-path tours and tour operators for families.

✔ **Mine the Internet, part two.** The Web is also the place to go for Toronto-specific information about activities and attractions for kids. For example, e-kids Toronto (www.e-kidstoronto.com) is targeted to Toronto residents, but it's a good way to discover activities that may be available to your children. Also, be sure to look for kid-friendly exhibitions at Toronto museums and other attractions so that you won't feel as if you're dragging your children through "another boring museum — again!"

✔ **Read up about Toronto (and about traveling with kids).** *How to Take Great Trips with Your Kids* (The Harvard Common Press) is full of good general advice that can apply to travel anywhere.

✔ **Plan ahead.** And involve the whole family. Some Toronto attractions are great for family members of all ages; others require patience and perhaps some headache medicine for the adults. In this book, whenever applicable, I've included parent alternatives to kid-specific activities and events (or vice versa) so that when your kids are off shopping for the latest trends in black outerwear and body-piercing accessories, you can be relaxing at a nearby outdoor cafe or bar with your favorite beverage.

✔ **Consider getting help.** I don't mean that you should have your head examined for bringing the kids along. Rather, look for babysitting resources that may be available through your hotel or through babysitting services such as Christopher Robin (☎ 416-483-4744; http://christopherrobin.homestead.com) so that you can get away for at least that one special evening out.

✔ **Ask about family packages or discounts.** Most Toronto attractions have family pricing that allows for a few dollars off your family's total admission fee. Also, check with your hotel to find out whether it offers any special family packages — financial or otherwise. It doesn't hurt to ask, and it may actually ease your travel budget.

Making Age Work for You: Tips for Seniors

Mention the fact that you're a senior citizen when you make your travel reservations. Although nearly all the major airlines have canceled their senior discount and coupon book programs, many hotels still offer discounts for seniors. In Toronto, people over the age of 65 qualify for reduced admission to theaters, museums, and other attractions, as well as discounted fares on public transportation.

Here are some other travel resources available for seniors:

✔ Members of **AARP** (formerly known as the American Association of Retired Persons), 601 E St. NW, Washington, DC 20049 (☎ 800-424-3410 or 202-434-2277; www.aarp.org), get discounts on hotels, airfares, and car rentals. AARP offers members a wide range of benefits, including *AARP: The Magazine* and a monthly newsletter. Anyone over 50 can join.

✔ **CARP** (Canada's Association for the Fifty-Plus), 27 Queen St. E., Suite 1304, Toronto, ON M5C 2M6 (☎ **416-363-8748;** www.50plus.com), offers similar benefits for Canadian seniors, including the *50Plus* magazine and CARP Travel, a full-service travel agency.

✔ Many reliable agencies and organizations target the 50-plus market. **Elderhostel** (☎ **877-426-8056;** www.elderhostel.org) arranges study programs for those aged 55 and over (and a spouse or companion of any age) in Canada and in more than 80 countries around the world. Most courses last five to seven days in Canada and the United States (2–4 weeks abroad), and many include airfare, accommodations in university dormitories or modest inns, meals, and tuition. Programs available for the Toronto area include theater packages and programs highlighting Toronto's cultural diversity.

✔ Recommended publications offering travel resources and discounts for seniors include the following: the quarterly magazine *Travel 50 & Beyond* (www.travel50andbeyond.com); *Travel Unlimited: Uncommon Adventures for the Mature Traveler* (Avalon); *101 Tips for Mature Travelers,* available from Grand Circle Travel (☎ **800-221-2610** or 617-350-7500; www.gct.com); *The Mature Traveler,* a monthly newsletter on senior travel, available by subscription (US$29.95 a year; www.thematuretraveler.com); *The 50+ Traveler's Guidebook* (St. Martin's Press); and *Unbelievably Good Deals and Great Adventures That You Absolutely Can't Get Unless You're Over 50* (McGraw-Hill).

Accessing Toronto: Advice for Travelers with Disabilities

Most disabilities shouldn't stop anyone from traveling. There are more options and resources out there than ever before. Nearly all the attractions, hotels, restaurants, and other destinations recommended in this book are accessible to travelers with disabilities. For those few that are not accessible, I've noted the specifics.

The Toronto Transit Commission, Toronto's public transit system (☎ **416-393-4636;** www.ttc.ca), is gradually improving its accessibility for persons with disabilities.

✔ As of this writing, 24 subway stations are accessible via elevators, including 9 stations in or around downtown Toronto, and 34 bus routes have accessible buses; accessible bus stops have the international wheelchair symbol on the bus stop post.

✔ Wheel-Trans offers door-to-door service for persons with disabilities. Fares are the same as on other TTC operations, and the service is available to Toronto visitors. Call ☎ **416-393-4111.**

▶ Streetcars are not wheelchair-accessible; in fact, the first step onto or off of streetcars is a steep one, so you may want to avoid the streetcar routes completely if you have any mobility concerns.

The following list offers some more resources available for travelers with disabilities:

▶ In Toronto, one of the best resources available is *Toronto with Ease,* a joint publication of the Disability Today Publishing Group and Tourism Toronto. This 48-page guide highlights (and congratulates) accessible attractions, hotels, restaurants, and shopping destinations in Toronto. To request a copy, contact Tourism Toronto, P.O. Box 126, 207 Queens Quay W., Toronto, ON M5J 1A7 (☎ **800-499-2514** or 416-203-2600; www.tourismtoronto.com).

▶ **Access to Travel** (www.accesstotravel.gc.ca) is a Government of Canada Web resource that offers information about accessible travel across Canada. The extensive Web site has links to accessibility Web sites and information about transportation facilities for people with disabilities.

▶ The **Centre for Independent Living in Toronto (C.I.L.T.)**, 205 Richmond St. W., Suite 605, Toronto, ON M5V 1V3 (☎ **416-599-2458**), provides referrals for accessible hotels and restaurants.

▶ **Access-Able Travel Source** (www.access-able.com) provides a comprehensive database of travel agents who specialize in trip planning for travelers with disabilities, as well as detailed information about accessible destinations around the world.

▶ Many travel agencies offer customized tours and itineraries for travelers with disabilities. **Accessible Journeys** (☎ **800-846-4537** or 610-521-0339; www.disabilitytravel.com) caters specifically to slow walkers and wheelchair travelers and their families and friends.

▶ Organizations that offer assistance to disabled travelers include the **Moss Rehab Hospital** (www.mossresourcenet.org), which provides a library of accessible-travel resources online; the **Society for Accessible Travel and Hospitality** (☎ **212-447-7284;** www.sath.org; annual membership fees: US$45 adults, US$30 seniors and students), which offers a wealth of travel resources for all types of disabilities and informed recommendations on destinations, access guides, travel agents, tour operators, vehicle rentals, and companion services; and the **American Foundation for the Blind** (☎ **800-232-5463;** www.afb.org), which provides information on traveling with Seeing Eye dogs.

▶ For more information specifically targeted to travelers with disabilities, the community Web site **iCan** (www.icanonline.net/channels/travel/index.cfm) has destination guides and several regular columns on accessible travel. Also check out the quarterly magazine *Emerging Horizons* ($14.95 per year, $19.95 outside the U.S.; www.emerginghorizons.com); **Twin Peaks Press** (☎ 360-694-2462; http://disabilitybookshop.virtualave.net/blist84.htm), offering travel-related books for travelers with special needs; and *Open World Magazine,* published by the Society for Accessible Travel and Hospitality (see above; subscription: $18 per year, $35 outside the U.S.).

Following the Rainbow: Resources for Gay and Lesbian Travelers

With Canada's largest gay community, Toronto is well accustomed to welcoming gay and lesbian visitors. The local community is centered around the intersection of Church and Wellesley streets, a neighborhood teeming with restaurants, bars, and shopping opportunities. The major event of the year, drawing nearly a million participants, is Pride Week (☎ 416-927-7433; www.pridetoronto.com) in late June, highlighted by the Pride Parade. Inside Out, the Toronto Lesbian and Gay Film and Video Festival, held annually in mid-May (☎ 416-977-6847; www.insideout.on.ca), features showings of over 250 films from Canada and around the world.

✔ The primary resource for news and community events and activities is *Xtra!,* a biweekly newspaper available at bookstores and other locations across Toronto. The *Xtra!* Web site also features an interactive community events page (www.xtra.ca).

✔ Many agencies offer tours and travel itineraries specifically for gay and lesbian travelers. In Toronto, **Rainbow High Vacations** (☎ 800-387-1240 or 416-962-2422; www.rainbowhighvacations.com) features packages both to and from Toronto, including "Get Married in Toronto" packages for travelers who wish to take advantage of an Ontario court's 2003 ruling that Canada's definition of marriage should include same-sex couples.

Outside Toronto, **Above and Beyond Tours** (☎ 800-397-2681; www.abovebeyondtours.com) is the exclusive gay and lesbian tour operator for United Airlines. **Now, Voyager** (☎ 800-255-6951; www.nowvoyager.com) is a well-known San Francisco–based gay-owned and -operated travel service. **Olivia Cruises & Resorts** (☎ 800-631-6277 or 510-655-0364; www.olivia.com) charters entire resorts and ships for exclusive lesbian vacations and offers smaller group experiences for both gay and lesbian travelers.

✔ The International Gay & Lesbian Travel Association (IGLTA) (☎ 800-448-8550 or 954-776-2626; www.iglta.org) is the trade association for the gay and lesbian travel industry, and offers an online directory of gay- and lesbian-friendly travel businesses; go to their Web site and click on "Members."

✔ The following travel guides are available at most travel bookstores and gay and lesbian bookstores, or you can order them from **Giovanni's Room** bookstore, 1145 Pine St., Philadelphia, PA 19107 (☎ **215-923-2960;** www.giovannisroom.com): *Frommer's Gay & Lesbian Europe,* an excellent travel resource; *Out and About* (☎ **800-929-2268** or 415-644-8044; www.outandabout.com), which offers guidebooks and a newsletter ten times a year packed with solid information on the global gay and lesbian scene; *Spartacus International Gay Guide* and *Odysseus,* both good, annual English-language guidebooks for gay men; the *Damron* guides, with separate, annual books for gay men and lesbians; and *Gay Travel A to Z: The World of Gay & Lesbian Travel Options at Your Fingertips* by Marianne Ferrari (Ferrari Publications; Box 35575, Phoenix, AZ 85069), a comprehensive gay and lesbian guidebook series.

Chapter 7

Taking Care of the Remaining Details

*T*hink of this chapter as your personal assistant for getting out the door with everything you need taken care of for your trip. This personal assistant reminds you to make sure that you have your passport (or other proof of citizenship), suggests what kinds of travel insurance to consider, offers tips on staying healthy while traveling, suggests where to go to rent a car (if you decide you need one), and then changes hats to become your personal concierge, helping you purchase your attraction and entertainment admissions ahead of time.

Do You Need a Passport?

A valid passport is the only legal form of identification accepted around the world. If you're traveling from the U.S., you don't technically need a passport to enter Canada; a valid proof of citizenship (such as a birth certificate) is all you require (but a driver's license isn't enough). However, if you have a valid passport, bring it. If you don't, getting a passport is easy, but the process takes some time. My recommendation: Make the effort to get a passport, if you can; having one helps speed the border-crossing process, and, of course, you'll then have it ready when you decide to take the family to Paris.

Applying for a U.S. passport

If you're applying for a passport for the first time, follow these steps:

1. Complete a **passport application** in person at a U.S. passport office; a federal, state, or probate court; or a major post office. To find your regional passport office, either check the **U.S. State Department** Web site, http://travel.state.gov/passport_services.html, or call the **National Passport Information Center (☎ 877-487-2778)** for automated information.

2. Present a **certified birth certificate** as proof of citizenship. (Bringing along your driver's license, state or military ID, or social security card is also a good idea.)

3. Submit **two identical passport-sized photos,** measuring 2-x-2 inches in size. You often find businesses that take these photos near a passport office. *Note:* You can't use a strip from a photo-vending machine because the pictures aren't identical.

4. Pay a **fee.** For people age 16 and over, a passport is valid for ten years and costs $85. For those 15 and under, a passport is valid for five years and costs $70.

Allow plenty of time before your trip to apply for a passport; processing normally takes three weeks but can take longer during busy periods (especially spring).

If you have a passport in your current name that was issued within the past 15 years (and you were over age 16 when it was issued), you can renew the passport by mail for $55. Whether you're applying in person or by mail, you can download passport applications from the U.S. State Department Web site at http://travel.state.gov/passport_services.html. For general information, call the **National Passport Agency (☎ 202-647-0518).** To find your regional passport office, either check the U.S. State Department Web site or call the **National Passport Information Center** toll-free number (☎ 877-487-2778) for automated information.

American Passport Express (☎ 800-841-6778; www.american passport.com) can process your first-time passport application in five to eight business days for $145, plus a $60 service fee; for renewals, the cost is $115 plus a $60 service fee. If you need the passport in three to five business days, the service fee is $100, and for a $150 service fee you can receive your passport in 24 hours.

Applying for other passports

The following list offers more information for citizens of Australia, New Zealand, and the United Kingdom.

- ✔ **Australians** can visit a local post office or passport office, call the **Australia Passport Information Service** (☎ **131-232** toll free from Australia), or log on to www.passports.gov.au for details on how and where to apply. Passports cost A$136 for adults and A$68 for those under 18.

- ✔ **New Zealanders** can pick up a passport application at any travel agency or Link Centre. For information, contact the **Passport Office,** Department of Internal Affairs, PO Box 10–526, Wellington (☎ **0800-225-050;** www.passports.govt.nz). Passports are NZ$80 for adults and NZ$40 for those under 16.

- ✔ **United Kingdom** residents can pick up applications for a standard ten-year passport (five-year passport for children under 16) at passport offices, major post offices, or a travel agency. For information, contact the **United Kingdom Passport Service** (☎ **0870-521-0410;** www.ukpa.gov.uk). Passports cost £42 for adults and £25 for those under 16.

Renting a Car (Or, Five Reasons Not to Rent a Car)

As opposed to most other major destinations, such as New York or London or Paris, where renting a car is really a poor option, deciding to rent a car while in Toronto is truly a matter of what you need, rather than what's most convenient. Navigating Toronto's streets and highways is not nearly as troublesome as doing so in the three cities mentioned above—the city layout is not confusing; parking is readily available (if at a fairly significant cost); and there are daily lulls in the city's traffic congestion.

If you're traveling with young kids and doing everything in Toronto via public transit is not an option, then the downside of renting a car will more than be offset by the convenience of being at the wheel and being able to cater to the needs of your children with a ready cooler full of juice boxes. Or, you may be planning a side trip to Niagara Falls or Stratford and need to rent a car to get there. But first, for the rest of you, here are five reasons why I think you really don't need to rent a car in Toronto:

- ✔ **You can ride the subway (or streetcar or bus) almost anywhere.** For tooling around Toronto, your best option is to make use of the city's comprehensive public transit system. You can get just about anywhere you need to go via subway, streetcar, or bus. And when public transit isn't convenient, taxi cabs are readily available, especially downtown and in the destination neighborhoods. (Chapter 8 has much more information about taking advantage of public transit, and in Chapter 13 I've included an itinerary that features hotels, restaurants, shopping, and attractions that are directly on, or within steps of, mass transit stops.)

✔ **Sometimes, walking makes the most sense.** If you're staying at a hotel in the heart of the city, many attractions are just a few minutes away on foot. In some cases, you can arrive at the attraction, pay the admission fee, and already be enjoying the visit in the amount of time it would take you to get to the subway station, walk down the stairs, hop on the next train, arrive at your destination station, climb the stairs, and then reach the attraction. Imagine, then, how much quicker walking would be than driving!

If you're not in a big hurry, walking offers the bonus of allowing you the flexibility to stop and smell the flowers (say, along the median that bisects University Avenue), or stop to enjoy a coffee or a pint, or to browse in a few shops along the way.

✔ **Parking fees are expensive — and everywhere.** Finding parking in Toronto is generally not a problem; paying for parking in Toronto can be. All-day rates at many of Toronto's downtown parking lots will run you C$15 to C$20 (US$12–US$16) or more (though on week-ends and holidays, your costs will be half that or even better).

And you can't get away from parking fees, even when you're exploring Toronto's neighborhoods. Unless you're lucky enough to find an open space on a purely residential street (in which case, you're probably taking the space of a dignified Toronto grandmother), you'll have to pay to park while you wander around The Beaches or Bloor West Village or Kensington Market. (If you *are* driving in Toronto, I have a few tips about parking in Chapter 8.)

✔ **Traffic will slow you down.** Whether you're stuck in rush-hour traffic on the Gardiner Expressway, returning from a day in The Beaches, or stopping and going (and stopping and going) behind a streetcar on King Street West, if you do a lot of driving around Toronto you *will* get stuck in traffic at some point.

Just like in your hometown, some drivers in Toronto can be reckless (a.k.a. stupid). You know the kind: the ones who exit off a highway — from the *far left* lane. These drivers represent a greater danger to visitors driving around Toronto for the first time; you're already a bit distracted because you're trying to *find* that same exit, and you may not even notice the offending driver approaching from your left.

✔ **Gas is on the pricey side.** If you're visiting from the U.S., you may have a bit of sticker shock when you fill up your tank (your rental car's tank, that is). Gas prices in Toronto usually range from C70¢ to C80¢ per liter, which translates to roughly C$2.65 to C$3.05 per gallon. Even with a favorable exchange rate, you're looking at any-where from US$2.17 to US$2.50 per gallon, which is still higher than in most U.S. markets.

The rest of this section offers some tips for making sure you get what you pay for, and that you don't pay for what you really don't need in a rental car.

Getting the best deal

Car rental rates vary even more than airline fares. The price depends on the size of the car, the length of time you keep it, where and when you pick it up and drop it off, where you take it, and a host of other factors. Asking a few key questions may save you hundreds of dollars.

 ✔ Weekend rates may be lower than weekday rates. If you're keeping the car for five or more days, a weekly rate may be cheaper than the daily rate. Find out whether the rate is the same for pickup Friday morning as for Thursday night.

 ✔ Some companies may assess a drop-off charge if you don't return the car to the same rental location; others, notably National, don't.

 ✔ Check whether the rate is cheaper if you pick up the car at a location in town rather than at the airport.

 ✔ Find out whether age is an issue. Many car rental companies add a fee for drivers under 25, while some don't rent to them at all.

 ✔ If you see an advertised price in your local newspaper, be sure to ask for that specific rate; otherwise you may be charged the standard (higher) rate. Don't forget to mention membership in AAA/CAA, AARP/CARP, and trade unions. These memberships usually entitle you to discounts ranging from 5 percent to 30 percent.

 ✔ Check your frequent-flier accounts. Not only are your favorite (or at least most-used) airlines likely to have sent you discount coupons, but most car rentals add at least 805 kilometers (500 miles) to your account.

 ✔ As with other aspects of planning your trip, using the Internet can make comparison shopping for a car rental much easier. You can check rates at most of the major agencies' Web sites. Plus, all the major travel sites — **Travelocity** (www.travelocity.com), **Expedia** (www.expedia.com), **Orbitz** (www.orbitz.com), and **Smarter Living** (www.smarterliving.com), for example — have search engines that can dig up discounted car-rental rates. Just enter the car size you want, the pickup and return dates, and location, and the server returns a price. You can even make the reservation through any of these sites.

Adding up the charges

In addition to the standard rental prices, other optional charges (and some not-so-optional charges, such as taxes) apply to most car rentals. The *Collision Damage Waiver* (CDW), which requires you to pay for damage to the car in a collision, is covered by many credit card companies. Check with your credit card company before you go, so that you can avoid paying this hefty fee (as much as C$25/US$21 a day).

The car rental companies also offer additional *liability insurance* (if you harm others in an accident), *personal accident insurance* (if you harm yourself or your passengers), and *personal effects insurance* (if your luggage is stolen from your car). Your insurance policy on your car at home probably covers most of these unlikely occurrences. However, if your own insurance doesn't cover you for rentals or if you don't have auto insurance, definitely consider the additional coverage (ask your car rental agent for more information). Unless you're toting around the Hope diamond, and you don't want to leave that in your car trunk anyway, you can probably skip the personal effects insurance, but driving around without liability or personal accident coverage is never a good idea. Even if you're a good driver, other people may not be, and liability claims can be complicated.

Some companies also offer *refueling packages,* in which you pay for your initial full tank of gas up front and can return the car with an empty gas tank. The prices can be competitive with local gas prices, but you don't get credit for any gas remaining in the tank. If you reject this option, you pay only for the gas you use, but you have to return the car with a full tank or face charges of C$3 to C$4 a gallon for any shortfall. If you usually run late and a fueling stop may make you miss your plane, you're a perfect candidate for the fuel purchase option.

Finally, don't forget to factor in your taxes and surcharges. In addition to the 15 percent GST/PST combination (see Chapter 4 for more about Toronto-area taxes), you'll pay two or three bucks for various fees and surcharges. And if you rent your car at Toronto's Pearson airport, you face an additional 14.61 percent "premium location charge."

Playing It Safe with Travel and Medical Insurance

Three kinds of travel insurance are available: trip-cancellation insurance, medical insurance, and lost luggage insurance. Here is my advice on all three.

- ✔ **Trip-cancellation insurance** is a good idea if you signed up for an escorted tour and paid a large portion of your vacation expenses up front (for information on escorted tours, see Chapter 5). Trip-cancellation insurance covers three emergencies — if a death or sickness prevents you from traveling, if a tour operator or airline goes out of business, or if some kind of disaster prevents you from getting to your destination.

- ✔ Buying **medical insurance** for your trip doesn't make sense for most travelers. Your existing health insurance should cover you if you get sick while on vacation (although if you belong to an HMO, check to see whether you're fully covered while in Canada).

✔ **Lost luggage insurance** is not necessary for most travelers. Your homeowner's or renter's insurance should cover stolen luggage if you have off-premises theft coverage. Check your existing policies before you buy any additional coverage. If an airline loses your luggage, the airline is responsible for paying $2,500 per bag on domestic flights. On international flights (including U.S. portions of international trips), baggage is limited to approximately $9.07 per pound, up to approximately $635 per checked bag.

Some credit cards (American Express and certain gold and platinum Visa and MasterCards, for example) offer automatic flight insurance against death or dismemberment in case of an airplane crash if you charged the cost of your ticket.

If you're interested in purchasing travel insurance, try one of the following companies:

✔ **Access America** (☎ **866-807-3982**; www.accessamerica.com)

✔ **Travel Guard International** (☎ **800-826-4919**; www.travelguard.com)

✔ **Travel Insured International** (☎ **800-243-3174**; www.travelinsured.com)

✔ **Travelex Insurance Services** (☎ **800-457-4602**; www.travelex-insurance.com)

Don't pay for more insurance than you need. For example, if you need only trip-cancellation insurance, don't buy coverage for lost or stolen property. Trip-cancellation insurance costs about 6 to 8 percent of the total value of your vacation.

Staying Healthy When You Travel

Getting sick will ruin your vacation, so I strongly advise against it (of course, last time I checked, the bugs weren't listening to me any more than they probably listen to you).

If you have health insurance, be sure to carry your insurance card in your wallet. Most U.S. health insurance plans and HMOs cover at least part of the cost of out-of-country hospital visits and procedures if insurees become ill or are injured while traveling. Most require that you pay the bills up front at the time of care, issuing a refund after you return and file all the paperwork. For information on purchasing additional medical insurance for your trip, see the previous section.

Talk to your doctor before leaving on a trip if you have a serious and/or chronic illness. For conditions such as epilepsy, diabetes, or heart problems, wear a **Medic Alert Identification Tag** (☎ 800-825-3785; www.medicalert.org), which immediately alerts doctors to your condition and gives them access to your records through Medic Alert's 24-hour hotline.

With the exception of certain HMOs and Medicare/Medicaid, your medical insurance should cover medical treatment — even hospital care — overseas. However, most out-of-country hospitals make you pay your bills at the time of treatment. And in a worst-case scenario, there may be the high cost of emergency evacuation. If you require additional medical insurance, try **MEDEX International** (☎ 800-527-0218 or 410-453-6300; www.medexassist.com) or **Travel Assistance International** (☎ 800-821-2828; www.travelassistance.com (for general information on services, call the company's Worldwide Assistance Services, Inc., at ☎ 800-777-8710).

If you're traveling to Toronto during the hottest months in summer, you should take some standard precautions against mosquitoes, as a preventive measure against the West Nile virus. As with SARS, your level of concern should be minimal; six West Nile cases were reported in Toronto during the summer of 2004. For more information about the kinds of precautions to take (or to get an update about the virus's impact in Toronto), the City of Toronto's Web site (www.city.toronto.on.ca/health/) has some good advice.

Worrying about SARS

In 2003, Toronto had the distinction of being the only North American city to really have to deal with severe acute respiratory syndrome (SARS), the illness that made international headlines, with Toronto the site of 40 of the more than 800 deaths worldwide. SARS cases began to appear in the greater Toronto area in mid-March, and Toronto stepped into high gear to contain the illness, with quarantine orders, hospital limitations, and delays for non-urgent surgery. In less than four months, Toronto's efforts had paid off — in early July 2003, the World Health Organization declared Toronto to be SARS-free.

Should you worry? As of this writing, little is known about whether SARS will return to *any* region. And in Toronto specifically, it's been determined that nearly everyone who contracted the illness had come in contact with an infected person in a health care facility. The illness was never spread in the general community.

Staying Connected by Cellphone

If your cellphone service is with a major provider, chances are good that you'll be able to use it in the Toronto metropolitan area. Check with your local provider before leaving home, to find out what service is available in Toronto and what it will cost you per minute.

The three letters that define much of the world's **wireless capabilities** are GSM (Global System for Mobiles), a big, seamless network that makes for easy cross-border cellphone use throughout dozens of countries worldwide. In the U.S., T-Mobile, AT&T Wireless, and Cingular use this quasi-universal system; in Canada, Microcell and some Rogers customers are GSM, and all Europeans and most Australians use GSM.

For many, **renting** a phone is a good idea. While you can rent a phone from any number of overseas sites, including kiosks at airports and at car rental agencies, you're probably better off renting before you leave home. That way you can give loved ones and business associates your new number, make sure the phone works, and have the phone on hand while traveling to Toronto.

Phone rental isn't cheap. You'll usually pay $40 to $50 per week, plus airtime fees of at least a dollar a minute. However, local rental companies often offer free incoming calls within their home country, which can save you big bucks. The bottom line: Shop around.

Two good wireless rental companies are **InTouch USA** (☎ **800-872-7626**; www.intouchglobal.com) and **RoadPost** (☎ **888-290-1606** or 905-272-5665; www.roadpost.com). Give them your itinerary, and they'll tell you what wireless products you need. InTouch will also advise you, for free, on whether your existing phone will work overseas; simply call ☎ **703-222-7161** between 9 a.m. and 4 p.m. EST, or go to http://intouchglobal.com/travel.htm.

Accessing the Internet Away from Home

Today's travelers have any number of ways to check their E-mail and access the Internet on the road. Of course, using your own laptop — or even a PDA (personal digital assistant) or electronic organizer with a modem — gives you the most flexibility. But even if you don't have a computer, you can still access your E-mail and even your office computer from cybercafes.

It's hard nowadays to find a city that *doesn't* have a few cybercafes. Although there's no definitive directory for cybercafes — these are independent businesses, after all — a couple places to start looking are at www.cybercaptive.com and www.cybercafe.com.

Aside from formal cybercafes, Toronto's **public libraries** have banks of computers set up for free Internet access so that you can check one of the Web-based E-mail account services. Avoid **hotel business centers** unless you're willing to pay exorbitant rates.

Most major airports now have **Internet kiosks** scattered near their gates. These kiosks, which you'll also see in shopping malls, hotel lobbies, and tourist information offices around the world, give you basic Web access for a per-minute fee that's usually higher than cybercafe prices. The kiosks' clunkiness and high prices mean you should avoid them whenever possible.

To retrieve your E-mail, ask your **Internet Service Provider (ISP)** if it has a Web-based interface tied to your existing E-mail account. If your ISP doesn't have such an interface, you can use the free **mail2web** service (www.mail2web.com) to view and reply to your home E-mail. For more flexibility, you may want to open a free, Web-based E-mail account with **Yahoo! Mail** (http://mail.yahoo.com). (Microsoft's Hotmail is another popular option, but Hotmail has severe spam problems.) Your home ISP may be able to forward your E-mail to the Web-based account automatically.

If you need to access files on your office computer, look into a service called **GoToMyPC** (www.gotomypc.com). The service provides a Web-based interface for you to access and manipulate a distant PC from anywhere — even a cybercafe — provided your "target" PC is on and has an always-on connection to the Internet (such as with Road Runner cable). The service offers top-quality security, but if you're worried about hackers, use your own laptop rather than a cybercafe computer to access the GoToMyPC system.

If you are bringing your own computer, the buzzword in computer access to familiarize yourself with is **Wi-fi** (wireless fidelity), and more and more hotels, cafes, and retailers are signing on as wireless "hotspots" from where you can get high-speed connection without cable wires, networking hardware, or a phone line. You can get Wi-fi connection in one of several ways. Many laptops sold in the past year have built-in Wi-fi capability (an 802.11b wireless Ethernet connection). Mac owners have their own networking technology, Apple AirPort. For those with older computers, an 802.11b/**Wi-fi card** (around US$50) can be plugged into your laptop. You sign up for wireless access service much as you do cellphone service, through a plan offered by one of several commercial companies that have made wireless service available in airports, hotel lobbies, and coffee shops, primarily in the U.S. (followed by the U.K. and Japan). **T-Mobile Hotspot** (www.tmobile.com/hotspot) serves up wireless connections at more than 1,000 Starbucks coffee shops nationwide. **Boingo** (www.boingo.com) and **Wayport** (www.wayport.com) have set up networks in airports and high-class hotel lobbies. **iPass** providers also give you access to a few hundred wireless hotel lobby setups. Best of all, you don't need to be staying at the Four Seasons to use the hotel's network; just set yourself up on a nice couch in the lobby. The companies' pricing policies can be byzantine, with a variety of monthly, per-connection, and per-minute plans, but in general you pay around US$30 a month for limited access — and as more and more companies jump on the wireless bandwagon, prices are likely to get even more competitive.

Some places provide **free wireless networks** in cities around the world. To locate these free hotspots, go to www.personaltelco.net/index. cgi/WirelessCommunities.

In addition, major Internet Service Providers (ISP) have **local access numbers** around the world, allowing you to go online by simply placing a local call. Check your ISP's Web site or call its toll-free number and ask how you can use your current account away from home, and how much it will cost. If you're traveling outside the reach of your ISP, the **iPass** network has dial-up numbers in most of the world's countries. You'll have to sign up with an iPass provider, who will then tell you how to set up your computer for your destination(s). For a list of iPass providers, go to www.ipass.com and click "Individual Purchase." One solid provider is **i2roam** (www.i2roam.com; ☎ 866-811-6209 or 920-235-0475).

Wherever you go, bring a **connection kit** of the right power, and phone adapters, a spare phone cord, and a spare Ethernet network cable — or find out whether your hotel supplies them to guests.

Keeping Up with Airline Security

With the federalization of airport security, security procedures at U.S. airports are more stable and consistent than ever. Generally, you'll be fine if you arrive at the airport **1 hour** before a domestic flight and **2 hours** before an international flight; if you show up late, tell an airline employee and she'll probably whisk you to the front of the line.

Bring a **current, government-issued photo ID** such as a driver's license or passport. Keep your ID at the ready to show at check-in, the security checkpoint, and sometimes even the gate. (Children under 18 do not need government-issued photo IDs for domestic flights, but they do for international flights to most countries.)

In 2003, the TSA phased out **gate check-in** at all U.S. airports. And **e-tickets** have made paper tickets nearly obsolete. If you have an e-ticket you can beat the ticket-counter lines by using airport **electronic kiosks** or even **online check-in** from your home computer. Online check-in involves logging on to your airlines' Web site, accessing your reservation, and printing out your boarding pass — and the airline may even offer you bonus miles to do so! If you're using a kiosk at the airport, bring the credit card you used to book the ticket or your frequent-flier card. Print out your boarding pass from the kiosk and simply proceed to the security checkpoint with your pass and a photo ID. If you're checking bags or looking to snag an exit-row seat, you will be able to do so using most airline kiosks. Even the smaller airlines are employing the kiosk system, but always call your airline to make sure these alternatives are available. **Curbside check-in** is also a good way to avoid lines, although a few airlines still ban curbside check-in; call before you go.

Security checkpoint lines are getting shorter than they were during 2001 and 2002, but some doozies remain. If you have trouble standing for long periods of time, tell an airline employee; the airline will provide a wheel-chair. Speed up security by **not wearing metal objects** such as big belt buckles. If you've got metallic body parts, a note from your doctor can prevent a long chat with the security screeners. Keep in mind that only **ticketed passengers** are allowed past security, except for folks escorting passengers with disabilities, or children.

Federalization has stabilized **what you can carry on** and **what you can't.** The general rule is that sharp things are out, nail clippers are okay, and food and beverages must be passed through the X-ray machine — but that security screeners can't make you drink from your coffee cup. Bring food in your carry-on rather than checking it, as explosive-detection machines used on checked luggage have been known to mistake food (especially chocolate, for some reason) for bombs. Travelers in the U.S. are allowed one carry-on bag, plus a "personal item" such as a purse, briefcase, or laptop bag. Carry-on hoarders can stuff all sorts of things into a laptop bag; as long as it has a laptop in it, it's still considered a personal item. The Transportation Security Administration (TSA) has issued a list of restricted items; check its Web site (www.tsa.gov/public/index.jsp) for details.

Airport screeners may decide that your checked luggage needs to be searched by hand. You can now purchase luggage locks that allow screeners to open and re-lock a checked bag if hand-searching is necessary. Look for Travel Sentry certified locks at luggage or travel shops and Brookstone stores (you can buy them online at www.brookstone.com). These locks, approved by the TSA, can be opened by lug-gage inspectors with a special code or key. For more information on the locks, visit www.travelsentry.org. If you use something other than TSA-approved locks, your lock will be cut off your suitcase if a TSA agent needs to hand-search your luggage.

Part III
Settling into Toronto

The 5th Wave   By Rich Tennant

"Welcome to the Toronto Arms. Can I give give you a hand?"

In this part...

What are the first things you're likely to want to do when you arrive in Toronto? Find your hotel and get a bite to eat. This part helps you with both. Chapter 9 runs down the information you need to book your lodging in Toronto, including listings of the city's best hotels. Chapter 10 introduces you to the gastronomic delights of Toronto, including where to find the best on-the-go grub for your on-the-go sightseeing days. This part also includes a chapter on discovering the city's best neighborhoods and getting your bearings in Toronto once you've arrived.

Chapter 8

Arriving and Getting Oriented

● ●

In This Chapter

▶ Arriving from outside Canada

▶ Getting to your hotel

▶ Scouting out Toronto's neighborhoods

▶ Finding more information

▶ Negotiating the mean streets of Toronto — by subway, car, or feet

● ●

*I*f you're arriving from outside Canada, your obvious first step is to get into the country, which I cover at the beginning of this chapter. You'll also discover how to get to the heart of Toronto (and to your accommodations) once you're within the city limits, whether you're coming by plane, by car, or even by train. (See Chapter 5 for details on getting to Toronto from outlying areas.)

After settling in, you'll want to immerse yourself in the city. Exploring Toronto's distinctive neighborhoods is very much like entering a new city simply by crossing a street. Toronto is relatively easy to navigate in a number of different ways — in particular, by using its accessible and multi-spoked public transit system — but one of the most enjoyable (and most reflective of the city's multifaceted culture) is to explore its communities. This chapter offers a detailed look into some of Toronto's most fascinating neighborhoods, as well as how to get around easily among them.

Navigating Your Way through Passport Control and Customs

U.S. residents arriving in Canada generally do not need a passport to get into and out of the country. However, you may find the process of getting across the border or through the customs line at the airport a bit more straightforward if you have a passport.

If you absolutely can't get your hands on a passport before you depart, you'll need a birth certificate to establish your country of origin, as well as photo identification. If you're not a U.S. citizen, you'll need your naturalization or alien-registration documents as well. Ideally, though, you'll have your passport in hand — check out Chapter 7 well in advance of your trip so that you can obtain the necessary documents and ensure your border-crossing goes as smoothly as possible.

If you're traveling to Canada from the United Kingdom, Australia, or New Zealand, you will need a valid passport to enter the country. (Chapter 7 has the information you need when applying for a passport.)

Passing through the immigration and customs checkpoints is, of course, more than just establishing your identity and confirming your country of origin; you also need to keep in mind your limits for bringing goods into and taking goods out of Canada. This section discuss what kind of stuff and how much of it you can bring in; for details on what you can take home with you, check out Chapter 12.

Chances are you won't be arriving in Canada with anything but the personal belongings you need to last you through your stay. However, if you do plan to bring in any items to be left in the country — for example, a wedding present for your cousin in Etobicoke, or your own supply of beer because you just can't get enough of that Pabst Blue Ribbon — you should know what will trigger duty and excise taxes.

- ✔ **Alcohol:** You can bring with you — duty- and tax-free — either 1.5 liters (about 50 ounces) of wine, 1.14 liters (about 39 ounces) of liquor, or 8.5 liters of beer or ale (the equivalent of a 24-pack of that good ol' Pabst Blue Ribbon).

- ✔ **Tobacco:** Without paying duty or taxes, you can bring into Canada a total of 200 cigarettes, 50 cigars, and 200 grams (7 ounces) of tobacco.

- ✔ **Gifts:** For that cousin in Etobicoke (pronounced eh-*toe*-beh-koh, for the uninitiated), you can bring in a wedding gift but it must be worth C$60 (US$49) or less.

- ✔ **Perishables:** Limited amounts of food products are allowed in from the U.S. For more details on quantities and types of meat, vegetables, dairy, and so on that you can bring with you, check out the Canada Border Services Agency Web site at www.cbsa-asfc.gc.ca.

Making Your Way to Your Hotel

You've made it! You're in Toronto! It doesn't matter anymore how you *got* to Toronto, just that you're *in* Toronto. So, where do you go now? This section helps you navigate the city upon arrival, getting yourself and your case of Pabst Blue Ribbon to your accommodations from the airport, the highway, or the train station.

Arriving by plane

If you fly to Toronto, you're likely to arrive at Toronto Pearson International Airport (named for Lester B. Pearson, who served as prime minister of Canada during the 1960s), which is northwest of downtown. (A few commuter flights — mostly from Ottawa — do fly into and out of Toronto Island Airport, which is just a ten-minute ferry ride from downtown Toronto.)

Getting to the city's core takes you anywhere from 30 minutes (if driving or taking a cab — add 10 to 15 minutes if you're traveling during rush hour) to an hour (if using mass transit). The following list outlines your options:

✔ **Driving yourself:** After picking up your rental car (see Chapter 7 for tips and details) and emerging from the terminal, look for Highway 427 South. Once you're heading south on the 427, look for the Gardiner Expressway heading east, which takes you into downtown (you'll know you're going the right way when you see the CN Tower as you approach downtown). Then follow the directions provided by your hotel — you did ask for directions, didn't you? — or have a passenger call your hotel to guide you to your destination (no cellphone use while driving, please!).

✔ **Hiring a ride:** Taxi service is plentiful throughout Toronto, and especially so from the airport. A taxi ride from Pearson to downtown Toronto will run you C$43 (US$35).

A great option for just a few dollars more (C$47/US$39) is to hire a limousine or town car from one of the many limousine services available — you can reserve in advance. Here are a couple of limo services to consider:

- **Aerofleet Services:** ☎ 800-268-0905
- **Airline Limousine:** ☎ 800-263-5466

✔ **Hopping on the hotel shuttle:** Check with your hotel to find out whether it offers a shuttle or limousine service to and from the airport. Failing that, Airport Express offers 24-hour bus service to downtown Toronto, with a route that includes a number of downtown hotels including the Westin Harbour Castle, the Holiday Inn on King, and the Delta Chelsea. Plan on 35 to 55 minutes, depending on your destination and traffic. The adult fare is C$15.50 (US$13) one-way, and C$26.75 (US$22) round-trip; children under 12 travel free if with an adult, and a 10 percent discount is available for one-way student and senior travel. For more information, call ☎ 905-564-3232 or check out the Web site at www.torontoairport express.com.

✔ **Going by public transit:** Toronto's subway system does not reach Pearson airport. To get downtown via mass transit, you'll need to take a bus to the nearest subway station and then ride the subway line to your ultimate stop. Plan on about an hour for this trip, which is your least expensive alternative (C$2.50/US$2.05). Your route options follow, each of which you can catch on the arrivals level of terminals 2 or 3:

- **#192 Airport Rocket:** Takes you to the Kipling station on the Bloor–Danforth line

- **#58A Malton:** Takes you to the Lawrence West station on the Spadina line

- **#307 Eglinton West:** Takes you to the Eglinton West or Eglinton stations on the Spadina line

Arriving by car

Getting to Toronto by car is relatively easy; see Chapter 5 for details about coming from points east, west, and south. Once you get into the greater Toronto area, however, traffic congestion and the occasionally confusing directional signs may pose some challenges for getting to your accommodations. However, this section should help you work your way into the heart of Toronto; for explicit directions to your hotel, you should contact the reservations desk before you arrive.

✔ **If coming in from the west,** you'll probably be traveling Highways 401 or 402 once you enter Ontario from Michigan. These two highways merge outside of London, Ontario (about 2 hours west of Toronto), with Highway 401 taking you the distance to Toronto. The 401 runs east to west through the northern part of the greater Toronto area, so once you hit the city you'll have to head south to get to your downtown hotel.

The 401 from London to Toronto is one of the busiest non-urban stretches of highway in Ontario. If traffic is especially heavy, an alternative is to take the Highway 403 turnoff, just east of Woodstock. This highway links with the Queen Elizabeth Way (QEW), which in turn becomes the Gardiner Expressway, which takes you right into downtown Toronto.

✔ **If coming in from the east,** your best bet is, again, the 401. Remember that this highway runs through the northern part of Toronto, so just about any southbound exit off the 401 (such as Yonge Street, Bathurst Street, or the 404, a.k.a. the Don Valley Parkway) will get you headed toward downtown Toronto.

Watch out for the directions you may get from one of the online mapping services. You may be directed to get off the 401 at Highway 2. Unless you're sure that the 401 has come to a complete standstill ahead, you're better off staying on this six-lane highway. Highway 2 becomes Kingston Road on the way into the city, and it'll take you a good extra half-hour to navigate the local traffic and traffic lights along the way.

✔ **If coming in from the south,** your only choice is the QEW from the New York–Ontario border. This highway becomes the Gardiner Expressway as you get closer to Toronto, and the Gardiner takes you directly into the heart of Toronto. Enjoy the majesty of the CN Tower and the Rogers Centre (formerly known as the SkyDome) on the horizon as you get closer.

Arriving by train

Keep in mind that you *can* get to Toronto via train (see Chapter 5 for details), and once you arrive, your final journey to your hotel is likely to be the easiest of the options discussed in this section.

All trains pull in to Union Station, in the heart of Toronto's Financial District — just across the street from the Fairmont Royal York, and just a few blocks north of Toronto's waterfront. Union Station also has a subway stop on the Spadina line, so you have easy access to other hotels that are on or near the subway route.

Getting to Know the Neighborhoods

Don't be surprised to hear local residents identifying themselves as from "The Beaches" or "Rosedale" or "The Kingsway," rather than as residents of Toronto. You're still talking with the locals; it's just that the locals tend to break down their status as Torontonians into subcategories — in this case, its neighborhoods.

Toronto neighborhoods can be defined by their cultural and ethnic makeup, by their income class, or by the primary activity that takes place in the area. This section introduces you to the neighborhoods that you're most likely to visit up close (or at least saunter through) during your visit to Toronto. To find out where these neighborhoods lie, have a look at the "Toronto Neighborhoods" map later in this chapter.

The Annex

A loosely defined area of grand residential homes, the University of Toronto campus and residences, and Bloor Street shopping and restaurants, The Annex originated as an area that was — you guessed it — annexed by the city of Toronto in the late 1800s. Its borders vary depending on whom you ask, but generally the area is considered to stretch from Bathurst Street to Avenue Road (west to east) and from Dupont Street to Harbord Street (north to south).

Bloor Street is this neighborhood's public core, with a blend of locally owned stores and restaurants enticing residents and visitors alike. But the real draw of this area is its stunning single-family homes, the grandest ranging in age from 70 to 120 years old. The Bata Shoe Museum is the only attraction in the heart of The Annex, though destinations such as the Royal Ontario Museum and Queen's Park (home of the Ontario Legislature) lie just south of its hazy borders.

Toronto Neighborhoods

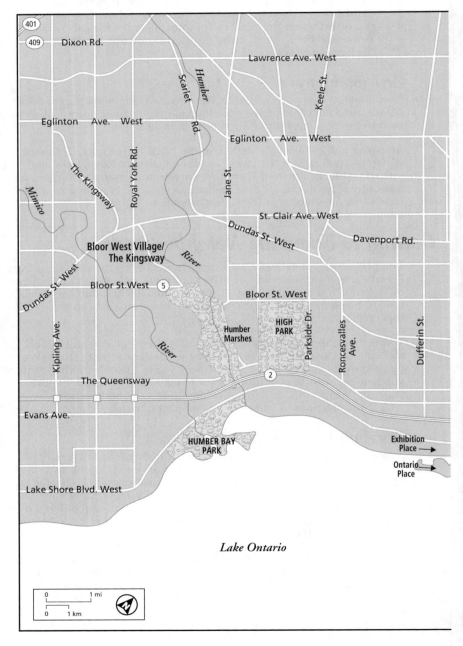

Toronto Neighborhoods

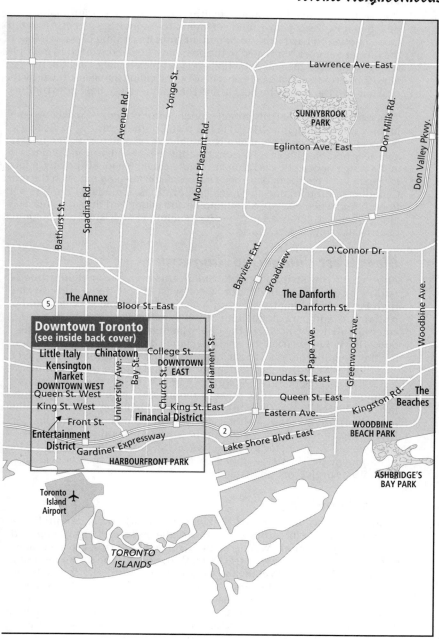

The Beaches

Once a summer destination for wealthy 19th-century Torontonians, The Beaches now lures year-round residents to its inviting streets, located close enough to Lake Ontario to benefit from its cooling breezes. Most of the former summer "cottages" in the area have been converted to multiple-family residences in semi-detached and four-plex homes. And the relaxed atmosphere of the area has been a beacon for young families, drawn by the proximity to the water, the beach, and the unique shopping opportunities.

This narrow strip of neighborhood stretches from roughly Coxwell Avenue in the west to Fallingbrook Road in the east, but the heart of The Beaches is Queen Street East. This major thoroughfare on a streetcar line boasts a variety of dining choices — from takeout to take-out-your-gold-card — and a range of eclectic and almost rabidly exclusive local shops. (In fact, for years local residents have been successful in keeping out even the most Canadian of brand-name shopping corporations, including Chapters and Roots.) And when you're done shopping and eating and drinking your way along Queen Street, head just one block south for a leisurely stroll on the boardwalk along Lake Ontario.

Bloor West Village/The Kingsway

Another narrow strip of neighborhood, this area (two neighborhoods, really) is centered around Bloor Street, west of downtown Toronto and High Park, stretching to Islington Avenue. The shops, services, and restaurants and bars along Bloor Street would make a good living if they catered only to the needs of the upper-income residential households bordering it. But even so, the area merchants do much to attract visitors, hosting neighborhood festivals and street fairs throughout the summer. The Bloor West Village Festival in mid-July and the Taste of the Kingsway festival in early September — with its samplings from the area's many restaurants, cafes, and bars — are perennial favorites. In this region, the historic Old Mill Inn — Toronto's first industrial building — hosts weddings and other posh events at its hotel and restaurant, located on the Humber River. Book and film lovers should be sure to stop at the Chapters Runnymede location; far from the typical big-box chain store, it's in the old Runnymede Theatre, complete with high ceilings, theater seating, and former projectors on display.

Bloor/Yorkville

A fairly small area, the Bloor/Yorkville neighborhood is definitely the most fashionable in Toronto, boasting high-class shopping, dining, and lodging choices. From Avenue Road to Yonge Street (west to east) and Scollard Street to Charles Street (north to south), the hub of activity centers on Yorkville Avenue and Cumberland and Bloor streets. Here you'll find storied establishments including the Four Seasons and the Park Hyatt, as well as the expensive clothiers and boutiques that cater to these hotels' clientele. Look nearby for the Royal Ontario Museum, but realize that the main attraction here is the moneyed — and those who love to see the moneyed walk through their doors.

Chinatown

Much like any major metropolitan city, Toronto is home to a number of areas that could rightly be called Chinatown. The largest of these, however, is located just west of University Avenue in an area bordered by College and Dundas streets (north to south) and Spadina Avenue (to the west). Brimming-with-character Asian shops and fruit-and-vegetable markets line the streets, along with a wealth of Chinese (and other Asian-cuisine) restaurants. Tucked in this neighborhood, you'll also find the Art Gallery of Ontario (AGO), a worthy destination on any itinerary.

The Danforth

Heading east, Bloor Street becomes Danforth Avenue after crossing over the Don Valley Ravine. The core of this area (locally known as The Danforth) is also referred to as Greektown, with its collection of Greek restaurants and tavernas, but the area is also becoming known for its nightlife and nighttime dining opportunities. The street is a hotbed of activity on warm (and cool) weekend evenings (and into the weekend mornings), with most of the action taking place between Pape and Broadview avenues.

Downtown

Downtown Toronto covers such a wide expanse it's difficult to restrict this designation to a specific location. Running from Spadina Avenue to Jarvis Street (west to east) and from College Street to Front Street (north to south), this area is the core of Toronto and also encompasses Chinatown and the city's Financial and Entertainment districts. Here you'll find the headquarters of some of Canada's largest corporations, including the big banks; choices for theatergoers ranging from Broadway-style productions to local-troupe presentations; a broad spectrum of cuisine selections; and most of Toronto's finest hotels. Check out this area for a visit to the Hockey Hall of Fame and the St. Lawrence Market.

Entertainment District

This area along King Street West hosts many of Toronto's entertainment venues, including the Roy Thomson Hall, and theaters such as the Royal Alexandra and the Princess of Wales. But Toronto's entertainment options aren't limited to King Street West; other jewels in the city's entertainment crown are the Canon Theatre on Yonge Street; Massey Hall, a concert hall just around the corner on Shuter Street; and the Hummingbird Centre on Front Street. Select the King West area for your accommodations (a number of reasonable hotels are located nearby), and you can take in a show or two as well as some fine pre- and post-theater dining.

Harbourfront and the Islands

This lake-centered area provides a variety of options for the visitor to Toronto. From the wide selection of antiquing venues to the cultural offerings of the Harbourfront Centre, you can easily devote a day to the shopping, dining, and festival-going possibilities on the mainland side of the water.

Hop on the ten-minute ferry to the Toronto Islands and you can relax and unwind with leisurely strolls through the city-run parks and gardens ... or, whip your kids into a frenzy at the Centreville Amusement Park, with its host of amusement rides, fast-food snacking, and carnival-style fun and games.

Kensington Market

This haven for shoppers, stretching from College to Dundas streets (north to south) and Bathurst Street to Spadina Avenue (west to east), has long been an apex of local merchant bargaining and bartering. Once Toronto's Jewish center, the area continues to adapt to Toronto's ever-changing and growing cultural landscape, today featuring shops and restaurants from around the world. The neighborhood's genteel confusion is part of its charm, as merchants continue to hawk their wares from the area's sidewalks and storefronts.

Little Italy

While this traditionally Italian-heritage neighborhood has long boasted the trattorias, restaurants, cafes, and shops to cater to both residents and visitors, Little Italy now mirrors the larger city of Toronto in its acceptance of a diversity of cultural groups, including immigrants from other Mediterranean countries and Asia. The area still acknowledges its origins with annual celebrations including the Taste of Italy festival. The hub of activity in this neighborhood is along College Street, west of Bathurst Street, but you'll find elements of it north to Harbord Street and south to Dundas Street.

Queen Street West

One of the trendier areas of Toronto, Queen Street West picks up steam as it heads west from University Avenue. With landmarks such as the Campbell House and the Citytv building, Queen Street West draws shoppers to a dazzling diversity of eclectic shops, boutiques, antiques stores, and alternative vendors, many of which sit side by side with some of the more fashionable brand-name establishments, such as Roots, Club Monaco, and Guess. The dining choices reflect the same diversity. A visit to Queen Street West would not be complete without voicing your opinion at Citytv's Speaker's Corner — a loonie may bring you your 15 seconds of fame on this popular showcase of both local talent and the truly talentless.

West Queen West

You won't find this street on any establishment's official address; instead, head west of Bathurst Street on Queen Street West to explore a neighborhood that's quickly becoming the place to be in Toronto. (Many former residents of Queen West to the east of Bathurst have moved west to avoid the skyrocketing rents of that more "fashionable" area.) A sign of this neighborhood's coolness is the popular success of the new Drake Hotel, a lodging and dining establishment that also hosts live performances from comedy to music to poetry and more.

Finding Information after You Arrive

For your last-minute tourist-type needs (or for another resource while planning your trip to Toronto), the **Toronto Convention & Visitors Association** office is on Toronto's waterfront, at 207 Queens Quay West, in the Queen's Quay Terminal at Harbourfront (☎ **800-499-2514** or 416-203-2600; www.torontotourism.com). The office is open Monday to Friday, 9 a.m. to 5 p.m.

The **Ontario Visitor Information Centre** is a convenient place to stop if you want to combine shopping with tourist research. Located in the Eaton Centre at Yonge and Dundas streets, its hours of operation are Monday to Friday 10 a.m. to 9 p.m.; Saturday 9:30 a.m. to 6 p.m.; and Sunday noon to 5 p.m.

Getting Around Toronto

Whether you're planning on a long weekend or two weeks in Toronto, figuring out the best way to get from point A to point B can just about make or break your stay. Your personal stress-o-meter will certainly benefit more from lingering a few extra minutes in that particularly fascinating exhibition at the ROM than from languishing in a traffic lineup heading north on Bay Street. The rest of this chapter is all about navigating Toronto.

Far and away your best option in most cases is to hop on the TTC, Toronto's reliable and conveniently placed subway system. You can get to most of the city's major attractions and neighborhoods via the subway; if the subway won't get you there, a connection with a bus or a streetcar will usually finish the job. But you can make your way around Toronto using other resources, including the city's many taxicabs, your own vehicle, or your own two feet — or, in the best scenarios, all of the above.

Mapping out a strategy

You'll have greater success getting around Toronto with a good map or two. The maps in this book are an excellent starting point, especially for finding locations that I recommend. In addition, a good online and very interactive map is maintained by the City of Toronto at www.toronto.ca/torontomaps. You can search for a specific address (such as that of your hotel) or you can just look around a particular intersection (say, Yonge and Dundas, which takes you to the location of Dundas Square, Toronto's newest open public square).

Once you've typed in your destination, you can look for nearby landmarks using the map's layers and legend frame. Select the "Things To Do" check box and then click the "Map It" button, and you'll find colored dots that correspond to parks, attractions, museums, and other locations. Click the "Identify" button (one of the nine icons along the top of the page; this one is identified by a lowercase "i"), and the area below the map shows information such as the attraction's address, hours of operation, and Web site.

Finally, select the "Aerial View" check box, and you can see what Dundas Square looked like from above as it was being constructed.

Negotiating Toronto on mass transit

With just over 68km (about 42.5 miles) of subway line, 306km (190 miles) of streetcar track, and thousands more kilometers covered by bus, getting around Toronto via the city's public transit system is the easiest and most reliable option for visitors. (Toronto residents take advantage of the system quite well themselves; the Toronto Transit Commission [TTC] records over 400 million passenger trips each year.)

The system is accessible just about any time of day or night. Subways run Monday through Saturday from 6 a.m. to 1:30 a.m., and on Sundays from 9 a.m. to 1:30 a.m. Most buses and streetcars run from 5 a.m. to 1:30 a.m. on weekdays, with reduced schedules on weekends. However, many of the major bus and streetcar routes in town operate all night as well; look for a stop with a reflective blue band. You can get detailed route and schedule information on the TTC Web site at www.ttc.ca.

Your fare options are reasonable as well, starting with a one-way fare (including transfer) anywhere in the city for C$2.50 (US$2.05) for adults, C$1.70 (US$1.40) for students age 13 to 19 and seniors age 65 and over, and C$.60 (US$.50) for children age 2 to 12.

When boarding a bus, streetcar, or subway with a one-way fare, *always* get a transfer ticket, even if you have no plans to use it. You won't be able to get one after you board, and you never know when you may change your mind along the way and hop off to catch a connecting vehicle. On a bus or streetcar, ask the driver for a transfer as you board and pay your fare; on the subway, machines just inside the turnstiles dispense transfers at the push of a button.

Unless you need only a single ticket for one-time use, you're better off with one of the TTC's day passes or multiple-token options:

- ✔ **Single day pass:** For C$8 (US$6.55), one person can ride all over town, on any regular routes, on Monday through Friday. The pass is good beginning at 9:30 a.m. through to the end of service. Saturday and Sunday day passes are valid all day long.

- ✔ **Family day pass:** That same C$8 (US$6.55) will give a family of up to six members unlimited travel on any regular TTC routes all day Sunday and holidays. A family pass is valid for a maximum of two adults, and all kids must be age 19 and under.

- ✔ **Multiple-fare purchase:** If a day pass isn't for you (say, you're planning just a handful of transit trips at irregular times over a period of several days), then you can purchase a set of tokens (or tickets) for a reduced price. You can buy five or ten tokens (or tickets) at a time, and you'll save around 15 percent compared to single purchases of five or ten one-way fares.

- ✔ **GTA Weekly Pass:** One final option if you're planning to use the TTC a lot is the Greater Toronto Area (GTA) Weekly Pass. This pass costs C$41.25 (US$34) per week and is valid from Monday to Monday during the week of purchase. With this pass, you can also use the neighboring transit systems in Mississauga, Brampton, and York Region (though it's unlikely you'll have any reason to). The GTA Weekly Pass is more of a commuter's pass, though with the pass you do save nearly 25 percent compared to a week's worth of day passes.

You can buy single one-way fares as you board the system. You must purchase day passes and multiple tokens at one of the TTC's subway stations. The GTA Weekly Pass is available at selected stations only; call the TTC at ☎ 416-393-4636 for details.

By subway

As I note a number of times throughout this book, using the subway is the easiest and most efficient way to see the sights in Toronto. With two major lines (described in more detail in two nearby sidebars) that work their way into and out of downtown, the subway can take you within steps (or, on occasion, a couple of blocks) of nearly all the hotels, restaurants, attractions, and so on that are mentioned in this book. (Two more extension lines — Sheppard and Scarborough — operate in the far north and far east of Toronto, respectively, and so are generally not useful to tourists.) To find out whether a particular hotel, restaurant, or attraction is close to one of the TTC subway stations, just check the listing details that follow individual reviews in Chapters 9, 10, and 11 where I list the nearest station.

Round and round it goes . . .

Well, you won't really go in circles when riding the subway, but the **Yonge–University–Spadina** line will take you in an incomplete oval up and down and around the downtown core. The line follows Yonge Street north and south, from Finch Avenue, about 16km (10 miles) north of the downtown area, to King Street. Then it makes a quick east-west turn to hit the stop at Union station before heading north-south again along University Avenue, Spadina Road, and, farther north, Allen Road, ending up at Sheppard Avenue, about 14km (9 miles) north of the downtown core.

With 14 stations in downtown Toronto, this line (the shape of a skinny U), has plenty of on-and-off access points so that you can easily get from, say, your hotel room at the Fairmont Royal York to the Eaton Centre for some shopping. And in some cases, you never even have to venture outdoors: Five stations (Dundas, Queen, King, Union, and St. Andrew) are directly connected to the PATH underground walkway, with its connections to hotels, shopping, restaurants, attractions, and more (see the section "Walking the streets of Toronto" for more about the PATH walkway).

The Yonge–University–Spadina line includes ten stations with elevator access, seven of them in the downtown core: St. George, Queen's Park, Union, Queen, Dundas, and Bloor–Yonge. Every station except Rosedale and Summerhill has escalators.

Getting on and off the subway is also a happy exercise in efficiency. Simply purchase a token (or pass, or set of tokens as described in the preceding section) at the station kiosk, slip the token through the token slot on the turnstile, and head for the landing area for the train that's headed in the direction you want to go. (Don't worry if you're unsure of the direction, subway maps are located in every station.)

If you're not sure about which train goes where, the TTC staff inside the kiosks are generally helpful — as long as it's not during rush hour — or ask for a copy of the *Ride Guide,* a TTC map showing complete subway, streetcar, and bus routes, as well as city highlights. (Or take along the tear-out Cheat Sheet at the front of this book, which includes a subway route map.)

By streetcar

The TTC operates 11 streetcar routes throughout Toronto — look for the 500 series of lines on the TTC's *Ride Guide.* (For example, the 501 line runs east to west from The Beaches to Etobicoke, along Queen Street, The Queensway, and Lake Shore Boulevard.)

Streetcars are a pleasant way to observe the hustle and bustle of many of Toronto's major thoroughfares. And if your plan is to enjoy the busy streets of Toronto, riding the streetcar is a good way to preview the hot spots before you set out for them on foot.

Go west (or east), young subway rider

The Bloor–Danforth line is the TTC's primary east-west subway line, and it cuts right through downtown Toronto on its northern edge. The line stretches west as far as Etobicoke (the Kipling station is about 13km/8 miles from the intersecting downtown area) and east to Scarborough (the Kennedy station is nearly 16km/10 miles from downtown).

This line has six stations in the vicinity of major destinations in this part of the downtown area: Bathurst, Spadina, St. George, Bay, Bloor–Yonge, and Sherbourne. Two of these stations (Bay and Bloor–Yonge) are connected to a much smaller underground walkway that connects the major shopping and business buildings in the area (see the section "Walking the streets of Toronto," later in this chapter, for more about this walkway).

The Bloor–Danforth line includes seven stations with elevator access, four of them in the downtown area: Bathurst, Spadina, St. George, and Bloor–Yonge. Every station has escalators.

If you're in a big hurry, though, you may want to consider the subway or a cab (or, in some cases, even walking would be faster). Streetcar tracks run down the center of some of Toronto's busiest streets, so streetcar operators have to fight traffic and observe stoplights like the rest of the drivers on the street; the journey to your destination may be much more stop-and-go than you'd like.

Because streetcars have to stay on tracks in the center of the street, you essentially have to walk across one-quarter of the street when getting on and off the streetcar. Although often this quarter of the street is taken up by parked cars, you're likely to see a car or two trying to pass a streetcar on the right, potentially endangering streetcar passengers. Getting on is usually not a problem; before stepping off the curb, you can easily take a quick look to the left for any oncoming cars. But take extra care in getting *off* the streetcar; before you take that last step to the pavement, peek around the side of the streetcar to make sure no other vehicles are careening wildly toward you. Technically, other traffic is supposed to stop when a streetcar's doors are open (in fact, the doors have a stop sign on them), but not every driver observes the stop (amazing, eh?).

Streetcar tracks do occasionally shut down for repairs. Also, streetcars themselves may break down en route, thereby suspending all service in the same direction on that route. In situations like these, buses provide backup service on the same schedules and using the same stops.

By bus

If you're using Toronto's mass transit system exclusively, you'll most likely have to board a bus at some time. A few of the more popular destinations, such as the Ontario Science Centre and the Toronto Zoo, are not near subway or streetcar lines, so you'll have to ride the subway as far as it will take you and then transfer onto a bus for the final leg of your journey (unless you clamber into a cab; see the next section).

Toronto buses are just like your buses back home: big, noisy, occasionally uncomfortable, and sometimes crowded, and you may end up sitting next to someone whose most recent shower was to celebrate the millennium. But the bus will get you where you need to go, and, barring a major traffic snafu, will do it in reasonably good time.

Remember to pick up your transfer ticket every time you board the subway, streetcar, or bus. Chances are that the only time you'll ride the bus is after transferring from the subway or streetcar line, so you don't want to have to pay a second one-way fare to finish your trip.

Hailing a taxi

Cabs are plentiful in Toronto, especially in the downtown area. For the most part, you can get from the east end of downtown to the west end of downtown for under ten bucks (unless you run into some heavy traffic — the meter clicks over every 30 seconds if you're not moving). Your meter starts at C$2.75 (US$2.25), and you're charged C$1.32 (US$1.10) per kilometer thereafter (the meter clicks in 25-cent increments.)

You can hail a cab from any intersection in Toronto, but you'll meet with more consistent success if you look for a taxi queue in front of a hotel or major office building. Make sure that you select the cab at the front of the line; you don't want to trigger a scuffle between taxi drivers.

If you need to call for a taxi, here are a few of the major — and reliable — cab companies in town. Each of these companies also carries a large fleet of minivans for larger groups and vehicles that are accessible for passengers with disabilities.

- ✔ **Beck Taxi:** ☎ 416-751-5555; www.becktaxi.com
- ✔ **Crown Taxi:** ☎ 416-750-7878; www.crowntaxi.com
- ✔ **Royal Taxi:** ☎ 416-777-9222; www.royaltaxi.ca

Making your own way: Driving around Toronto

As you may have noted in other sections of this book, my strongest recommendation remains that you don't drive in Toronto. If you drive *to* Toronto (as opposed to flying), you'll get more out of your trip if you just leave the car parked in the hotel lot and use public transit, taxicabs, or your feet to get around town.

While you'll probably pay through the nose for your hotel parking spot (some charge close to C$30/US$25 for overnight parking), you'll avoid paying through the ear and throat too when you park at or near all the attractions you visit (or, worse, for restaurant valet parking).

Downtown Toronto does have some on-street parking, though traditional meters have gone the way of the Yugo. Each block with on-street parking has a machine where you insert your coins or your credit card (no paper money) to pay for an allotment of parking time. If you need to park for only a couple of hours, on-street parking is your cheapest option — assuming you can find a spot — with downtown rates at a mere C\$2 (US\$1.65) an hour (for a maximum of 2 hours). Keep in mind, though, that on-street parking has restrictions during rush hour. If you're parked on the street during one of these restricted times, your car *will* be towed — count on it.

If you insist on driving (see Chapter 7 for tips on car rentals), read the next section for a few tips and reminders about doing so safely and efficiently.

Remembering the rules of the road

Driving in Toronto is not unlike driving in any other North American city when it comes to traffic laws and courteous driving habits. And if you're used to dealing with headache-inducing traffic back home, you'll feel right at home on Toronto's streets and highways. But here are a few specific considerations to keep in mind:

- ✔ **Speed limits:** Speed limits are posted in kilometers, so if you bring a car in from the U.S. you'll have to observe the small-print numbers on your speedometer. Highway speed limits range from 90 to 100 kilometers per hour (kmph), which works out to around 55 to 62 miles per hour (mph). Speed limits on city streets can range from 30 to 70 kmph, but most downtown thoroughfares are posted at 50 kmph.

  When they aren't stop-and-go and bumper-to-bumper, Toronto-area highways such as the Gardiner Expressway, the 401, and the QEW can seem to resemble a NASCAR straightaway, with all lanes running between 110 and 120 kmph. And, unfortunately, you'll quite regularly spot drivers reaching speeds of 130 or 140 kmph — usually just before they zoom across three lanes of heavy traffic to exit the highway from the passing lane. When traffic is not at a standstill, your best — and safest — bet is to keep up with the pace of the vehicles around you (the 110-to-120-kmph set, that is).

- ✔ **Right turn on red:** You can turn right on a red light in Toronto after you've made a complete stop. Make sure to watch for pedestrians and cyclists in the crosswalk in front of you before you make your turn, however (see the upcoming sections on pedestrians and cyclists). Also, remember that many downtown-Toronto streets are one-way; don't make yourself stand out like a sore-thumbed tourist — and risk serious injury to much more than just your thumb — by turning the wrong way onto a one-way street.

- ✔ **Seating arrangements:** Drivers and passengers must wear seat belts; Toronto and Ontario law enforcement agencies regularly conduct random spot checks for seat belt violations. Also, in Ontario, drivers are responsible for making sure that all passengers under the age of

16 are properly secured, either by car seat or seat belt, whether in the front seat or back, and children under age 13 are safest in the back seat, away from any potential point of impact.

✔ **Left-turn lights:** Toronto has a couple of different left-turn signals (or advanced greens, as the locals call them). The most common is a flashing green light, which allows drivers facing the same direction to either turn left (from the left-turn lane, of course) or proceed straight (or turn right); the opposing line of drivers still has a red light. Once the green light stops flashing, drivers in the left-turn lane should stop, as the opposing traffic (and pedestrians) will start to enter the intersection. You'll also see left-turn signals with a green arrow pointing to the left; when your turn is over, the green arrow will briefly turn yellow before disappearing.

✔ **Streetcar courtesy:** It's illegal to pass a streetcar on the right when its doors are opened for passengers getting on or off. It's common sense to not pass a streetcar on the right, period. If you get stuck behind a slow-moving streetcar, just relax and enjoy the ride; who knows, you may spot an out-of-the-way restaurant to try.

✔ **Watch for violators:** Some Torontonians just give driving in Toronto a really bad name. You're almost sure to observe that aforementioned driver going 140 on the 401 before crossing over in front of you to exit the highway. In the city, some drivers seem to habitually run very yellow or red lights. My best advice is to drive defensively: be prepared for the worst and pleasantly surprised when you see the best.

Looking out for folks on two feet

Torontonians cross the street anytime, anywhere. If there's an opening in traffic the size of the narrowest of alleyways, they're off and running — right to the middle of the road, from where they can watch for the narrowest of openings in the traffic coming from the *other* direction.

As a driver in this strange asphalt land, it's tempting to anticipate that a pedestrian may cross in front of you at any time, but don't — that kind of tentative driving is a recipe for being rear-ended, and at the very least you'll be cursed at by the drivers behind you. Instead, the best course of action is what your driver's ed instructor (hopefully) told you: be aware of your surroundings, and remember that your surroundings include Toronto's many walkers and cyclists.

Toronto's major thoroughfares are littered with *pedestrian crossovers.* Though they technically don't "cross over" anything, they're strategically placed in heavy foot-traffic locations where a traffic light is inconvenient or a good distance away. These crossovers are marked by yellow signs that span the street and have flashing yellow lights that pedestrians activate when they're ready to cross. What to watch for as you approach these crossovers? Look for the flashing yellow lights and a pedestrian with arm extended, pointing to indicate their intention to cross the street.

Don't even think about passing a car or streetcar that's stopped at a pedestrian crossover. Not only is it bad form (and dangerous to pedestrians who may be hidden by the stopped vehicle), but it's also illegal (within 30m — about 100 feet — of the crossover).

Remember that pedestrians have the right of way at traffic-light intersections when they have the walk signal. Remember also that, as in any city with walk signals, most folks keep on a-going when the walk signal has changed to a don't-walk signal.

Looking out for folks on two wheels

If you're driving downtown, you're sure to meet cyclists. Many of them will be bicycle couriers, darting in and out from between cars as they try to maneuver their way through traffic as quickly as possible en route to their next delivery.

Toronto also has an active corps of recreational and commuter cyclists who make good use of the city's 35km (22 miles) of on-street bike lanes. These lanes are painted with a diamond and an outline of a bicycle: downtown, the primary ones are these:

- ✔ Sherbourne Street, a north–south lane stretching from Lake Shore Boulevard to Bloor Street;

- ✔ Gerrard and College streets, an east–west lane that follows Gerrard and then College from Parliament to Bathurst streets; and

- ✔ St. George Street, a north–south lane from Queen to Bloor streets.

Toronto has many other streets that are designated as signed bike routes, and cyclists use these and other Toronto streets quite regularly. Here are a few tips for driving your car safely on Toronto's bicycle-friendly streets:

- ✔ **Check your mirrors, and your blind spot:** Especially when getting out of your car after parking on the street, check your mirrors and turn around to check your blind spot *before* you open your street-side door. Plowing into a suddenly opened car door is one of the leading causes of serious cycling injuries and deaths.

- ✔ **Watch your right turns:** Cyclists can easily be hidden from your sightline when you're making a right-hand turn, especially from a stopped position. You may be so focused on making sure that no cars are coming from the left that before making your turn you forget to check to your right one last time for any pedestrians or cyclists.

- ✔ **Cyclists posed as pedestrians:** Cyclists may use the pedestrian crossovers as well, so keep an eye out for the flashing yellows discussed in the preceding section.

Toronto's Underground

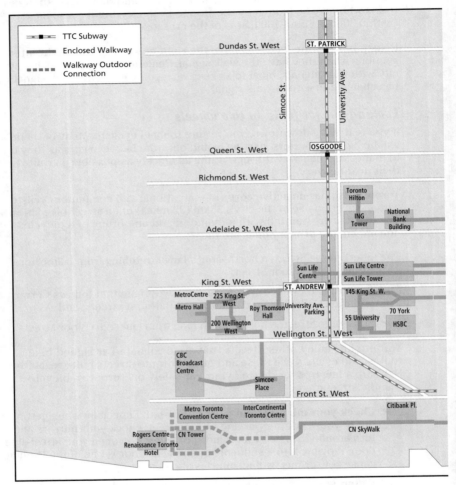

Toronto's Underground

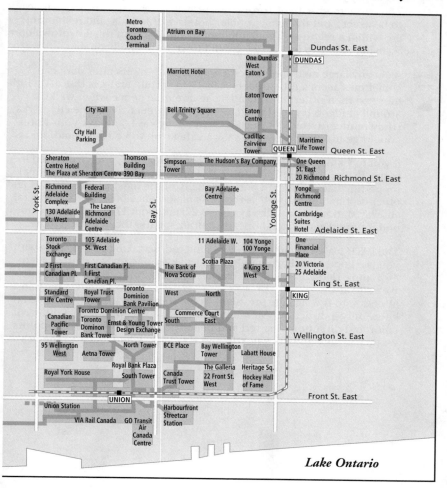

Walking the streets of Toronto

The entire mega-city of Toronto is sprawling (641 sq. km/248 sq. miles, to be exact), but the most popular hotels, attractions, and restaurants are within a relatively small number of city blocks in the downtown core. So using your two feet to get around town is definitely doable.

As in any large metropolitan city, walking the streets after dark can sometimes seem a little treacherous — in certain areas of the city a little more so than others. As always, use common sense when walking around at night: try to stay on well-lighted streets, avoid the city parks (they're nicer to look at during the day anyway), and ask your hotel concierge for clear directions for a safe stroll to your destinations.

If you're visiting Toronto during the colder seasons, you've no need to restrict your walking. Toronto's PATH underground walkway is perfect for getting back and forth between many of the most popular hotels and other destinations, as well as the city's major office buildings and several subway stations. The walkway covers 27km (about 17 miles) and includes underground access to shops, restaurants, bars, theaters, and more.

The PATH walkway can be a bit convoluted, so taking a map along with you is a good idea. Fortunately, I've provided one for you here, called "Toronto's Underground." You can also get one from the City of Toronto's Web site at www.city.toronto.on.ca/path/index.htm. Or, pay close attention to the signage prevalent in the walkway. Finally, if you need to know only a direction, each letter in PATH corresponds to a different color and direction: P is red and heads south, A is orange and points west, T is blue and goes north, and H is yellow and leads to the east.

Chapter 9

Checking In at Toronto's Best Hotels

Even if you time your visit to coincide with a major trade show or citywide festival, you should have no trouble finding a place to stay in Toronto for the length of your visit. This chapter offers some thoughts about the kinds of accommodation available in the city, as well as your best options for overnight stays.

You should also have no trouble finding a place that will be happy to take lots of your Canadian cash (credit cards also welcome). Yes, you will probably pay a lot for your room — one of the consequences of visiting any cosmopolitan business center such as Toronto (or New York or London). But this chapter helps you take some of the sting out of these costs, with suggestions for making sure you get the most out of your lodging dollar.

The bulk of this chapter, however, reviews a couple of dozen hotels to help you narrow down your choices when deciding where to stay during your Toronto visit. Along with their status as some of the best lodging options in the city, one of the primary criteria for a hotel making it into this chapter is location, location, location. For example, the suburban community of Mississauga may have a top-notch hotel or two, but you'll find little to do in this otherwise pleasant city, and unless you really want to stay close to the airport you'll spend way too much time and money getting to Toronto's best attractions.

Picking the Kind of Place That Suits Your Style

Because of the location of most of your touring options, your best bet for lodging in Toronto is going to be a downtown (or near-downtown) hotel. The section, "Finding the Perfect Location," later in this chapter, gives you the scoop on *where* you should look; this section offers some information about *what kind of lodging* is readily available for your visit to Toronto.

Hotels where you feel right at home

All the big hotel chains have set up shop in Toronto — Hyatt, Holiday Inn, Howard Johnson — including those that don't start with the letter *H*. What you get from these hotels is familiarity. You're generally safe to expect that a Sheraton in Toronto will offer pretty much the same experience as a Sheraton in Tacoma.

These chain hotels are a great option if all you really need is a clean, comfortable, safe place to sleep — with a nice big TV to help you wind down — after a long day of seeing the sights, eating hearty meals, taking in a show, or all of the above. Your chances for finding a hotel that's especially kid-friendly are better at the chains: most of them offer amenities such as indoor swimming pools that the kids can look forward to after a looooong day of museum-hopping. You may also be able to cut some costs if you choose a hotel chain that's linked with one of your frequent-flier accounts.

Chain hotels are not such a great option if you're looking for something unique to Toronto, or for a hotel that blends in, both in style and in service, to its surrounding neighborhood. (For a discussion of these specialty hotels, see the next section.) Chain hotels may also be hit and miss when it comes to consistent service. But if you're comfortable enough with both their hits and their misses, and appreciate their familiarity, a chain hotel may be perfect for you.

Hotels that treasure their independence

Looking for a hotel that boasts a little more character than your standard Marriott? Maybe a hotel that understands its surroundings and does its best to fit right in? Then you'll want to consider one of Toronto's many fine independent, and usually locally run, hotels.

The best of the hotels in this category go out of their way to flaunt their individual style and service. In this category, you can find hotels that celebrate their longevity in the city; hotels that may cater to specific travelers, be they business travelers or travelers used to the gushy (and occasionally not-so-gushy) catering of plush accommodations; and hotels that absorb the ambience (and the clientele) of its neighborhood.

Many hotels in this category also offer a slightly higher brand of customer service, though not necessarily the kinds of service and amenities that cater to families, particularly in the downtown core.

Bed-and-breakfast options

If you're a veteran bed-and-breakfast traveler, and welcome the kinds of unique inn-style accommodation that a bed-and-breakfast in a busy metropolitan setting can offer, Toronto has a few choices for you to consider. (Find bed-and-breakfast contact information later in this chapter). However, for a variety of reasons, going the bed-and-breakfast route may not be your best choice of accommodation when visiting Toronto:

- ✔ **Limited availability:** Toronto just isn't a big bed-and-breakfast city; the prime real estate is taken up by office buildings and hotels and luxury homes in neighborhoods that are exclusively for homes. Even the destination neighborhoods (such as The Beaches or Bloor West Village) have few options when it comes to bed-and-breakfasts.

- ✔ **Limited parking:** Where you can find a bed-and-breakfast, you're not likely to find easy parking. Few B&Bs have their own parking facilities, so you're expected to hunt down street parking just like the locals do.

- ✔ **Limited to adults:** Well, not exclusively, but many B&Bs in Toronto (and elsewhere) do not welcome children, or else they welcome children only over a certain age. If you're planning a family vacation to Toronto, a bed-and-breakfast is probably not an option for you.

Finding the Perfect Location

Because of Toronto's welcoming and accessible public transit system, choosing an area in which to stay is not as critical as it may seem for such a large, spread-out city. (See Chapter 8 for more about Toronto's mass transit.) Find a hotel in one of the areas discussed in this section and you'll be within easy walking distance, or have flexible transit options, to just about any attraction in Toronto.

For more information about these and other Toronto neighborhoods, check out Chapter 8. For more about the destinations discussed here, see Chapter 11.

Downtown

Book a room in the area that I call downtown Toronto (bounded by Spadina Avenue and Jarvis Street, west to east, and College and Front streets, north to south), and you'll have easy access to most of Toronto's Financial District, and much of its best shopping and dining choices, which you can find along Queen and King streets heading west of University Avenue.

This 4-sq.-km ($1^1/2$-sq.-mile) area has some great attractions too, from arts to sports to shopping. Among the sights in this area are the Art Gallery of Ontario, the Hockey Hall of Fame, and the St. Lawrence Market.

North of downtown

North of College Street and south of Eglinton Avenue is a large area that encompasses what some call Midtown and what others call Uptown. What you need to know, however, is how to get to Bloor/Yorkville, Church/Wellesley, and The Annex and Rosedale, respectively, prime neighborhoods for high-class shopping and accommodations, gay-friendly restaurants and bars, and posh residential streets with stately Toronto homes.

Find a hotel in this area and you're within minutes of such destinations as the Royal Ontario Museum, Queen's Park, and the Yorkville shopping (and celebrity-sighting) district.

The Entertainment District

Does your Toronto vacation include theater and music, as well as some great pre- and post-performance wining and dining? Toronto's Entertainment District has several hotels that cater to the whims of visiting theatergoers. In this area, you're also within a stone's throw (just try to resist the temptation!) of the eclectic shopping strips along Queen Street West.

Harbourfront on the lakeshore

Choose among several hotels along Queens Quay and you'll be in a good location for your visits to the CN Tower, the Rogers Centre (formerly known as the SkyDome), and Harbourfront Centre. You can also practically step outside your hotel and on board one of the several cruise ships that negotiate Lake Ontario, or hop on the ferry to the Islands.

If you're planning a gourmet's tour of Toronto, however, this area may not be a good resting place for you. You'll find that the better restaurants in town are several blocks north of the waterfront.

Staying near the airport

Unless one of the reasons for your trip to Toronto is to visit with long-lost relatives who live in Toronto's west end, spending your nights near the airport is not a good choice. Toronto's Lester B. Pearson International Airport is a fine facility — albeit perpetually under construction, as any good airport is — but it's a long half-hour drive into Toronto's center (longer during rush hour), where you'll spend a good chunk of your transportation budget on parking. A taxi into downtown is not much better, either timewise or pricewise: Fare from the airport to downtown will cost you at least C$40 (US$33). Finally, there's no easy way in or out of the airport area via public transit; the airport is not on a subway line, and getting there requires a bus ride of 20 to 45 minutes.

However, if you've scheduled a 6 a.m. flight home, you may want to consider spending your last night in Toronto near the airport. You'll still need an early wake-up call to make sure that you get to the airport in plenty of time to work your way through the various check-in and customs lineups, but at least you'll gain another half-hour of sleep. At just about any airport location, including the following, you'll find shuttle service readily available:

✔ **Radisson Suite Hotel Toronto Airport** (640 Dixon Rd.; ☎ **800-333-3333** or 416-242-7400; www.radisson.com/torontoca_airport): Each guest room (C$182/US$149) includes a separate living room, where you can spread out all your clothes and souvenirs for easier packing.

✔ **Sheraton Gateway Hotel** (Terminal 3; ☎ **800-325-3535** or 905-672-7000; www.sheraton.com/gatewaytoronto): This hotel is the only airport-area location that's attached to the airport, and you'll pay more for its convenience (rack rate is C$309/US$253). Of course, you can make some of that up by turning in your rental car a day early.

✔ **Fairfield Inn & Suites Toronto Airport** (3299 Caroga Dr.; ☎ **800-603-7307** or 905-673-9800; www.marriott.com): This reasonable option (C$149–C$169/US$122–US$139) has little to offer in the way of nearby dining options, but the new Marriott property (opened in 2004) offers roomy suites that will comfortably fit a family for the one last night in Toronto before an early morning flight. And the indoor pool opens early.

Finding the Best Room at the Best Rate

In all but the smallest accommodations, the rate you pay for a room depends on many factors — chief among them being how you make your reservation. A travel agent may be able to negotiate a better price with certain hotels than you can get by yourself. (That's because the hotel often gives the agent a discount in exchange for steering his or her business toward that hotel.)

Room rates (even rack rates; see definition below) change with the season, as occupancy rates rise and fall. But even within a given season, room prices are subject to change without notice, so the rates quoted in this book may be different from the actual rate you receive when you make your reservation. Be sure to mention membership in AAA, AARP, frequent-flier programs, corporate rewards programs — or your Uncle Joe's Elks lodge in which you're an honorary inductee, for that matter, if that works — when you call to book. You never know when the affiliation may be worth a few dollars off your room rate.

After you make your reservation, asking one or two pointed questions can go a long way toward making sure you get the best room in the house. Always ask for a corner room. They're usually larger, quieter, and have more windows and light than standard rooms, and they don't always cost more. Also ask if the hotel is renovating; if it is, request a room away from the renovation work. Inquire, too, about the location of the restaurants, bars, and discos in the hotel — all sources of annoying noise. And if you aren't happy with your room when you arrive, talk to the front desk. If they have another room, they should be happy to accommodate you, within reason.

Finding the best rate

When was the last time you paid the sticker price on a new car? Or bought a home without offering lower than the asking price? Or stopped at a yard sale and paid the full 25¢ for the paperback out of an old card-board box? Paying for a hotel room falls into the same category — always, always negotiate.

The *rack rate* is the maximum rate a hotel charges for a room. It's the rate you get if you walk in off the street and ask for a room for the night. You sometimes see these rates printed on the fire/emergency exit diagrams posted on the back of your door.

Hotels are happy to charge you the rack rate, but you can almost always do better. Perhaps the best way to avoid paying the rack rate is sur-prisingly simple: Just ask for a cheaper or discounted rate. You may be pleasantly surprised.

Despite what you just read, the quoted prices in this chapter for lodging reviews are the rack rates. This does not mean that you're going to end up paying exactly what you'll find here; it simply means that quoting the rack rates is the most accurate way I know of to give you a realistic sense of what one hotel in Toronto costs when compared with others.

Here are some more ideas for getting a reduced rate on your room:

- ✔ **Supply, meet demand:** Try to book a hotel room at just about any busy destination the week before you arrive and you're likely to pay through the nose, if you're lucky enough to find a room at all. Expand your options — both in price and in amenities — by reserving your room as soon as you know your travel dates. Remember that you can keep looking for a cheaper rate right up until around 4 p.m. of the day you arrive (which is generally the time after which the hotel will go ahead and charge you for a room that you've guaranteed with a credit card).

- ✔ **Visit during the off-season:** In Toronto, that's basically during January and February, though you may be able to garner less expensive lodging during the spring and fall. At any time of the year, however, you may run into a convention or trade show that can fill up the city's hotel rooms (and cash registers) in a hurry. Chapter 3 has more information about deciding when to visit Toronto.

- ✔ **Package your stay:** Package and escorted tours can sometimes include a significantly lower room rate (the tour operators or bundlers get reduced rates by ensuring hotels that a certain number of rooms will be full). Of course, you may also give up some travel flexibility, especially with an escorted tour, by booking your room as part of a package. Check out Chapter 5 for more about travel packages.

- ✔ **Call the hotel directly:** Especially if you're looking to stay in one of the chain hotels, you may not get the best rate by calling the chain's toll-free reservations line. Call the hotel directly to find out whether any hotel-specific specials or discounts are available. For example, local franchises may offer a special group rate for a wedding or family reunion, but they may neglect to tell the central booking line. Your best bet is to call both the local number and the toll-free number and see which one gives you a better deal. It may be well worth the couple of bucks you spend on long-distance charges.

Surfing the Web for hotel deals

Shopping online for hotels is generally done one of two ways: by booking either through the hotel's own Web site or through an independent booking agency (or a fare-service agency such as **Priceline**). These Internet hotel agencies have multiplied in mind-boggling numbers of late, competing for the business of millions of consumers surfing for accommodations around the world. This competitiveness can be a boon to consumers who have the patience and time to shop and compare the online sites for good deals — but shop they must, for prices can vary considerably from site to site. And keep in mind that hotels at the top of a site's listing may be there for no other reason than that the hotel paid to get the placement.

Of the "big three" sites, **Expedia** (www.expedia.com) offers a long list of special deals and "virtual tours" or photos of available rooms so you can see what you're paying for (a feature that helps counter the claims that the best rooms are often held back from bargain-booking Web sites). **Travelocity** (www.travelocity.com) posts unvarnished customer reviews and ranks its properties according to the AAA rating system. Also reliable are **Hotels.com** and **Quikbook.com**. An excellent free program, **TravelAxe** (www.travelaxe.net), can help you search multiple hotel sites at once, even ones you may never have heard of — and conveniently lists the total price of the room, including the taxes and service charges. Another booking site, **Travelweb** (www.travelweb.com), is partly owned by the hotels it represents (including the Hilton, Hyatt, and Starwood chains) and is therefore plugged directly into the hotels' reservations systems — unlike independent online agencies, which have to fax or e-mail reservation requests to the hotel, a good portion of which get misplaced in the shuffle. More than once, travelers have arrived at the hotel, only to be told that they have no reservation. To be fair, many of the major sites are undergoing improvements in service and ease of use, and Expedia will soon be able to plug directly into the reservations systems of many hotel chains — none of which can be bad news for consumers. In the meantime, it's a good idea to **get a confirmation number** and **make a printout** of any online booking transaction.

In the opaque Web site category, where you submit a bid for a mystery hotel somewhere in Toronto, **Priceline** (www.priceline.com) and **Hotwire** (www.hotwire.com) are even better for hotels than for airfares; with both, you're allowed to pick the neighborhood and quality level of your hotel before offering up your money. Priceline's hotel product even covers Europe and Asia, though it's much better at getting five-star lodging for three-star prices than at finding anything at the bottom of the scale. On the downside, many hotels stick Priceline guests in their least desirable rooms. Be sure to go to the **BiddingforTravel** Web site (www.biddingfortravel.com) before bidding on a hotel room on Priceline; it features a fairly up-to-date list of hotels that Priceline uses in major cities. For both Priceline and Hotwire, you pay up front and the fee is nonrefundable. *Note:* Some hotels do not provide loyalty-program credits or points or other frequent-stay amenities when you book a room through opaque online services.

The pros and cons of online booking

It's hard to pass up the convenience of browsing for hotels online when deciding where to stay in a particular destination. It's also hard to pass up some of the deals you may find at the online booking services recommended in the section "Surfing the Web for hotel deals." For example, a search of Expedia (both the Canadian and the U.S. sites) in the fall of 2004 found a rate of C$114 (US$96) per night for a weekend in March 2005 at the Metropolitan Hotel. That same weekend booked through the Metropolitan's own online booking service offered a rate of C$169 (US$139) per night, and the hotel's rack rate for that period starts at C$350 (US$287). Your "Expedia special rate" would save you roughly 35 to 60 percent in lodging costs.

That's a great saving, but remember that hotels typically set aside only a certain number of rooms to offer to online booking services for their "special rates." And usually, those rooms are of a specific quality. Guests who pay nightly rates that are closer to the hotel's rack rates are going to be first in line for a hotel's best rooms — the ones that are most recently renovated and updated, have the best views, or are farthest away from the noise that's a part of every hotel (elevators, ice machines, music from the hotel bar, and so on).

If you're going to accept an online bargain, you're likely to get what you pay for. That doesn't mean you're getting a bad deal; you still get to take advantage of a hotel's amenities, ambient charm, and food and drink facilities — everyone pays the same for these. And the low end on, say, the Metropolitan's room-quality scale still gives you a pretty decent room. Just keep in mind that you probably aren't going to end up in that upper-floor suite with the Egyptian cotton linens and in-room Jacuzzi that you were hoping for.

Booking to fit your itinerary

Before you start distributing your credit card number to various hoteliers in the Toronto area, consider how you're building your itinerary so that you can maximize the amount of hotel you can get for your money. Rates can vary daily, so consider what you may pay in a hotel in Toronto's Financial District on a Wednesday night versus what that same room will cost you on a Saturday night.

Because Toronto is the center of much of Canada's business and financial world, the city's hotels rely heavily on business travelers who are generally more likely to pay a higher "top dollar" than vacationers, whose "top dollar" has no risk of acrophobia. However, business travelers tend to travel during the week, when the business needs tending to, so hotels may have weekends during the year when many rooms are not booked.

Your negotiating power usually increases if you're trying to book in a fairly exclusively business area for a couple of weekend nights. When researching your hotel options, make sure to watch in your local newspaper for hotel-chain ads that trumpet great weekend rates at select locations; if you can match one of these locations with your weekend in Toronto, you'll be able to save extensively.

If your vacation includes a side trip to the theater-festival towns of Stratford or Niagara-on-the-Lake, remember that the opposite may be true in terms of weekend versus weekday availability, if not rates. The theater crowd is generally lighter during the week, with the towns filling up for weekend performances. Hotel and bed-and-breakfast availability can be tighter during Friday and Saturday nights, though most bed-and-breakfasts don't vary their rates.

Finding a Room when There's No Room at the Inn

On any given week in Toronto, especially during spring and summer, the city's hotels may be crammed full with conventioneers, trade show attendees, festival-goers, or simply more tourists like you. So it definitely pays to book your accommodations as early as possible after you've established your travel dates.

However, I also know that there are times when booking early just isn't a possibility. Maybe you garnered one of those great cyber-airfares that airlines offer to fill empty seats on weekend flights — the kind that require you to buy your airline ticket on Wednesday for a Friday flight, leaving you in Toronto on a Friday night just hoping to find a vacant room somewhere.

You do have a few options before you arrive in Toronto without a place to lay your head (or your suitcase, if you had time to pack one between that Wednesday ticket purchase and your Friday departure).

- ✔ **Head back to your computer.** You have about 36 hours before you take off on that quick weekend flight. Try one of the online booking services discussed in the preceding section. These services are a fast and easy way to find a list of possibilities, though you should still pick up the phone to reserve, given the last-minute nature of your visit.

- ✔ **Check out the chain hotel Web sites.** Some hotels are now offering weekend-only specials (either via E-mail or through their Web site only) similar to the airline cyber-style fares. You may get lucky and find a Toronto hotel to your liking.

- ✔ **Call on the locals. Tourism Toronto** (☎ **800-499-2514** or 416-203-2500; www.torontotourism.com) can work with you to find a room when none seems to be in sight.

✔ **Consider a bed-and-breakfast.** Though bed-and-breakfast accommodations tend to fill up fairly well in advance, you may be able to take advantage of another traveler's cancellation. The **Toronto Bed & Breakfast Reservation Service** (☎ **877-922-6522** or 705-738-9449) works with a dozen or so B&Bs in Toronto; this service's Web site (www.torontobandb.com) has links to B&B description pages. **The Downtown Toronto Association of Bed and Breakfast** (☎ **416-410-3938;** www.bnbinfo.com) is another free service, matching your accommodation and location preferences with a B&B or guesthouse that most closely meets your needs. Keep in mind, however, that many B&Bs do not welcome children.

✔ **Go back to school.** Many residence buildings at the University of Toronto offer housing for non-students during the summer. No central summer residence agency exists, so you have to check with the individual residences. Contact the university's student housing service (☎ **416-978-8045**) for a list of residences and phone numbers.

Toronto's Best Hotels

The hotels listed here are the cream of the crop, the crème de la crème, the whipped cream with a cherry on top . . . you get the idea. If none of these suit your fancy — or if you can't wriggle your way into one of them — the "Runner-up Hotels" section later in this chapter offers a few alternatives.

The accommodations reviewed in this chapter are organized alphabetically. Each review lists the neighborhood in which the hotel resides, in case you're interested in staying in a particular area of the city — you can also find a hotel on the "Toronto Accommodations" map and then turn to its review. For even more convenience, the end of this chapter includes a couple of indexes, one listing hotels by neighborhood, the other listing by price.

If you're traveling with kids, look for reviews accompanied by this icon to find hotels that offer amenities and special programs that appeal to children. Because most hotels offer some kind of discount or free stay for kids accompanied by an adult, I've awarded this icon only to those accommodations that go out of their way to make families with kids feel welcome.

A few select hotels in this chapter earn this coveted icon. You won't just find the icon next to the single-dollar-sign hotels; hotels that earn this icon provide significant value for the money you spend there, such as premium five-star service in a three-star location.

Each review here includes a dollar-sign symbol to indicate the *rack rate* price range for each hotel. Table 9-1 tells you what you can expect in terms of room size, amenities, and other accommodation features in each of the five price categories.

Toronto Accommodations

ACCOMMODATIONS

10 Cawthra Square **27**
Annex Guesthouse
  Bed and Breakfast **1**
Best Western Primrose **24**
  Hotel
Bond Place Hotel **21**
Cambridge Suites Hotel **16**
Clarion Selby Hotel **28**
  & Suites
Delta Chelsea **23**
The Drake Hotel **2**
Fairmont Royal York **12**
Four Seasons Hotel **30**
The Grand Hotel & Suites **22**
Hilton Toronto **18**
Holiday Inn on King **4**
Hotel Le Germain **5**
Hotel Victoria **14**
Howard Johnson **32**
  Downtown
InterContinental **8**
  Toronto Centre
Le Royal Meridien **15**
  King Edward
Marriott Courtyard **25**
Metropolitan Hotel **19**
  Toronto
Novotel Toronto Centre **11**
Park Hyatt **31**
Radisson Plaza Hotel **9**
  Admiral
Renaissance Toronto **7**
Sheraton Centre Toronto **17**
Soho Metropolitan **6**
The Strathcona Hotel **13**
The Sutton Place Hotel **26**
Toronto Marriott Eaton **20**
  Centre
Travelodge Toronto **3**
  Downtown West
Westin Harbour Castle **10**
Windsor Arms **29**

Table 9-1	Key to Hotel Dollar Signs	
Dollar Sign(s)	**Price Range**	**What to Expect**
$	C$100 (US$82) and under	Rooms are available in Toronto for these prices; you just have to know where to look. During summer, your best bet for these rates are at various university residence houses around town. Of course, many of the rooms are singles, so you may be bunking alone (but some do have meal plans available, so at least you don't have to *eat* alone). Virtually no amenities here — you may be lucky to have linens provided, and don't even think about a private bath — but you'll be able to save your loonies and toonies for the rest of your itinerary.
$$	C$100–C$175 (US$82–US$144)	Hotels in this category tend to be from the lower-end chains (such as Howard Johnson or Choice Hotels), or they're smaller independent operations that have few amenities or that may be just out of the downtown core. Rooms in this category will be on the small side, but comfortable, though they may or may not have air-conditioning. You will have a private bathroom — even in the bed-and-breakfasts in this price range — but the selection of showering and/or bathing facilities varies (some rooms offer bathtub only). Amenities are also bare-bones: few pools, even fewer fitness facilities; and you'll probably have to go off-site for a meal.
$$$	C$175–C$250 (US$144–US$205)	You won't find too much difference in the quality of rooms and facilities at hotels in this category from hotels in the preceding category. The big difference here? Location, location, location. Generally, rooms in this category remain fairly standard fare: moderate in size, less so in creative design. And you'll have much more consistency in the quality and efficiency of bathrooms. Amenities are likely to be a (small) step up: the hotel will have a pool (or one nearby) and probably a restaurant or two.
$$$$	C$250–C$325	Just shy of the crème de la crème (see below) is this (US$205–US$267) category of hotels in which you'll really begin to notice what you're paying for. These next two categories are for travelers who consider the quality of their hotel room to be an integral part of their trip. Public areas are more ornate, with comfortable seating that's suitable for people-watching; for celebrity-watching, you'll likely need to move one category up. These hotels usually have multiple restaurants and bars on-site; many of your not-so-basic amenities, such as on-site massage and expanded fitness and activity centers; and a concierge service to point you in the right direction.

Dollar Price Range Sign(s)	What to Expect
$$$$$ C$325 (US$267) and above	For the ultimate splurge, try one of the handful of hotels in this category. All, of course, are centrally located, with the most opulent of settings and the most luxurious of styles. The rooms are sumptuous, with all the features the most wired-up business traveler would need, and then some; you may even find rooms that are individually designed — no cookie-cutter artwork here. Bathrooms are lavish, with high-end brand-name (or self-branded) toiletries. And you have the best in spa and fitness facilities available to you, if not at the hotel, then just around the corner.

Don't forget to factor in any taxes you'll pay when budgeting for your lodging costs. The government tacks on an extra 12 percent to your room rate (7 percent GST plus 5 percent provincial lodging tax).

The Hotels

Bond Place Hotel
$$ Downtown

Though its rooms are on the small side, the Bond Place Hotel is a surprisingly great value. Right in the heart of Toronto — just a block north of the Eaton Centre and quite close to a variety of entertainment venues, including Massey Hall and the Winter Garden Theatre — this hotel offers some of the best special rates in downtown Toronto, though some areas of the surrounding neighborhood are a bit dodgy. Although at these prices you're almost certain to share the hotel with a tour group or two, this is one hotel where it pays big-time to negotiate out of their rack rates. Rooms have standard amenities, and their smallness evokes a kind of New York feel, but a 1999 renovation is still holding its own; rooms are clean and well maintained, and the bathrooms are fully serviceable with shower/tub combinations. The hotel offers a wide range of room configurations; for example, 23 rooms have a pair of twin beds plus either one double or one three-quarter bed tucked off in a small alcove — great for families with kids. Ask for a room on the higher floors; some have a great view of the city. The lobby-level restaurant is adequate in a pinch, and room service is inconveniently not available for breakfast, so try heading a couple of blocks north to Elm Street for some good eateries. If you decide to stay in for an evening, the basement-level bar offers the hotel's only entertainment, a couple of pool tables and dartboards; the Bond Place has no pool or fitness facilities. Overnight parking is reasonable, but off-site; the lot is across Dundas Street.

*See map p. 110. 65 Dundas St. W. ☎ **800-268-9390** or 416-362-6061. Fax: 416-360-6406.* www.bondplacehoteltoronto.com. *TTC: Dundas station. Parking: C$14 (US$11). Rack rates: C$149 (US$122) double. AE, DISC, MC, V.*

Cambridge Suites Hotel
$$$$$ Downtown

The first hotel outside of Nova Scotia for this luxury suite chain, the Cambridge Suites is a roomy — albeit somewhat spendy — lodging option in the heart of downtown Toronto. The two-room suites are well designed for the business traveler — the Cityscape suites even include an in-suite fax machine — and the living room includes a fold-out sofa, ideal for traveling families. The rack rates are extravagantly high, but with some advance planning you may be able to experience the Cambridge brand of luxury for around C$200 (US$164). The linens are fashioned from Egyptian cotton, making for a luxurious sleep (there's that word again!). Suites include a mini-fridge and microwave for snacking or breakfast, which can save you a few bucks over the hotel's pricey (and inconsistent) restaurant, Resto Portico.

See map p. 110. 15 Richmond St. E. ☎ *800-463-1990 or 416-368-1990. Fax: 416-601-3751.* www.cambridgesuitestoronto.com. *TTC: Queen station. Parking: C$16 (US$13). Rack rates: C$449–C$524 (US$368–US$430) double. AE, DC, DISC, MC, V.*

Clarion Selby Hotel & Suites
$$ Downtown

A late-19th-century Victorian mansion belonging to the Gooderham family (of Gooderham & Worts Distillery fame), this renovated quaint hotel is on the outer edges of what's generally considered downtown Toronto, but its proximity to the Sherbourne subway station (just across the street) makes the Selby a reasonably priced alternative with easy access to Toronto's sights. The Selby is not the place to stay if you're looking for top-of-the-line amenities; it remains a pretty basic hotel, with cozy, high-ceilinged guest rooms in a variety of layouts, reflecting the quirkiness that comes with creating a hotel out of a lovely older home. The furnishings, however, do attempt to match the style of the building, making the guest rooms somewhat more homey than those in your typical Clarion facility. And only recently were the last of the private bathrooms installed, reducing the already limited space of some of the guest rooms, but some retain the charm of the mansion's days gone by with beautifully restored clawfoot tubs. The hotel has 12 suites, including a handful with large bathroom and Jacuzzi tub. There's little to see and do in the vicinity, but the nearby subway stop makes the inconvenient location bearable. Parking is available on-site, but is limited to 36 spaces.

See map p. 110. 592 Sherbourne St. ☎ *416-921-3142. Fax: 416-923-3177.* www.hotelselby.com. *TTC: Sherbourne station. Parking: C$10 (US$8). Rack rates: C$120–C$159 (US$98–US$130) double. AE, DC, DISC, MC, V.*

Delta Chelsea
$$–$$$$$ Downtown

Self-proclaimed "Canada's largest hotel," this facility offers nearly 1,600 guest rooms that do help it stand out for its vastness. The Delta Chelsea is also self-proclaimed "Toronto's entertainment hotel," but you'll find others, such as the Holiday Inn on King and the Sheraton Centre Toronto, that are a bit closer to the major Toronto theaters. Hype notwithstanding, this popular hotel has plenty to offer, especially for families traveling with kids. The Chelsea has two indoor pools: one is for adults only, and the other is on a second-floor recreation area that features the Children's Creative Centre — a playroom offering games, crafts, and scheduled activities for kids age 3 to 12. Teens are welcome too, with the hotel's Starcade Centre showcasing pool, air hockey, and video games. And for parents, an in-house theater babysitting service is available nightly — four hours for C$25 (US$21) per family. Rooms are a bit small, though the hotel features a few "Family Fun Suites" complete with separate bedrooms and sundry knickknacks for the kids. You'll pay more for parking here than in many other locations.

See map p. 110. 33 Gerrard St. W. ☎ *877-814-7706 or 416-595-1975. Fax: 416-585-4375.* www.deltachelsea.com. *TTC: College station. Parking: C$22 (US$18). Rack rates: C$129–C$399 (US$106–US$327) double. AE, DC, DISC, MC, V.*

The Drake Hotel
$$–$$$$ Queen West

If you're such a frequent traveler that you proudly boast about your room size as if you're selecting a shirt size, The Drake may just be for you (its rooms are self-sized at S, M, L, and XL). On the other hand, if you're just the uptight kind of traveler who feels he must boast about his shirt size, The Drake is probably not for you. Eclectic is the operative word here. This newly opened antiestablishment establishment is a beautiful refurbishing of a century-old flophouse that shares the cultural perspective of its neighbors in Toronto's growing West Queen West neighborhood. The rooms are called Crash Pads and range in size from 14 to 36 sq. m (150 to 385 sq. ft.), and each features high-speed Internet access, flat-screen TVs, CD/DVD players, and glass showers. An entertainment space features live performances from comedy to music to poetry and more.

See map p. 110. 1150 Queen St. W. ☎ *866-372-5386 or 416-531-5042. Fax: 416-531-9493.* www.thedrakehotel.ca. *TTC: Osgoode station, and then 501 Queen streetcar west. No onsite parking. Rack rates: C$159–C$259 (US$130–US$212). AE, MC, V.*

Fairmont Royal York
$$$–$$$$ Financial District

Opened in 1929 as the Royal York Hotel, this Canadian Pacific Hotel property was, at the time, the tallest building in the British Commonwealth. Fairmont took over the day-to-day operations when it merged with CP in 1999, but the Royal York continues to set Toronto hospitality standards for opulence and service — the staff go out of their way to put the accommodate in accommodations — and it continues to host the rich and famous (and those who film the rich and famous; the hotel is a popular site for Toronto-area film shoots. Its location opposite Union Station makes the Royal York a prime base for business and leisure travelers alike: at the doorstep of Toronto's Financial District, within steps of the Hummingbird Centre for the Performing Arts and the Hockey Hall of Fame, and still with a fairly open view of Lake Ontario (looking past the growing number of lakeside condos) on the hotel's south side.

The hotel's ornate lobby is a draw for people-watching (and celebrity-sighting, if you're into that sort of thing), and the rich wood-paneled Library Bar is one of the city's finest hotel bars (see Chapter 16). Guest rooms vary in size, though they share most amenities; room rates reflect the rooms' diversity as well as their location (the Signature Rooms, for example, are all above the 12th floor, with extra features such as CD players, plusher mattresses, a view of the lake, and a higher price tag). Room décor throughout is up to the Fairmont chain's elegant standards. Bathrooms are fairly uniform in size — as is expected in older hotels — and completely uniform in amenities, including shower/tub combination.

In many ways, the Royal York is almost a city within a city. The building itself equals the expanse of Toronto's massive Union Station. The health club features over a dozen weight and resistance machines; an indoor pool, Jacuzzi, and kids' wading pool; and private treatment rooms for on-site massages. The hotel ties into the PATH underground walkway (See map in Chapter 8) with its own concourse of restaurants, shops, and services either run by or leased out by the hotel. The Japanese steakhouse chain Benihana is a bit of an odd restaurant choice for such an elegant hotel, but the EPIC restaurant presents a more formal — and appropriate for the setting — dining option, including a breakfast buffet with just about the freshest fare in town. In addition to these and five other dining establishments on-site, the in-room menu is as extensive as you'll find anywhere, and the hotel staff includes both a resident bath sommelier and Canada's only tea sommelier.

See map p. 110. 100 Front St. W. ☎ *800-257-7544 or 416-368-2511. Fax: 416-368-9040.* www.fairmont.com. *TTC: Union station. Parking: C$31 (US$25). Rack rates: C$189–C$289 (US$155–US$237) double. AE, DC, DISC, MC, V.*

Four Seasons Hotel
$$$$$ **Bloor/Yorkville**

With 32 stories and 380 guest rooms and suites, the Four Seasons at least attempts to place a premium on wide-open spaces. The guest rooms in this chic hotel — in one of Toronto's chicest neighborhoods — range from 30 to 39 sq. m (325 to 425 sq. ft.); the suites go way up from there. Each room is designed with maximum comfort in mind, from the cozy duvets to the restful sitting areas to the plush marble bathrooms with shower and tub combinations. The hotel provides a complete range of spa and fitness amenities, and your dining options include the perpetually highly rated Truffles, though the Bloor/Yorkville neighborhood has such a diversity of restaurant options that you're better served to get out of the hotel for your brightest stars make the Four Seasons their Toronto home — Hollywood celeb types can be here for weeks at a time for a film shoot in Toronto — and the hotel was a longtime host of the Toronto International Film Festival (until the Delta Chelsea took over that role in 2003). So you're certain to spend a good chunk of your vacation budget if the Four Seasons is your destination, which you may consider worth it for its location near great shopping and dining and things to do (the Royal Ontario Museum, for example, is just a couple of blocks south), not to mention some star-gazing of the celebrity type.

See map p. 110. 21 Avenue Rd. ☎ ***800-819-5053*** *or 416-964-0411. Fax: 416-964-2301.* www.fourseasons.com. *TTC: Bay station. Parking: C$30 (US$25). Rack rates: C$355–C$425 (US$291–US$349) double. AE, DC, DISC, MC, V.*

The Grand Hotel & Suites
$$–$$$ **Downtown**

Though not in the most attractive part of town, this suite hotel on the eastern edge of downtown Toronto offers a relatively trouble-free lodging experience at a decent price. Guest rooms are a bit on the small side to really do justice to the term "suite," but many nice amenities are tucked into that little space, including a kitchenette with mini-fridge, two-element stove, and microwave, and a full complement of entertainment options including CD, VCR, *and* DVD players. For the traveling family, the Grand Deluxe Room offers a separate sleeping area (its small size prevents me from calling it a bedroom), a pull-out sofa for the kids, and two TVs to minimize family "discussions" about the viewing of *Coronation Street*. Or the Junior Suite offers a bit more room (and French doors to separate the sleeping areas) for only about C$50 (US$41) per night more. In keeping with the theme of the rooms, the marble bathrooms are a bit small but clean and functional. The rooftop patio features two outdoor Jacuzzis that are open year-round, with bar service available during the summer. The rooftop offers one of the best views of the city, nice given the lack of aesthetic enjoyment available in the surrounding neighborhood, which is definitely the significant drawback to a stay here. Except for the Grand's lovely Citrus restaurant opposite the lobby, few restaurant options are nearby. The Dundas subway station is the closest, but it's a good six-block walk; another option is the 505 Dundas W. streetcar, which takes you into downtown with transfer opportunities at the Dundas and St. Patrick subway stations. Better yet, let the pleasant and professional doormen hail a cab for you; the money you save on your room rates could be put to good use in taxiing around Toronto.

See map p. 110. 225 Jarvis St. ☎ ***877-324-7863*** *or 416-863-9000. Fax: 416-863-1100.* www.grandhoteltoronto.com. *TTC: Dundas station. Parking: C$19 (US$16). Rack rates: C$169–C$239 (US$139–US$196) double. AE, DC, DISC, MC, V.*

Hilton Toronto
$$$–$$$$ **Financial District**

With its location practically in the heart of Toronto's Financial District, the Hilton Toronto is a major draw for business travelers. However, the Hilton is just about the most central hotel in terms of proximity to places to see and things to do — you're within a kilometer or two (a mile or so) of just about every major downtown attraction — making it a good home-base choice for rummaging around downtown Toronto. Guest rooms are pretty standard fare, though a recent full-scale renovation included the introduction of sleeker, more modern furnishings. The public areas are a bit more impressive, including a couple of quality dining choices: The popular (and pricey) Ruth's Chris Steak House chain has prime location here, and TUNDRA focuses on presenting an inventive menu of Canadian cuisine.

See map p. 110. 145 Richmond St. W. ☎ *800-445-8667 or 416-869-3456. Fax: 416-869-3187.* www.toronto.hilton.com. *TTC: Osgoode station. Parking: C$27 (US$22). Rack rates: C$219–C$299 (US$180–US$245) double. AE, DC, DISC, MC, V.*

Holiday Inn on King
$$$–$$$$ **Entertainment District**

If your Toronto vacation includes a show or two, the Holiday Inn on King may just be your most logical choice of accommodations. In fact, it's also within easy walking distance of a half-dozen other destinations, including the CN Tower. The calling card of this hotel is its amenities — and there are many, from the rooftop outdoor swimming pool (open May through September) to the newly reequipped fitness center to the in-room spa services (not directly affiliated with the hotel, but you can make arrangements in the lobby); also on-site are the Mahogany Lounge, a classic scotch-and-cigars meeting place, and the Laugh Resort Comedy Club. The rubber duckie and night-light that are standard in each bathroom will appeal to your sense of whimsy; your practical side will appreciate the standard shower/tub combinations. Guest rooms have that Holiday Inn look to them, comfortable if not aesthetically inspiring, though check back in a year or so, as current renovation plans are to install hardwood flooring in every room. For a downtown location, the rooms are surprisingly large.

Don't worry about the hotel's restaurants: it's not that they're bad or good, it's just that you'll have so many other options in this Theater District neighborhood. With more than ten restaurants just across King Street (ranging from Cajun to French to Indian and more), and dozens more in the surrounding blocks, you'll find plenty of choices for your post- and pre-theater outings.

See map p. 110. 370 King St. W. ☎ *800-263-6364 or 416-599-4000. Fax: 416-599-7394.* www.hiok.com. *TTC: St. Andrew station. Parking: C$18 (US$15). Rack rates: C$239–C$279 (US$196–US$229) double. AE, DC, DISC, MC, V.*

Hotel Le Germain
$$$$$ Entertainment District

Sleek and open, at once luxurious and homey, this relatively new addition to the Toronto hotel scene (fall 2003) is a study in moderate indulgence. Tucked away in a narrow two-block-long street (almost an alleyway) between John and Peter streets, its intimate location and almost-hidden entrance suggest exclusivity (the equally veiled entrances of two hip nightspots across Mercer Street — the restaurant Rain and the bar Shmooze — enhance that feel). But once you're inside, you'll feel at home and pampered — quite a combination! — thanks to the inviting two-story lobby with floor-to-ceiling windows and a connected library, the efficiently courteous front-desk staff and concierge, and the three fresh apples set out for guests in the elevator waiting area on each floor.

The emphasis is on space and openness at this Toronto location of the Boutiques Hotel properties — the first location outside of Quebec. The two-story lobby is only the beginning: You'll find high ceilings throughout; guest rooms are bright and spacious; each of the hotel's four suites has a private walk-out balcony; and one suite has two levels, ideal for business travelers looking for a private space to wine and dine clients. Standard in every unit are lush Egyptian cotton linens, flat-screen TVs, and free high-speed Internet access (wireless is available in the lobby). And the prevailing sense of openness extends to each guest room's bathroom: glass partitions separate the bathroom from the main area of the guest room (with elegant wood blinds to close for a little privacy, if you desire). The hotel offers about a 50/50 split of shower-only and shower/tub combination bathrooms, but even tub aficionados will appreciate — no, make that adore — the rain shower that's standard in each room.

See map p. 110. 30 Mercer St. ☎ **866-345-9501** *or 416-345-9500. Fax: 416-345-9501.* www.germaintoronto.com. *TTC: St. Andrew station. Valet parking: C$25 (US$21). Rack rates: C$395–C$495 (US$324–US$406) double. AE, DC, DISC, MC, V.*

Hotel Victoria
$$ Financial District

Built in 1909 and fully renovated in the late 1990s, Toronto's second-oldest hotel (after the King Eddy) is one of Toronto's best hotel bargains. The owners have preserved the genuine and classy feel of old-style hotelier while adding the modern in-room amenities required of a downtown hotel. And an even more recent conversion of the second floor — from meeting space to eight additional guest rooms (bringing the total to 56 units) — introduced a more modern alternative, complete with halogen desk lamp and crisp bold furnishings, for guests who prefer chic over charm. To be expected with a hotel of its age, the Victoria's guest rooms are generally on the small side, though two front units on each floor take advantage of a little more space to offer a mini-fridge and coffee area. Bathrooms are uniformly tasteful, with marble floor (and tile in those rooms — all but eight — with shower/tub combinations) and pedestal basin sinks standard throughout.

The hotel has no restaurant on-site (a continental breakfast is provided with the room rate) and there's no parking exclusively available with the hotel, but you can get by without either. The Hotel Victoria is just a couple of blocks from the King subway station, and a variety of dining options are within easy walking distance in all directions. The hotel's single elevator is a bit slow, so you may have to wait for a ride during peak hours.

See map p. 110. 56 Yonge St. ☎ *800-363-8228 or 416-363-1666. Fax: 416-363-7327.* www.hotelvictoria-toronto.com. *TTC: King station. No on-site parking. Rack rates: C$105–C$159 (US$86–US$130) double. AE, MC, V.*

InterContinental Toronto Centre
$$$–$$$$ Financial District

A $30-million reconstruction effort has turned this former Crowne Plaza location into one of Toronto's newest luxury offerings. This InterContinental (a second Toronto InterContinental is in the Bloor/Yorkville district) opened in September 2003, presenting a bit of a boutique-hotel look in a luxury-hotel package. The renovated lobby and other public areas are a study in rich, dark hues and huge, open spaces. All the guest rooms were also renovated in the changeover to InterContinental status, and they have maintained their spaciousness while adding a touch of comfortable charm to room furnishings. Additionally, 90 Club InterContinental rooms were added for the more discerning — and likely business — traveler; these rooms offer little extra touches of luxury and efficiency, including Egyptian cotton linens and high-speed Internet access. Guests can use the facilities of the Victoria Spa on the hotel's third floor, including spa pool and whirlpool; its exercise room is a visual masterpiece, with hardwood flooring and stunning stone structures separating exercise "cubicles" — oh, and there are also some weight and resistance machines, if you want something to do while you enjoy the original design. The on-site restaurant, Azure, caters to hotel guests for breakfast (with a standard buffet), the local business crowd for lunch, and local gourmands for dinner (with limited success). The InterContinental's location on the fringes of both the Financial and Entertainment districts, however, opens up a number of diverse off-site dining options.

See map p. 110. 225 Front St. W. ☎ *800-422-7969 or 416-597-1400. Fax: 416-597-8128.* www.torontocentre.intercontinental.com. *TTC: Union station. Parking: C$19 (US$16). Rack rates: C$179–C$319 (US$147–US$262) double. AE, DC, DISC, MC, V.*

Le Royal Meridien King Edward
$$$$–$$$$$ Downtown

The "King Eddy" just turned 100. Built in 1903, this Toronto landmark has over those 100 years hosted the best and the brightest, from Kipling to Twain, Caruso to McCartney and Lennon (and Harrison and Starr), Roosevelt to de Gaulle. Now a part of the Le Meridian brand of luxury hotels, the hotel retains the charm and sophistication that introduced itself to Toronto as the city's "first luxury hotel." It's a testament to how luxury hotels used to be made, with elegant furnishings, long, wide hallways, and opulent yet inviting public areas. The guest rooms are all beautifully décorated, with many of the most up-to-date modern amenities (including flat-screen plasma TVs in some rooms). Marble bathrooms are well appointed and amply sized. Travelers with a disability should note that only four rooms are wheelchair-accessible, all on the second floor.

See map p. 110. 39 King St. E. ☎ 800-543-4300 or 416-863-9700. Fax: 416-367-5515. www.lemeridien-kingedward.com. TTC: King station. Valet parking: C$28 (US$23). Rack rates: C$300–C$450 (US$246–US$369) double. AE, DC, DISC, MC, V.

Metropolitan Hotel Toronto
$$$$$ Downtown

One of two locations in Toronto operated by Metropolitan Hotels (a third is in Vancouver), this hotel seems to have endured some inattention while its younger sister — the Soho Metropolitan — was completed and opened (early in 2003). But with the Soho complete, work is now ongoing at this not-at-all-ugly sister, in the hotel's first major renovation since 1993. Rooms yet to be updated suffer the expected challenges, such as outdated furnishings, but in no way diminish the appeal of this proud facility. Renovated rooms boast a more modern and crisp look, with muted tones highlighted by dark-blond wood paneling; beds offer the comfort of down duvets and Frette linens. Guest rooms are consistently smaller than those available at other downtown hotels, and the bathrooms are especially tightly confined, though serviceable with shower/tub combinations.

Amenities are top-drawer at the Metropolitan, from its highly popular complimentary limo service and progressive fitness center with indoor pool and Jacuzzi, to its highly acclaimed restaurants: Hemispheres, with its great blend of Canadian and international cuisine, and the Cantonese experience at Lai Wah Heen (see review in Chapter 10) are both fine dining experiences, and among the best in Toronto hotel offerings. And these restaurants will come in handy when your search for inspiring dining nearby comes up empty; the surrounding area reflects the bureaucratic "charm" of its primary residents, including Toronto's City Hall and the U.S. Consulate.

See map p.110. 108 Chestnut St. ☎ 800-668-6600 or 416-977-5000. Fax: 416-977-9513. www.metropolitan.com/toronto. TTC: St. Patrick station. Parking: C$19 (US$16). Rack rates: C$350–C$460 (US$287–US$377) double. AE, DC, DISC, MC, V.

Park Hyatt
$$$–$$$$ Bloor/Yorkville

While the Hollywood elite tend to prefer the Four Seasons, its neighbor to the east (reviewed earlier in this chapter), many professional sports teams and athletes have a soft spot for the Park Hyatt — high praise considering the number of fine alternatives so close to the two primary sports venues: the Rogers Centre and the Air Canada Centre. The two towers of this luxury hotel — if you have a choice, opt for the North Tower with its larger rooms — sit conveniently on the corner of Bloor Street and Avenue Road in the Bloor/Yorkville neighborhood, just across Bloor Street from the Royal

Ontario Museum. Its prime location is ideal for easy access to much of the city's best shopping and dining and attractions, but you may need to kick yourself out the door so that you don't spend your entire holiday enjoying the luxury and amenities of the Hyatt.

Boasting the largest guest rooms in the city, the Hyatt's rooms average about 46 sq. m (500 sq. ft.), with standard guest rooms coming in at between 28 and 37 sq. m (300 and 400 sq. ft.). And a full-scale, full-hotel renovation just completed in early 2003 modernizes these expansive rooms, with large marble bathrooms housing shower/tub combinations, two-line telephones, and in-room fax/printer/copier machines. Pulling yourself away from your room, you may be drawn to the Park Hyatt's in-house Stillwater Spa facilities, with 17 treatment rooms offering everything from the standard facials, pedicures, and massages to some more specialized treatments such as hydro-therapy and shiatsu. Finally, the renowned Roof Lounge atop the South Tower is equally well known for attracting Toronto's literary elite and for its stunning city skyline view — one of the best in the city.

See map p. 110. 4 Avenue Rd. ☎ *416-925-1234. Fax: 416-924-4933.* http://park toronto.hyatt.com. *TTC: Bay station. Parking: C$30 (US$25). Rack rates: C$319–C$409 (US$262–US$335) double. AE, DC, DISC, MC, V.*

Radisson Plaza Hotel Admiral
$$$ Harbourfront

From its name to its guest rooms' large windows to the nautical theme pervading its public areas, the Radisson Admiral dives to great depths to acknowledge its waterfront setting overlooking Lake Ontario. And the view is definitely its most attractive feature, so aim for a lakeside room when making your reservation. A recently completed renovation has improved the Radisson from a standard, somewhat worn-down hotel to a reasonably priced, comfortable hotel with a less-than-ideal location for getting out and about. The Harbourfront area is a bit slim on places to go and things to do; the area's restaurant options are abysmal, so you'll have to head toward downtown for a decent bite to eat. And while the closest subway station is Union station, you'll either need to walk the 1.5km (just under 1 mile) to the station or hop on the 509 Harbourfront streetcar to make a connection. But if the setting, complete with a rooftop pool with a splendid view of the lake, appeals to you, you can't do much better than the Radisson.

See map p. 110. 249 Queens Quay W. ☎ *800-333-3333 or 416-203-3333. Fax: 416-203-3100.* www.radisson.com/torontoca_admiral. *TTC: Union station, and then 509 Harbourfront streetcar west. Parking: C$18 (US$15). Rack rates: C$179–C$249 (US$147–US$204) double. AE, DC, DISC, MC, V.*

Sheraton Centre Toronto
$$$$–$$$$$ Downtown

One of the most prominent convention hotels in town, its prime location — just on the northern edge of Toronto's Financial District, with only Nathan Phillips Square coming between it and City Hall — is a major reason why.

(Over 7,800 sq. m/84,000 sq feet of meeting space also helps.) The guest rooms are more stylish (if not spacious) than you may expect from a down-town business hotel, with rich, bold colors: some have queen-size sleigh beds; all have adequately sized bathrooms with shower/tub combinations. Explore the amenities beyond your room and you may be hesitant to even venture outdoors. The two-story lobby, encircling a greenery-filled atrium, is comfortable and spacious enough for semi-private meeting and greeting. None of the three restaurants are outstanding, but you don't need to avoid them, either; remember that you're also not far from the fashionable Queen West neighborhood, where you have a dazzling array of dining options. A light and airy fitness center, with nearly floor-to-ceiling windows, features primarily weights and resistance machines. The indoor/outdoor pool is open year-round (the outdoor portion is well heated), with poolside bar service during the warmer months. And if all that ain't enough, the hotel courtyard features almost a hectare (over 2 acres) of greenery and rushing — well, closer to trickling — water in its Waterfall Garden. But even with all that's available in-house, make sure you do head outside; you're a block from the Eaton Centre, across the street from the Nathan Phillips Square reflecting pool (a favorite for ice skating in winter), next door to the large Bay department store, and centrally located enough to take a casual walk to destinations such as the Hockey Hall of Fame, the Art Gallery of Ontario, and of course the previously mentioned Queen Street West neighborhood.

*See map p. 110. 123 Queen St. W. ☎ **800-325-3535** or 416-361-1000. Fax: 416-947-4854.* www.sheraton.com/centretoronto. *TTC: Osgoode station. Valet parking: C$33 (US$27). Rack rates: C$310–C$370 (US$254–US$303) double. AE, DC, MC, V.*

Soho Metropolitan
$$$$–$$$$$ Entertainment District

To badly misuse a well-worn cliché, you're not in Kansas anymore, Toto. This stylish and luxurious hotel is one of two new "boutique" hotels to open in Toronto in 2003. (The other is the Hotel Le Germain, reviewed previously in this chapter.) With an emphasis on intimacy in a tight open space (you'll understand the apparent contradictions when you arrive), the Soho successfully combines sophisticated service with innovative touches. The hotel has a small number of accommodations — only 86 guest rooms and suites — with an attention to personal comfort that starts with the lobby staff. Each guest room is uniformly long and large (averaging 56 sq. m/600 sq. ft.), featuring a separate dressing area, cozy down duvets, and Frette bed linens, and equipped with state-of-the-art electronic drapery, lighting, and privacy controls. The safe comes complete with an outlet to recharge your laptop's battery. The spacious bathrooms feature heated marble tiles on the floor, a glass-enclosed shower, and a separate — and large — tub. The fitness area includes an indoor pool and Jacuzzi (rare for a boutique hotel), along with a dozen weight and resistance machines.

The Soho features a trio of dining options, ranging from the casual Senses Bakery and Cafe, with an assortment of stunningly prepared sweets luring diners and passersby alike, to the supremely upscale, and extremely pricey, Sen5es (yes, the "5" is in the name) Restaurant, open for dinner only, Wednesday through Saturday.

See map p. 110. 318 Wellington St. W. ☎ *416-599-8800. Fax: 416-599-8801. www.metropolitan.com/soho. TTC: St. Andrew station. Parking: C$20 (US$16). Rack rates: C$305–C$385 (US$250–US$315) double. AE, DC, DISC, MC, V*

The Strathcona Hotel
$–$$$ Financial District

This small hotel, tucked away between the two tines of the fork that includes University Avenue and York Street, is about as different as you can get from the Royal York, not only in location (they're on opposite sides of York Street) but also in experience. That's not to say that the Strathcona is a *bad* experience, it's just quite different from the opulent experience of the Royal York. From the unpretentious yellow-and-green color scheme to the smallish, European-style rooms that predominate below the eighth floor, this hotel offers a spartan alternative to the luxury of other down-town hotels. But everything is fresh and clean and up to date; a recent renovation emphasized efficiency in smaller spaces over state-of-the-art décor and amenities. And the Strathcona clearly recognizes the value of its location; in the heart of Toronto's Financial District it sets aside all rooms above the eighth floor as its Corporate Rooms, with extras such as a desk, phone with two lines and dataport, coffeemaker, and daily news-paper. (These rooms also draw a fair number of residual guests who can't fit into the Royal York.)

On-site amenities are minimal, limited to a couple of restaurants: the York Street Cafe, just off the lobby, for breakfast and lunch; and The Pub, in the hotel's lower level, for lunch, dinner, and drinks. The Strathcona has a fee-per-use arrangement with the Wellington Fitness Club next door, which includes sauna, whirlpool, and steamroom. No parking is available on-site; the recommended lot is a couple of blocks west, off Wellington Street.

See map p. 110. 60 York St. ☎ *800-268-8304 or 416-363-3321. Fax: 416-363-4679. www.thestrathconahotel.com. TTC: Union station. No on-site parking. Rack rates: C$99–C$179 (US$81–US$147) double. AE, DC, MC, V.*

The Sutton Place Hotel
$$$$$ Bloor/Yorkville

The high-ceilinged lobby adorned with cherry-wood wingback chairs, the tastefully appointed guest rooms, and even the serene pool, suggest a kind of casual opulence here on the outside fringe of Toronto's trendiest neigh-borhood — something you may not expect to find, based on the hotel's boxy and utilitarian outside appearance. With a fairly small amount of units (just under 300), the Sutton Place still manages to provide a number of comfortable amenities that you may have trouble finding in other similarly sized accommodations. The indoor pool is also on the small side, but the pool area is inviting and a sundeck is adjacent for the warmer months. Weights and a handful of resistance machines await you in a cozy exercise room with nearby sauna. Guest rooms are very comfortable and quite spacious, with a wide spectrum of furnishings, both in color and in style. Bathrooms don't quite match the spaciousness of the guest rooms, but are nonetheless serviceable. The Sutton Place's location is not ideal — you're several blocks south of the center of the Bloor/Yorkville neighborhood—but the Wellesley subway station is just steps away, and a few good restaurants (including the acceptable Accents location in the hotel) are close at hand. The touch of class with a significantly lower price tag than, say, the Four Seasons, makes the location easier to stomach.

See map p. 110. 955 Bay St. ☎ *800-268-3790 or 416-924-9221. Fax: 416-924-1778.* www.toronto.suttonplace.com. *TTC: Wellesley station. Parking: C$20 (US$16). Rack rates: C$365–C$410 (US$299–US$336) double. AE, DC, MC, V.*

Toronto Marriott Eaton Centre
$$$–$$$$ **Downtown**

Forget Cozumel or Cayman; this hotel is a paradise — for shoppers, at least — a veritable consumer's resort. With a direct connection to the Eaton Centre, you never have to step on sidewalk to take in some serious shopping. It's a bit on the small side, but an indoor pool, Jacuzzi, and fitness center occupy the top floor, and a couple of passable dining options further improve your ability to check in without stepping out . . . until you check out. If you need a reminder of what life is like on the outside, many rooms offer a pleasant view of the city to the north, and some overlook the quaint Church of the Holy Trinity right next door. The rooms themselves are comfortable and spacious enough to welcome a family and kids and a couple of armfuls of shopping bags. Customer service here is among the best in Toronto, with plenty of knowledgeable staff on hand to assist you and direct you around town once you finally decide to venture out of doors.

See map p. 110. 525 Bay St. ☎ *800-905-0667 or 416-597-9200. Fax: 416-597-9211.* www.marriott.com. *TTC: Dundas station. Parking: C$19 (US$16). Rack rates: C$179–C$299 (US$147–US$245) double. AE, DC, DISC, MC, V.*

Monday, Monday

Okay, it's not likely to involve a retrospective of The Mamas and the Papas, but you can appreciate some fine classical and culturally diverse concerts at the Church of the Holy Trinity, located just outside the Eaton Centre and under the nose of the Toronto Marriott Eaton Centre. The church sponsors a noon-hour concert every Monday during the summer months (C$5 donation is requested) in its sanctuary. The location is remarkable for both its aesthetic and acoustic beauty. For information about schedules, call ☎ **416-598-4521**.

For a slightly less sophisticated activity, try to ascribe some meaning to the various crests that encircle the church's outdoor structure as you overlook it from one of the Marriott hotel's lower-level rooms, its Parkside restaurant, or one of the Eaton Centre's restaurants (Mr. Greenjeans has the best view, if not the most inspiring food).

Travelodge Toronto Downtown West
$$–$$$$ Entertainment District

The only motel in downtown Toronto (though it takes pains to call itself a hotel), this popular and cheap destination is a gold mine if you're looking for a place to park your car and your sightseeing-weary body in a pleasant and comfortable resting place. Room rates are about the best in downtown, and parking rates are clearly the best — free. But with no on-site amenities, this place is very basic lodging: clean, comfortable beds, large guest rooms with a utilitarian bathroom, and free continental breakfast. Here, you're situated on one of the best shopping, dining, and entertainment thoroughfares in the city, and the King streetcar takes you quickly into the downtown core. You won't find a bargain like this in a location like this in too many metropolitan destinations.

See map p. 110. 621 King St. W. ☎ ***800-578-7878*** *or 416-504-7441. Fax: 416-504-4722.* www.travelodgetorontodowntown.com. *TTC: St. Andrew station and then 504 King streetcar west. Free parking. Rack rates: C$109–C$259 (US$89–US$212) double. AE, DC, DISC, MC, V.*

Westin Harbour Castle
$$$$–$$$$$ Harbourfront

The Westin is a clear choice for one of the best views of Lake Ontario in Toronto (the other is the Radisson, farther west on Queen's Quay). However, the area offers little outside the hotel and its outstanding amenities. There's some nearby shopping at the small Queen's Quay Terminal (a trip to Tilley Endurables makes it worth at least a brief visit), and the restaurant options are geared toward the tour-bus crowd. You really have to decide whether the view is worth the extra travel to get around town to the highlights.

Guest rooms tend to be small, but they're very comfortable and highly appointed. Not all rooms have a lake view, so for your best shot at getting one you need to request a lake view room when you reserve (while you're at it, try for the south tower, which lies slightly toward the lake ahead of the north tower and houses the adults-only Toula Restaurant on its top floor). If you get stuck on the non-lake side, remember that the fifth-floor indoor pool and Jacuzzi has a lakeside view, as do the sundeck and tennis court that are open during warmer months, and the spa and massage services include some lake-view treatment rooms.

See map p. 110. 1 Harbour Sq. ☎ ***888-625-5144*** *or 416-869-1600. Fax: 416-869-0573.* www.westin.com/harbourcastle. *TTC: Union station, and then 509 Harbourfront streetcar. Valet parking: C$30 (US$25). Rack rates: C$279–C$419 (US$229–US$344) double. AE, DC, DISC, MC, V.*

Windsor Arms
$$$$–$$$$$ **Bloor/Yorkville**

Once considered one of Toronto's finest hotels, attracting royalty, millionaires, and celebrities, the Windsor Arms descended into mediocrity and eventually receivership in the 1980s and early 1990s. But it has revived, thanks to a meticulous — and très expensive — reconstruction, reopening in 1999 with 26 luxury suites and 2 oversized rooms. Many rooms boast fireplaces, and all are at least 46 sq. m (500 sq. ft.) in size. Frette linens and limestone bathroom floors are just two of the luxury in-room amenities. And, if you're so inclined, 24-hour butler service is available.

See map p. 110. 18 St. Thomas St. ☎ **416-971-9666**. *Fax: 416-921-9121.* www.windsorarmshotel.com. *TTC: Bay station. Parking: C$25 (US$21). Rack rates: From C$295 (US$242) double. AE, DC, MC, V.*

Runner-up Hotels

10 Cawthra Square
$$–$$$ **Church–Wellesley Village** One of three bed-and-breakfasts located within steps of one another, this renovated mansion is in the heart of the primary gay-friendly neighborhood in Toronto, just east of Church and Wellesley streets. Each of the three locations offers stylish accommodations with private baths and period furnishings, and 10 Cawthra Square has spa and massage services available. Wedding packages in these luxe mansions are also popular. *See map p. 110. 10 Cawthra Square.* ☎ *800-259-5474 or 416-966-3074.* www.cawthrasquare.com.

Annex Guesthouse Bed and Breakfast
$–$$ **The Annex** Skirting the edges of both Little Italy and Chinatown, and close to Bloor/Yorkville, this cozy bed-and-breakfast is a welcome resting place for travelers concentrating on Toronto's art offerings — the Royal Ontario Museum, the Art Gallery of Ontario, and the Gardiner Museum are within easy walking distance. One of the three units is a top-floor suite, complete with kitchenette area, deck, and private bath with shower-tub combination. The other three units are ideal for families traveling together (two of the rooms have a twin bed only) and share a bath with shower. *See map p. 110. 241 Lippincott St.* ☎ *416-588-0560.* www.annexguesthouse.com.

Best Western Primrose Hotel
$$ **Downtown** Overlooking Allan Gardens, the Best Western Primrose is an average downtown Toronto hotel with reasonable rates for its central location. The hotel is a short three blocks from the College subway station, and a cab ride to any downtown activity is short and well priced. Rooms are standard chain-hotel fare: generally clean and comfortable, if aesthetically uninspiring. The rooftop heated pool with its city view is a nice draw for summer travelers. Parking is available but limited. *See map p. 110. 111 Carlton St.* ☎ *800-565-8865 or 416-977-8000.* www.torontoprimrosehotel.com.

Howard Johnson Downtown

$$–$$$ **Bloor/Yorkville**   If your lodging requirements are simply for bare-bones accommodations in a convenient location, the Howard Johnson is a good bet. In the only way you're likely to see Howard Johnson, Four Seasons, and Park Hyatt in the same sentence, the three hotels are just steps apart in the ritzy Bloor/Yorkville area; you can experience the highfalutin shopping (including Hazelton Lanes practically next door) and dining options in the area without the highfalutin hotel costs of its pricey neighbors. The hotel has no amenities on-site — and no sharing agreements with any of its neighbors — so all you're getting here is a place to rest and rejuvenate before the next day's sightseeing. *See map p. 110. 89 Avenue Rd.* ☎ *800-446-4656 or 416-964-1220.* www.the.hojo.com.

Marriott Courtyard

$$$ **Downtown**   If you've stayed at any of Marriott's hundreds of Courtyards, you know what you're in for at this location on the north end of downtown Toronto. If you appreciate this kind of familiarity in your lodging choice, the Courtyard is probably your best bet in Toronto. But you'll find yourself in an area that's not very close to the major attractions, so be prepared to spend some time on the subway (the College station is a block away). *See map p. 110. 475 Yonge St.* ☎ *800-847-5075 or 416-924-0611.* www.courtyard.com.

Novotel Toronto Centre

$$$$ **Financial District**   An early 2003 renovation has turned this conveniently located hotel into a good bet for Toronto visitors. Located on the southern edge of downtown, the Novotel provides easy access to the Hockey Hall of Fame and the Hummingbird Centre (just a block away), and is an easy four-block walk to the CN Tower. Guest rooms have that familiar chain-hotel feel, but they're a good size, with the modern updates that you'd expect from a recent renovation (fully equipped and well-designed bathrooms, upgraded furnishings, and so on). *See map p. 110. 45 The Esplanade.* ☎ *416-367-8900.* www.novotel.com.

Renaissance Toronto Hotel

$$$$$ **Entertainment District**   With 70 rooms that overlook the field at the Rogers Centre, this hotel is a baseball (or Canadian football) fan's dream. Of course, those 70 rooms can be more than double the rate you would pay for another room in the hotel with a less inspiring view. Besides the sports-viewing venue, other recreational options on-site include an indoor pool and whirlpool and fully stocked fitness center. But be warned — unless you really want to splurge for a room from which you can watch a Major League Baseball game, you're probably better off staying elsewhere; the hotel itself is a bit utilitarian and drab, and expensive drab at that. *See map p. 110. One Blue Jays Way.* ☎ *800-237-1512 or 416-341-7100.* www.renaissancehotels.com.

Index of Accommodations by Neighborhood

The Annex
Annex Guesthouse Bed and Breakfast ($-$$)

Bloor/Yorkville
Four Seasons Hotel ($$$$$)
Howard Johnson Downtown ($$)
Park Hyatt ($$$-$$$$)
The Sutton Place Hotel ($$$$$)
Windsor Arms ($$$$-$$$$$)

Church–Wellesley Village
10 Cawthra Square ($$-$$$)

Downtown
Best Western Primrose Hotel ($$)
Bond Place Hotel ($$)
Cambridge Suites Hotel ($$$$$)
Delta Chelsea ($$-$$$$$)
The Grand Hotel & Suites ($$-$$$)
Hotel Le Germain ($$$-$$$$$)
Clarion Selby Hotel & Suites ($$)
Le Royal Meridien King Edward ($$$$-$$$$$)
Marriott Courtyard ($$$)
Metropolitan Hotel Toronto ($$$$$)
Sheraton Centre Toronto ($$$$-$$$$$)

Toronto Marriott Eaton Centre ($$$-$$$$)

Entertainment District
Holiday Inn on King ($$$-$$$$)
Hotel Le Germain ($$$$$)
Renaissance Toronto Hotel ($$$$$)
Soho Metropolitan ($$$$-$$$$$)
Travelodge Toronto Downtown West ($$-$$$$)

Harbourfront
Radisson Plaza Hotel Admiral ($$$)
Westin Harbour Castle ($$$$-$$$$$)

Financial District
Fairmont Royal York ($$$-$$$$)
Hilton Toronto ($$$-$$$$)
Hotel Victoria ($$)
InterContinental Toronto Centre ($$$-$$$$)
Novotel Toronto Centre ($$$$)
The Strathcona Hotel ($-$$$)

Queen West
The Drake Hotel ($$-$$$$)

Index of Accommodations by Price

$
Annex Guesthouse Bed and Breakfast (The Annex)
The Strathcona Hotel (Financial District)

$$
10 Cawthra Square (Church–Wellesley Village)
Annex Guesthouse Bed and Breakfast (The Annex)
Best Western Primrose Hotel (Downtown)

Bond Place Hotel (Downtown)
Clarion Selby Hotel and Suites (Downtown)
Delta Chelsea (Downtown)
The Drake Hotel (Queen West)
The Grand Hotel & Suites (Downtown)
Hotel Victoria (Financial District)
Howard Johnson Downtown (Bloor/Yorkville)
The Strathcona Hotel (Financial District)
Travelodge Toronto Downtown West (Entertainment District)

$$$

10 Cawthra Square (Church–Wellesley Village)
Delta Chelsea (Downtown)
The Drake Hotel (Queen West)
Fairmont Royal York (Financial District)
The Grand Hotel & Suites (Downtown)
Hilton Toronto (Financial District)
Holiday Inn on King (Entertainment District)
Hotel Le Germain (Downtown)
InterContinental Toronto Centre (Financial District)
Marriott Courtyard (Downtown)
Park Hyatt (Bloor/Yorkville)
Radisson Plaza Hotel Admiral (Harbourfront)
The Strathcona Hotel (Financial District)
Toronto Marriott Eaton Centre (Downtown)
Travelodge Toronto Downtown West (Entertainment District)

$$$$

Delta Chelsea (Downtown)
The Drake Hotel (Queen West)
Fairmont Royal York (Financial District)
Holiday Inn on King (Entertainment District)
Hotel Le Germain (Downtown)
InterContinental Toronto Centre (Financial District)
Le Royal Meridien King Edward (Downtown)
Novotel Toronto Centre (Financial District)
Park Hyatt (Bloor/Yorkville)
Sheraton Centre Toronto (Downtown)
Soho Metropolitan (Entertainment District)
Toronto Marriott Eaton Centre (Downtown)
Travelodge Toronto Downtown West (Entertainment District)
Westin Harbour Castle (Harbourfront)
Windsor Arms (Bloor/Yorkville)

$$$$$

Cambridge Suites Hotel (Downtown)
Delta Chelsea (Downtown)
Four Seasons Hotel (Bloor/Yorkville)
Hilton Toronto (Financial District)
Hotel Le Germain (Entertainment District)
Le Royal Meridien King Edward (Downtown)
Metropolitan Hotel Toronto (Downtown)
Renaissance Toronto Hotel (Entertainment District)
Sheraton Centre Toronto (Downtown)
Soho Metropolitan (Entertainment District)
The Sutton Place Hotel (Bloor/Yorkville)
Westin Harbour Castle (Harbourfront)
Windsor Arms (Bloor/Yorkville)

Chapter 10

Dining and Snacking in Toronto

*P*ull up a chair and order your favorite beverage. This chapter introduces you to some of Toronto's best dining experiences — the ones that unfold right before your eyes with course after course of excellent cuisine, whether it be fine and fancy or great and greasy. You'll find a thorough listing — well, definitely thorough enough to keep your palate pleased for several visits to Toronto, not just your first — of some of the best, most popular, and most accessible restaurants in the city. Each restaurant listing includes what you can expect to pay for your meal, in which neighborhood you'll be paying for it, and what type of cuisine you'll be paying for. Finally, at the end of the chapter, you'll find handy indexes that break down each restaurant discussed here by those same criteria: neighborhood, cuisine, and price.

Toronto is a gastronome's delight, and many Torontonians are delighted to partake any — and, for some, every — day of the week. After you've spent some time sorting out your dining options in the city, you'll understand why: Toronto is chock-full of culinary experiences of all shapes, sizes, and structures. That is, given the cultural diversity of the city; its status as a business, financial, and entertainment center; and its splendidly varied architectural landmarks, you'd be hard pressed to name a cuisine, a restaurant theme, or even an unusual venue that Toronto hasn't tried. The point of all this is to plan ahead before you step out to find your evening meal.

My advice is to anticipate that just about every restaurant you try to visit is going to be full, so make your reservations as early as you can once you've settled into town. (In some very rare cases, you should reserve before you get to town; I tell you about those places in this chapter.) Even if you don't make reservations for one of the more popular dining hot spots as early as you should, call and find out if you can get in. People often cancel reservations at the last minute, or the restaurant may not be booked up in the first place.

Getting the Dish on the Local Scene

Toronto is a restaurant-lover's dream. Local residents have every day of the year to check out the hottest new offering, check back with an old favorite, or check into some of the international cuisine readily available all over town. Of course, Torontonians also have the whole year to pick up a lot of very pricey checks. To really sample the latest and greatest of Toronto's restaurants, you will have to part with a significant portion of your travel budget.

Tasting some of Toronto's dining trends

Here are a few ideas for discovering what kinds of epicurean experiences await you in Toronto:

- **Ask around.** The best hotels have people on staff who provide this very service. Check with your concierge (or front-desk staff, at some of the less sophisticated hotels). Not only is it quite likely that they'll know about some of the city's most talked-about dining alternatives, but chances are that one or two of them may be just around the corner.

- **Ask around some more.** Get acquainted with your hotel's other guests. Chat with them around the breakfast-buffet table or in the hotel hot tub. You're likely to meet a few who travel to Toronto on a regular basis, most likely with a business expense account. Find out where they like to eat.

- **Read up before you go.** With so many restaurants in the city, Toronto also has quite a few resources that try to keep up with the city's dining trends. Use the Web to find out what some of these writers and reviewers are saying about Toronto restaurants:

  - *Toronto Life* **magazine:** This Web site (www.toronto life.com) has an effective search feature in its restaurant guide, where you can search for a restaurant by type of cuisine, by neighborhood, and by price range. Then, when you find one that interests you, have a look at what the magazine's reviewers have to say about it. You can also review each month's current issue; there's a regular dining section that discusses the happenings in Toronto's restaurant scene.

- **Chowhound:** At www.chowhound.com, you can just about find it all. This message board offers (by and large) uncensored discussion about restaurant trends in ten regions around North America, including Toronto and Montreal. A sampling of recent (and popular) subjects runs from comparing New York and Toronto restaurants, to finding the best samosas (or beer or pizza or sushi or just about anything else) in town, to recommending the best fill-in-the-blank (Chinese, Thai, Mexican, and so on) restaurant. But be prepared: Though the Toronto board is fairly new (2003), you still need to be prepared to wade through a ton of messages — many of the trivial and/or petty variety.

- **MenuPalace:** This site is a Toronto restaurant Web portal (www.menupalace.com); it doesn't feature reviews, or even any subjective content. But it's a great place to do some browsing to find a few restaurants to consider before you arrive in Toronto. The site creates, designs, and hosts individual Web sites for restaurants listed on the portal. One caveat: While the site does include a thorough list of restaurants (by cuisine, by neighborhood, and so on), it does not provide links to independent Web sites created by restaurants on their own.

- **Toronto newspapers:** The Saturday edition of most of the newspapers available in Toronto includes a restaurant review; some of them you can link to online. Check out, for example, Jacob Richler's weekly review in the *National Post* at www.canada.com/toronto/features/aroundtown/dining. You can also find regular reviews in the *Toronto Star* and *The Globe and Mail.*

Finding the top dining areas

When in Toronto, it's hard *not* to find a top dining area, but the city does have a few standard consistently hot spots. To start, your best options are in and around downtown Toronto, including the diverse neighborhoods that encircle the central business area. You'll be able to scout out a representative number of quality restaurants near whatever hotel you've selected as your home base.

If you want to venture outside the area surrounding your accommodations, here are a few select neighborhoods that have a wide variety of dining options:

- **Little Italy:** Particularly along College Street, this neighborhood's main thoroughfare, the variety of restaurants has increased as the neighborhood has become known less for the Italian heritage of its residents than for its excellent cuisine choices.

✔ **Bloor/Yorkville:** If you want to keep attracting the celebrities who frequent the Four Seasons or the Park Hyatt, you have to keep up with the culinary times. And many restaurants in this hip and stylish region do just that. This area also caters to the many office buildings and condominiums scattered in and around this seemingly exclusive neighborhood. But don't feel excluded; you'll find some fine meals here.

✔ **King Street West:** When you're home to several of the major theater and entertainment venues in town, you're certain to have one or two restaurants nearby. King Street West and the blocks surrounding it have plenty of options for your pre- or post-theater meal. Or sneak in while the theatergoers are at the show for a slightly more intimate experience. Whenever you choose to eat, a diversity of cuisines awaits you.

✔ **Chinatown:** As in similar neighborhoods in many other major cities, diners know what to expect here: the best of the best in Chinese and other Asian cuisine. But, locals know that, especially along the tiny strip that is Baldwin Street, two blocks north of Dundas Street, you'll find even more variety — and much of it quite good — from Indian to French to Malaysian to Italian.

These are but a few suggestions; this list could also include the Financial District, where, appropriately, you'll generally find the highest-priced restaurants in the city; Bloor West Village, which features fine and casual dining that caters to local residents and neighborhood visitors alike; The Beaches, with its focus on light and reasonably quick fare so that you can get back to your window-shopping or boardwalk-ambling; The Danforth, with its collection of Greek establishments that mingle with some of the city's trendier spots; and on and on. You're never too far from someplace with tasty offerings in Toronto.

Eating like a local

Not even the locals can afford to take on the mission of patronizing the cream of the crop of Toronto's restaurants on a regular (or even semi-regular) basis. So this section helps you discover the tricks of the diners who manage to balance the occasional pricey splurge with the more modest goal of finding good, reasonably priced meals, day in and day out. And if you really want to make like a lemming and follow the residents to a good meal, you'll find some other ideas here as well.

✔ **Scour the neighborhoods.** Residents of Toronto's diverse neighborhoods have to eat too — and they regularly do so without leaving their home turf. It may be a local pub that consistently serves cold beer and piping-hot fish and chips, or a Chinese restaurant that dishes up the spiciest (and tastiest) Singapore noodles in town, or a breakfast spot with lines of weekend patrons waiting out front for a table. As you wander through the shops and sundries in one of Toronto's neighborhoods, ask for recommendations. And make sure that you ask the right people: If it's a true insider's perspective you're after, chances are you'll learn more from the proprietor of an independent bookstore than from the afternoon-shift barista at a chain coffee shop.

✔ **Eat out — literally.** Locals know that the first sign of spring is not budding trees or blooming gardens. Instead, especially for Toronto diners, the first sign of spring is the seemingly overnight explosion of outdoor seating areas. Torontonians love their alfresco dining. And it's easy to see why. Spring through fall, Toronto offers many sunny and warm opportunities to eat and drink outside, and the city's sidewalks are narrow enough that you always have a great table for people-watching. In fact, some downtown sidewalks have just enough room for a table for two and single-file pedestrians.

✔ **Takeout is a good thing.** Everyone suffers the occasional day when, even if you could get the best table in the house at a local dining fave, you're too dispirited or exhausted to occupy it. For Torontonians, the next best thing is to order in. Some of the best meals in Toronto arrive in (environmentally incorrect) plastic bags and Styrofoam containers. You may have to ask your concierge or other hotel staff for recommendations of places that deliver to your hotel's neighborhood, but chances are they'll pull out a hefty stack of carry-out menus large enough to rival your average Torontonian's refrigerator door. And Toronto's takeout is no longer just for pizza or egg rolls; you can often find good Indian or Greek or even Fusion cuisine nearby that's available for takeaway or delivery.

✔ **Line up for a shawarma.** What's a shawarma? With origins in the Middle East, it's spit-roasted meat — usually lamb, chicken, or beef — shaved off the spit and sometimes then grilled with onions or peppers. Here, you can find it served in a pita with tahini, hummus, and hot sauce, usually in tiny, out-of-the-way storefront locations or even the occasional street-vendor cart. It's (about) four bucks well spent. And you can line up for more than shawarmas. Take your pick from an embarrassment of street-vendor riches: from hot dogs (of course) to fries to falafels to stir-fry. You'll have to jockey for a place in line with local workers on their lunch break, but the quick meal at a low price is hard to beat during a long day of sightseeing. For more about meals on the go, see the section "Dining and Snacking on the Go," later in this chapter.

Wrapping up the details

You're all dressed up and you're looking for someplace to go. This section covers some of the last-minute details that you should consider before you make that final choice for your evening meal (one of the details is that you really don't have to get all that dressed up).

✔ **Making reservations:** Remember that part of the hipness quotient of a hot restaurant is directly related to the amount of effort required to get a table. For a table at locations such as Susur or Bymark you need to make a reservation — sometimes weeks in advance. (See the sidebar "When you really want to break bread in the best," later in this chapter, for a list of the hottest restaurants, and therefore hardest-to-get tables, in Toronto.)

For less trendy spots, you often can walk in and be seated within minutes. But when in doubt, make a reservation. You can always check with your hotel concierge to find out if a reservation is necessary, but why take the chance? Besides, the concierge will likely be happy to make the reservation for you.

✔ **Dressing to dine:** Smart casual is about as fancy as you'll need to get. You'll see diners in business dress, especially in the Financial District, but unless you've booked one of the trendy private dining rooms, you can probably leave your jacket and tie at the hotel — along with your jeans and Birkenstocks.

✔ **Lighting up:** All Toronto restaurants and bars are smoke-free — well, almost. Establishments can still have a designated smoking area, but it must be a fully enclosed, self-contained room with its own separate ventilation system. Needless to say, you won't find very many of these.

Trimming the Fat from Your Budget

You probably don't need anyone to tell you how to limit your meal costs while in Toronto; you'll no doubt do the same things you do at home — with the exception of stocking up on groceries to prepare the evening meal. But I do have a few ideas to help you save a loonie or two:

✔ **Save your finest dining dollars for one big splurge.** Remember that Toronto boasts more than 7,000 restaurants. I'm here to tell you — and common sense dictates — that the city is crawling with mid-priced restaurants with perfectly appetizing (and often delicious) food. If you're traveling on a fairly tight meal budget, sample from these mid-range eateries — many of the ethnic-inspired restaurants are in this price range — and limit your really big splurge to one fine night out.

✔ **Opt for lunch over dinner.** If you've heard nothing but great things about the restaurant down the street from your hotel, but the dinner menu is just too overpriced for your liking, check to see whether they have a lunch menu. A lunch entree is often less expensive than the same or a similar dinner entree at many restaurants.

✔ **Or, eat light (and cheaply) during the day to save up for dinner.** Your hotel may offer breakfast with your room rate, and while you risk the fact that the spread won't be all that impressive, that's at least one meal you can strike from your travel budget. Save up all that breakfast money, and you can upgrade to a fancier dinner or two. A light lunch — or a hot dog from one of Toronto's many street-vendor carts — can also free up some cash for your evening meal.

✔ **Feast in the neighborhood.** Eating out in the neighborhoods that lie outside the downtown area may result in a saving of a few bucks. And don't overlook what the residents may have to say about some of the local haunts; such "haunts" are often popular in part because of their value.

✔ **Drink locally.** No, this isn't a suggestion to raid your hotel room's minibar (actually, avoiding the minibar entirely is another wise tip for cutting your meal costs). Ask the waitstaff or wine steward to recommend a good local bottle of wine. Ontario wineries offer some nice vintages, and at a significantly lower price than that of wines shipped in from, for example, California or British Columbia or Australia. And beginning in 2005, Ontario restaurants may allow you to bring your own wine.

Remember also that the full goods and services tax (GST) and provincial sales tax (PST) apply to your meals, so an additional 15 percent will be added to your tab. (And it's the nonrefundable kind of GST.) It's almost enough to make you consider a run to the local grocery store. Also, Ontario adds a 10 percent liquor tax to alcohol sold in restaurants.

Toronto's Best Restaurants

The dining scene in Toronto is in constant flux. New restaurants come; others fade away. I've tried to select only establishments that are well entrenched or that seem likely to be in business for the foreseeable future. But if you discover that an eatery mentioned here has closed its doors, no worries: Another chef is likely to quickly set up shop at the same location. And finally, don't accept this chapter as the final word on where to eat in Toronto. Check with your hotel concierge about other establishments in your area; she may be able to squeeze you in at one of the hottest dining gigs in town.

Knowing what the $ symbols mean

For the most part, dining out in Toronto is not an inexpensive proposition. (For some tips on where to go without spending more loonies than you care to, skip forward to the section "Dining and Snacking on the Go.") Dining in Toronto ranges from modestly pricey and low-key to black-bedecked, end-of-business-day "casual." So that you have an idea what you're going to have to fork over for a particular meal, the listings here include a dollar symbol ($), which gives you an idea of the range of costs for a restaurant's main courses. When figuring your eating-out budget, remember to factor in your personal dining habits: Must every meal start with an appetizer? Are you a dessert person? Both? Is a meal incomplete without a good bottle of wine, or will just a glass suit you?

All of these extras will add to your dining costs, but the ranges given in these listings will offer you a good idea of how restaurants stack up against one another.

Here's the breakdown of the dollar signs you can find in this chapter's reviews:

$	Under C$10 (US$8.20)
$$	C$10–C$20 (US$8.20–US$16)
$$$	C$20–C$30 (US$16–US$25)
$$$$	Over C$30 (US$25)

As with the hotel listings in Chapter 9, you'll notice that most reviews here sport more than one dollar-sign category. This is meant to give you the clearest possible sense of a restaurant's prices. So if a particular restaurant offers main courses in the range of C$15 to C$32 (US$12–US$26), it merits two to four dollar signs. Also, if a listing mentions a restaurant's lunch menu as a dining option, the dollar signs (and price ranges) will reflect that.

Finding a meal right where you are

Okay, I admit it. The restaurants reviewed in this chapter — most of which are indicated on the "Toronto Dining" map — do not represent *all* the best restaurants in Toronto. Why? I could take the easy way out and tell you that Toronto has so many restaurants that would end up on anyone's top-ten list it's impossible to mention them all in this small space. But I do have a couple of (I think) legitimate reasons for not reviewing all the "best."

- ✔ **When traveling, proximity is a consideration.** As a new (or, at least, infrequent) visitor to Toronto, you may feel a little overwhelmed when it comes to finding and getting to destinations that are out of the downtown core (that is, where I expect most of you reading this book will stay). Some terrific restaurants are located a good distance away from downtown, and thus potentially out of the comfort zone of many readers.

  This chapter reviews many terrific restaurants that are within a reasonable (preferably, by foot or public transit) distance of the lodging suggestions discussed in this book.

- ✔ **When traveling, time is often a consideration.** And time constraints may affect you whether you're sightseeing, shopping in Toronto's top neighborhoods, or making the opening curtain of a Broadway-style show. When you're ready to take a shopping or touring break, you'll likely want a quick bite to eat before getting back to the task at hand. Or you may want to enjoy a reasonably quick dinner before catching the 8 p.m. show at the Royal Alexandra. None of these situations calls for a dining experience, as memorable as it may be, that lasts for two or three hours.

Toronto Dining

DINING

360 Revolving Restaurant 10
Adega 25
Alice Fazooli's! Italian 17
　　Crabshack
Babur 21
Bangkok Garden 26
Barberian's 24
Bedford Academy 30
Biff's 6
Big Daddy's 15
The Black Bull 20
Brassaii 12
Brick Street Bakery 1
Bymark 8
C'est What? 2
Café Nervosa 37
Canoe 8
Dhaba 14
Dunn's Famous 16
　　Bar & Grill
Flo's 38
Fred's Not Here 14
Fressen 19
Happy Seven 28
Hernando's Hideaway 4
Irish Embassy Pub & Grill 5
John's Italian Caffé 27
Lai Wah Heen 22
Le Papillon 3
Mildred Pierce 13
Mövenpick Marché 7
North 44 36
Pangaea 30
Pearl Harbourfront 9
The Pilot Tavern 35
Queen Mother Cafe 21
Reuben S. 14
The Rivoli 18
Sassafraz 33
Scaramouche 39
The Senator 23
Sushi Inn 32
Susur 13
Wayne Gretzky's 11
　　Restaurant

In this chapter, you'll find recommendations for restaurants that are fairly close to most of Toronto's major attractions, shopping districts, and nightlife venues. For tips about grabbing a *really* quick bite, check out the section "Dining and Snacking on the Go," later in this chapter.

✔ **When on a budget, cost is *the* consideration.** Especially if you're visiting Toronto with kids, you probably can't — or don't want to — count on spending $200 or $300 very often for an evening meal. And Toronto has plenty of offerings where you can do just that, when you add up the starters and the drinks and the wine and the dessert and the tips and the valet parking and the ATM fees for that last-minute run when your partner tells you that she thought *you* were going to get the cash.

Most of the restaurants reviewed in this chapter fall into the two- to three-dollar-sign range.

Because I don't want to leave you completely empty-handed if you're an honorary Toronto gastronome, the sidebar "When you really want to break bread in the best" later in this chapter offers a list of the city's more memorable dining offerings. For more detailed reviews of many of Toronto's finest restaurants not mentioned here, pick up a copy of *Frommer's Toronto* (published by Wiley Publishing, Inc.).

360 Revolving Restaurant
$$$–$$$$ Downtown   CONTINENTAL

Okay, so right off the bat, here's a restaurant that ignores the cost considerations discussed earlier in this chapter. But, if you ride to the top of the CN Tower you may find yourself tempted to have a meal atop the world's tallest free-standing structure. In fact, size definitely matters here: the world's tallest wine cellar plus the largest revolving restaurant equals the most money you can spend at 360m (1,200 ft.). And you will spend a lot at this award-winning, if overpriced, destination — it is a destination, not a local's hangout — but the elevator ride is thrown in (woo-hoo!). The menu emphasizes Canadian fare where possible, with special attention paid to meats and seafood prepared with innovative flavors in not-so-innovative ways (there's lots of roasting and searing going on). For example, arctic char may be served on pumpkin orzo with a sea scallops and lemon tarragon broth; for the less inventive, the now-declassé prime rib is tender and delicious enough to bring it back in style. For a tourist destination restaurant, this is one of the best, though how lofty that praise may seem depends on your own experiences with tourist eateries. But, of course, the view is part of the experience; Toronto at night is a beautiful sight. But keep in mind that you can save a few bucks by reserving this experience for lunch — and the prix fixe menu will save you a few more.

Two other in-tower cafes are less inspiring, though also less expensive: **Horizon's Café** offers more of a bar environment with the requisite nachos and spring rolls; **MarketPlace Café** provides a food-court-style meal.

See map p. 138. 301 Front St. W. ☎ *416-362-5411.* www.cntower.ca. *Reservations required. TTC: Union station. Main courses: C$29–C$35 (US$24–US$29) lunch, C$30–C$48 (US$25–US$39) dinner; C$44 (US$36) prix fixe lunch, C$47–C$67 (US$39–US$55) prix fixe dinner. AE, DC, MC, V. Open: Daily 11 a.m.–2 p.m.; Sun–Thurs 4:30–10 p.m., Fri–Sat 4:30–10:30 p.m.*

Adega
$$–$$$ **Downtown**   **PORTUGUESE**

This modest eatery is slightly removed from Toronto's Little Portugal neighborhood (which is centered around Dundas Street west of Bathurst Avenue), but the Portuguese menu here focuses on seafood, much as may be expected from the seafaring nation. The modesty of the eatery applies to its main floor, with an intimate layout made for hushed conversations (or boisterous ones, when the standard tables for two are squeezed together to accommodate larger groups); several private alcoves provide more intimacy. The restaurant, however, makes good use of its second floor and its wine cellar (*adega* is Portuguese for cellar) for private functions and much larger groups. A taste of the Mediterranean is served up as you begin your meal, with a sampling of olives and breads and olive oil. Entrees are balanced toward the Atlantic side of the seafood ledger, with both Mediterranean and continental influences. For the true Iberian experience, go for the Petisco's appetizer platter, with grilled chouriço (a Portuguese sausage), sardines, and squid, as well as Portuguese goat cheese and prosciutto. An extensive lineup of fairly priced Portuguese wines accompanies the menu, and outdoor seating is available during the warmer months.

See map p. 138. 33 Elm St. ☎ *416-977-4338.* www.adegarestaurante.ca. *Reservations recommended. TTC: Dundas station. Main courses: C$18–C$29 (US$15–US$24). AE, DC, MC, V. Open: Mon–Fri 11 a.m.–3 p.m.; Mon–Sat 5 p.m.– 11 p.m.*

Akane-ya
$$ **The Beaches**   **JAPANESE**

On the east end of Queen Street East in The Beaches, this tiny, tiny location offers decidedly upscale Japanese and sushi cuisine. The best seats in the house are the half-dozen at the sushi bar; you have barely another dozen to choose from if the sushi bar is full up. But never mind the too-cozy coziness; everything from the elegantly prepared sushi to tempura to teriyaki is done to near perfection. The fixed-price options may save you a buck or two, but why sacrifice the satisfaction of sampling the great variety of sushi at à la carte prices?

2214A Queen St. E. ☎ *416-699-0377. Reservations recommended. TTC: 501 Queen streetcar east. Main courses: C$15–C$20 (US$12–US$16). AE, DC, MC, V. Open: Mon–Sat 5:30–10:30 p.m., Sun 5–10 p.m.*

Alice Fazooli's! Italian Crabshack

$–$$$ **Entertainment District**   **ITALIAN**

Any restaurant that willingly — even enthusiastically — places six children under the age of ten at a table separate from their six parents should be considered kid-friendly by anybody's standards. This actually happens at Alice Fazooli's, where the servers have just as much fun with the kids as the kids have with them. Of course, the warehouse setting doesn't do much to drown out the restaurant's sounds, so you may not be able to hear your kids having so much fun — which could be a good or a bad thing, depending on your perspective. This is a local chain, with four other locations scattered around Toronto (this is the only one actually in Toronto proper), and the food evokes a kind of upscale chain-restaurant feel: not as lackluster as your basic Applebee's or TGI Friday's; not as stirring as, say, The Palm or Ruth's Chris. The focus, as the name indicates, is on seafood with an Italian flair, and it's all fairly basic, yet nicely prepared. But, as with other chains, they tend to try to do a little bit of everything; you can also sample steaks, ribs, and even a nice New Orleans–style bouillabaisse. When in doubt, however, go with a sampling of starters; the coconut shrimp is the best around, and a couple of thin-crust pizzas (the goat cheese with portobello is terrific) will satisfy even the finickiest of kids (or adults). If you plan an evening meal at Alice Fazooli's before a play or event at one of several downtown venues, the after-dinner cab is on them.

See map p. 138. 294 Adelaide St. W. ☎ *416-979-1910. Reservations recommended. TTC: St. Andrew station. Main courses: C$8–C$22 (US$6.55–US$18) lunch, C$10–C$26 (US$8.20–US$21) dinner. AE, DC, MC, V. Open: Sun–Wed 11:30–1 a.m., Thurs–Sat 11:30–2 a.m.*

Allen's

$$–$$$ **The Danforth**   **IRISH-AMERICAN**

With 228 single-malt scotches on hand behind its long oak bar, and over a hundred beers to choose from (including a dizzying array of Belgian brew), it's understandable that Allen's is a regular recipient of many of those "Best of . . ." awards that the local rags hand out now and again. In addition to the plentiful variety of drink, Allen's provides its patrons with pretty fair food as well. Notable for its attention to the burger (a thick slab of ground steak, cooked to your specifications, onto which you can add such favored accompaniments as sautéed mushrooms and onions, peameal bacon, and a variety of cheeses), the rest of the regularly changing menu offers Irish recipes, refined for the urban and business connoisseurs that fill this popular eatery during the weekday lunch hour. But my favorite part about Allen's is the way it makes you feel like you have your own neighborhood pub. From the ever-pleasant servers, who ensure your comfort without rushing you out the door, to the rack of some of the world's best newspapers, available for perusing whether dining alone or with a fellow news junkie, to its patio out back, away from the noisy bustle of the Danforth and shaded by tall willows, Allen's is a refreshing break.

143 Danforth Ave. ☎ 416-463-3086. www.allens.to. *Reservations not accepted. TTC: Broadview station. Main courses: C$10–C$26 (US$8.20–US$21). AE, DC, MC, V. Open: Mon–Fri 11:30 a.m.–11 p.m., Sat–Sun 11 a.m.–11 p.m.*

Aunties and Uncles
$ Little Italy   BREAKFAST/LIGHT FARE

This homey place may just remind you of your favorite aunt's kitchen — you know, the one that always seemed to have fresh bread baking. The décor and furnishings are retro, and the food's always fresh. Practically everything here centers around the tiny restaurant's famous challah bread; from breakfast toast to French toast, these light and airy fresh-baked loaves are the bread of choice. The lunch offerings include original and inspiring combinations of ingredients for refreshing salads and amazing made-to-order sandwiches on the aforementioned challah. The popularity of this eatery increases with the temperature, when the outdoor patio opens.

74 Lippincott St. ☎ 416-324-1375. Reservations not accepted. TTC: Queen's Park station, and then the 506 Carlton streetcar west. Main courses: C$5–C$8 (US$4.10–US$6.55). No credit cards. Open: Tues–Sun 9 a.m.–4 p.m.

Babur
$–$$ Queen West   INDIAN

Specializing in tandoori — and not too bad with rotis — Babur is a mainstay in the Queen West neighborhood. A plentiful lunch buffet at a great price (C$11/US$9) draws the visitors who come to this district for its eclectic shopping as well as the business workers who cross nearby University Avenue for the selection of veggie and meat curries, naan, salads, and desserts. The dinner menu doesn't disappoint either, with the terrific butter chicken, mango chicken, and goan fish curry. Vegetarian dishes work equally well, including the tandoor-prepared shashlik paneer and a nice lentil entree, daal tarka. Babur doesn't really feel like a typical Indian place — aside from the mouthwatering aroma, of course — but there's no mistaking the genuineness of its craft. This eatery is a nice waystation on your journey up and down Queen Street West.

See map p. 138. 273 Queen St. W. ☎ 416-599-7720. Reservations not accepted. TTC: Osgoode station. Main courses: C$8–C$15 (US$6.55–US$12). AE, MC, V. Open: Daily 11:45 a.m.–2:30 p.m., 5–10:30 p.m.

Use these handy Post-It® Flags to mark your favorite pages.

Bangkok Garden
$$–$$$$ Downtown   THAI

One of Toronto's original Thai restaurants, the Bangkok Garden remains a popular destination for locals and visitors — its doors are just outside the Elm Street entry of the Delta Chelsea. With Adega and Barberian's also on the block (and all reviewed here), Elm Street has itself a nice miniature restaurant row happening. The Bangkok Garden's décor is truly garde-nesque, with tall greenery and teak finishes in an atrium-like, two-level dining room. Many of its authentic furnishings hail direct from Thailand, setting up an atmosphere for what the restaurant calls a "truly Thai" dining experience. And it is an experience, without doubt, but one that you pay a slight premium for. Toronto has a number of Thai places around town that offer a meal that's as good as or better than Bangkok Garden, but without the atmosphere. Nevertheless, a visit here is well worth your while. Dishes are categorized as hot, salty, sour, or sweet — perfect for a party of four if you're into some sampling — worthy choices include the crab pad thai and the red vegetable curry. Or try the weekday lunch buffet or Sunday brunch buffet to really experience all the senses.

See map p. 138. 18 Elm St. ☎ **416-977-6748**. www.bangkokgarden.ca. *Reservations recommended. TTC: Dundas station. Main courses: C$10–$C36 (US$8.20–US$30). AE, DC, MC, V. Open: Daily 11:30 a.m.–2:30 p.m., 5–10 p.m.*

Barberian's
$$$–$$$$ Downtown   STEAKHOUSE

Yes, it's a splurge — and a big one, at that, though the highest end of the price range is reserved for the largest of the artery-cloggers (12- to 24 - ouncers) — but if you're in the mood for a big, juicy steak, and want something a little different from the Morton's or Ruth's Chris experience that you can get back home (and in Toronto, too), then Barberian's is the place for you. This eatery opened in 1959, and it retains its dark and clubby and classically steakhouse-y feel. The menu of highly regarded and highly flavorful steaks is just steps from the Delta Chelsea, and only a few blocks northwest of the Canon Theatre — steak and a show is a tempting possibility. If you're not a red-meat enthusiast, I'll resist the temptation to recommend the nearby Bangkok Garden or Adega — chances are that you're only considering Barberian's because you're traveling *with* a red meat enthusiast — and instead suggest the lemon-grilled capon or the salmon steak, both laudable choices. But when in Rome, go for the steak. It won't disappoint.

See map p. 138. 7 Elm St. ☎ **416-597-0335**. www.barberians.com. *Reservations required. TTC: Dundas station. Main courses: C$25–C$49 (US$21–US$40). AE, DC, MC, V. Open: Daily 5 p.m. to midnight, Mon–Fri noon to 2:30 p.m.*

Bedford Academy
$–$$ The Annex   PUB FARE

Don't let the library/study setting or the steady stream of customers from the nearby University of Toronto or even the scholarly name fool you; the Bedford Academy is more watering hole than ivory tower — granted, a watering hole with an upscale pub menu, but a watering hole nonetheless. The Bloor/Yorkville location draws the business lunchers (as well as the scattered shoppers) for weekday lunch, and the good selection of beers (18 on tap) and comfortable patio draw the after-work and weekend crowds. The menu offers the usual pub standards with a Bloor/Yorkville kind of touch (portobello mushroom burger with pommes frites, anyone?), and a pleasant selection of soups and salads suggest a cozy bistro as well.

See map p. 138. 36 Prince Arthur Ave. ☎ *416-921-4600. Reservations not required. TTC: St. George station. Main courses: C$8–C$15 (US$6.55–US$12). AE, DC, MC, V. Open: Daily 11 a.m.–3 a.m.*

Biff's
$$–$$$$ Financial District   CONTINENTAL

Strolling past Biff's in the early evening, the muted entry lighting and the alluring out-front seating suggest a fine bistro meal before heading across the street to the St. Lawrence or the Hummingbird for a play. Step inside, however, and the bistro transforms into downtown hot spot, tables buzzing with the conversation of Toronto's suits from the nearby financial centers. The menu, though, remains decidedly bistro-like, starting with the wild-mushroom soup, which barely glances at the puree setting before heading to your table with clear evidence that actual mushrooms remain, or the delectable spinach, endive, and pear salad, topped with walnuts and Roquefort dressing. Both starters are available at lunch or dinner, but the lunch menu most fully conjures up memories of Parisian eateries, from the omelette du jour (with pommes frites, of course) to a flavorful baked tarragon chicken and mushroom dish. The servers are among the most efficient in the city; Biff's recognizes its surroundings — lunch diners needing to return to the office; the pre-theater crowd rushing to finish their desserts and coffees before the lights dim. Oddly, however, an early closing time prevents most theatergoers from rounding out an evening with a Biff's crème brûlée or profiteroles.

See map p. 138. 4 Front St. ☎ *416-860-0086.* www.biffsrestaurant.com. *Reservations recommended. TTC: Union station. Main courses: C$14–C$22 (US$11–US$18) lunch, C$24–C$33 (US$20–US$27). AE, DC, MC, V. Open: Mon–Fri noon to 2:30 p.m.; Mon–Wed 5–10 p.m., Thurs–Sat 5–11 p.m.; closed Sun.*

Big Daddy's
$–$$$ Entertainment District   CAJUN

Just steps from the Royal Alexandra Theatre and Roy Thomson Hall, this New Orleans–style eatery does its best to emulate New Orleans frivolity, which is a tough feeling to conjure when walking through a cold, sharp, autumn wind along King Street. But step down (Big Daddy's is below street level) to pick up your Mardi Gras beads, step up to the Oyster Bar for a selection of the gulf's (and the Maritimes') finest, or step into the kitschy Voodoo Lounge and, well, it's Toronto's own Canadian French Quarter (worth about 21¢ down in the Big Easy). The food comes pretty close too, with a nice balance of traditional blackened shellfish and chicken and a surprisingly disparate assortment of pastas. The jambalaya linguine redefines this traditional Cajun rice dish with grilled chicken and shrimp, and the seafood jalapeño/cilantro fettucine creates a nice combination of distinct spicy flavors when served with the same creole cream sauce. Don't come here expecting to eat light: Big Daddy's is a carb-loading, heavy-cream type of place. Expect to leave stuffed.

See map p. 138. 212 King St. W. ☎ **416-599-5200.** www.bigdaddys.ca. *Reservations recommended. TTC: St. Andrew station. Main courses: C$9–C$25 (US$7.40–US$21) lunch, C$13–C$30 (US$11–US$25) dinner. AE, DC, MC, V. Open: Mon 11:30 a.m.–11 p.m., Tues–Fri 11:30–1 a.m., Sat 4 p.m.–1 a.m., Sun 4–11 p.m.*

The Black Bull
$–$$ Queen West   PUB FARE

Washington, D.C., has its cherry blossoms, Wrigley Field has its ceremonial first pitch, and Toronto has its Black Bull. The unofficial first day of spring in Toronto is the day that this tavern opens its massive patio, ready to take in the chilled sun and the brisk step of Queen West residents bold enough to bring out the first pair of shorts. It ain't fancy — quite often, an intimidating lineup of Harleys welcomes your arrival — but the pizzas, burgers, nachos, and such move quickly, and the beer flows freely. A couple of pool tables are indoors, but there's really no reason to come here but for the patio; it seats close to 200 and still there are days when a table is hard to find.

See map p. 138. 298 Queen St. W. ☎ **416-593-2766.** *Reservations not required. TTC: Osgoode station, and then walk — it's spring, after all. Main courses: C$7–C$13 (US$5.75–US$11). AE, MC, V. Open: Daily 11 a.m.–2 a.m.*

Bonjour Brioche
$ Queen East   BAKERY/CAFE

Known primarily for its baked goods, this tiny cafe boasts some delectable breakfast and lunch options as well. Opened a few years after Hello Toast (see listing later in this chapter) was established down the street — Bonjour Brioche? Hello Toast? Hello? — the dining menu is limited but the food is fresh and top-notch. The baked French toast is just the right combination of sweet and crunchy — kind of a French toast casserole. Sandwiches are the primary lunch fare, most served on a deliciously fresh baguette, but consider the daily quiche instead for something heartier.

812 Queen St. E. ☎ **416-406-1250.** *Reservations not accepted. TTC: 501 Queen streetcar east. Main courses: C$5–C$9 (US$4.10–US$7.40). Cash only. Open: Tues–Fri 8 a.m.–5 p.m., Sat 8 a.m.–4 p.m., Sun 8 a.m.–3 p.m.; closed Mon.*

Brick Street Bakery
$ Distillery District   LIGHT FARE

Located just inside the main entrance of the Gooderham & Worts distillery complex, Toronto's exciting new shopping and dining destination in what's known as the Distillery District, the Brick Street Bakery is a throwback to what must have been the simpler marketplace times of the distillery's heyday. (A chicken tarragon pie and a couple of loaves of organic sourdough? "Let's call it ten bucks." And no need to even ring it up on the antique cash register.) There's enough room here to select your sweet, find out what's fresh out of the oven (I could swear they were wood-burning stoves), add whatever it is to your order, and head back outside. Sandwich choices include chicken, beef, pork, and lamb (perhaps on a couple of slices of that organic sourdough); chutneys and spiced-up mayonnaises serve as not-overpowering condiments. Delicious and very reasonably priced pastries range from scones and cookies to tarts and bread pudding. But what may bring you back before you even leave the distillery are the savory pies (including the aforementioned chicken tarragon — the steak and stout is equally enthralling), which are often either just out of the oven or just about to come out of the oven. ("I'll have some potato, leek, and cheddar pies out in five minutes; I'll hold one for you if you'd like to come back." Seriously.)

See map p. 138. 55 Mill St. ☎ *416-214-4949. TTC: 504 King streetcar east, and then the 72 bus south at Parliament St. Main courses: C$6–C$7 (US$4.90–US$5.75). No credit cards. Open: Sun–Wed 11 a.m.–7 p.m., Thurs–Sat 11 a.m.–9 p.m.*

Café Nervosa
$$–$$$ Bloor/Yorkville   ITALIAN

If you're a fan of *Frasier,* like I am, you're probably asking yourself that age-old chicken-and-egg question: Which came first, this restaurant or the Seattle coffee bar? (Okay, so you're probably not dweebish enough to ask yourself that question. But if you did, you'll be interested to hear that the fictional coffee bar is the inspiration for this bistro's name.) This cozy, yellow, Victorian house is a natural draw for the celebrity-spotters who migrate to the Yorkville part of the Bloor/Yorkville neighborhood. (For your best view of the sidewalk action, opt for the main patio, which follows the corner around Yorkville and Bellair avenues; the rooftop patio is stranded out back, but is an ideal setting for more intimate outdoor dining.) Café Nervosa has a hearty selection of salads, including a pair that are big enough for a pair — the pollo e formaggio di capra is the best bet, mixed greens with grilled chicken, wild mushrooms, goat cheese, and sun-dried tomatoes. The options for thin-crust pizza are even more plentiful, from your anything-but-basic margherita pie to an intimidating funghi e formaggio (two varieties of mushrooms, two varieties of soft cheeses, and prosciutto). Toss in a boisterous cappuccino, and attentive servers who deliciously disappear after you get your coffee, and you're set for a solid hour of people-watching.

See map p. 138. 75 Yorkville Ave. ☎ **416-961-4642**. www.cafenervosa.ca. *Reservations required for parties of 5 or more only. TTC: Bay station. Main courses: C$10–C$25 (US$8.20–US$21). AE, DC. MC, V. Open: Sun–Wed 11 a.m.–11 p.m., Thurs–Sat 11 a.m. to midnight.*

C'est What?
$–$$ **St. Lawrence Market**   **PUB FARE**

It's not really what you'd traditionally call pub fare — just good, casual, eclectic cuisine that happens to be in a pub, complete with 29 beers on tap. When maneuvering the crowds at the St. Lawrence Market, resist the "carrion call" of the Churrasco chicken sandwich or the Carousel peameal bacon in a bun and head for this dungeon-level eatery for a pint or two and a diverse blend of starters, sandwiches, and entrees. Popular fare includes its original minced lamburger, a surprisingly lean buffalo burger, and Porter beef ribs, marinated in the home-crafted Coffee Porter. A nice lighter choice on the lunch menu is the French Quarter, combining shaved ham, maple syrup, melted cheddar, and roasted red-pepper mayonnaise on a bun. And the late-night fare has plenty of snacking options to accompany your beer-tasting — the Al's Cask Ale and the Coffee Porter are must-tastes. Open and serving food until 2 a.m. every night, C'est What? is a natural answer to that age-old post-theater question: "Say, how about we grab a bite to eat?"

See map p. 138. 67 Front St. E. ☎ **416-867-9499**. www.cestwhat.com. *Reservations not accepted. TTC: King station. Main courses: C$6–C$16 (US$4.90–US$13). AE, MC, V. Open: Daily 11:30 a.m.–2 a.m.*

Dhaba
$–$$ **Entertainment District**   **INDIAN**

The restaurants that beckon tourists on King Street West between John and Peter streets are known for their garish, faux-trendy, suck-you-in signage — the kind about which the locals know better — and très convenient real estate in the very heart of the Entertainment District. With one or two better-than-average exceptions, these eateries offer mainstay, less-than-inspiring fare that caters to the mediocre expectations of out-of-towners who simply don't know where else to turn. Dhaba — smack in the middle of that restaurant row — rises above the rest, literally and figuratively. Up 21 steps (no elevator) to a narrow room that houses a pair of tandoors, this Indian restaurant boasts a "healthwise" menu that, whether fat-free or fat-full, is among the best in the city. Tandoori is the preparation of choice, with particular emphasis on chicken dishes — I counted 14 of them, not including the tandoori platter, with three of its four dishes of the fowl variety. Not that there's anything wrong with that, of course; the butter chicken is remarkable, and the chicken biryani is a nice less-spicy rice dish. These dishes and others are fine for the dinner crowd, but Dhaba is all about an amazing C$10.95 (US$9) lunch buffet, when you can sample

from 50 items (though that number includes the requisite salads and desserts — try the rice pudding), including butter chicken, tandoori chicken, and a changing menu of meat, fish, and vegetable curries.
See map p. 138. 309 King St. W. ☎ *416-740-6622. Reservations recommended for dinner. TTC: St. Andrew station. Main courses: C$10–C$20 (US$8.20–US$16). AE, DC, MC, V. Open: Daily 5–10:30 p.m.; Mon–Fri 11:45 a.m.–2:30 p.m., Sat–Sun noon to 3 p.m.*

Dos Amigos
$–$$ The Annex   MEXICAN

A tiny, somewhat bizarre dining room, in an out-of-the-way and seemingly desolate location — sounds great! Let's go now! Really, though, you should, because outstanding and authentic Mexican restaurants are notoriously hard to find in Toronto, and this one may just be the best of the best. Dos Amigos is the kind of place that appreciates tastes and textures, not how many chili peppers should be listed next to the spiciest dishes on the menu. Start with one of seven margaritas or a crisp bottle of Dos Equis and a fresh round of guacamole. Entrees well worth considering include the pollo con mole (chicken swimming in a rich, unsweetened chocolate sauce) or a selection of taquitos (chicken, pork, and beef) that are accompanied by a couple of homemade salsas. And they do very nice things with seafood — this is definitely (and thankfully) not your mama's Chi-Chi's.
1201 Bathurst St. ☎ *416-534-2528.* www.dos-amigos.ca. *Reservations recommended. TTC: Dupont station, and then the 26 Dupont bus west and the 7 Bathurst bus north. Main courses: C$8–C$19 (US$6.55–US$16). AE, MC, V. Open: Tues–Thurs 5–10:30 p.m., Fri–Sat 5–11 p.m., Sun 5–10:30 p.m.*

Dunn's Famous Bar & Grill
$–$$ Entertainment District   DELI

Established in Montreal in 1927, Dunn's quickly became something of a local institution before moving on to Ottawa, Edmonton, and, now, Toronto. Taking up residence between the Princess of Wales and Royal Alexandra theaters, this location is somewhat more upscale in design than its Ottawa or Montreal colleagues. The design may be by design, though, given that it's just across the street from the massive Metro Hall, which houses the administrative offices for the City of Toronto. Thus, Dunn's draws heavy business-area traffic during the day, but its proximity to the Entertainment District makes it a natural for the theater crowd at night. However, the food remains decidedly low-key, with an emphasis on size over style (or, in some cases, substance), and it begins with a huge smoked-meat sandwich for five bucks. What you gain in savings, however, is taken away in time lost due to slow and indifferent service, though perhaps it's just a matter of newness (this location opened in fall 2003). The smoked meat here is good, not great — for great, head a block west, to Reuben S. (reviewed later in this chapter). The menu does offer quite a bit more variety than your standard deli (though do you really want fish and chips from a deli?), but the quality is hit-and-miss, with nothing terribly awful or awesome. Don't expect great here, but you can expect an adequate and casual meal that works well just before you head next door to the theater.

See map p. 138. 284A King St. W. ☎ *416-599-5464. Reservations not necessary. TTC: St. Andrew station. Main courses: C$5–C$16 (US$4.10–US$13). AE, MC, V. Open: Mon 7:30 a.m.–8 p.m., Tues–Fri 7:30 a.m.–11 p.m., Sat 9 a.m.–11 p.m., Sun 9 a.m.–8 p.m.*

Fiesta Azteca
$–$$ **Leaside**   **MEXICAN**

This shopping district on Bayview Avenue north of downtown is ideally designed for the laid-back browser. Its wide sidewalks and bright, open storefronts make for lots of strolling (and lots of strollers — the baby-carrying kind) and leave room for sunny sidewalk seating. But when partaking in this casual meandering, do you really want a heavy Mexican meal to slow you down? In a word, yes. Actually, in another word, guacamole — it's the best in the city. So at the very least, take a break with a margarita and a bowl of fresh tortilla chips to accompany the hearty guacamole — mixed with chunks of tomato and onion and a hint of pico de gallo, it's served in a dark marble mortar and pestle that somehow manages to look like a heavy sombrero. The main dishes lack the inventiveness of those served at Dos Amigos (reviewed earlier in this chapter), but the standard brew of enchiladas, burritos, and such are freshly prepared in a kitchen that sits at the front of the restaurant (kids love to line up to watch the action) and are commonly offered with a choice of four flavorful sauces. The green tomatillo sauce is the best; creamy and full of texture, it works very well with a chicken enchilada. And, yes, sidewalk seating is an option.

1618 Bayview Ave. ☎ *416-482-9998. Reservations not accepted. TTC: Davisville station, and then the 11+ Davisville bus north. Main courses: C$7–C$16 (US$5.75–US$13). AE, MC, V. Open: Daily noon to 10 p.m.*

Flo's
$–$$ **Bloor/Yorkville**   **DINER**

Inside, counter seating, Formica tabletops, big and comfy booths; outside, closely positioned, slightly unstable tables and chairs on a metal balcony, the extension of a narrow, winding, metal staircase that leads to this second-floor casual eatery on ritzy Yorkville Avenue. Go for the inside seating: It's comfortable, and large windows draw in the light that you miss by not sitting on the balcony — and you won't miss the tight quarters and servers dancing and darting around the balcony tables. But once you've settled, expect some of the best casual fare that the city has to offer. All the diner basics are done with just a slight uptick in style — burgers with roasted red peppers or Brie; tuna or chicken melts on thick challah bread; and fabulously thick milk shakes, with daily special flavors — the strawberry-rhubarb is divine — and smoothies. Breakfasts are delicious here too, and the coffee is a hearty roast and strong. Flo's is nearly always busy — it's a good business lunch spot during the week and a nice choice for weekend shoppers or Sunday brunchers — so expect a lineup outside and a wait inside. But use the time to enjoy your dining companion or the newspaper; it's well worth the wait.

See map p. 138. 70 Yorkville Ave. ☎ *416-961-4333. Reservations not accepted. TTC: Bay station. Main courses: C$6–C$13 (US$4.90–US$11). AE, MC, V. Open: Mon–Thurs 7:30 a.m.–10 p.m., Fri–Sat 8:30 a.m.–11 p.m., Sun 9 a.m.–10 p.m.*

Fred's Not Here
$$–$$$ Entertainment District   ECLECTIC

The open kitchen is the showpiece of this steady, fairly expensive location along the King Street restaurant row. The menu is true eclecticism, with so many directions that it's hard to know where to go. That's not necessarily a bad thing, just a bit of a jumble. You can go Thai; you can go bistro. You can grill 'em; you can smoke 'em. You can toss in a bit of Cajun; or you can bring out the big guns and go with that crown prince of eclectic dining: ostrich (which, in case you're wondering, tastes a bit more like veal than chicken). Your most reliable option, among all these choices, is to go with something off the grill. Whether it's steak, seafood, or pork, it's usually done right. Whichever you choose, the best route is through the remarkable baked lobster and crab soup. And Fred's (restaurateur Fred Luk) usually *not* here; perhaps he's tending to one of his other four Toronto restaurants.

See map p. 138. 321 King St. W. ☎ *416-971-9155. www.fredsnothere.com. Reservations recommended. TTC: St. Andrew station. Main courses: C$15–C$30 (US$12–US$25). AE, DC, MC, V. Open: Mon–Fri 11:30 a.m.–2:30 p.m.; Sun–Wed 5– 10 p.m., Thurs–Sat 5–11 p.m.*

Fressen
$$ Queen West   VEGETARIAN

This vegan restaurant (technically, lacto-ovo vegetarian) has achieved a fair bit of attention of late, if not for its appetizing, upscale, and inspiring food, then for its perpetually in-line skating owner/chef Stephen Gardner, whom you can often see at work in the kitchen with the restaurant's open-concept design. No reliance on tofu and bland salads here; Fressen is gourmet dining in its most natural and fine state. Breads are baked in-house and served fresh with an olive tapenade. If dining with a dyed-in-the-wool carnivore, note that the portobello "steak" is tender and "meaty," and the black-bean corn wrap entree is filling and complemented with a flavor-filled jalapeño sauce. Especially when busy, service can be slow, but the atmosphere and anticipation make the delay bearable. Fressen is open during the day only on weekends, with a popular Saturday and Sunday brunch, when eggs are also served.

See map p. 138. 478 Queen St. W. ☎ *416-504-5127. Reservations recommended. TTC: Osgoode station, and then 501 Queen streetcar west. Main courses: C$12–C$14 (US$9.85–US$11). AE, MC, V. Open: Sun–Thurs 5:30–10 p.m., Fri–Sat 5:30–11 p.m.; Sat–Sun 10:30 a.m.–3:30 p.m.*

Garden Gate Restaurant
$ The Beaches   CHINESE/CANADIAN

Informally known around the neighborhood as "The Goof" (for some burnt-out neon lights a few years back on a sign out front that normally says "GOOD FOOD"), the narrow, burnt-orange booths at this tiny corner location are nearly always filled with local Beaches residents. Sure, the Cantonese-style Chinese is "GOOD FOOD," and hot and familiar to anyone from any North American city of any size, but a couple of their Szechuan entrees are the best options on the menu. The thick Szechuan noodles come with chicken and shrimp in a spicy Szechuan sauce, and the Singapore Rice Vermicelli is perfectly spiced with the curry prominently flavored and overloaded with fresh green peppers (my suggestion: substitute chicken for the shrimp — the big chunks of fresh, moist chicken breast beat the tiny frozen shrimp any day of the week). Of course, if you're in the mood for the Canadian part of The Goof's Chinese-Canadian cuisine, it's hard to beat a bacon-and-egg breakfast for under five bucks or a steaming hot turkey sandwich with gravy-covered crinkle-cut french fries, just like the old Jones Cafe back in 1960s Middle America. Kids will love the chicken balls, freshly made milk shakes, and the coin-operated jukeboxes along one wall that still occasionally work. Old-fashioned counter seating is on the other wall where you can get a good view of the food being prepared (really, you can watch the food being prepared from anywhere in this tiny restaurant).

2379 Queen St. E. ☎ 416-694-9696. Reservations not accepted. TTC: 501 Queen streetcar east. Main courses: C$5–C$9 (US$4.10–US$7.40). MC, V. Open: Sun–Thurs 8 a.m.–10 p.m., Fri–Sat 8 a.m.–11 p.m.

Happy Seven
$ Chinatown   CHINESE

At this classic Cantonese restaurant you don't want to avoid the seafood — the Happy Seven specializes in it, with over 30 seafood dishes, including some straight-from-the-tank offerings (a subtle warning for those who prefer not to see their meal swimming before they eat). This modest place is equal parts inviting and open and colorful and kitschy. In addition to the great selection of seafood, the huge menu is full of soup offerings, with the standards (the best hot and sour I've ever had, eggdrop, wonton) as well as a number of quite inventive ones, such as the surprisingly sweet melon and crabmeat soup. For the main dishes, anything with scallops is a hit, and the seafood fried rice is served heaping with an abundance of fresh vegetables. If you're feeling courageous, ask for the pink menu with its not-so-standard dishes, including frog legs, fried pigeon, and again some nice scallops dishes. Happy Seven is open until 5 a.m., if you end up near Chinatown with a late-night craving for *anything* to eat.

See map p. 138. 358 Spadina Ave. ☎ 416-971-9820. Reservations not accepted. TTC: Spadina station, then 510 Spadina streetcar south. Main courses: C$7–C$15 (US$5.75–US$12). MC, V. Open: Daily 4 p.m.–5 a.m.

Hello Toast
$–$$ Queen East   **BRUNCH/LIGHT FARE**

Its name is the brainchild of humorist Fran Lebowitz, though it's unknown whether she's aware of it. When questioning the naming of a New York eatery (Bonjour Croissant), Lebowitz pondered the idea of going to Paris and opening a place called Hello Toast. This quirky east-end restaurant does have a certain toast theme to it (including a collection of imaginatively displayed toasters), and it's best known for its weekend brunches, which always draw a long line of would-be diners. Sadly, the weekend lineup is not always about the brunch's popularity; service can be just shy of abysmal, but the cinnamon French toast or the eggs Benedict or the thick challah toast keeps the regulars coming back. Hello Toast offers a lighter selection of salads, light entrees, and pasta during the week and on weekend evenings. But go for the brunch — and go early, or expect to wait in a long line.

993 Queen St. E. ☎ *416-778-7299. Reservations not accepted. TTC: 501 Queen streetcar east. Main courses: C$8–C$13 (US$6.55–US$11). AE, MC, V. Open: Mon–Fri 11 a.m.–4 p.m., Sat–Sun 10 a.m.–4 p.m.; Tues–Sat 6–10 p.m.*

Hernando's Hideaway
$–$$ St. Lawrence Market   **MEXICAN**

Teals and yellows and stripes adorn the walls and tables of this restaurant offering Tex-Mex-style cuisine in a bit of a hidden-away location near the St. Lawrence and Hummingbird centers and just east of the Financial District. This colorful place exudes bright and cheery — and the massive margaritas definitely contribute. Hernando's is the kind of Mexican restaurant where diners should have few expectations. They make no pretensions toward being authentic; this is Mexican-style food for a North American diet (well, north-of-the-Rio-Grande North America). But what they do, they do well. Fajitas are hot and sizzling, using fresh vegetables and pico de gallo and other generous trimmings (the vegetarian fajitas introduce zucchini and broccoli and carrots to the tortilla). The menu is loaded with the standard a la carte options (tacos, enchiladas, burritos) that can also be ordered with one of an array of combination plates. It's fun, easy eating, and a comfortable and fast spot for pre- or post-theater eating and drinking.

See map p. 138. 52A Wellington St. E. ☎ *416-366-6394.* www.hernandoshideaway. com. *Reservations accepted only for groups of 8 or more. TTC: King station. Main courses: C$8–C$20 (US$6.55–US20). AE, MC, V. Open: Mon–Thurs 11:30 a.m.–11 p.m., Fri 11:30 a.m. to midnight, Sat noon to midnight, Sun 3–10 p.m.*

When you really want to break bread in the best

Where do you go in Toronto when Hernando's Hideaway just won't cut it as a fine dining experience? Toronto has dozens of high-end, cutting-edge cuisine, pricey restaurants that help keep the city's gourmands happy, especially when you throw in the best of the best hotel restaurants (such as EPIC at the Royal York or TUNDRA at the Hilton — it's obviously a prerequisite to uppercase your best hotel eateries). If your Toronto experience will not be complete without a meal at this type of establishment, this sidebar suggests some of the city's most highly regarded restaurants.

- ✔ **Brassaii** (461 King St. W.; ☎ **416-598-4730**; www.brassaii.com): Just to prove the point that you don't have to break the bank to enjoy an inventive meal, Brassaii offers unassuming entrees for under C$30 (US$25). But for a variety of unique offerings, share a handful of appetizers.

- ✔ **Bymark** (66 Wellington St. W.; ☎ **416-777-1144**; www.bymark.ca): Anecdotally known for its C$33 (US$27) hamburger (with accompaniments such as porcini mushrooms, Brie, and shaved truffle), and as a second Toronto restaurant for Mark McEwan, owner of North 44 (see below).

- ✔ **Canoe** (66 Wellington St. W., 54th floor; ☎ **416-364-0054**; www.canoe restaurant.com): Boasting one of the best views of any Toronto restaurant (albeit from the top of a boring old Canadian bank tower), the menu focuses on Canadian fare more than most Toronto establishments. Don't be surprised to find offerings such as caribou or Atlantic lobster.

- ✔ **Mildred Pierc**e (99 Sudbury St.; ☎ **416-588-5695**): This very elegant setting is somewhat out of the downtown core, but worth the drive (or cab ride). With a menu that is primarily Asian-inspired (try the lychee martini), it may be one of Toronto's most romantic dining establishments.

- ✔ **North 44** (2537 Yonge St.; ☎ **416-487-4897**; www.north44restaurant.com): Despite its Canadian-inspired name (it's Toronto's latitude line), the menu here is not Canadian at all. But its globe-trotting inspirations (including Mediterranean, Asian, and Italian) will make it easy for you to forgive.

- ✔ **Pangaea** (1221 Bay St.; ☎ **416-920-2323**; www.pangaearestaurant.com): An inviting and blended décor of metal and dark wood foreshadow a fusion-inspired take on Canadian ingredients.

- ✔ **Scaramouche** (1 Benvenuto Pl.; ☎ **416-961-8011**; www.scaramouche restaurant.com): Another stellar view — this one from north of downtown (book way ahead for a window seat) — to accompany a classically inspired menu; think foie gras, roasted seafood, and grilled meat prepared classically well.

- ✔ **Susur** (601 King St. W.; ☎ **416-603-2205**; www.susur.com): Currently, the hottest hot-for-the-moment location in Toronto, splurge for the tasting menu, a seven-course experience that changes daily and is served according to volume (the main course is served first).

The Host
$–$$ The Annex   INDIAN

This elegant, if somewhat poorly lit, location is a reliable place for upscale Indian cuisine. Located just west of the ritzy Bloor/Yorkville neighborhood, The Host gets its share of a regular business crowd for its lunch buffet. But you get the real experience of the place during dinner hours, with an emphasis on chicken curry and vegetarian dishes. The makhni is an extra-spicy version of chicken tikka masala; ambi nicely combines chicken and mango. Tandoor dishes are done nicely here as well: the mirch tikka has a bold green chili flavor. While the varied menu courteously includes spiciness ratings, you can pretty much count on any dish having a bit of a kick to it.

See map p. 138. 14 Prince Arthur Ave. ☎ *416-962-4678.* www.welcometohost. com. *Reservations recommended. TTC: St. George station. Main courses: C$9–C$17 (US$7.40–US$14). AE, DC, MC, V. Open: Daily 11:45 a.m.–2:30 p.m.; Mon–Thurs 5–10:30 p.m., Fri–Sat 5–11 p.m., Sun 5–10 p.m.*

Il Fornello
$$–$$$ The Danforth   ITALIAN

Yes, it's a chain. How does a chain restaurant end up in a travel guidebook? Well, it's a local chain, which ought to count for something. (Ah yes, you say, but the Olive Garden was once a local chain also.) And its locations are generally where locals and visitors like to go, which ought to count for something more. (Fine, but what about all the talk about Greektown on the Danforth?) But really, it's also about a pretty decent and reliable meal at a good price. (Okay, here's where I step in: Don't go when you're in a hurry, as the kitchens tend to be uniformly slow.) But here's where the charm of Il Fornello applies: This homey bistro offers a calm environment in which friends and family meet, a respite for business travelers after a day of meetings, and a wide range of simple and flavorful pastas and pizzas that appeal to a family of picky eaters — all this for a mid-range dining-out price. Menus vary slightly from location to location, but the pizzas are thin-crust with standard and so-called gourmet toppings (including artichoke hearts, pesto and pine nuts, and escargot). Pasta dishes include a selection of linguines and fettucines and so forth, and are not overwhelmingly large. With such a varied menu, this is one place where the members of your party may want to order separate items and then swap bites.

Other locations in Toronto include 35 Elm St., just outside the Delta Chelsea (☎ **416-598-1766**); 214 King St. W., in the Entertainment District (☎ **416-977-2855**); and in The Beaches at 1968 Queen St. E. (**416-691-8377**).

576 Danforth Ave. ☎ *416-466-2931.* www.ilfornello.com. *Reservations recommended. TTC: Pape station. Main courses: C$12–C$25 (US$9.85–US$21). AE, DC, MC, V. Open: Mon–Thurs 11:30 a.m.–10 p.m., Fri 11:30 a.m.–11 p.m., Sat–Sun 10:30 a.m.–10 p.m.*

Irish Embassy Pub & Grill
$–$$$ Financial District   PUB FARE

Established in a 19th-century former bank building, this popular pub is appropriately smack-dab in the heart of Toronto's Financial District, a great location for the business lunch crowd as well as for travelers staying at the nearby Hotel Victoria or Royal York or any of the half-dozen hotels in this thriving (at least during the day) area. And its late hours make the Irish Embassy a natural destination for theatergoers exiting the St. Lawrence and Hummingbird centers just a block or so away. With both pub seating and a separate dining room, you can go for the bar menu loaded with the classic pub favorites (pizza, burgers, Irish stew, fish and chips) or the dinner menu with many of the same offerings plus a few more upscale entrees. Emphasis is on meat and potatoes, with the honors for greatest variety going to the spuds (colcannon mash and chive mash are just a couple of the options), but a couple of vegetarian entrees are available as well. If you're hoping for a relatively quiet meal (for a pub, anyway), stay away during Maple Leafs and Raptors game nights; the pub's proximity to the Air Canada Centre makes it a popular pre-game destination.

See map p. 138. 49 Yonge St. ☎ *416-866-8282.* www.irishembassypub.com. *Reservations recommended. TTC: King station. Main courses: C$11–C$15 (US$8–US$11) lunch; C$11–$C24 (US$9–US$20). AE, DC, MC, V. Open: Daily 11:30 a.m.–2 a.m.*

John's Italian Caffé
$$ Chinatown   PIZZA/ITALIAN

This restaurant is actually just outside Toronto's Chinatown, but it's a good alternative destination if you aren't in the mood for Asian cuisine. John's Italian Caffé is in a cozy little strip of eclectic eateries along a one-block stretch of Baldwin Street that is convenient to Chinatown, Kensington Market, and the Art Gallery of Ontario. A casual setting with one of the lovelier outdoor patios in the city, John's offers up an equally casual menu rich in pastas, paninis, and pizzas, with a dash of the eatery's trademark pesto (nearly all of its dishes feature the basil-intensive sauce). Pizza is available by the slice or whole (with over 40 toppings to choose from if you want to design your own), but make sure you try one of the deliciously fresh panini sandwiches, such as the chicken panini with dijon, roasted red peppers, and provolone, or the aptly named Hero panini, John's version of the stereotypical construction worker's favorite meat sandwich.

See map p. 138. 27 Baldwin St. ☎ *416-596-8848. Reservations not necessary. TTC: St. Patrick station. Main courses: C$10–C$19 (US$8.20–US$16). AE, MC, V. Open: Sun–Thurs 11 a.m.–11 p.m., Fri–Sat 11 a.m.–2 a.m.*

Lai Wah Heen
$$–$$$$ Downtown   CHINESE

The only thing typically hotelish about this hotel restaurant is its incon-sistent service, but the accolades are plentiful for this spot on the second floor of the Metropolitan Hotel — including best dim sum in North America, according to the *New York Times* and *Gourmet* magazines. Not having sampled all the dim sum in North America (or Toronto, for that matter) I can't vouch for these claims; but it's pretty good here, which makes this atypical hotel restaurant one of the few reviewed in this book. All dishes are prepared after ordering, which may account for some of the slowness in service, but also surely accounts for the freshness and flavor of each piece, from the standards, such as steamed seafood dumplings, steamed rice rolls (with seafood or meat), and fried spring rolls, to the not-so-standards, such as the luscious fried lobster roll with mango.

See map p. 138. 108 Chestnut St. ☎ 416-977-9899. www.metropolitan.com/lwh. *Reservations recommended. TTC: St. Patrick station. Main courses: C$18–C$42 (US$15–US$34); C$3.50–C$7 (US$2.85–US$5.75) dim sum. AE, DC, MC, V. Open: Daily 11:30 a.m.–3 p.m., 5:30–10:30 p.m.*

Lemon Meringue
$$–$$$$ Bloor West Village   BISTRO

For a delectable pastry or an equally delicious meal, Lemon Meringue is one of the more fashionable stops in the homespun-trendy Bloor West Village neighborhood. An evening meal can be a bit pricey, especially after an afternoon of successful shopping, so my recommendation is for a midday shopping break, with late lunch and dessert to rejuvenate those browsing-weary feet. You can't go wrong with one of the fresh salads, such as a Thai beef tenderloin salad or the inventive warm roasted vegetable and bread salad, served with goat cheese crusted with toasted pumpkin seeds. Save a bit of room for one of the signature tarts, prepared in either a shortbread or puff pastry crust and filled with several choices of fresh fruit and/or sweets. But the tarts are only one option among a sea of cream pies, mousses and crèmes brûlées, and, of course, lemon meringue. If you stroll by the restaurant during one of the neighborhood's several summer festivals (such as the Bloor West Village Festival in July), you can enjoy a refreshing glass of ice-cold fresh-squeezed lemonade for just a couple of bucks.

2390 Bloor St. W. ☎ 416-769-5757. www.lemonmeringue.com. *Reservations accepted for dinner only. TTC: Jane station. Main courses: C$11–C$14 (US$9–US$11) lunch; C$26–C$32 (US$21–US$26) dinner. AE, MC, V. Open: Tues–Fri 11 a.m.–3:30 p.m., Sat brunch 9:30 a.m.–3:30 p.m.; Tues–Thurs 5:30–10 p.m., Fri–Sat 5:30–10:30 p.m.*

Le Papillon
$$–$$$ St. Lawrence Market   QUÉBÉCOIS

A selection of more than 20 entree and dessert crêpes, a steaming mug of traditional French onion soup suffocating in a layer of pungent Swiss cheese, a starter menu rich in pâtés, and of course warm fresh breads — it's all a recipe for comfort food, French-Canadian style. For a more conventional entree, try the tourtière (a traditional Québécois meat pie filled with pork, veal, and beef) or the delightful filet de porc à la bordelaise, moist pork tenderloin served in a red wine sauce with mushrooms and red peppers. Among the crêpe offerings, the crêpe bourguignonne is a flavorful take on the boeuf bourguignon, and the crêpe Jean-Pierre features a variety of tastes with its spinach, broccoli, onion, feta cheese, and spicy tomato sauce filling. For dessert, why "settle" for a crème caramel or a sorbet (both delicious), when the crêpe banane royale is calling, with its banana, almond, and ice cream filling, covered with a sinful chocolate rum sauce and fresh whipped cream. Le Papillon is just around the corner from the St. Lawrence and Hummingbird centers, so you may want to make it a sweet post-theater dessert destination.

See map p. 138. 16 Church St. ☎ 416-363-3733. www.lepapillon.ca. *Reservations recommended. TTC: Union station. Main courses: C$14–C$25 (US$11–US$21); C$9–$14 (US$7.40–US$11) crêpes. AE, DC, MC, V. Open: Tues–Fri noon to 2:30 p.m.; Tues–Wed 5–10 p.m., Thurs 5–11 p.m., Fri 5 p.m. to midnight; Sat 11 a.m. to midnight, Sun 11 a.m.–10 p.m.*

Mövenpick Marché
$–$$ Financial District   CONTINENTAL

Located in the BCE Place building (the same building that houses the Hockey Hall of Fame), the Mövenpick Marché is an unusual dining experience, to say the least. Not quite restaurant, not quite cafeteria, the concept requires you to wander around from station to station in search of something that will pique your appetite. Food stations offer pretty standard fare — there's a salad stop, several entree stops, a dessert stop — and the theme is Swiss specialties and other European dishes. The trays are a bit on the small side, so you have to plan your meal accordingly (or else make several round-trips from your table), but you can select your ingredients on certain dishes and make small talk with the chef and other diners while your order is being prepared. Kids will enjoy the process if not the pizzas, french fries, and a few other kid-friendly items. Don't miss a stop at the dessert cart; it's the best part of the meal here.

See map p. 138. 42 Yonge St. ☎ 416-366-8986. Reservations not accepted. TTC: King station. Main courses: C$9–C$15 (US$7.40–US$12). AE, MC, V. Open: Daily 7:30 a.m.–2 a.m.

Narula's
$ India Bazaar   INDIAN

While a fair distance east from downtown, this four-block stretch of Gerrard Street East is a hectic array of restaurants, shops, and markets that cater to significant portions of Toronto's South Asian population as well as neighboring east-end communities. Especially during the weekend, it's worth a streetcar ride from downtown for the neighborhood-fair atmosphere, complete with outdoor merchandise racks and the tempting aroma of street-vendor foods ready for your order. This tiny eatery a few blocks west of Coxwell Avenue has an all-vegetarian menu that's served up cafeteria-style with few bells and whistles and plenty of ideal flavors and textures. The thali meal includes a rotating selection of three curried dishes served in a kitschy prison-style three-compartment metal plate with a side of flatbread and basmati rice. Other menu items such as poori, samosas, and nice light soups make this a delightful and inexpensive find and worth the journey out of your way. On Tuesdays, every menu item (except drinks) is just two bucks, so expect a lineup.

1438A Gerrard St. E. ☎ 416-466-0434. Reservations not accepted. TTC: 506 Carlton streetcar east. Main courses: Under C$5 (US$4.10). No credit cards. Open: Tues–Sun 12:30–9:30 p.m.

Pearl Harbourfront
$–$$ Harbourfront   CHINESE

In the Queen's Quay Terminal, an otherwise nondescript shopping center (except for the Tilley Endurables location), the Pearl is just about the best restaurant on the waterfront (except for the ultra-chic, adults-only Toulà Restaurant and Bar at the Westin Harbour Castle). Skylights add illumination and the dining room is usually busy, but the restaurant definitely has a more formal air to it than other Chinese restaurants in the city. The menu leans heavily toward Cantonese and Szechuan specialties, such as pineapple chicken fried rice — served in a carved-out pineapple — and Singapore noodles. And the dim sum is quite appetizing as well. Some Vietnamese dishes are also on the menu.

See map p. 138. 207 Queens Quay W. ☎ 416-203-1233. Reservations recommended. TTC: Union station, and then 509 Harbourfront streetcar west. Main courses: C$9–C$18 (US$7.40–US$15). AE, MC, V. Open: Daily 11 a.m.–2 p.m. for dim sum, 5–10 p.m. for dinner.

The Pilot Tavern
$–$$ Bloor/Yorkville   PUB FARE

If ever Toronto had a competition for watering-hole landmark, The Pilot would be right at the top of the list. It opened in 1944 and the World War II–inspired theme continues today in some of its décor. In 1972 The Pilot moved to its current location, bringing its original bar over with the move (legend has it that a group of Pilot regulars physically carried the bar to its new home), and the spot includes what many call the best rooftop patio in the city. The third-floor Flight Deck is open during the warmer months, and you can order from the full menu and from the full bar on deck; the view is not the greatest (lots of Bloor/Yorkville buildings in your sightline), but the atmosphere is cozy and welcoming to sun-worshipers. The menu offers above-average pub fare, from burgers to fish and chips to surprisingly tasty Thai noodles, and you don't want to miss out on the fresh-cut fries, which have established a bit of a cult following. For a weekend break from the Bloor/Yorkville shopping frenzy, The Pilot features weekend afternoon jazz, Saturday from 3:30 to 6:30 p.m. and Sunday 3 to 6 p.m.

See map p. 138. 22 Cumberland St. ☎ *416-923-5716.* www.thepilot.ca. *Reservations not necessary. TTC: Bloor–Yonge station. Main courses: C$8–C$18 (US$6.55–US$15). AE, MC, V. Open: Mon–Thurs 11–1 a.m., Fri–Sat 11 a.m.–2 a.m., Sun noon to 8 p.m.*

Queen Mother Café
$$ Queen West   THAI

Adults only are welcomed inside this dark dining area, with small intimate tables and wooden booths (although, during the summer months you can dine with kids on the lively backyard patio). But if you must leave the kids to enjoy room service back at the hotel, you must — this longtime (since 1987) local hangout is worth the sacrifice. One of the first Thai restaurants in Toronto, the Queen Mother has since incorporated other Asian and South Asian cuisines into its menu, including Laotian, Japanese, and Indian. Vegetarians are well cared for: In addition to a few menued items, many dishes (including the delectable pad thai) can be ordered vegetarian-style. The pad thai (or any of the noodle dishes) is a good bet, but don't overlook entrees such as the ping gai (marinated chicken breast served with a spicy lime coriander sauce) or the seafood hot pot (an assortment of fresh fish, shrimp, and calamari simmered with veggies in a curry coconut sauce).

See map p. 138. 206 Queen St. W. ☎ *416-598-4719. Reservations not accepted. TTC: Osgoode station. Main courses: C$10–C$19 (US$8.20–US$16). AE, MC, V. Open: Mon–Sat 11:30 a.m.–1 a.m., Sun noon to midnight.*

Quigley's
$–$$ The Beaches   BISTRO

Quigley's has one of the least hectic outdoor patios in the city: it's situated on a relatively quiet corner at the east end of The Beaches where the foot traffic is mostly made up of local residents, the vehicle traffic is fairly light, and you don't get the flow of residents, tourists, and workers that you find at more central locations. And really, the three-tiered patio here is just about the only reason to stop at Quigley's. (Indoor seating is limited to the bar in front and a narrow bank of tables in the back.) The food is reliable, if not remarkable, with a variety of salads, pastas, and Asian-inspired dishes taking up the most space on the menu. The single-serving thin-crust pizzas are a good choice; try the grilled chicken (with peppers, zucchini, smoked bacon, and chevre, among other toppings) and the Mediterranean (with green olives, artichokes, capers, and feta) and then share them amongst yourselves. Jazz musicians perform on Sunday afternoons and evenings.

2232 Queen St. E. ☎ *416-699-9998. Reservations not accepted. TTC: 501 Queen streetcar east. Main courses: C$7–C$20 (US$5.75–US$16). AE, MC, V. Open: Mon–Fri 11 a.m.–2 a.m., Sat–Sun 9 a.m.–2 a.m.*

The Real Jerk
$–$$ Queen East   CARIBBEAN

With its corrugated metal awnings, vinyl tablecloths, and even "palm trees," you'd almost think that you'd stepped off the Queen East streetcar and into an out-of-the-way eatery on some lightly traveled road on a Caribbean island. Well, maybe not. But the food and atmosphere will at least help you reminisce about some little place that you did happen to find when last in the Cayman Islands or Jamaica. The variety of dishes offered is just about the greatest in the city, ranging from starters such as patties, fried plantain, and cod fritters to nine selections of rotis to curry and jerk meat, seafood, and vegetarian entrees. You can even find ackee and codfish on the menu here. You can't miss on any of the rotis, and the jerk chicken is appropriately spicy and flavorful; for something a little lower on the heat gauge, go for one of the curried dishes. And if you have the option to add rice and peas to your entree, go for it; in my opinion, the dish, when done well, is the Caribbean's greatest contribution to good eating — and The Real Jerk does it well.

709 Queen St. E. ☎ 416-463-6055. Reservations not needed. TTC: 501 Queen streetcar east. Main courses: C$8–C$14 (US$6.55–US$11). AE, MC, V. Open: Mon 11:30 a.m.–10 p.m., Tues 11:30 a.m.–11 p.m., Wed–Thurs 11:30 a.m. to midnight, Fri 11:30–1 a.m., Sat 2 p.m.–1 a.m., Sun 3–11 p.m.

Rebel House
$–$$ Rosedale   PUB FARE

Just slightly off the beaten path — at least the beaten path as taken by this book — the Rebel House is a bit of a local's hangout. And it's designed as such, with two very narrow dining levels that don't accommodate too many customers (though the back patio helps out during warmer months). As with any good tavern, the beer is the draw here, with a great selection of Ontario microbrews to go along with the more traditional national and international brands. Foodwise, it's fairly atypical pub fare, focusing instead on Canadian fare, which is almost as prevalent as the beer. You may consider the venison braised in dark ale; old-fashioned meatloaf, served with roasted-onion mashed potatoes, lima bean succotash, and mushroom gravy; lamb and ale stew; and other comfort foods. The Rebel House is known for its poutine, a Québécois dish that's somewhat similar to the cheesy fries you may find in the U.S. It's french fries mixed with cheese curds and covered with gravy — an acquired taste.

1068 Yonge St. ☎ 416-927-0704. Reservations not accepted. TTC: Rosedale station. Main courses: C$8–C$18 (US$6.55–US$15). AE, MC, V. Open: Mon–Sat 11:30 a.m.–11 p.m., Sun 11:30 a.m.–10 p.m.

Reuben S.

$–$$ **Entertainment District   DELI**

Walk through the front door here and you'll hear a voice booming out to you, "Any table! Help yourself!" Classy, this place is not. "Have you been here before? You like smoked meat? You gotta get the combo — comes with fries and slaw." Did I mention the booming voice? "How about a cold Black Cherry with that?" Smoked meat is the name of the game here at Reuben S. They use only Schwartz meats out of Montreal, which are brined and smoked on-site; ask for a quick tour — if they're not too busy, you'll likely get a look at the smoker. (Corned beef, smoked veal, beef tongue, and spiced turkey breast are also smoked on-site.) The nearly 3-inch-tall sand-wiches pack in just the right mix of lean and fat to achieve perfectly moist smoked meat on rye. Smoked meat is even offered as a side on the grilled dinner entrees (rib steak and grilled chicken, for example). And yes, do get the combo: the fries are fresh cut and the slaw is vinegar- not mayo-based.

See map p. 138. 327 King St. W. ☎ *416-596-9201. Reservations not accepted. TTC: St. Andrew station. Main courses: C$6–C$17 (US$4.90–US$14). AE, DC, MC, V. Open: Sun–Tues 11 a.m.–4 p.m., Wed–Sat 11 a.m.–9 p.m.*

The Rivoli

$–$$ **Queen West   BISTRO**

Operated by the same folks who run the nearby Queen Mother Café (with the same adults-only restriction — except on its outdoor patio), The Rivoli is a bit of a multiplex entertainment venue that just happens to serve an Asian fusion cuisine as a little sidebar. (Actually, the Side Bar is The Rivoli's on-site version of a martini bar that also serves as a DJ-led music hall on Thursdays through Saturdays.) An upstairs pool hall has 13 tables mixed in with a separate bar and lounge that features nightly music. And the famed Rivoli Backroom has hosted an eclectic mix of music, comedy, readings, and, more recently, monthly writers' discussion groups (titled "This is not a reading series") hosted in association with Pages Books & Magazines down the street. The Backroom has played host to such rising (at the time) acts as the Indigo Girls, Beck, and Blue Rodeo. The food? Well, in this intimate and casual bistro environment the emphasis is on South Asian, Caribbean, and continental, as well as some good vegetarian offerings (the vegan filet mignon is Asian-inspired: a tofu steak marinated in Asian spices and served with a miso gravy). Noodle dishes are also a good bet, or go for the Rivoli Burger, served on an egg bun and topped with caramelized onions.

See map p. 138. 332 Queen St. W. ☎ *416-597-0794.* http://rivoli.ca/. *Reservations not accepted. TTC: Osgoode station, and then 501 Queen streetcar west. Main courses: C$8–C$10 (US$6.55–US$8.20) lunch, C$14–C$20 (US$11–US$16) dinner. AE, MC, V. Open: Daily 11:30 a.m.–2 a.m.*

Sassafraz
$$-$$$$ Bloor/Yorkville CONTINENTAL

This restaurant has taken a critical beating in recent years, though a change in ownership (and chef) is starting to bring back a bit of the buzz. It's still one of the best spots in Toronto for people-watching, if not necessarily the best for fine food. Your best bet is to stay away during dinner, consider it for (highly priced) lunch on a sunny day when you can bask at one of its outdoor tables (try the jerk chicken salad served with plantain chips or the Caesar salad offered with tortilla strips instead of those inconsistent croutons), or make it a stop for a weekend brunch, which is more casual and less pricey and served up with live jazz on both Saturdays and Sundays. The French toast is prepared with egg bread and served with a wildberry compote and orange and vanilla whipped cream, and the huevos rancheros features chorizo sausage and a tasty chipotle pico de gallo.

See map p. 138. 100 Cumberland St. ☎ *416-964-2222.* www.sassafraz.ca. *Reservations recommended. TTC: Bay station. Main courses: C$17–C$26 (US$14–US$21) lunch, C$24–C$39 (US$20–US$32) dinner; C$14–C$25 (US$11–US$21) brunch. AE, DC, MC, V. Open: Daily 11:30 a.m.–2 a.m.*

Senator Diner
$-$$ Downtown DINER

This self-proclaimed Toronto landmark (claiming to be the city's oldest restaurant, dating from 1928) looks every bit the part of a mature downtown neighborhood eatery, down to the high ceilings, Formica tabletops, counter seating, and checkerboard-patterned linoleum floors. The Senator also offers the status quo diner-type offerings (entrees is not a term that easily rolls off the tongue when discussing diner food) such as corned beef hash, meatloaf, chili, and made-to-order burgers. There's also a very commendable fish and chips, which may or may not qualify as diner food but definitely qualifies as a good bet here, with its fresh halibut and not-too-greasy chips. Some other un-diner-like items have also made their way onto the menu, though you're probably better off sticking with the standard greasy-spoon fare. Jazz musicians perform upstairs Tuesdays through Sundays at Top O' The Senator (see Chapter 16).

See map p. 138. 253 Victoria St. ☎ *416-364-7517. Reservations not necessary. TTC: Dundas station. Main courses: C$8–C$15 (US$6.55–US$12). AE, MC, V. Open: Mon–Fri 7:30 a.m.–3 p.m., Sat–Sun 8 a.m.–3 p.m.; Tues–Sat 5–10 p.m.*

Sushi Inn
$-$$ Bloor/Yorkville JAPANESE

For just about the most reasonable Japanese meal in Toronto — in price, service, and efficiency — the Sushi Inn delivers good and fresh sushi, huge and beautifully presented bento boxes, and tender teriyaki. And the location is great for a quick meal during a day of shopping or before an evening of carousing in the trendy Bloor/Yorkville neighborhood. The seating area is small, and tables are crammed together trying to fill every possible nook and cranny, so you may need to wait without a reservation, but be patient (or make a later reservation and do some more shopping) — what awaits you is worth it. The edamame starter dish is heaping and served piping hot; the California rolls are among the best in Toronto. For your main course, the highlight of the fabulous bento boxes (the silver box is a good choice) is the beautiful tempura vegetables, again, served piping — no, blisteringly — hot, so your palate will appreciate your breaking them up before biting into them. Chicken or beef teriyaki are equally appetizing and tender, served with just the right amount of sauce (that is, not smothered). And save room for a small scoop of green-tea ice cream — very refreshing.

See map p. 138. 120 Cumberland St. ☎ 416-923-9992. Reservations recommended. TTC: Bay station. Main courses: C$7–C$17 (US$5.75–US$14). AE, MC, V. Open: Sun–Thurs 11:30 a.m.–11:30 p.m., Fri–Sat 11:30 a.m. to midnight.

Tulip Steak House
$–$$ Queen East   DINER

The name is a bit of a misnomer — the Tulip is not your typical steakhouse in the Morton's or Ruth's Chris or Barberian's manner. The Tulip's menu does feature a few steaks, reasonably priced if not reasonably tender, but the real draw here is good, old-fashioned greasy-spoon diner fare, headlined by sizable breakfasts and delivered by efficient waitresses. Expect a long lineup out the door for the weekend breakfast hours. It's been around for over 50 years (which you won't need to question, once you see its 1950s vinyl seating décor), and it's worth a quick stop in the morning on your way to The Beaches (just hop off the 501 Queen streetcar at Coxwell Avenue, about ten blocks west of where The Beaches' action is). If you must go for a steak, the T-bone is the best bet here; it's big and juicy and the fat just glistens when it's hot off the grill.

1606 Queen St. E. ☎ 416-469-5797. Reservations not accepted. TTC: 501 Queen streetcar east. Main courses: C$7–C$18 (US$5.75–US$15). AE, DC, MC, V. Open: Mon–Sat 7 a.m. to midnight, Sun 7 a.m.–11 p.m.

Wayne Gretzky's Restaurant
$$–$$$ Entertainment District   CANADIAN

You probably couldn't place this restaurant in a more ideal setting if you set it down in the middle of Maple Leaf Gardens. It's just steps from the Rogers Centre (formerly known as the SkyDome), a few more steps from the Air Canada Centre, and right in the heart of Toronto's most touristy restaurant region. The food is above-average theme-restaurant fare; this is the kind of place where you can't go wrong with a burger and fries or even a nice salad, but keep clear of the dishes that require a more deft culinary touch. And the entrees are on the spendy side, but about what you'd expect when you have a place like this that is driven more by celebrity than by cuisine. Nevertheless, older kids especially will have a great time gawking at the Great One's memorabilia, whiling away the food preparation time at an air hockey table, or just taking in the whole restaurant-cum-sports bar experience (even if they can't get into the sports bar proper). Summer diners can enjoy the Oasis, the restaurant's rooftop patio.

See map p. 138. 99 Blue Jays Way. ☎ **416-979-PUCK.** *Reservations recommended. TTC: St. Andrew station. Main courses: C$10–C$25 (US$8.20–US$21). AE, MC, V. Open: Mon–Thurs 11:30–1 a.m., Fri–Sat 11:30 a.m.–2 a.m., Sun 11:30 a.m.–11 p.m.*

Dining and Snacking on the Go

Eating on the go is as Canadian as, well, Swiss Chalet. Not that you'd really want to make a quick dash for one of the many Swiss Chalets in and around downtown Toronto; the rotisserie-intensive, quasi-fast-food, quasi-sit-down chain is actually an adequate choice for a quick and fairly inexpensive meal, especially for families. But you can find a much greater variety of cheap eats and meals on the go while making your way around town. This chapter helps you know where to look.

For the location of many of the places discussed in this section, refer to the "Toronto Dining" map earlier in this chapter.

Why stopping to eat doesn't have to slow you down

You're on a roll. It's your designated shopping day while in Toronto, and you just can't face the idea that you have to set the shopping bags down for a bite to eat. Besides, isn't all that mall or department store food just plain dull? Well, that's not necessarily so. Between the many neighborhood shopping districts, with shopper-friendly (read: quick) eateries nearby, and a few in-store surprises, you can have a pretty decent meal for a fair price and get right back to the shopping racks.

The following list offers a few suggestions on opportunities for eating out while on the shopping trail (for details on Toronto's major shopping destinations, check out Chapter 12):

✔ **Antiques on Queen East:** The more underrated of the two antiques shopping districts on Queen Street (see Chapter 12), this area between Carlaw Avenue and Leslie Street features nearly a dozen small and eclectic stores (look for the sidewalk displays of recently purchased items). Head west on Queen to **Hello Toast,** 993 Queen St. E., one block east of Carlaw (☎ **416-778-7299**) for an adequate weekday lunch. Better yet, plan for a weekend shopping day in this area and begin with Hello Toast's justifiably renowned brunch. You'll need to get there before it opens (at 10 a.m.) to avoid the long lines of locals, but the cinnamon French toast is well worth the effort. For Caribbean cuisine, including a great selection of rotis, head farther west on Queen to **The Real Jerk,** 709 Queen St. E., at Broadview (☎ **416-463-6055**). It's a slightly longer hike — and you'll pass an adult entertainment venue on the way — but The Real Jerk offers the best variety of Caribbean cuisine in Toronto.

Snacking for the health-conscious shopper

When spending time in Toronto's neighborhoods — shopping or just walking around — you can pick up a healthy snack quite easily, and it won't take much time out of your schedule. Just pop in to one of the several fruit and vegetable stands (storefronts, really) that cater primarily to local residents. For a reasonable price you can pick up a pint of strawberries, a couple bananas, maybe even a bag of baby carrots; while you're there, pick up a small bunch or bouquet of flowers to spruce up your hotel room. If you're concerned about the cleanliness of your fruit and veggies, grab a couple of bottles of water so you can rinse off your stash while sitting at a nearby park bench.

✔ **Department-store souvlaki?** It's not where you'd expect to find surprisingly appetizing souvlaki, but the aisleside cafe on the lower level of **The Bay** on Queen and Yonge streets (also accessible via the PATH walkway) is the exception that proves the rule. This cafe is so low-profile it doesn't even have a name. If you're not in the mood for Greek, the amazingly diverse menu also includes rotis, lasagna, jerk chicken, and meat patties, with entrees ranging in price from C$6 to C$9 (US$4.90–US$7.40).

✔ **Queen West alternative(s):** The stretch of Queen Street West from University to Spadina avenues has dining alternatives as diverse as the free range of shops and services along what was once the most "alternative" strip in Toronto. For a healthy option, Fresh by Juice for Life, 336 Queen St. W. (☎ **416-599-4442**), is a vegetarian chain that does a thriving takeaway business and features rice bowls, salads, and wraps (C$6–C$9/US$4.90–US$7.40) to accompany its dozens of juice and soy shake offerings. There are two other locations: 521 Bloor St. W. (☎ **416-531-2635**) and 894 Queen St. W. (☎ **416-913-2720**).

Where to look for the best of these "health food" outlets? Almost any neighborhood shopping district will do, but head for Bloor West Village (try the **Green Thumb Fruit Market**, 2294 Bloor St. W., in the heart of this popular shopping district), or find the best of the best in the Kensington Market neighborhood (such as the **Oxford Fruit** stand at 255 Augusta Ave.).

Locating Toronto's hidden gems for cheap eats

Need to satisfy your pizza craving? Are you committed to your vacation habit of finding the best fish and chips wherever you are? What about local breakfast haunts, or terrific (and terrifically inexpensive) Chinese, or a good local burger? Or maybe you're just curious about where to sample reasonably priced food that reflects the city's cultural diversity? This section directs you to a few inexpensive Toronto dining landmarks.

Frying up the fish and chips debate

Not much can rile up a bunch of dedicated gourmands more than a discussion about the best fish and chips: a similar debate rages on in Toronto. The old standby — Len Duckworth's, which has been around for 70-plus years — has longevity and loyalty on its side, not to mention the basic grease-stained brown-paper-bag mentality that appeals to the working-class chippy. Not in its favor are its two locations on the east side that attract plenty of locals and not too many others (2638 Danforth Ave.; ☎ 416-699-5865; and 2282 Kingston Rd.; ☎ 416-266-0033).

Two newer entries in this city's fish and chips wars can be found in slightly more visitor-friendly environs. At **White Bros. Fish Co.** in The Beaches (2248 Queen St. E.; ☎ 416-694-3474), halibut is the whitefish of choice, accompanied by not-too-greasy fresh-cut fries and fresh salads and chowder. This location is on the eastern fringes of the heavily foot-trafficked neighborhood, but it's small enough to regularly attract lineups outside its door. It's open Tuesday through Sunday, 4 to 9 p.m. (Fridays noon to 9 p.m.).

Chippy's, on the other side of town but also on the fringes of a popular Queen Street neighborhood (893 Queen St. W.; ☎ 416-866-7474), tries to raise the bar for fish and chips establishments by offering salmon and shellfish as alternatives to the preferred (at least to this writer) halibut or even cod. Prices are a bit higher as well, raising the fish and chips threshold dangerously close to the ten-dollar line. Chippy's is open Monday through Thursday, noon to 9 p.m., and Friday and Saturday until 11 p.m..

For fish and chips in a pub setting, inconsistency is the watchword, but you do get to enjoy the benefit of proximity to a number of Toronto attractions. One good option is the **Jersey Giant** (71 Front St. E.; ☎ 416-368-4095), ideally located for fish and chips and a pint following a morning at the St. Lawrence Market.

Sampling from a cultural smorgasbord

With the diversity of its population ever expanding, it's impossible to list all the choices that are on Toronto's ethnic buffet. So here are just a few of the city's more popular (and easily accessible) and inexpensive alternatives:

> ✔ **Rotis:** To call this delight a "Caribbean burrito" is unfair, though the origin of the description is easy to understand (a usually curried filling is engulfed in a tortilla or similar kind of flatbread and folded up not unlike a burrito). **The Real Jerk** (709 Queen St. E.; ☎ 416-463-6055) is worth a trip to the east end of downtown (hop on the Queen streetcar heading east) for one of its nine rotis, all under C$7 (US$5.75). A little pricier, and on the opposite end of

Queen, **Ghandi's** (554 Queen St. W.; ☎ 416-504-8155) offers a nice selection of Indian rotis.

✔ **Shawarmas and falafels:** Middle-Eastern eateries are popping up all over Toronto in small storefront and market booths, and these tasty pita sandwiches are uniformly cheap and made-to-order. **Mediterranean to Go**, practically hiding in a miniature restaurant row just south of the Delta Chelsea (4 Elm St.; ☎ 416-585-9276), is not exactly the most welcoming place in the city, but the offerings are fresh, the sauces generously applied, and the prices low. In the Annex, **Ghazale's** (504 Bloor St. W.; ☎ 416-537-4417) has good falafels, but the chicken shawarmas are the draw; both are under four bucks.

✔ **Sample 'em all:** Head for **Kensington Market,** where you'll find ethnic food places scattered throughout. Work your way through the maze of storefronts and people for Caribbean, Portuguese, Chinese, and more in the way of cultural sampling.

Picking up a pizza

For variety — and amazing pizza — you can't pass up **Amato** (534 Queen St. W.; ☎ 416-703-8989). It's on the western edge of the funky Queen Street West neighborhood, and the atmosphere takes its cue from its surroundings. With plenty of seating for large groups and families, and a wide variety of toppings and side dishes, Amato is a casual and comfortable respite to recharge your calorie reserves after a few hours' traipsing up and down this eclectic shopping strip. A number of locations scattered throughout the city offer 24 varieties of pizza for just C$3.50 (US$2.85) a slice, including one shop near Yonge and College (429 Yonge St.; ☎ 416-977-8989), on the northern edge of downtown, and a takeout-only booth tucked away in a small mini food court farther east in the heart of Queen Street West (238 Queen St. W.; ☎ 416-591-6661).

On the east side of town, two neighborhood pie-makers deserve a mention. **Magic Oven,** just north of the Danforth (788 Broadview Ave.; ☎ 416-466-0111), offers the best crust in town, with whole-grain or organic options, and a huge variety of vegetarian specialty pizzas. And the meat pizzas aren't too shabby either. In The Beaches — the Upper Beaches, actually — tables at **The Copper Pipe Pizza Pub** fill quickly in its small storefront location on Kingston Road, about a half mile north of Queen Street (924 Kingston Rd.; ☎ 416-690-6081). Locals come back regularly for the thin crust and gourmet toppings, as well as the two-for-one pizzas on Tuesday nights. If you're in a hurry, keep in mind that service can be touch-and-go, especially on those Tuesday nights.

Each of the above locations offers limited delivery, so you may be out of luck if you want to have one of these pies delivered to your hotel. If you're going the delivery route your options are plentiful, but the best pizza of the most widely available delivery outlets is **Pizza Nova** (16 locations in Toronto; for delivery, call ☎ 416-439-0000), with the most consistently fresh toppings and a surprisingly good Caesar salad.

Omelettes and onion rings

No, not together — though if you find a place that offers onion rings as a substitute for seasoned home fries, let me know.

If you've tired of room service or your hotel's buffet choices, or you merely want a late-morning, greasy-spoon, bacon-and-egg breakfast instead of a midday lunch in a crowded bistro, head for The Beaches and the **Sunset Grill** (2006 Queen St. E.; ☎ 416-690-9985). This cozy eatery — open for breakfast and lunch only — turns around quick and large-portioned breakfasts at very reasonable prices, especially if you're in time for the breakfast specials (they end at 10 a.m.). Omelettes are huge — leaving little room on your plate for the seasoned home fries — though occasionally they're a little heavy on the cheese, making them a bit too greasy. For a nice alternative, try one of their egg-white frittatas: light and fluffy and with a little more topping variety. Expect a long lineup on weekend mornings, and don't count on using your American Express (or your Visa, for that matter); the Sunset Grill takes cash only.

What once was Flo's Diner, in an old-fashioned diner-style building, is now just **Flo's** (70 Yorkville Ave.; ☎ 416-961-4333), in a much less interesting location above a Great Canadian Bagel Company outlet in the tony Bloor/Yorkville neighborhood — though its access via a winding, narrow, outdoor, metal staircase is an adventure (you can also get to Flo's via an inside elevator). The menu remains diner-ish, with upscale flourishes (see the complete review earlier in this chapter), and breakfasts are no exception. No watered-down diner coffee here — it's dark and strong and freshly brewed — and fresh juices are standard, as are refreshing smoothies incorporating those juices. You won't get the speedy service of a typical diner either, but bring the morning paper — it's worth the wait.

For burgers (and onion rings) look for **Lick's**, a Toronto fast-food institution with a dozen locations, including the perpetually busy branch in The Beaches (1960 Queen St. E.; ☎ 416-362-5425) and the uptown outlet near Yonge and Eglinton. Or stop at the Kingston Road location (2383 Kingston Rd.) on your way to or from the Toronto Zoo. Go for the atmosphere as much as for the food; while you wait for your order you can enjoy the serenade from Lick's employees, who put a whole new spin on the expression "whistle while you work." Burgers (including chicken, turkey, and vegetarian options) are grilled while you wait, and you can select from a variety of condiments. Attention, U.S. burger consumers: Don't expect the bland, almost tasteless patty you find at American burger stalwarts; Lick's "Homeburgers" are flavored with spices to add a little zest to your burger experience. If you want to avoid the zest, try the chicken burgers ("Chick'n Lick'n"), with just plain ol' barbecue sauce.

Another made-to-order burger location is **Groucho's Gourmet Burgers** (1574 Bayview Ave.; ☎ 416-482-3456) in the Leaside neighborhood. In addition to the fresh ground beef grilled to your specifications, fresh toppings are the draw here. Go gourmet with your burger by adding such accompaniments as roasted garlic, sun-dried tomatoes, and sautéed mushrooms, eggplant, and sweet peppers.

Spotting the fry truck (and other street vendors)

Ah, there's nothing like strolling casually through Nathan Phillips Square in July, admiring the innovative creativity of the artists participating in the annual Toronto Outdoor Art Exhibition, the smell of grease wafting through the air. Yes, welcome to downtown Toronto, where the fry truck is both a meeting place ("meet me at 12:15 in front of the fry truck") and a welcome, if somewhat oily, treat for a weary traveler. For just a few bucks (depending on the size of your order you'll pay anywhere from C$2.50–C$4.00/US$2.05–US$3.30), you can leave with a near armload of french fries. Make sure to load up on the condiments you desire: malt vinegar, salt, ketchup, mayo, mustard — it's all there.

Of course, you can find **fry trucks** in Toronto locations other than on Queen Street beside Nathan Phillips Square — they are fry *trucks,* after all — especially at outdoor draws such as Ontario Place and Exhibition Place. It's comforting to know that if you're ice skating at Nathan Phillips Square in winter the fry truck will be there, ready to sell you a helping of nice warm fries. Fry trucks offer more than just fries — including sodas to drink with your fries, hot dogs or burgers to accompany your fries, or even onion rings — but what people line up for are the fresh-cut, piping-hot fries; save your hot dog fix for Shopsy's, the ubiquitous **hot dog vendors**.

Some days, it seems as if you see a **Shopsy's** cart on every street corner in the city. The hot dogs are actually quite good — not a bad way to refuel if you're on foot and don't want to slow down to eat lunch. Each dog (usually beef, though veggie or chicken dogs are also available) has been previously boiled (some vendors have a grill to warm up your dog after you order) and is scored diagonally across the top before being served on a steamed roll. The vendors offer a variety of condiments to dress up your dog, though by the end of a lunch hour the bins can seem pretty well picked over. I'm partial to the banana peppers and red peppers, green olives, and sliced tomatoes, but other offerings include sauerkraut, chopped onions, sweet relish, and, for some unknown reason, bacon bits. For two bucks (or three, with a can of soda), you have yourself a pretty appetizing meal or snack.

You may also run across the occasional corn-on-the-cob vendor, or one of the handful of Chinese-food carts around town (try St. George Street near the University of Toronto for the greatest selection). And in the heat of summer, you'll be able to dig up an ice cream treat or three. But for the ultimate street feast, make your way to one of several outdoor "Taste of" festivals in the city, such as the Taste of the Danforth or the Taste of Little Italy. Check out Chapter 3 for more details.

Giving in to the Canadian doughnut obsession

What is it about Canada and doughnuts? No one really knows for sure, but doughnuts are an integral part of the Canadian diet. Any doubt about their place in society was washed away at the opening of Ontario's first Krispy Kreme (a U.S.–based doughnut chain) outlet in Mississauga (a suburb of Toronto) in 2001. The store's first-day sales set a company-wide record, beating out opening-day sales figures for any of the chain's U.S. stores.

With only 14 stores in Canada — and none in Toronto proper — Krispy Kreme is not yet ready to challenge the supremacy of Canada's undisputed doughnut king, **Tim Hortons.** Founded in 1964 by Tim Horton (a 22-year veteran of the National Hockey League) and now owned by Wendy's International, the chain has more than 2,000 outlets across Canada and has extended its product line over the years to include bagels, muffins, sandwiches, and soups. Tim Hortons coffee — definitely *not* gourmet, but decent nonetheless — has legions of Canadian devotees who speak the language of the "double double" (that's two creams, two sugars).

Tim Hortons will probably disappoint those who've come to observe the true Canadian doughnut phenomenon in Toronto. Its expansion has been at the expense of the kind of small-town, meet-for-a-coffee-and-a-smoke, gossip-central feel that the mom-and-pop shops — and even some of the other chains — still have (facilitated by their separate smoking rooms). Other Toronto-area doughnut dealers include **Coffee Time, Country Donut,** and **Baker's Dozen,** which usually ends up with the "Best Donuts in Toronto" award whenever some local scribe is inclined to conduct a tongue-in-cheek review.

Sipping coffee and watching people

Yes, of course, **Starbucks** has one or two or eighty locations in Toronto. And they're generally all in convenient spots for a coffee and/or pastry break from sightseeing or shopping. But you don't have to give in to the arabica monolith to get a good cup of coffee here. A couple of Canadian coffeehouse chains are almost as prolific in Toronto as Starbucks — many a street corner has two or three of the competing chains within view of each other — and the city is home to a number of excellent independent shops that I heartily recommend.

First, the competing chains. **Timothy's World Coffee** started out in Toronto in the mid-1970s and now has over 60 locations in the Greater Toronto Area. A smaller, neighborhood-style coffeehouse, **PAM's Coffee & Tea** has nearly a dozen locations in the GTA. And the ugly stepsister of Toronto's coffee community — more for its aggressive expansion strategies and not the quality of its coffee, which I think is the best of these three options — **Second Cup** has well over 100 locations in the Toronto area, including storefronts in all area Home Depot stores.

For the freshest coffee — and to experience the greatest variety of flavor — you have to seek out the independent coffee shops that roast their own beans on-site. Here are the best that Toronto has to offer:

- ✔ Located in the recently rejuvenated Distillery District, **Balzac's Coffee** (55 Mill St.; ☎ 416-207-1709; www.balzacscoffee.com) is quickly establishing a reputation for roasting Toronto's best coffee — after years of successful roasting at its Stratford location (see Chapter 14).

- ✔ **Moonbean Coffee Company** (30 St. Andrews St.; ☎ 416-595-0327; www.moonbeancoffee.com) in Kensington Market offers juices, smoothies, and vegetarian-inspired finger foods to go along with its own blends and organic coffees.

- ✔ Staking its claim as the first on-site roastery in Toronto, **Coffee Tree Roastery** (2412 Bloor St. W.; ☎ 416-767-1077; www.coffeetree.ca) has been churning out rich coffee, such as the intensely flavored Millionaires Mixture, for nearly 20 years in Bloor West Village.

Having dessert first

Given Toronto's culinary success, it's not surprising that dessert lovers may also be equally pleased with what generally follows the main course at Toronto's finest restaurants. However, you can also find plenty of places that are more than happy to satisfy your sweet tooth — without all the preliminaries. Here are a few:

- ✔ While the **Bread and Roses Bakery** (2232 Bloor St. W.; ☎ 416-769-9898) features perfectly fine fresh breads, muffins, and other baked goods (as well as a nice cafe menu), the chocolate macaroons alone make the inevitable queue worth waiting out.

- ✔ Near the far eastern edge of The Beaches, **Ed's Real Scoop** (2224 Queen St. E.; ☎ 416-699-6100; www.edsrealscoop.com) lures ice-cream lovers to the eastern edge of The Beaches. The rich ice cream is made on-site, and flavors alternate by the week. If your timing is right, try the strawberry-rhubarb or the Callebaut milk chocolate — and then take a pint for the walk back.

- ✔ You can't mention **Greg's Ice Cream** (750 Spadina Ave.; ☎ 416-961-4734) in The Annex neighborhood without including these two simple words: roasted marshmallow. That flavor — and other odd yet equally inspiring creations — keeps Torontonians coming back year after year.

- ✔ It's a bit west of the downtown core, but the gelato at **La Paloma Gelateria & Café** (1357 St. Clair Rd. W.; ☎ 416-656-2340) justifies the cab ride. For true decadence it's hard to surpass the Ferrero Rocher, but the 50-plus other flavors take a good run at it.

- For its wide selection of takeaway sweets, ice cream, and popcorn (including caramel corn), kids will love the two locations of the **Nutty Chocolatier** (144 Yonge St.; ☎ **416-363-9009;** and 2179 Queen St. E., in The Beaches; ☎ **416-698-5548**). Loose chocolates are available by the gram (or pound), popular packaged chocolates and candies cater to the kids, and expat-Brits can satisfy their yen for British sweets.

- **Sen5es Bakery** (318 Wellington St. W.; ☎ **416-961-0055**), located on the main floor of the Soho Metropolitan Hotel, presents beautifully prepared — and pricey — desserts, with an emphasis on style (sometimes to the detriment of substance). The Raspberry Vanilla Bavarian and the Passionfruit Charlotte stunningly achieve both. Don't bother with the weak coffee; get your sweets to go and have coffee at a nearby Starbucks or Second Cup.

- Between Ed's Real Scoop (discussed above) and **Wanda's Pie in the Sky** (7A Yorkville Ave.; ☎ **416-925-7437**), located in the Bloor/Yorkville neighborhood, this advocate of all things strawberry and rhubarb can find contentment. Dozens of other fillings are regularly featured at this popular cafe, along with an assortment of cakes and cookies.

Index of Restaurants by Neighborhood

The Annex
Bedford Academy (Pub Fare, $–$$)
Dos Amigos (Mexican, $$–$$$)

The Beaches
Akane-ya (Japanese, $$)
Garden Gate Restaurant (Chinese, $)
Il Fornello (Italian, $$–$$$)
Quigley's (Bistro, $–$$)

Bloor West Village
Lemon Meringue (Bistro, $$–$$$$)

Bloor/Yorkville
Café Nervosa (Italian, $$–$$$)
Flo's (Diner, $–$$)
The Pilot Tavern (Pub Fare, $–$$)
Sassafraz (Continental, $$–$$$$)
Sushi Inn (Japanese, $–$$)

Chinatown
Happy Seven (Chinese, $)
John's Italian Caffe (Pizza/Italian, $$)

The Danforth
Allen's (Irish-American, $$–$$$)
Il Fornello (Italian, $$–$$$)

Distillery District
Brick Street Bakery (Light Fare, $)

Downtown
360 Revolving Restaurant (Continental, $$$–$$$$)
Adega (Portuguese, $$–$$$)
Bangkok Garden (Thai, $$–$$$$)
Barberian's (Steakhouse, $$$–$$$$)
Il Fornello (Italian, $$–$$$)
Lai Wah Heen (Chinese, $$–$$$$)
The Senator (Diner, $–$$)

Entertainment District
Alice Fazooli's! Italian Crabshack (Italian, $–$$$)
Big Daddy's (Cajun, $–$$$)
Dhaba (Indian, $–$$)
Dunn's Famous Bar & Grill (Deli, $–$$)
Fred's Not Here (Eclectic, $$–$$$)

Il Fornello (Italian, $$–$$$)
Reuben S. (Deli, $–$$)
Wayne Gretzky's Restaurant (Canadian, $$–$$$)

Financial District

Biff's (Continental, $$–$$$$)
Irish Embassy Pub & Grill (Pub Fare, $–$$$)
Mövenpick Marché (Continental, $–$$)

Harbourfront

Pearl Harbourfront (Chinese, $–$$)

India Bazaar

Narula's (Indian, $)

Leaside

Fiesta Azteca (Mexican, $–$$)

Little Italy

Aunties and Uncles (Breakfast/Light Fare, $)

Rosedale

Rebel House (Pub Fare, $–$$)

Queen East

Bonjour Brioche (Bakery/Cafe, $)
Hello Toast (Brunch/Light Fare, $–$$)
The Real Jerk (Caribbean, $–$$)
Tulip Steak House (Diner, $–$$)

Queen West

Babur (Indian, $–$$)
The Black Bull (Pub Fare, $–$$)
Fressen (Vegetarian, $$)
Queen Mother Cafe (Thai, $$)
The Rivoli (Bistro, $–$$)

St. Lawrence Market

C'est What? (Pub Fare, $–$$)
Hernando's Hideaway (Mexican, $–$$)
Le Papillon (Québécois, $$–$$$)

Index of Restaurants by Cuisine

Bistro

Lemon Meringue (Bloor West Village, $$–$$$$)
Quigley's (The Beaches, $–$$)
The Rivoli (Queen West, $–$$)

Breakfast

Aunties and Uncles (Little Italy, $)
Bonjour Brioche (Queen East, $)

Brunch

Hello Toast (Queen East, $–$$)

Cajun

Big Daddy's (Entertainment District, $–$$$)

Canadian

Wayne Gretzky's Restaurant (Entertainment District, $$–$$$)

Caribbean

The Real Jerk (Queen East, $–$$)

Chinese

Garden Gate Restaurant (The Beaches, $)
Happy Seven (Chinatown, $)
Lai Wah Heen (Downtown, $$–$$$$)
Pearl Harbourfront (Harbourfront, $–$$)

Continental

360 Revolving Restaurant (Downtown, $$$–$$$$)

Biff's (Financial District, $$–$$$$)
Mövenpick Marché (Financial District, $–$$)
Sassafraz (Bloor/Yorkville, $$–$$$$)

Deli

Dunn's Famous Bar & Grill (Entertainment District, $–$$)
Reuben S. (Entertainment District, $–$$)

Diner

Flo's (Bloor/Yorkville, $–$$)
The Senator (Downtown, $–$$)
Tulip Steak House (Queen East, $–$$)

Eclectic

Fred's Not Here (Entertainment District, $$–$$$)

Indian

Babur (Queen West, $-$$)
Dhaba (Entertainment District, $–$$)
Narula's (India Bazaar, $)

Irish-American

Allen's (The Danforth, $$–$$$)

Italian

Alice Fazooli's! Italian Crabshack (Entertainment District, $–$$$)
Café Nervosa (Bloor/Yorkville, $$–$$$)
Il Fornello (The Danforth and three other locations, $$–$$$)
John's Italian Caffe (Chinatown, $$)

Japanese

Akane-ya (The Beaches, $$)
Sushi Inn (Bloor/Yorkville, $–$$)

Light Fare

Aunties and Uncles (Little Italy, $)
Bonjour Brioche (Queen East, $)
Brick Street Bakery (Distillery District, $)
Hello Toast (Queen East, $–$$)

Mexican

Dos Amigos (The Annex, $$–$$$)
Fiesta Azteca (Leaside, $–$$)
Hernando's Hideaway (St. Lawrence Market, $–$$)

Pizza

John's Italian Caffe (Chinatown, $$)

Portuguese

Adega (Downtown, $$–$$$)

Pub Fare

Bedford Academy (The Annex, $–$$)
The Black Bull (Queen West, $–$$)
C'est What? (St. Lawrence Market, $–$$)
Irish Embassy Pub & Grill (Financial District, $–$$$)
The Pilot Tavern (Bloor/Yorkville, $–$$)
Rebel House (Rosedale, $–$$)

Québécois

Le Papillon (St. Lawrence Market, $$–$$$)

Steakhouse

Barberian's (Downtown, $$$–$$$$)

Thai

Bangkok Gardens (Downtown, $$–$$$$)
Queen Mother Cafe (Queen West, $$)

Vegetarian

Fressen (Queen West, $$)

Index of Restaurants by Price

$

Alice Fazooli's! Italian Crabshack (Italian, Entertainment District)
Aunties and Uncles (Breakfast/Light Fare, Little Italy)
Babur (Indian, Queen West)
Bedford Academy (Pub Fare, The Annex)
Big Daddy's (Cajun, Entertainment District)
The Black Bull (Pub Fare, Queen West)
Bonjour Brioche (Bakery/Cafe, Queen East)
Brick Street Bakery (Light Fare, Distillery District)
C'est What? (Pub Fare, St. Lawrence Market,)
Dhaba (Indian, Entertainment District)
Dos Amigos (Mexican, The Annex)
Dunn's Famous Bar & Grill (Deli, Entertainment District)
Fiesta Azteca (Mexican, Leaside)
Flo's (Diner, Bloor/Yorkville)
Garden Gate Restaurant (Chinese, The Beaches)
Happy Seven (Chinatown, Chinese)
Hello Toast (Brunch/Light Fare, Queen East)
Hernando's Hideaway (Mexican, St. Lawrence Market)
Irish Embassy Pub & Grill (Pub Fare, Financial District)
Mövenpick Marché (Continental, Financial District)
Narula's (Indian, India Bazaar)
Pearl Harbourfront (Chinese, Harbourfront)
The Pilot Tavern (Pub Fare, Bloor/Yorkville)
Quigley's (Bistro, The Beaches)
The Real Jerk (Caribbean, Queen East)
Rebel House (Pub Fare, Rosedale)
Reuben S. (Deli, Entertainment District)
The Rivoli (Bistro, Queen West)
The Senator (Diner, Downtown)
Sushi Inn (Japanese, Bloor/Yorkville)
Tulip Steak House (Diner, Queen East)

$$

Adega (Portuguese, Downtown)
Akane-ya (Japanese, The Beaches)
Alice Fazooli's! Italian Crabshack (Italian, Entertainment District)
Allen's (Irish-American, The Danforth)
Babur (Indian, Queen West)
Bangkok Garden (Thai, Downtown)
Bedford Academy (Pub Fare, The Annex)
Biff's (Continental, Financial District)
Big Daddy's (Cajun, Entertainment District)
The Black Bull (Pub Fare, Queen West)
Café Nervosa (Italian, Bloor/Yorkville)
C'est What? (Pub Fare, St. Lawrence Market)
Dhaba (Indian, Entertainment District)
Dos Amigos (Mexican, The Annex)
Dunn's Famous Bar & Grill (Deli, Entertainment District)
Fiesta Azteca (Mexican, Leaside)
Flo's (Diner, Bloor/Yorkville)
Fred's Not Here (Eclectic, Entertainment District)
Fressen (Vegetarian, Queen West)
Happy Seven (Chinatown, Chinese)
Hello Toast (Brunch/Light Fare, Queen East)
Hernando's Hideaway (Mexican, St. Lawrence Market)
Il Fornello (Italian, The Danforth and three other locations)
Irish Embassy Pub & Grill (Pub Fare, Financial District)
John's Italian Caffe (Pizza/Italian, Chinatown)
Lai Wah Heen (Chinese, Downtown)

Lemon Meringue (Bistro, Bloor West Village)
Le Papillon (Québécois, St. Lawrence Market)
Mövenpick Marché (Continental, Financial District)
Pearl Harbourfront (Chinese, Harbourfront)
The Pilot Tavern (Pub Fare, Bloor/Yorkville)
Queen Mother Cafe (Thai, Queen West)
Quigley's (Bistro, The Beaches)
The Real Jerk (Caribbean, Queen East)
Rebel House (Pub Fare, Rosedale)
Reuben S. (Deli, Entertainment District)
The Rivoli (Bistro, Queen West)
Sassafraz (Continental, Bloor/Yorkville)
The Senator (Diner, Downtown)
Sushi Inn (Japanese, Bloor/Yorkville)
Tulip Steak House (Diner, Queen East)
Wayne Gretzky's Restaurant (Canadian, Entertainment District)

$$$
360 Revolving Restaurant (Continental, Downtown)
Adega (Portuguese, Downtown)
Alice Fazooli's! Italian Crabshack (Italian, Entertainment District)
Allen's (Irish-American, The Danforth)
Bangkok Garden (Thai, Downtown)
Barberian's (Steakhouse, Downtown)
Biff's (Continental, Financial District)
Big Daddy's (Cajun, Entertainment District)
Café Nervosa (Italian, Bloor/Yorkville)
Fred's Not Here (Eclectic, Entertainment District)
Il Fornello (Italian, The Danforth and three other locations)
Irish Embassy Pub & Grill (Pub Fare, Financial District)
Lai Wah Heen (Chinese, Downtown)
Lemon Meringue (Bistro, Bloor West Village)
Le Papillon (Québécois, St. Lawrence Market)

Sassafraz (Continental, Bloor/Yorkville)
Wayne Gretzky's Restaurant (Canadian, Entertainment District)

$$$$
360 Revolving Restaurant (Continental, Downtown)
Bangkok Garden (Thai, Downtown)
Barberian's (Steakhouse, Downtown)
Biff's (Continental, Financial District)
Lai Wah Heen (Chinese, Downtown)
Lemon Meringue (Bistro, Bloor West Village)
Sassafraz (Continental, Bloor/Yorkville)

Part IV
Exploring Toronto

The 5th Wave
By Rich Tennant

"When the movie's about New York, they shoot it in Toronto. When it's about Paris or Russia, they shoot it in Toronto. So, when the producer asked us where we'd like to shoot a remake of 'Lawrence of Arabia,' the answer was easy."

In this part...

Finding something to do when visiting Toronto is not an impossible task; finding time to fit it all in just may be. Nevertheless, this part is the place to start. In the four chapters here, you'll read about the top Toronto sightseeing and shopping destinations. If you're looking for a little direction in planning your days in the city, this part also includes a chapter of a few suggested itineraries. Finally, if and when you've run through your wish list of things to do in Toronto, I suggest a couple of worthwhile day-trip destinations to consider.

Chapter 11

Discovering Toronto's Best Attractions

*O*f course, you could spend all your time in Toronto exploring the neighborhoods, walking the gardens, finding a hidden gem to buy, and sampling the city's gastronomic diversity — all of that is a great part of what coming to Toronto is all about. But why come all this way and not discover even more of what the city has to offer? This chapter gives you the lowdown on the premier attractions in Toronto, which you can use to plot out your sightseeing itinerary.

This chapter also introduces you to more variety in sightseeing options, broken down into several categories of specific interest. If you're visiting Toronto with the family, have a keen interest in the arts or architecture, appreciate the finer aspects of an exhilarating hockey or basketball game, or just want to explore the pathways, boardwalks, and trails that the city has to offer, this chapter is for you. Finally, if you just want a bird's-eye perspective of the city when you arrive, you can find several suggestions about touring Toronto from the lake, from the sidewalks, and from the streets.

After reviewing the recommendations in this chapter, if you still need a little guidance to build your Toronto itinerary, turn to Chapter 13, which includes four specific itineraries to consider. If you ever run out of things to do in Toronto, check out Chapter 14 for some exciting and entertaining destinations that are within a couple of hours' drive of Toronto.

Toronto is one of nine North American cities that have welcomed the San Francisco–based ticket-booklet innovation known as CityPass (☎ 888-330-5008; www.citypass.net). In Toronto, you can save big-time bucks (as much as C$55) on admission fees to six major attractions, all of which are discussed in this chapter — CN Tower, Art Gallery of Ontario, Royal Ontario Museum, Casa Loma, Ontario Science Centre, and Toronto

Zoo. With CityPass, you pay one price for admission to each of these six attractions; the pass is valid for nine days after you first use it. You can purchase your ticket booklet online before you leave home — in U.S. dollars only (US$35.17 adults, US$21.79 ages 4–12) — or at any of the six attractions in Canadian dollars (C$46 adults, C$28.50 ages 4–12).

Toronto's Top Sights

The "Toronto Attractions" map provided later in this chapter includes most of the destinations listed in this section and in the upcoming section "Finding More Cool Things to See and Do."

Allan Gardens
Downtown

Featuring six greenhouses that cover almost 1,500 sq. m (over 16,000 sq. ft.), Allan Gardens has been a horticultural destination in Toronto since 1860. The land was donated to the city by George William Allan, a Toronto cultural and political leader of the time, with the proviso that the property's use always be acceptable to the Toronto Horticultural Society. Most prominent in the 5-hectare (13-acre) complex — and in the most central location — is the glass-domed Palm House, and the five additional greenhouses each feature flora from distinct climates: the Arid House, the Tropical Landscape House, the Cool Temperature House, and the Tropical Houses. An additional greenhouse is being relocated to Allan Gardens from its current location at the University of Toronto, though its public use has yet to be determined. Note the afternoon closing hours, as this is an area of town in which you should take care after dark.

See map p. 181. Between Jarvis, Sherbourne, Dundas, and Gerrard sts. ☎ *416-392-7288. http://collections.ic.gc.ca./gardens/. TTC: College station. Admission: Free. Open: Mon–Fri 9 a.m.–4 p.m., Sat–Sun and holidays 10 a.m.–5 p.m.*

Art Gallery of Ontario
Downtown

A museum with a long history of showcasing Canadian art and artists, the Art Gallery of Ontario (AGO) also features international works in its open-design building full of natural and strategically artificial light. Permanent viewing options include the largest public collection of works by British sculptor Henry Moore and a rotating display of paintings from artists ranging from European masters to Canadian contemporaries. You can also visit The Grange, Toronto's oldest remaining brick house, and the original home of the AGO (at the time known as the Art Gallery of Toronto). The Grange still houses a few permanent displays, as well as hosts the occasional theatrical and spoken-art performances.

Toronto Attractions

ATTRACTIONS:
Air Canada Centre **13**
Allan Gardens **20**
Art Gallery of Ontario **5**
Bata Shoe Museum **2**
Campbell House **16**
Canadian Broadcasting Centre **7**
Casa Loma **1**
CN Tower **9**
Design Exchange **15**
Eaton Centre **19**
Famous Players Paramount **6**
George R. Gardiner Museum of Ceramic Art **4**
Harbourfront Centre **11**
Hockey Hall of Fame **14**
Riverdale Farm **21**
Rogers Centre **8**
Royal Ontario Museum **3**
Steam Whistle Brewing **10**
Textile Museum of Canada **17**
The Distillery District **22**
Toronto Islands **12**
Trinity Church **18**

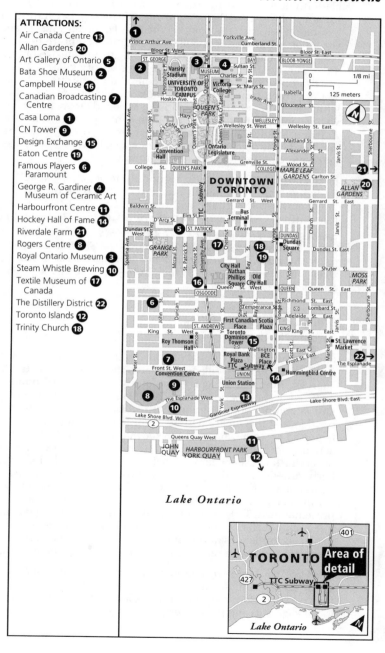

Recent exhibitions at the AGO have included a collection of 73 bronze sculptures designed by Edgar Degas (though created by the Hébrard foundry of Paris, with the approval of the Degas estate); an extensive exhibition featuring the paintings of Tom Thomson, one of Canada's famed Group of Seven artists; a collection of Inuit sculpture depicting celebratory movements; and a fun exhibition featuring lifesize photographs and some personal reflections of 19 of the security guards that monitor the AGO's collections. And 2004 welcomed an exhibition of paintings from J.M.W. Turner, James Whistler, and Claude Monet, organized in cooperation with Tate Britain in London and the Musée d'Orsay in Paris, as well as a well-regarded exhibition of early-20th-century Italian painter and sculptor Amedeo Modigliani. The Agora restaurant, open for lunch or brunch Wednesday through Sunday, features special menus that reflect the period and source of the AGO's major exhibitions.

In 2003, the AGO closed its second floor of gallery space, including its Canadian gallery, to much hue and cry; at time of writing, it remains unclear when the space will reopen. The AGO is planning extensive renovations — by the renowned Frank Gehry — to begin in 2005.

*See map p. 181. 317 Dundas St. W. ☎ **416-979-6648**. www.ago.net. TTC: St. Patrick station. Admission: C$12 (US$9.85) adults, C$9 (US$7.40) seniors and students, C$6 (US$4.90) children 6–15, free for children 5 and under; free admission Wed 6–8:30 p.m. Open: Tues 11 a.m.–6 p.m., Wed 11 a.m.–8:30 p.m, Thurs–Fri 11 a.m.–6 p.m., Sat–Sun 10 a.m.–5:30 p.m.*

Black Creek Pioneer Village
Toronto North

Located north of the heart of Toronto in the Downsview neighborhood, Black Creek Pioneer Village re-creates the day-to-day activities of a 19th-century Victorian village, complete with dozens of homes and shops restored to their period glory. The village centers around the family farm and accompanying buildings of the Daniel Stong family, who set up residence at this location in the early 1800s. Volunteer guides are dressed in period costume, and you can see many of the village's craftspersons in action, from blacksmith to tinsmith to weaver and more. Kids will also enjoy observing the resident farm animals. A variety of lovely floral, vegetable, and herb gardens grace the grounds, and you can purchase many hand-crafted items made at the village. The McNair Gallery in the village's Visitor Centre features rotating exhibitions; in 2004, the gallery featured a multimedia presentation of Toronto's involvement in the Underground Railroad slavery freedom movement of the 1850s and 1860s. Black Creek hosts music and dance performances during summer weekends; the entertainment focuses on music and dance representative of Canada's diverse cultures.

The **Half Way House** restaurant is open for lunch, including an outdoor barbecue during summer, and the village provides plenty of outdoor tables for a casual picnic. You can enjoy traditional holiday feasts during October (Thanksgiving) and December (Christmas). The village really comes alive for the yuletide season, with picturesque heritage lamplight reflecting off the crisp snow (if you've timed your visit with the snow), and hands-on demonstrations and activities geared toward the "festively inclined" (home-made decoration and present tips, for example). Call or check the Web site for other special events and holiday-related festivities throughout the year.

1000 Murray Ross Pkwy. (at Steeles Ave. and Jane St.), Downsview. ☎ 416-736-1733. www.blackcreek.ca. TTC: Finch station, then Steeles 60 West bus. Parking: C$6 (US$4.90). Admission: C$11 (US$9) adults, C$10 (US$8.20) seniors, C$7 (US$5.75) children 5–14, free for children 4 and under. Open: May–June Mon–Fri 9:30 a.m.–4:30 p.m.; Sat–Sun and holidays 10 a.m.–5 p.m.; July–Sept daily 10 a.m.–5 p.m.; Oct–Dec Mon–Fri 9:30 a.m.–4:00 p.m., Sat–Sun and holidays 10 a.m.–4:30 p.m. Closed Jan–Apr, Christmas Day and Boxing Day (Dec 26).

Canadian Broadcasting Centre
Entertainment District

The Canadian Broadcasting Corporation (CBC) has been Canada's national radio and television broadcaster since 1936, establishing a well-known reputation for solid international reporting while also trying to meet the entertainment demands of Canadian families. The CBC Museum showcases Canadian cultural history over the last 60-plus years while simultaneously featuring a history of the network's television and radio services, as well as its broadcast personalities. The museum also screens CBC programming from its archives throughout the day. Hour-long tours take you behind the scenes at CBC, including visiting the CBC Radio studios and CBC Television news sets, and the sound stages for currently airing CBC Television pro-grams. Call ahead to find out about sitting in the audience for a studio taping.

See map p. 181. 250 Front St. W. ☎ 416-205-8605. www.cbc.ca/facilities. TTC: Union station. Admission: Free to the museum; tours C$7 (US$5.75) adults, C$5 (US$4.10) seniors and students, free for children 3 and under. Open: Museum Mon–Fri 9 a.m.–5 p.m., Sat noon to 4 p.m.; tours Tues–Fri 9 a.m.–5 p.m.

CN Tower
Entertainment District

Par for the course for these kinds of attractions, the CN Tower is an expensive proposition, especially for a family. But in that classic struggle of supply versus demand, the tower supplies the preeminent view of Toronto and Lake Ontario, so it remains *the* requisite destination on any itinerary, even if you're paying more to ride to the top of this beacon than you would to visit Seattle's Space Needle or Paris's Eiffel Tower. At 540m (just over 1,800 ft.), the CN Tower is the world's tallest free-standing structure (Kuala Lumpur's Petronas Towers, at just under 450m [1,500 ft.] tall, qualifies more appropriately as the world's tallest *building*), and it serves as a communications tool for the Toronto region, with microwave receptors and antenna at its height.

Nevertheless, despite the cost of admission, the CN Tower is a must-see destination when visiting Toronto for the first time. The tower features four viewing areas, which you can visit depending on the amount of money you wish to spend. The **Look Out Level** is the first-rung viewpoint with an indoor observation deck at 341m (1,136 ft.), and an outdoor observation deck at 337m (1,122 ft.), as well as the famous (or infamous depending on your personal queasiness quotient) **Glass Floor,** from which you can look straight down and feel as if you're floating on air. You may as well hop up and down a time or two; everyone else does, and you won't be going anywhere. The **SkyPod** is the tower's highest observation point, and at 440m (1,465 ft.) it's as high as you can get anywhere without getting airborne. In between is the **360 Revolving Restaurant** (see Chapter 10) at 345m (1,150 ft.). Other also slightly overpriced dining options include the Horizons Café at the Look Out Level and the Marketplace Café at ground level.

For more to do beyond the awe-inspiring views, the tower complex features ground-level shopping (mostly souvenir kitsch), motion-simulated rides, an arcade, and an informative film about the tower's construction.

See map p. 181. 301 Front St. W., just east of the Rogers Centre (formerly known as the SkyDome). ☎ **416-868-6937.** www.cntower.ca. *TTC: Union station. Admission: Total Tower Experience (includes Look Out, Glass Floor, SkyPod, and more) C$32 (US$26) all ages; minimal tower experience (Look Out & Glass Floor) C$19 (US$16) adults, C$17 (US$14) seniors, C$14 (US$11) children 4–12, free for children 3 and under; call for other admission packages. Open: Daily (except Christmas Day) 9 a.m.–10 p.m.*

Design Exchange
Downtown

Housed in the former location of the Toronto Stock Exchange, the Design Exchange (DX) has become the stock-and-trade center for Canadian design. Its permanent collection is dedicated to the best Canadian-designed materials created in the post–World War II era, now with over 150 items in its collection, most of which is on display on the DX's first floor. The permanent collection includes primarily furniture, housewares, and lighting, but continues to grow to include such varied examples of modern Canadian industrial design as sporting equipment and medical equipment. The center also features three other exhibition rooms, where rotating exhibitions are presented, occasionally for an additional admission fee. Early 2004, for example, featured the North American premiere of the exhibition celebrating the life of Princess Diana with display material courtesy of the Althorp Estate, her family estate. The restaurant KUBO DX resides just next door to the Design Exchange and features a varied lunch menu and a dim sum menu.

See map p. 181. 234 Bay St., in TD Centre. ☎ **416-363-6121.** www.dx.org. *TTC: St. Andrew station. Admission: C$8 (US$6.55) adults, C$5 (US$4.10) students and seniors, free for children under 14. Open: Mon–Fri 10 a.m.–6 p.m., Sat–Sun noon to 5 p.m.*

The Distillery Historic District
Toronto East

A welcome new addition to Toronto, the Distillery Historic District opened in 2003 to rave reviews from critics, Torontonians, and visitors. On the site of the Gooderham & Worts Distillery, which operated from the 1830s until 1990 — and then served as a set for films ranging from *Chicago* to *X-Men* — 44 buildings are gradually being converted into industrial art spaces, restaurants, galleries, shops, and coffeehouses — a kind of mini-arts community just east of downtown. Major tenants include a second **Sandra Ainsley Gallery** (the original is downtown), focusing on glass art; the **Mill Street Brewery**, purveyor of organic beers offering on-site tours and a tasting bar; **Balzac's Coffee**, roasting its own beans on-site; and **Found Objects**, a fascinating, if cramped, gifts and housewares shop. And a couple of dozen local artists showcase their work — ranging from crafts to calligraphy to ceramics and more — in the **Case Goods Building** at the south end of the distillery campus. First stop, though, is the Distillery Visitor Centre where excellent tours focusing on the history and architecture of the complex start out. Summer weekends feature outdoor market-style shopping and concerts in the square, and the first couple of years have already featured successful festivals such as the **Distillery Jazz Festival.**

See map p. 181. 55 Mill St. ☎ 416-364-1177. www.thedistillerydistrict.com. *TTC: 504 King streetcar east, and then the 72 bus south at Parliament Street. Admission: Free entrance to complex; tours C$6 (US$4.90) adults, C$5 (US$4.10) seniors and students. Open: Daily 11 a.m.–7 p.m.*

Fort York
Toronto West

Fort York started out in 1793 as a simple garrison to defend what John Graves Simcoe, lieutenant governor of what was then known as Upper Canada, considered to be an ideal location for Upper Canada's capital. This town of York became Toronto in 1834, and the site of Fort York qualifies as well as any as the birthplace of Toronto. The Battle of York took place here during the War of 1812, and Fort York was destroyed as the Americans overtook the Canadian and British forces. It was subsequently rebuilt and used as a military outpost until the late 1800s and again during the two world wars. Open year-round, Fort York today has Canada's largest collection of original buildings from the War of 1812 period. During summer, activities include guided tours; guard demonstrations; period-living demonstrations; and music, drills, and munition firings.

100 Garrison Rd., off Fleet St., between Bathurst St. and Strachan Ave. ☎ 416-392-6907. www.fortyork.ca. *TTC: Bathurst station, then 511 Bathurst streetcar south. Admission: C$5 (US$4.10) adults, C$3.25 (US$2.65) seniors and youths 13–18, C$3 (US$2.45) children 6–12, free for children 5 and under. Open: Mid-May–Labour Day daily 10 a.m.–5 p.m.; September to mid-May Mon–Fri 10 a.m.–4 p.m., Sat–Sun 10 a.m.–5 p.m.*

Harbourfront
Waterfront

Toronto's waterfront is a bit of a city unto itself, complete with some office space and condos, a couple of hotels, a few (mostly uninspiring) restaurants, piers and quays for outdoor strolling, shops and markets for indoor strolling, and a sense of separation from the rest of the city, with its natural boundary (Lake Ontario) and its wholly unnatural boundary (the unsightly but heavily used Gardiner Expressway). You tend to come away with the impression that there's so much more that can be done with such prime space — and maybe that day will come — but it remains a pleasant enough area to spend a day, especially a warm sunny day when the temperature on the breezy lakefront is a few degrees cooler than amid the skyscrapers of downtown.

One of the best reasons to visit the Harbourfront is as a means of getting right out of the Harbourfront — right away — that is, hopping on one of the city's **ferries** to the Toronto Islands, where you can walk or bike along tree-lined paths, enjoy the pint-sized thrills of the Centreville Amusement Park, or sunbathe on the islands' southern beaches with a cool drink by your side (see the next section, "Finding More Cool Things to See and Do," for more about a day on the Islands). Ferries depart from the Toronto Ferry Docks at Bay Street and Queens Quay, just west of the Westin Harbour Castle; round-trip fares for the 10-minute trip are C$6 (US$4.90) adults, C$3.50 (US$2.85) seniors and students under 19, C$2.50 (US$2.05) for children 2 to 14, and free for children under 2.

Farther west along Queens Quay is the **Queen's Quay Terminal,** 207 Queens Quay W. (www.queens-quay-terminal.com), with dozens of retail shops and eateries. Most of the options are of the standard tourist variety, but you can find a branch of Tilley Endurables here (they make the famous Tilley Hat — see Chapter 12), and the Pearl Harbourfront restaurant offers a fine dim sum menu (see Chapter 10). The Premiere Dance Theatre stages modern dance performances in its intimate space, including the annual season of DanceWorks, a local independent dance troupe.

The **Harbourfront Centre,** 235 Queens Quay West (☎ **416-973-4000;** www.harbourfrontcentre.com), includes the Power Plant gallery, showcasing contemporary Canadian and international works; the Harbourfront Centre Theatre; and the York Quay Centre, with a collection of exhibition and performance spaces, including the Brigantine Room, home to the **Harbourfront Reading Series.** Outdoors, a concert stage faces the lake and hosts weekend performances during July and August. A small pond serves in warm weather as a stage for remote-control boat enthusiasts (and those who like to watch), and as a public skating rink in winter. The rink is open daily 10 a.m. to 10 p.m. (till 11 p.m. on Friday and Saturday), and admission is free. Skate rentals are available (C$7/US$5.75 adults and C$6/US$4.90 seniors and children).

A bit farther west, the **Toronto Music Garden,** 475 Queens Quay W., between Bathurst Street and Spadina Avenue, opened in 1999. Designed by landscaper Julie Messervy and inspired by Johann Sebastian Bach's *Suites for Unaccompanied Cello,* the garden's opening celebration was highlighted by Yo-Yo Ma's stirring interpretation of the piece. Each part of the garden represents a different section of the work.

See map p. 181. Queens Quay W., starting at the foot of Bay St. TTC: Union station, and then 509 Harbourfront streetcar west.

Hockey Hall of Fame
Financial District

With over 300 inductees in its registry, the Hockey Hall of Fame pays special attention to the history and lore of the National Hockey League, making it a nice fit here in this NHL-mad city. (For if Canada is mad for hockey — which it is — then Toronto is a bit over the top, especially when it comes to the NHL and the beloved Toronto Maple Leafs.) Among the permanent exhibits here are the original Stanley Cup trophy, memorabilia from the arenas of the "Original Six" NHL franchises, two theaters offering historic NHL highlights and Stanley Cup retrospectives, and even the Canadian loonie that was buried below center ice at the Salt Lake City Winter Olympics before the games in which Canada's men's and women's hockey squads each won 2002 gold medals. Kids and parents alike will enjoy the interactive exhibits, including a chance to take on goalie Eddie Belfour — or at least a simulated likeness of him — or to call your own NHL game.

See map p. 181. 30 Yonge St. (at Front St.), in BCE Place. ☎ *416-360-7765.* www.hhof.com. *TTC: Union station. Admission: C$12 (US$9.85) adults, C$8 (US$6.55) seniors and children 4–18, free for children 3 and under. Open: Late June to Labour Day Mon–Sat 9:30 a.m.–6 p.m., Sun 10 a.m.–6 p.m.; Sept to late June Mon–Fri 10 a.m.–5 p.m., Sat 9:30 a.m.–6 p.m., Sun 10:30 a.m.–5 p.m. Closed New Year's Day and Christmas Day, as well as one day in Nov for annual induction ceremony.*

Ontario Place
Harbourfront

Open daily from June through Labour Day (and on a few May and September weekends), this summer destination is a celebration of Toronto's waterside locale. Futuristic-looking structures of steel and glass seemingly suspend above Lake Ontario, offering opportunities to stroll, browse, and even eat out over the water. And attractions such as **Soak City** (a water park filled with play pool areas, huge waterslides, and water rafting and tube rides), bumper boats, and a log flume water ride all help to remind visitors of the lake's proximity.

Built in 1971 and still operated by the Government of Ontario, Ontario Place tries to provide thrills and chills for all ages. Older kids (and adults) will enjoy activities and rides such as the **Megamaze,** which is exactly what it sounds like — a large, multilayered maze featuring special effects and terrific sounds, and the **Mars Simulator Ride,** a virtual-reality ride that takes you to Mars and back. Younger kids are a high priority as well: the **H₂O Generation Station** is a large outdoor soft climbing structure, with slides, walkways, tunnels, towers, and more; the **Atom Blaster** is not as violent as the name implies, though kids do get to fire soft foam balls at one another; and the **O.P. Driving School** is one of the better amusement-park car-driving rides I've seen, complete with driving instructors to let kids know the rules of the road. And, of course, everyone "benefits" from the uninspiring fast-food fare (pizza, subs, burgers, fries, and so on) that the park considers fine dining.

For non-amusement park entertainment, the **Cinesphere** dome features IMAX movies year-round. Admission is C$9 (US$7.40) adults, C$7.50 (US$6.15) seniors and children 13 and under, or C$7 (US$5.75) general admission for weekday off-season showings. The **Molson Amphitheatre** offers canopied and open-sky seating for summer evening concerts. Recent performers have included Bryan Adams, Coldplay, Dave Matthews Band, and James Taylor. For concert and ticket information, call ☎ **416-260-5600** or check out the House of Blues Web site at www.hob.com.

955 Lakeshore Blvd. W., on the waterfront. ☎ ***866-663-4386*** *or 416-314-9900.* www.ontarioplace.com. *TTC: Bathurst station, and then 511 Bathurst streetcar south. Admission: Grounds admission C$13 (US$11) for ages 4 and up, free for children 3 and under; separate fees for rides and events; Play All Day pass C$29 (US$24) for ages 6 and up, C$17 (US$14) seniors, C$15 (US$12) children ages 4 and 5, free for children 3 and under. Open: July to Labour Day daily 10 a.m.–8 p.m.; June Mon–Fri 10 a.m.–4 p.m., Sat–Sun 10 a.m.–6 p.m.; late May and Sept weekends 10 a.m.–6 p.m.*

Ontario Science Centre
Toronto North

Located north of Toronto's downtown core, the Ontario Science Centre is a hands-on, interactive destination that keeps active learners of all ages entertained. The complex features over 800 hands-on exhibits, covering categories ranging from sports to geology to the inner body to outer space and beyond. Science enthusiasts will appreciate the variety of staff-presented demonstrations and hands-on science exhibits. Beginning in 2003, the Ontario Science Centre began a three-year "innovation renovation" called **Agents of Change,** that will include seven new exhibition areas. One of these new features, **KidSpark,** a learn-through-play space designed for kids ages 8 and under, opened in November 2003.

Also worth a visit are the **OMNIMAX Theatre,** with separate admission (C$11/US$9 adults, C$8/US$6.55 seniors and students 13–17, C$7/US$5.75 children 4–12), for its regular rotation of two to three IMAX films, and the gift shop operated by **Mastermind Toys,** a Toronto-area chain of quality toys, games, and books (see Chapter 12).

770 Don Mills Rd. ☎ *416-696-1000.* www.ontariosciencecentre.ca. *TTC: Pape station, and then 25 Don Mills bus north. Admission: C$14 (US$11.50) adults, C$10 (US$8.20) seniors and students 13–17, C$8 (US$6.55) children 4–12, free for children 3 and under. Open: Daily 10 a.m.–5 p.m. Closed Christmas Day.*

Paramount Canada's Wonderland
Vaughan (north of Toronto)

About an hour's drive north of downtown Toronto is the closest *major* theme park to the metropolitan area. Part of the Paramount Parks group that includes similar parks such as Great America near the San Francisco Bay Area, Carowinds outside Charlotte (NC), and Kings Island near Cincinnati, Canada's Wonderland offers more than 60 rides among its 200-plus attractions on over 120 hectares (300 acres) of park. The thrill rides feature more than ten different roller coasters, including **Canada's First Flying Coaster,** new in 2004, where riders lie prostrate in a suspended car that simulates the sensation of flying. You'll want your swimsuit for **Splash Works,** an 8-hectare (20-acre) water park that includes an outdoor wave pool, relaxing water floats, and not-so-relaxing water rides. **Hanna-Barbera Land** and **KidZville** offer plenty of rides, shows, and activities for the younger kids, including a kid-sized roller coaster.

9580 Jane St., Vaughan. ☎ *905-832-8131.* www.canadas-wonderland.com. *TTC: Yorkdale or York Mills station, and then Wonderland Express GO bus. Admission: Pay-One-Price Passport (includes unlimited rides and shows but not parking, special attractions, or Kingswood Music Theatre) C$50 (US$41) adults and children 7 and up, C$25 (US$21) seniors and children 3–6, free for children 2 and under; admission only (no rides) C$26 (US$21). Open: June 1–25 Mon–Fri 10 a.m.–8 p.m., Fri–Sat 10 a.m.– 10 p.m.; June 26–Labour Day daily 10 a.m.–10 p.m.; mid-May and mid-Sept to early Oct Sat–Sun 10 a.m.–8 p.m. Closed mid-Oct to mid-May.*

Dropping off the kids at Canada's Wonderland

If you're traveling with older kids — that is, those whom you think are old enough and responsible enough to make it through a day on their own — you may want to consider dropping them off at the front gates of Canada's Wonderland and getting away for a quiet adult retreat on your own. The **McMichael Canadian Art Collection** (see the next section, "Finding More Cool Things to See and Do") is just 9km (5¹/₂ miles) west of the theme park, and its hours are similar to the park's (opening at 10 a.m.).

After spending a few hours in the museum, you can while away the rest of the day in the nearby village of **Kleinburg** (www.kleinburgvillage.com), a country village with a core full of quaint shops and casual eateries.

Rogers Centre
Entertainment District

The home of Major League Baseball's Toronto Blue Jays and the Canadian Football League's Toronto Argonauts, the Rogers Centre is a massive, not altogether attractive, landmark between Toronto's downtown and water-front. (Formerly called the SkyDome, this station took on its new name in early 2005.) But the structure did put Toronto on the major sports-venue map when it was completed in 1989, the first domed arena with a retractable roof. In addition to the 65,000-plus seating capacity, the Rogers Centre houses a hotel (Renaissance Toronto Hotel) and four restaurants, all with windows that overlook the field.

Hour-long tours of the Rogers Centre operate daily (event scheduling per-mitting) and include a 15-minute film about the structure's construction. The walking tour also offers a 45-minute behind-the-scenes look at the media center, a private SkyBox, the Club seats, the Blue Jays Memorabilia Suite, the opportunity to see a dressing room, and a stroll onto the field. Call ahead to try to time your visit so that no event is going — that way you can venture onto the field surface.

See map p. 181. Front and John sts. ☎ **416-341-2770.** www.rogerscentre.com. *TTC: Union station. Admission: C$12.50 (US$10) adults, C$8.50 (US$7) seniors and students (ages 12–17), C$7 (US$5.75) children 5–11, free for children 4 and under. Open: Daily 11 a.m.–3 p.m.*

Royal Ontario Museum
Bloor/Yorkville

The Royal Ontario Museum ("the ROM" — rhymes with *mom*) is Toronto's premier museum, devoted to Canadian and international culture, heritage, and natural history. The ROM boasts Canada's largest collection of museum items — more than 5 million. The museum is located in a prime location in the ritzy Bloor/Yorkville neighborhood, just across Bloor Street from the Park Hyatt Hotel. Beginning in 2003, the ROM began a massive renovation project, dubbed Renaissance ROM, which is scheduled for completion in December 2006 and will incorporate over 23,000 sq. m (nearly 250,000 sq. ft.) of new exhibition space. Parts of the museum will remain open throughout the reconstruction, and the ROM is even hosting daily renovation tours (at 1:30 p.m., free with museum admission). Other galleries, such as the popular **T.T. Tsui Galleries of Chinese Art** and the **Discovery** and **Byzantine galleries,** are closed during the renovation.

The international reputation of the ROM is enhanced by its diverse Asian collections. The **H.H. Levy Gallery** showcases textiles, paintings, and wood prints from East Asia, and the **Christopher Ondaatje South Asian Gallery** has a twofold focus: the history and geology of the region in the Moments in Time hall; and the Personal Adornment hall, which displays objects of dress and accessories with commentary on their meaning within their contextual culture.

The galleries celebrating the ancient civilizations of Greece, Rome, and Egypt remain open during the ROM's reconstruction. And the **Samuel European Galleries** continue to present displays representing European style from the Middle Ages to the present day, with period rooms focusing on furnishings, arts, textiles, and elements of warfare.

For families, **Hands-on Biodiversity** is an interactive permanent gallery that focuses on non-human diversity, that is, the interrelational workings of plants and animals. Much of this gallery is dedicated to viewing and identifying representations of plants and wildlife, but the gallery does include a few living exhibits, including a working beehive and a living stream stocked with fish and plant life native to Ontario. The fascinating **Bat Cave** will enthrall older kids with its diorama of bats and their predators.

Special exhibits are presented in the **Garfield Weston Exhibition Hall**, usually with a separate admission. Past exhibitions have included Art Deco 1910–1939, Peter Rabbit's Garden, and in spring 2004, Eternal Egypt: Masterworks of Ancient Art from the British Museum. And Friday nights, normally quiet at museums, are now the ROM's busiest nights: its ROM Friday Nights program offers free admission to the museum (and reduced admission to special exhibits), as well as special performances, food, and drink based on various holiday and multicultural themes.

See map p. 181. 100 Queen's Park. ☎ *416-586-5549.* www.rom.on.ca. *TTC: Museum station. Admission: Weekdays C$15 (US$12) adults, C$12 (US$9.85) seniors and students, C$10 (US$8.20) children 5–14; weekends C$18 (US$15) adults, C$15 (US$12) seniors and students, C$10 (US$8) children 5–14; free for children 4 and under, and for all Fri 4:30–9:30 p.m. Open: Sat–Thurs 10 a.m.–6 p.m.; Fri 10:00 a.m.–9:30 p.m. Closed New Year's Day and Christmas Day.*

Steam Whistle Brewing
Downtown

This brewery began production in early 2000 and has quickly established itself as producing one of the best local brews in the city. The brewery set up shop in an old Canadian Pacific Railway roundhouse — a roundhouse was a building used to store and repair steam locomotives, hence the beer's name — and Steam Whistle makes use of some of the roundhouse's steam equipment for non-beer-production activity. You can pick up Steam Whistle's pilsner at Beer Stores and LCBO liquor stores around Toronto, and many local restaurants and bars serve the beer in bottles or on tap.

For an interesting behind-the-scenes look at the microbrewing process, the brewery offers half-hour tours (on the hour) that include a visit to the Steam Whistle brewhouse, the fermentation vessels, and the bottle shop, ending with a sample at the tasting bar. The tour also offers a more detailed background discussion of the brewery and the roundhouse.

See map p. 181. 255 Bremner Blvd. ☎ *416-362-2337.* www.steamwhistle.ca. *TTC: Union station. Admission: C$4 (US$3.30); kids can tour but can't taste. Open: Mon–Sat noon to 6 p.m.*

Toronto Zoo
Toronto North

The Toronto Zoo provides a fun and educational experience for families traveling with kids of all ages, though it's not in the most accessible of locations. The zoo is owned and operated by the City of Toronto (despite the fact it resides in the city of Scarborough, which since 1998 has been a part of the "megacity" of Toronto), and houses over 5,000 animals on its 284 hectares (710 acres).

Organized by geography, zoo highlights include the **African Rainforest,** including the popular **Gorilla Rainforest Exhibit,** and the **African Savanna** and the **Canadian Domain** sections. Most areas of the zoo feature both indoor and outdoor exhibition areas. The zoo features a few rides to go along with the animal exhibits, including camel and pony rides, and the Zoomobile, an open-air tram that transports visitors around the facility, complete with running commentary. All rides require an additional fee.

Unless you enjoy extended public transit rides on subway cars *and* buses with multiple transfers, you'll want to drive. The easiest route — if not always the speediest, depending on the volume of traffic on Highway 401 — is to head north of the city to Highway 401 and then east to the Meadowvale Road exit (#389). Zoo parking is C$8 (US$6.60) per vehicle.

Meadowvale Rd., north of Hwy 401 in Scarborough. ☎ **416-392-5900.** www.torontozoo.com. *TTC: Sheppard–Yonge station or Don Mills station, and then 85 Sheppard East bus. Admission: C$18 (US$15) adults, C$12 (US$9.85) seniors, C$10 (US$8.20) children 4–12, free for children 3 and under. Open: mid-May to Labour Day daily 9 a.m.–7:30 p.m., mid-March to mid-May and Labour Day to mid-Oct daily 9 a.m.–6 p.m., mid-Oct to mid-March daily 9:30 a.m.–4:30 p.m. Closed Christmas Day.*

Finding More Cool Things to See and Do

You've taken in the CN Tower, and you've marveled at the artificial grandeur that is the Rogers Centre. You've got your day planned for the Toronto Zoo, or maybe the Ontario Science Centre. But Toronto offers so much more to see and do than the top attractions listed earlier in this chapter. In the following sections, I introduce you to even more variety in sightseeing options, broken down into several categories of specific interest. If you're visiting Toronto with the family, have a keen interest in the arts or architecture, appreciate the finer aspects of an exhilarating hockey or basketball game, or just want to explore the pathways, boardwalks, and trails that the city has to offer, this section is for you.

Exploring Toronto with kids in tow

Unless you're traveling in the kid-friendly meccas of Orlando or even Anaheim, you'd be hard-pressed to find a destination that is more welcoming to families than Toronto, especially for the younger set — of kids, that is. In addition to the obvious choices involving the Toronto Zoo or the Ontario Science Centre — great attractions for your younger ones — or even the quaint authenticity of Black Creek Pioneer Village (all discussed in the preceding section), Toronto offers other worthy experiences.

Centreville Amusement Park
Toronto Islands

Located on Centre Island, Centreville Amusement Park has over 30 rides to go along with more than a dozen food outlets and a variety of carnival-style games and activities. The park is clearly designed for families with younger kids. The majority of the rides are best enjoyed with a child under four feet tall; in fact, admission prices are based on the height of visitors. The young'uns just about have the run of the place, with such classics as the Antique Carousel and a 16-cage Ferris wheel, or the pleasant train ride through the park and the slightly thrilling Kermitt Froggs Bouncing Bog. Also on-site, the Far Enough Farm is a small petting farm with domestic animals such as donkeys, horses, sheep, goats, pigs, and even emus. Older kids will enjoy some of the rides (such as the Log Flume Ride and the Monster Coaster, which, sadly, is not much of a monster) and carnival games, but you may find that your teenagers will become a bit bored by the second hour. Just outside Centreville, however, are a few independently operated activities, such as a bungee-jump contraption and a rock-climbing wall, that teens may enjoy (for a separate C$10/US$8.20 fee).

Centreville does not have a separate entrance, so families are welcome to wander in and out of the park (and around the islands) throughout the day, an ideal plan if you want to take a break from the rides for a nice picnic on the island grounds. And four times daily during summer, a children's theater performs on Centre Island, just along the walkway on the way to Centreville.

See map p. 181. Toronto Islands. ☎ **416-203-0405**. www.centreisland.ca. *TTC: Union station, and then 509 Harbourfront streetcar west. Admission: All-day pass C$23 (US$19) all ages over 4 feet tall, C$16.50 (US$13.50), children under 4 feet tall; individual ride tickets C70¢ (US60¢); family ride pass for family of four C$72 (US$59); ferry to the islands C$6 (US$4.90) adults, C$3.50 (US$2.85) seniors and students 15–19, C$2.50 (US$2.05) children 2–15, free for children under 2. Open: Victoria Day–Labour Day Mon–Fri 10:30 a.m.–5 p.m., Sat–Sun 10:30 a.m.–8 p.m.; early May and late September Sat–Sun 10:30 a.m.–6 p.m.*

Riverdale Farm
Cabbagetown

This rural oasis in the heart of the city imitates 19th-century Ontario farm life, with a full complement of farm animals such as horses, cows, goats, sheep, pigs, and chickens. On-site live demonstrations take place throughout the day, offering kids and adults insight into the day-to-day operations of a farm, including cow and goat milking and egg collecting. Adults will enjoy the well-kept floral and herb gardens just inside the main entrance and elsewhere around the farm. Note that Riverdale Farm is *not* a feeding farm, though kids can get up close and personal with the animals under the supervision of the helpful staff. A snack bar (mostly hot and cold beverages and sweets) and gift shop (with mostly hand-crafted items) are operated by the non-profit Friends of Riverdale Farm, which also sponsors a weekly organic farmers' market on Tuesdays from May to October.

See map p. 181. 201 Winchester St., east of Parliament St. ☎ *416-392-6794.* www.toronto.ca/parks/riverdalefarm.htm. *TTC: Castle Frank station, and then 65 bus south to Winchester St. Admission: Free. Open: Daily May–Oct 9 a.m.– 6 p.m., Nov–Apr 9 a.m.–5 p.m.*

Exploring Toronto with teens

Wondering what to do with your teenagers? Well, if you have teenagers like many of the ones I know, you understand they're happiest when they're pretty much on their own. But I do have a few ideas about things to do in and around Toronto that may interest them, starting with Paramount Canada's Wonderland theme park north of the city, the Hockey Hall of Fame for your sports-minded teens, the Distillery for a casual hanging-out kind of place (all three reviewed earlier in this chapter), and an afternoon of shopping along eclectic Queen Street West (see Chapter 12). And since hanging out seems to be what most teenagers do best, here are a few other prime spots.

Eaton Centre
Downtown

Step inside this massive indoor mall on a weekend afternoon and you'll understand why it's self-proclaimed as "one of the most visited tourist attractions in Toronto" — though don't ask me how they sort out the shoppers as Toronto visitors or Toronto residents. Eaton Centre has nearly 300 shops and restaurants within its five-layer, multitiered structure, with Sears serving as the flagship retailer (Sears bought out the old Eaton's Department Store chain in the late 1990s). The Bay, Canada's preeminent department store (see Chapter 12), is not technically in the Eaton Centre, but its store at Queen and Yonge streets unofficially serves as the other bookend flagship retailer.

All the usual suspects have branches here, including Old Navy, Gap, Indigo Books & Music, Roots, Club Monaco, and, just opened in the fall of 2004, a branch of the chic fashion retailer H&M. But really, your teens won't be focused so much on where they can shop; the shopping is secondary. The Eaton Centre simply presents a great central location for them to hang out away from the folks.

See map p. 181. 220 Yonge St., between Dundas W. and Queen W. sts. ☎ *416-598-8700.* www.torontoeatoncentre.com. *TTC: Queen or Dundas station. Open: Mon–Fri 10 a.m.–9 p.m., Sat 9:30 a.m.–7 p.m., Sun noon to 6 p.m.*

Famous Players Paramount
Entertainment District

Parents may find this 14-screen movie theater an example of extreme-neon, ear-blasting multiplex gone bad, but your teens will likely think of it as just another day at the movies. No subtlely lost here: The sound level, lighting, and branding are all at peak levels. In addition to the 14 standard-screen venues, the Paramount has an IMAX theater, which offers both popular feature films and special IMAX-format runs. Food options aren't just limited to overpriced popcorn and soda pop; you can also choose from overpriced Pizza Hut, Burger King, Taco Bell, and other well-known teenage fast-food junkie havens. And for a little entertainment before and/or after the movie, the Tech Town game room is sure to please the most avid gamers in your family. For non-moviegoers (a.k.a. chaperoning parents), a Chapters bookstore is just around the corner on John Street, complete with an in-house Starbucks to help you pass the time.

See map p. 181. 259 Richmond Ave. W. ☎ *416-368-6089.* www.famousplayers.com. *TTC: Osgoode station. Open: Daily noon to midnight.*

Playdium
Mississauga

It's totally and completely out of the way from just about anywhere, but for a full-day's sensory-overload experience for older kids, a trip west of Toronto to Mississauga may be the ticket. This massive game house has over 200 games and simulators, as well as attractions such as batting cages, go-cart rides, and mini-golf. The games range from basic pinball and table hockey to interactive, virtual-reality activities such as Indy car racing, hang gliding, and golf. There's over 3,700 sq. m (40,000 sq. ft.) of frenetic fun and games here, as well as the usual snack-bar-quality food offerings. All in all, an ideal place for your kids to while away a few hours.

99 Rathburn Rd., next to the Square One Shopping Centre in Mississagua; take the Gardiner Expressway (which becomes the QEW) west, exit at Hurontario St., and head north about 5km (3 miles). ☎ *905-273-9000.* www.playdium.com. *Admission: Play cards start at C$10 (US$8.20) for 45 game credits, but are available in any amount (about C20¢/US16¢ per credit); call for Wed and Sat night unlimited play offers; attractions priced separately. Open: Mon–Thurs noon to midnight, Fri noon to 2 a.m., Sat 10–2 a.m., Sun 10 a.m. to midnight.*

Toronto's art appreciation tour

In addition to the museums recommended earlier in this chapter, Toronto has a few more specialized museums to consider. Tourists with foot fetishes more than welcome . . .

Bata Shoe Museum
The Annex

A mecca for all Imelda Marcos wanna-bes, this museum houses over 10,000 shoes in its collection that goes back more than 4,500 years. In addition to footwear from ancient civilizations such as Egypt, Greece, and Rome, the museum traces the history of the shoe (or, I guess more correctly, the shoes) through the centuries and across the continents. And for the fashionista- and celebrity-conscious, the museum's so-called "Walk of Fame" presents the frequently outlandish footwear of the famous from entertainment, politics, sports, and the arts.

See map p. 181. 327 Bloor St. W. ☎ 416-979-7799. www.batashoemuseum.ca. *TTC: St. George station. Admission: C$6 (US$4.90) adults, C$4 (US$3.30) seniors and students, C$2 (US$1.65) children, C$12 (US$9.85) family (2 adults, 2 childen); free admission Thurs after 5 p.m. Open: Tues–Wed and Fri–Sat 10 a.m.–5 p.m.; Thurs 10 a.m.–8 p.m.; Sun noon to 5 p.m.*

Gardiner Museum of Ceramic Art
Bloor/Yorkville

The Gardiner is the only museum in Canada dedicated exclusively to ceramics. Opened in 1984, the museum was founded to showcase the extensive ceramics collection of Toronto philanthropists and entrepreneurs George and Helen Gardiner. In the intervening 20 years, the collections have nearly doubled in size, leading to an expansion that began in 2004. The Gardiner's collection includes some of the most remarkable collections of ceramics from the Americas, as well as pottery and porcelain from Europe and China.

Shut down for all of 2004 and most of 2005, the musuem facility is scheduled to open with a new third floor in the fall of 2005. But the Gardiner continues to host exhibitions with the cooperation of friendly nearby facilities. For example, the fall of 2005 promises a significant exhibition on Picasso's ceramic work to be displayed at the University of Toronto Art Centre.

See map p. 181. 111 Queen's Park. ☎ 416-586-8080. www.gardinermuseum.on.ca. *TTC: Museum station. Call for post-expansion admission fees and hours.*

McMichael Canadian Art Collection
Kleinburg

An impressive stone and timber structure marks the location of the permanent collection of renowned Canadian landscape artists Tom Thomson and the Group of Seven, as well as their contemporaries. The McMichael is Canada's pre-eminent Canadian art exhibitor, and in addition to the collections of Thomson and the Group of Seven (Franklin Carmichael, Lawren Harris, A.Y. Jackson, Frank Johnston, Arthur Lismer, J.E.H. MacDonald, and Frederick Varley, for those who are keeping score), the museum features an extensive collection of Inuit and First Nations art.

10365 Islington Ave., Kleinburg. ☎ **905-893-1121.** www.mcmichael.com. *Admission: C$15 (US$12) adults, C$12 (US$9.85) seniors and students, C$30 (US$25) family (maximum of 5, with no more than 2 adults); free for children 5 and under. Open: May–Oct daily 10 a.m.–5 p.m.; Nov–Apr daily 10 a.m.–4 p.m.*

Textile Museum of Canada
Downtown

This relatively unique museum — one of only eight dedicated to this genre and the only one in Canada — contains a collection of more than 10,000 works, ranging from quilts and carpets to cloths and fabrics from a variety of cultural and religious heritages. Occasional special exhibitions are free with admission.

See map p. 181. 55 Centre Ave. ☎ *416-599-5321.* www.museumfortextiles.on.ca. *TTC: St. Patrick station. Admission: C$8 (US$6.55) adults, C$6 (US$4.90) seniors, students, and children 5–14. C$22 (US$18) family (maximum of 5, with no more than 2 adults); free for children 4 and under. Open: Tues, Thurs–Fri 11 a.m.–5 p.m.; Wed 11 a.m.–8 p.m.; Sat–Sun noon to 5 p.m.*

Finding Toronto's architectural highlights and stately homes

Toronto offers a number of architectural wonders (and a few oddities, as well), and I've listed some highlights here. If touring public (or even private) buildings of all shapes and genres, consider a trip to Toronto during the last weekend of May. **Doors Open Toronto** is a free once-a-year event when more than 100 buildings of architectural or historic significance open their doors for public viewing. Many locations feature guided tours. Most of the buildings represented are either closed to the public during the rest of year or normally charge some kind of admission fee. For details, contact the Doors Open Toronto office with the City of Toronto (☎ **416-338-0628;** www.doorsopen.org).

Campbell House
Downtown

Built in 1822 (before Toronto came to be), this once-private home was built by William Campbell, who would go on to become chief justice of what was then Upper Canada. The home was moved from its original location in the old city of York in 1973 and subsequently restored to its nearly original Georgian splendor.

See map p. 181. 160 Queen St. W. ☎ *416-597-0227. TTC: Osgoode station. Admission: C$4.50 (US$3.70) adults, C$3 (US$2.45) students, C$2.50 (US$2.05) seniors, C$2 (US$1.65) children. Open: Mon–Fri 9:30 a.m.–4:30 p.m.*

Casa Loma
The Annex

This early-20th-century castle may not be to everyone's tastes, but you have to admire it for its sheer audacity. The labor of love of one Sir Henry Pellatt, an entrepreneur perhaps best known as founder of Toronto's first electric monopoly, the castle is stunning in its complexity of design, if not somewhat overwhelming. Make sure to leave enough time to explore the dramatic stained-glass dome (in the Conservatory, Colonel Mustard) and the lovely 2.4-hectare (6-acre) garden.

See map p. 181. 1 Austin Terrace. ☎ *416-923-1171.* www.casaloma.org. *TTC: Dupont station. Admission: C$12 (US$9.85) adults, C$7.50 (US$6.15) seniors and students 14–17, C$6.75 (US$5.55) children 4–13; free for children 3 and under. Open: Daily 9:30 a.m.–5 p.m. (last admission at 4 p.m.). Closed New Year's Day and Christmas Day.*

Church of the Holy Trinity
Downtown

In what some would call a most unholy location — practically in the heart of the Eaton Centre shopping mall — the Church of the Holy Trinity is a peaceful oasis amid a cacophony of capitalism. In fact, one of the best views of the 19th-century Anglican church is from the window seats at Mr. Greenjeans, a family restaurant in the Eaton Centre. Tours of the unpretentious church are not available; an existing and somewhat activist laity call this congregation home. However, concerts, art exhibitions, and other community events are regularly scheduled — some with an admission charge, some without. On Mondays during summer, you can enjoy a free (though a $5 donation is encouraged) lunchtime concert series that starts at 12:15 p.m. The concerts are mostly of a classical bent, and many take advantage of the church's pipe organ. Check the church's Web site or call ahead for arts events.

See map p. 181. 10 Trinity Square. ☎ *416-598-4521.* www.holytrinitytoronto.org. *Admission: Free for Music Mondays summer concert series ($5 donation encouraged); other events vary in cost. Open: No public tours available; weekly services Sun 9 a.m. and 10:30 a.m., Wed at noon.*

Discovering Toronto's sporting and entertainment life

Chapters 15 and 16 feature more details about the entertainment scene in Toronto, including music venues and Broadway-caliber theater. For a public and ground-level glimpse of Canada's best and brightest in the arts and sporting worlds, check out **Canada's Walk of Fame** (☎ 416-367-9255; www.canadaswalkoffame.com). Reminiscent of the more populous Hollywood Walk of Fame, the 83 stars along King Street West feature such Canadian celebrities as Dan Aykroyd, Jim Carrey, Céline Dion, Bobby Orr, and even Monty Hall of *Let's Make a Deal* fame. The stars line up in front of the Princess of Wales and Royal Alexandra theaters, as well as around Roy Thomson Hall (Toronto's premier concert stage). Induction ceremonies take place in June of each year.

Sports fans can find just about every variety of professional sports in Toronto at some point during the year. The biggie, of course, is NHL hockey, with fan interest in the local Toronto Maple Leafs at rabid levels. So, without some serious connections, you're not likely to get a Leafs ticket (and if you do, count on spending some serious coin — in 2003, the *average* ticket price was just under US$57). Other professional franchises are based in Toronto, however — including minor league hockey — if you hope to catch a game or two during your visit.

✔ **Hockey:** The NHL's Toronto Maple Leafs (www.mapleleafs.com) play a 41-game home schedule (plus a handful of pre-season games) at the Air Canada Centre. What few single-game tickets you may be able to get are available only through Ticketmaster (☎ **416-872-5000;** www.ticketmaster.ca) and range in cost from C$40 to C$185 (US$33–US$152) — at least in pre-lockout prices.

The Leafs' minor league hockey affiliate moves from St. John's, Newfoundland, to begin play in Toronto in 2005. The American Hockey League team will play its home games in Ricoh Coliseum at Exhibition Place (☎ **416-263-3000;** www.ricohcoliseum.com); call for ticket prices and schedule.

✔ **Basketball:** The NBA's only Canadian franchise is based in Toronto. The Raptors (www.raptors.com) play a 41-game home schedule at the Air Canada Centre. Single-game tickets are available through Ticketmaster (☎ **416-872-5000;** www.ticketmaster.ca) and range in cost from C$36 to C$180 (US$30–US$148).

✔ **Football:** You won't find the NFL variety in the land of the Canadian Football League (three-down territory, larger field, faster-paced game than the American version). The Toronto Argonauts (www.argonauts.ca), who won the 2004 Grey Cup Championship (the "Super Bowl" of the CFL), play a 9-game home schedule at the Rogers Centre. Single-game tickets are available through Ticketmaster (☎ **416-872-5000;** www.ticketmaster.ca) and range in cost from C$15 to C$50 (US$12–US$41).

✔ **Baseball:** With the Montreal Expos heading for the U.S. capital city, the Toronto Blue Jays (www.bluejays.com) is the only Major League team based in Canada. The two-time World Series winners play in the cavernous Rogers Centre (the retractable roof opens up on warm summer days and evenings). Single-game tickets are available through Ticketmaster (☎ **416-872-5000;** www.ticketmaster.ca) and range in cost from C$9 to C$62 (US$7–US$51).

✔ **Lacrosse:** Another popular Canadian sport (in fact, Canada's national sport is lacrosse, not hockey), the still-fledgling National Lacrosse League has its flagship franchise in Toronto. The Rock (www.torontorock.com) play at the Air Canada Centre and offer just about the best sports value in town, with single-game tickets C$21 to C$46 (US$17–US$38).

For tennis fans, the men's and women's professional tours stop in Toronto every other year. When the women are playing the Rogers Cup tournament in Toronto (as they are in 2005), the men's tournament, Tennis Masters Canada, takes place in Montreal. The tours alternate locations each year.

The PGA Tour (professional men's golf tour) has one stop each year in Canada, rotating among several courses in Ontario, Quebec, and British Columbia. Check the Bell Canadian Open Web site (www.e.bell.ca/cdnopen) to find out whether the tournament is in the Toronto area during your visit.

Taking a brisk walk or a long bike ride

The city of Toronto tries to be pedestrian-friendly and cyclist-friendly, offering a variety of walking trails and bike lanes and trails for the road-weary. However, because of the area's high volume of car traffic, conditions for walkers and bikers are not always as safe as they could be. Use common sense when exploring the area's trails and paths and keep in mind that drivers aren't always prepared to share the road (or crosswalks) with non-motorized vehicles. Chapter 8 has more details about walking and cycling around Toronto.

Among the many areas where walkers and bikers are welcome, the following four are the cream of the crop — and of course, quite populated on the most glorious days of spring, summer, and fall.

- ✔ **The Beaches:** Running east from Ashbridge's Bay Park to Silver Birch Avenue, a wide wood-planked boardwalk meanders about 3km (about 2 miles) along the shore of Lake Ontario. Most of the board-walk lies about two blocks south of Queen Street East, the heart of The Beaches community with its myriad shops and restaurants (see Chapter 10). On sunny weekends, the boardwalk is dense with pedestrians and their children and/or dogs. A paved lane runs parallel to the boardwalk and is best left to cyclists and in-line skaters.

No castaways on these islands

You won't find Gilligan or the skipper wandering around the Toronto Islands. Ferry service runs every half hour or so during the peak summer months — less frequently and more irregularly during the rest of the year — and the area is loaded up with paved walkways and bike paths that all lead back to one ferry dock or another.

But if you do end up losing your bearings while traversing the Islands, just scan the treeline until you spot the top of the CN Tower. Once you spot the tower, you can head in its direction, and you're sure to find your way back to the Centre Island Dock, ready to hop aboard the next available ferry.

✔ **High Park:** This 160-hectare (400-acre) city park in the west end of Toronto features the usual park amenities (baseball and soccer fields, picnic areas and playgrounds), and is also a popular spot for residents of the surrounding neighborhoods for pleasant evening walks and casual family bike outings. During summer, High Park is also home to **CanStage's Dream in High Park,** an annual outdoor tradition that features a two-month run of a Shakespeare play in the park's amphitheater.

✔ **Martin Goodman Trail:** A 20-km (12-mile) paved path that spans nearly the entire breadth of Toronto along its lakeshore, this stretch offers plenty of opportunity for long walks and rides with lake vistas and urban viewscapes (tall buildings and overcrowded roadways to help you keep grounded). Not that you'll be alone on this heavily used path, especially in its busiest sections west of downtown.

✔ **Toronto Islands:** You're only ten minutes away from really getting away from it all — meaning no cars, no business suits, no cellphones (not really about the cellphones, but one can dream) — with a short ferry ride to Toronto Islands, just south of the city's lakeshore. The city-operated ferries run regularly throughout the day, usually full with commuters (who live primarily on Ward's Island) and day-trippers headed for the tranquil trails and beaches or the slightly more hectic Centreville Amusement Park, all located on the main Centre Island.

Seeing Toronto by Guided Tour

You've made your way into Toronto, and now you're looking for some ideas about how to best shape your sightseeing itinerary. This is where guided tours come in: hop on a bus or join a walking tour, enjoy a quick overview of what Toronto has to offer, and then head back to the hotel or to a local coffee shop to strategize about where to start, what to include, and how to prioritize.

Toronto offers several interesting ways to see the city from this kind of perspective. Tour-bus companies provide unique ways of being shown around town, with opportunities to hop on and hop off along the way. Walking tours focus on introducing you to the open outdoor spaces that Torontonians take pride in enjoying and showing off. And, for a more long-distance perspective of the city, the view from a boat deck on Lake Ontario is one of the best.

Keep in mind that most of the tours discussed in this chapter simply drive, cruise, or hike you *by* Toronto destinations. You generally have to return on your own to actually get *into* a destination.

Seeing Toronto from the south — cruising on Lake Ontario

If you have a chance to do nothing else while in Toronto, don't miss the view of Toronto's skyline from the waters of Lake Ontario: it's one of the city's best offerings. And the easiest (and cheapest) way to enjoy this vista is to hop aboard one of the City of Toronto's ferry boats that run from the Harbourfront to the Toronto Islands (see the review of the Centreville Amusement Park earlier in this chapter for details).

However, the ferries are bare-bones cruising — get on, cross the lake, get off — no narration, no food, no drink, and sometimes no seating. For a slightly more luxurious ride, a number of cruise tours operate along the lakefront. Most include some kind of narration and refreshment service; all are an informative and entertaining way to see the city from a distance.

✔ **Great Lakes Schooner Company:** Launched in 1930 as a European commercial sailing ship, the *Kajama,* a 50-m (165-foot), three-masted schooner, now sails Lake Ontario on 90-minute unnarrated day tours of the harbour and Toronto Islands (☎ **416-203-2322;** www.greatlakesschooner.com). The ship is fully licensed, so you can enjoy your favorite beverage (and some assorted snacks) while on board — though you may be asked to help hoist the main sail, so keep that in mind before placing your drink order. Boarding at the foot of Lower Simcoe Street just east of the Radisson Hotel Admiral, the ship sails three times daily from July through Labour Day, and once a day during June. Prices are C$19.95 (US$16) for adults, C$17.95 (US$15) for seniors, and C$10.95 (US$9.45) for children.

✔ **Mariposa Cruise Line:** Two boats in this line's fleet of seven, the *Oriole* and the *Showboat,* depart from the Harbourfront's Queen's Quay Terminal for a one-hour narrated sightseeing Harbour Tour that circles Toronto's harbour, the highlight of which is a brief excursion into the waterways of the Toronto Islands and a cruise by the Gibraltar Point Lighthouse (☎ **800-976-2442** or 416-203-0178; www.mariposacruises.com). The five daily departures operate from mid-May through September and feature a cash bar and a selection of snacks. Two- to three-hour lunch, dinner, and Sunday brunch cruises are also available. Prices for the sightseeing cruise are C$16.50 (US$14) for adults, C$15.00 (US$12) for seniors and students ages 12 to 17, and C$11.50 (US$9.45) for children ages 4 to 11; children under 4 are free.

✔ **Toronto Hippo Tours:** Kids will love this 90-minute narrated tour by land and sea (☎ **877-635-5510** or 416-703-4476; www.torontohippotours.com). The 40-passenger amphibious bus showcases the standards on land (the Hockey Hall of Fame, the Eaton Centre, City Hall, and so on) before unnervingly splashing into Lake Ontario for a view of the city skyline and Ontario Place. No food or drink is available on board. Tours begin at 151 Front St. W., at Simcoe Street, and run daily from May through October, from 11 a.m. to 6 p.m. Fares are C$35 (US$29) for adults, C$30 (US$25) for seniors and students ages 13 to 17, and C$23 (US$19) for children ages 3 to 12; children under 3 are free, and a family rate package is available.

Walking with the talk — Toronto walking tours

For a more in-depth look at Toronto and its environs, walking tours offer the benefit of informative (and usually entertaining) guides who can talk the talk while walking the walk. And the best walking tours in Toronto appeal to travelers and locals alike with an interest in a specific subject matter, be it food, art, architecture, history, or more. This section introduces you to some of the more enjoyable Toronto walking tours.

✔ **A Taste of the World:** With as many as nine weekly (and sometimes twice-weekly) themed walking and cycling tours of Toronto neighborhoods, you're sure to find as many (or more) local residents as tourists taking in one of these unique tours (☎ 416-923-6813; www.torontowalksbikes.com). Themes focus around food, including tours of Toronto's Chinatown, a walk through Kensington Market, and concentrated looks at neighborhood cuisine, ghosts (great fun for the kids), and literature, including an homage to Charles Dickens' single visit to Toronto in 1842. Walks are scheduled from May through October and last from just over 2 hours (for the ghost and literary walks) to just under 4 hours (for the food tours). Rates for the shorter walks are C$15 (US$12) for adults, C$13 (US$11) for seniors and students, and C$9 (US$7.40) for children under 12; the food walks will cost you C$35 (US$29) for adults, C$30 (US$25) for seniors and students, and C$22 (US$18) for children under 12. Call ahead about the cycling tours; some years, no regular bike tours are scheduled, although private tours may be available.

✔ **Art InSite:** Local visual arts columnist Betty Ann Jordan leads free 90-minute walking tours of Toronto's private studios and art galleries, with outings regularly scheduled for the first Thursday of each month (except January) for the city's major art districts, such as Bloor/Yorkville and Queen Street West. Private tours and a Friday art walk that features more diverse citywide visits are also available for a charge. For more info, call ☎ 416-979-5704 or visit the Web site at www.artinsite.com.

A whirlwind tour by air

For an amazing, if somewhat expensive, view of Toronto by air, consider a helicopter tour. Operated by The Helicopter Company, two city tours and a few other specialty tours (such as birthday flights and romantic interludes) allow you to hover over the city for an expansive view of its highlights (and lowlights — the city's waterfront development is somewhat controversial and a bit of an eyesore, for example). The two city tours are extremely quick (9 and 16 minutes, respectively); don't expect to fill up a videotape's worth of footage, but you will have ample photo ops in those few minutes. City tours cost C$80 and C$150 (US$66 and US$123) per person, plus the ferry fare to get to the Island Airport from which flights originate. Flights can sometimes be delayed or canceled because of weather, so call before you set out (☎ 416-203-3280; www.helitours.ca).

- ✔ **City Walks:** Sponsored by Civitas Cultural Resources, these downtown Toronto tours are offered on weekends, with regular rotations around the Union station/St. Lawrence Market area, focusing on the area's history and architecture. Special tours can also be arranged for other prominent areas of the city. Tours are C$12 (US$9.85), and free for children under 12. Call ☎ 416-966-1550 for more information or to book a tour.

- ✔ **ROMwalks:** Volunteers from the Royal Ontario Museum lead these free tours of Toronto neighborhoods, focusing on areas with the greatest architectural and historical interest, including destinations that may already have their own organized tours. If you have to choose, however, go for the ROMwalk; the Queen's Park ROMwalk, for example, is far more informative and filled with juicy tidbits than the Ontario Legislature's sponsored tour. Each walk begins in the area to be walked; they last between one and two hours and run from late May through September. For a schedule of walks or for more information, call ☎ 416-586-8097 or check online at www.rom.on.ca.

- ✔ **Walk Historic Paths:** Organized by Heritage Toronto, a charitable organization with links to the City of Toronto, this neighborhood walking tour program features walks to the city's most historic sites, led by volunteer guides (storytellers, really) who share the intimate secrets behind each walk's destination. Walks share insights from the history of Toronto's neighborhoods, streets, and historic buildings, among other subjects. Each walk is offered only once, and the schedule of walks runs from April through October. Walks are free of charge, though some are limited to Heritage Toronto members. Contact Heritage Toronto for a brochure of their upcoming walks, or view their schedule online (☎ 416-338-3886; www.heritagetoronto.org).

Seeing the city on two wheels

The **Toronto Bicycling Network (TBN),** a member-based recreational bicycling club, hosts regularly scheduled rides from March through December (weather permitting) throughout the Greater Toronto Area for cyclists of all levels and on a variety of surfaces. Non-members are welcome to participate in most scheduled rides for a C$5 (US$4.10) fee. When the bicycles are stored away for the winter, TBN also sponsors ice-skating and cross-country-skiing programs. For more information, contact the TBN hotline at ☎ 416-760-4191, or check the online schedules at www.tbn.on.ca.

Touring and commuting at the same time — bus tours of Toronto

Sure, you may feel a bit like a tourist geek, especially if you're perched atop one of the city's open-air double-decker buses, but touring by bus is *the* best introduction you'll get to *any* city, including Toronto. As a bonus, the bus tours discussed in this section allow you to get on and off at scheduled stops for the duration of your fare. It's almost as if you're sightseeing and commuting all at the same time.

✔ **Gray Line:** The mother of all city bus tour providers, Gray Line (☎ **800-594-3310** or 416-594-3310; www.grayline.ca) offers four sightseeing tours in Toronto — including a combined bus and harbour-cruise tour — but the Hop-On Hop-Off City Tour gives you the most flexibility for seeing the city to begin your visit. From a double-decker bus (or a trolley bus during the winter), you can see many of the top attractions in Toronto, and have the freedom to hop off at any of the 20-plus stops to take a closer look. Tour tickets are valid for two days, and you can also sit in on the complete 2-hour narrated tour (time well spent if for no other reason than the tour's entertaining guides). The buses start running at 10 a.m. daily, and fares for the four tours range from C$32 to C$39 (US$26–US$32) for adults, C$28 to C$38 (US$23–US$31) for seniors, and C$17 to C$26 (US$14–US$21) for children ages 4 to 11; children under 4 are free, and family rates are available.

✔ **ShopDineTour Toronto:** Toronto's newest — and most exciting — bus tour entry, ShopDineTour includes many of Toronto's fashionable neighborhoods as part of its tour route. The Jump-On Jump-Off tour includes neighborhoods such as Greektown on the Danforth, The Beaches, and Queen Street West, in addition to the regular tourist attraction and hotel stops. Operating from May through October, the trolley and open-air double-decker buses feature running commentary from lively guides. The 2-day tour ticket costs C$30 (US$24) for adults, C$26 (US$21) for seniors and students, and C$15 (US$12) for children ages 6 to 13; children 5 and under are free. For more information, call ☎ **416-463-7467** or check online at www.shopdinetourtoronto.com.

Chapter 12

Shopping the Local Stores

. . . .

In This Chapter
▶ Checking out the Toronto shopping landscape
▶ Sticking with the brand names
▶ Finding the motherlode(s) of marketplaces
▶ Discovering the best Toronto shopping districts
▶ Searching for something specific

. . . .

For variety, style, and bargains, Toronto rivals the biggest U.S. shopping meccas, including New York, Chicago, or San Francisco. You have so much to choose from — so many stores offering just about anything you can think of, so many hidden and little-known independent shops to discover, and so many price ranges to consider — that even several trips to the big city will never allow you to cover it all (though you'll have fun trying).

Toronto also has its share of U.S. brand-name chains occupying retail space on its streets, underground, and in its malls. You'll have no trouble finding U.S. favorites such as Old Navy, the Gap, Eddie Bauer, Pottery Barn, Restoration Hardware, The Disney Store, Williams-Sonoma, Foot Locker, and more. For U.S. visitors, what you'll find in these locations is pretty much what you can find at home; prices may be a little higher (in Canadian dollars, of course), but a favorable exchange rate may lower them for you somewhat (check out Chapter 4 for further discussion about the benefits — and possible drawbacks — of the exchange rate).

But what Toronto really has to offer shopping-wise is a wide range of shops that cater to as wide a range of clientele. The city is bursting with small independent shops in out-of-the-way places (but also in the best shopping neighborhoods) where you can pick up merchandise of all sorts at reasonable prices. This chapter directs you to these great shopping districts and helps you create a plan of attack for when you get there; at the end of the chapter, I provide a brief index of the shopping covered in this book, organized by type of merchandise.

Surveying the Shopping Scene

Before you start pounding the pavement and meandering through the malls, there are three things about shopping in Toronto that you should keep in mind:

- ✔ **You are going to pay a lot for that muffler.** And that toque. And those mittens. (The same goes for merchandise that's not even winter-related.) Plenty of deals are ripe for the taking in Toronto, but you'll also find items that will make a significant dent in your wallet.

- ✔ **You won't have to go too far.** As with so many other day-to-day dealings and activities that go in Toronto, good shopping is found within many of the city's neighborhoods — a few specific neighborhoods, in fact (see the section "Searching Out the Best Shopping Neighborhoods," later in this chapter). With the best shopping bets confined to a few blocks in a neighborhood or one of Toronto's most comprehensive malls, you can most likely get your intended shopping done without a lot of extra walking, driving, or parking.

- ✔ **Take the subway.** Especially in the downtown shopping districts and malls, the cost of parking is about as high as it gets in Toronto. Save your money for your purchases and ride the subway or walk. If you end up buying that backyard rotisserie you've been looking for, you can always hail a cab for the ride back to your hotel.

Where the money goes

As Canada's largest city, as well as its business and financial center, and with its appeal to the so-called Hollywood elite, Toronto has a reputation for sophisticated (and pricey) shopping, a reputation that's somewhat deserved. And the prices will seem steeper depending on where you come from — most other Canadians find Toronto shopping to be exorbitantly expensive.

But for visitors from south of the border or from Europe, the draw of high-class shopping and favorable currency is almost too much to pass up. Even with its drop in value during 2004, the U.S. dollar still goes nearly a quarter of the way further in Toronto than it does at home. One euro earns you more than a buck and a half in Canadian currency, and the British pound is practically gold — it's worth a toonie and then some (a coffee and doughnut will set you back the equivalent of about 90p).

Remember that the goods and services tax (GST) and the provincial sales tax (PST) tack an additional 15 percent on to any purchases — automatically cutting in half that 30-percent-off-everything sale that sounded so promising. However, with careful planning, you can get back much of your GST (which, at 7 percent, is the smaller of the two add-ons) through the tax rebate program for non-residents. For any purchases you make to qualify for the rebate, each individual receipt must be at least C$50, before taxes. So, that vintage NHL Original Six collector plate may seem like a great deal at $49.95, but you better be prepared to talk them up a nickel so that you can get back your C$3.50 in GST.

If you're not a resident of Canada, don't go overboard with your spending; you still have to get your goods back into your home country. (If you *are* a resident of Canada, you already know not to go overboard with your spending; likely you can buy half again as much merchandise back home in Moose Jaw.) The upcoming section "Taking stuff home" has more detail about what pre-duty spending limits are for residents of the United States, the United Kingdom, Australia, and New Zealand.

When the money goes: shopping hours

For most shopping districts, stores open at or around 10 a.m. (an hour or two later on Sundays). From there, hours of operation become a little convoluted:

- ✔ **Mall shopping:** The major (and usually more outlying) malls, such as the Eaton Centre and the Yorkdale Shopping Centre, have the longest hours, staying open until 9 p.m. during the week and as late as 9 p.m. on Saturdays. The less major (they can't really be called minor) malls, such as Hazelton Lanes in Bloor/Yorkville, have more civilized evening hours, open until 6 or 7 p.m. Monday through Saturday.

- ✔ **Neighborhood shopping:** It's not that the sidewalks roll up at a designated hour, but most shops that you'll find in and around neighborhoods outside downtown close their doors by 7 or 8 p.m. Not to worry: You'll find plenty of eating and drinking establishments willing to take your post-shopping dollar.

- ✔ **Downtown shopping:** In the Financial District, proprietors tend to go home with the rush-hour crowd — but there's not much to shop for around there anyway. Elsewhere in the downtown core, however, stores generally stay open until 7 p.m. Monday through Wednesday (and, often, Saturday) while hanging on until 8 or 9 p.m on Thursday and Friday.

- ✔ **Sunday shopping:** All bets are off for Sundays. Shopping hours are all over the map; most consistently, however, shops open either at 11 a.m. or noon and close around 5 p.m.

Taking stuff home

For U.S. residents, as long as your stay in Canada is longer than 48 hours, you're eligible for a US$800 duty-free personal exemption on goods that you can take home with you, which includes a maximum of 200 cigarettes and 100 cigars (no Cubans, of course) and 1 liter (1 quart) of an alcoholic beverage. If your stay is shorter than 48 hours, your personal exemption is US$200.

For more information about what you can and cannot take home with you to the U.S., look for the *Know Before You Go* online brochure at www.customs.gov.

The following list offers details about customs requirements if you're returning from Canada to the U.K., Australia, or New Zealand:

- ✔ **For U.K. residents:** Duty-free, you can return home with as much as 200 cigarettes, 100 cigarillos, 50 cigars, or 250g (about 8 oz.) of tobacco; 60cc (60ml, or a little over 2 oz.) of perfume; 2 liters of still table wine; 250cc (250ml, or about 8.5 oz.) of eau de toilette; 1 liter of liquor (34 oz.) or 2 liters (68 oz.) of fortified wine, sparkling wine, or liqueurs such as port and sherry; and an additional £145 worth of other goods including gifts and souvenirs. For more information, contact HM Customs and Excise (☎ **0845-010-9000** or 020-8929-0152; www.hmce.gov.uk).

- ✔ **For Australian residents:** Your duty-free limits are 250 cigarettes or 250g (about 8 oz.) of other tobacco products; 1,125ml (about 38 oz.) of alcohol; and an additional A$400 worth of other goods. For additional information, contact the Australian Customs Service (☎ **1300-363-263** or 02-6275-6666; www.customs.gov.au).

- ✔ **For New Zealand residents:** Before having to pay duty, you can return home with 200 cigarettes, 250g (about 8 oz.) of tobacco, 50 cigars, or a combination of all three not weighing more than 250g; 4.5 liters of wine or beer and one bottle of other alcoholic beverage not to exceed 1,125ml (about 38 oz.); and an additional NZ$700 worth of other goods. For more details, contact the New Zealand Customs Service (☎ **0800-428-786**; www.customs.govt.nz).

Checking Out the Big Names

As with just about any shopping excursion these days, checking out the big names is more than just finding the most cavernous department store (of which Toronto has a few). You now also have to think about big and *branded* shopping names — the kind of names that trigger an immediate reaction: "Hmm, Nike. Just do it." This section introduces you to the big names in Toronto. To find out where the big names are, refer to the "Toronto Shopping" map, later in this chapter. (Oh, and there is a Nike store in Toronto. You can find it in the Bloor/Yorkville neighborhood at 110 Bloor St. W.; ☎ 416-921-6453.)

Pure Canadian: Exploring the big national stores

With over 15 percent of the total Canadian population residing in the Greater Toronto Area, all the nationwide Canadian stores have set up shop — or have flagship stores — here.

Toronto Shopping

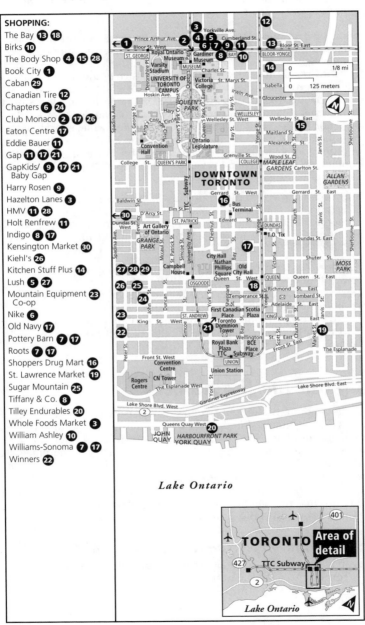

SHOPPING:

The Bay **13** **18**
Birks **10**
The Body Shop **4** **15** **28**
Book City **1**
Caban **29**
Canadian Tire **12**
Chapters **6** **24**
Club Monaco **2** **17** **26**
Eaton Centre **17**
Eddie Bauer **11**
Gap **11** **17** **21**
GapKids/ **9** **17** **21**
  Baby Gap
Harry Rosen **9**
Hazelton Lanes **3**
HMV **11** **28**
Holt Renfrew **11**
Indigo **8** **17**
Kensington Market **30**
Kiehl's **26**
Kitchen Stuff Plus **14**
Lush **5** **27**
Mountain Equipment **23**
  Co-op
Nike **6**
Old Navy **17**
Pottery Barn **7** **17**
Roots **7** **17**
Shoppers Drug Mart **16**
St. Lawrence Market **19**
Sugar Mountain **25**
Tiffany & Co. **8**
Tilley Endurables **20**
Whole Foods Market **3**
William Ashley **10**
Williams-Sonoma **7** **17**
Winners **22**

The Bay
Downtown

The Hudson's Bay Company opened its first department store in Calgary, Alberta, in 1884, following a couple hundred years of fur trading in western Canada. Hudson's Bay is now responsible for a trio of store chains, one of which is The Bay, with two downtown stores — including this one that is accessible via the PATH underground walkway (see Chapter 8) — and several others around Toronto. With everything from fashions to housewares to appliances and more, in dozens of name-brand lines as well as their own, The Bay is one of those stores where if you wait long enough, something of interest to you will go on sale. Of course, service is hit and miss (mostly miss), so you may in fact find yourself literally waiting for the next big sale. A second downtown location at 44 Bloor St. E. (☎ 416-972-3333; TTC: Bloor–Yonge) has shorter hours Monday through Wednesday.

See map p. 210. 176 Yonge St. ☎ 416-861-9111. TTC: Queen station. Open: Mon–Fri 10 a.m.–9 p.m., Sat 9:30 a.m.–7 p.m., and Sun noon to 6 p.m.

Birks
Bloor/Yorkville

Move over, Tiffany & Co. — Canada has its own blue-box jeweler. Birks opened first in Montreal in 1879 and now has 38 stores in Canada; the Bloor/Yorkville location is the flagship of eight Toronto-area stores. The Birks brand denotes luxury and elegance, and its product line, including jewelry, watches, and silver, is high-end in both price and design. (Birks also designs and manufactures much of its offerings.) The store's iconic blue box (a different shade of blue from Tiffany's) was introduced in 1944, adding brand appeal to the company's reputation for fine jewelry.

See map p. 210. 55 Bloor St. W. ☎ 416-922-2266. TTC: Bay station. Open: Mon–Thurs & Sat 10 a.m.–6 p.m., Fri 10 a.m.–7 p.m., Sun noon to 5 p.m.

Canadian Tire
Bloor/Yorkville

On the fringes of both Bloor/Yorkville and the Rosedale neighborhoods, this Canadian Tire store is just one of 20 in the Greater Toronto Area (one of more than 1,000 across Canada). The store was founded in 1922 as a car-parts outlet and has grown into a multifaceted retailer at which car-repair parts and services still dominate but which also includes tools, electrical, home improvement materials, home products, sporting goods, and much more. With so much variety in these superstores, it's the weekend get-away-from-the-spouse-and-kids-for-an-hour-or-two oasis for Canadians everywhere. Buy something here and you'll receive the highly recognizable Canadian Tire Money, which you can use on any future purchase — or, if you don't plan to return, drop it in the donation bin on your way out the door so that it can be used by charitable organizations.

See map p. 210. 839 Yonge St. ☎ 416-925-9592. TTC: Bloor–Yonge station. Open: Mon–Fri 9 a.m.–9 p.m., Sat 8:30 a.m.–7 p.m., and Sun 10 a.m.–6 p.m.

Chapters/Indigo
Bloor/Yorkville

Under the corporate banner Indigo Books & Music Inc., these two bookstore chains represent the majority slice of Canada's retail book market by the longest of shots: over 250 stores across Canada, including two other smaller chains — Coles and SmithBooks. The modus operandi of each store is similar: multiple floors of books to choose from, discounted bestsellers and deep-discount racks, a great selection of magazines and CDs and DVDs, comfortable seating to encourage longer browsing, and a cafe. The two stores listed below are practically neighbors in the Bloor/Yorkville neighborhood. Other Toronto stores include an Indigo at the Eaton Centre (☎ 416-591-3622) and a Chapters in the Entertainment District (142 John St.; ☎ 416-595-7349).

Indigo Books & Music also operates the self-proclaimed **World's Biggest Bookstore,** 20 Edward St. (☎ 416-977-7009), two blocks south of the Delta Chelsea and one block north of the Eaton Centre. The boast in the name may be hard to prove (or disprove), but the store does offer about 27km (about 17 miles) of bookshelves, with a focus on discounted books, as well as magazines, videos and DVDs, and software.

See map p. 210. Chapters: 110 Bloor St. W. ☎ *416-920-9299. Indigo: 55 Bloor St. W.* ☎ *416-925-3536. TTC: Bay station. Open: Mon–Thurs 9 a.m.–10 p.m., Fri–Sat 9 a.m.–11 p.m., and Sun 10 a.m.–10 p.m.*

Harry Rosen
Bloor/Yorkville

At almost 3,000 sq. m (32,000 sq. ft.) and with three levels of shopping, this flagship store in a 17-store Canadian chain features the most renowned lines in men's clothing, shoes, and accessories, including Bruno Magli, Ermenegildo Zegna, Burberry, and its own high-end label. The look definitely favors traditional (read: enduring) over novel (read: faddish), and that look spans from formal to business to casual. But Harry wouldn't be Harry without its dedication to service — from personal shoppers to resolving clothing emergencies to lifetime alterations, Harry's got your back (and cuff).

See map p. 210. 82 Bloor St. W. ☎ *416-972-0556. TTC: Bay station. Open: Mon–Wed 10 a.m.–7 p.m., Thurs–Fri 10 a.m.–9 p.m., Sat 10 a.m.–6 p.m., Sun noon to 5 p.m.*

Holt Renfrew
Bloor/Yorkville

This fashion department store carries the most extensive line of haute couture designers in Canada, from Armani to Zegna, from Bellissimo to McCartney. And Holt Renfrew draws the big-name designers — not just their product lines, but the designers themselves — for exclusive showcase events and shows at this flagship Toronto store. Personal services such as a store concierge and personal shoppers add to the swanky experience. *See map p. 210. 50 Bloor St. W. ☎ 416-922-2333. TTC: Bay station. Open: Mon–Wed & Sat 10 a.m.–6 p.m., Thurs–Fri 10 a.m.–8 p.m., Sun noon to 6 p.m.*

Mountain Equipment Co-op
Entertainment District

Outdoors enthusiasts need look no farther than this nonprofit co-operative store that specializes in gear and equipment for the whole family, including clothing for all seasons — available even for newborns — along with the backpacks and other gear you'll need to carry it to your next trekking (or canoeing or biking) experience. And if you need gear on a shorter-term basis — say, for a last-minute camping trip to Algonquin Park — you can take advantage of MEC's rental program. Outdoor activity workshops are held regularly throughout the year, and on weekends you can try your hand at rock climbing — in the store! If you find something to take home with you — or you want to try out the rock climbing — you have to join the co-op; lifetime membership is five bucks.
See map p. 210. 400 King St. W. ☎ 416-340-2667. TTC: St. Andrew station, then King streetcar west to Spadina. Open: Mon–Wed 10 a.m.–7 p.m., Thurs–Fri 10 a.m.– 9 p.m., Sat 9 a.m.–6 p.m., Sun 11 a.m.–5 p.m.

Roots
Bloor/Yorkville

Roots has not so quietly become recognized as the official Canadian sports-wear supplier, and the Toronto-based company is — again, not so quietly — making inroads in the lucrative U.S. market. Since 1998, Roots has been the "official outfitter" for Canada's Olympic teams — that is, Roots designs the ceremonial and competitive clothing for all Canadian athletes. And for the 2002 Salt Lake City Winter Games and the 2004 Athens Summer Games, Roots created the team wear for the U.S. Olympic team as well; the company will be the U.S. official outfitter at least through the 2008 Games.

In this and other Toronto retail locations, you can follow the post-Olympic crowds to get the latest in Canadian Olympic team fashion. The Roots logo — which you're sure to spot all over town — is on sweatshirts, T-shirts, fleece tops, and more; the company has expanded to include lines for kids and infants, and a Roots Home Store is north of Bloor/Yorkville at 195 Avenue Rd. (☎ 416-927-8585; TTC: Dupont).
See map p. 210. 100 Bloor St. W. ☎ 416-323-3289. TTC: Bay station. Open: Mon–Wed 10 a.m.–8 p.m., Thurs–Fri 10 a.m.–9 p.m., Sat 11 a.m.–7 p.m., and Sun noon to 6 p.m.

Shoppers Drug Mart
Downtown

Canada's largest drugstore chain, Shoppers Drug Mart has a select few 24-hour stores in the Toronto area; this one is the only 24-hour location downtown, just a block from the Delta Chelsea and a few blocks north of the Eaton Centre. Here you can find your standard over-the-counter medications, a wide range of toiletries and beauty care items, and a few odds and ends in the food and snack aisle. A location in Bloor/Yorkville (360 Bloor St. W.; ☎ 416-961-2121) is open every night until midnight.

See map p. 210. 700 Bay St.. ☎ 416-979-2424. TTC: College station. Open: 24 hours daily, year-round.

Winners
Entertainment District

Winners is the T.J. Maxx of Canada — in fact, it is operated by the same firm that runs T.J. Maxx and Marshall's, two of the biggest discount (they prefer "off-price") clothing chains in the U.S. While these kind of, er, off-price retailers typically set up shop in suburban areas, this rare downtown location runs like the rest of 'em — off-the-rack, occasional brand-name clothing, shoes, and accessories, as well as some housewares. Expect a bit of a mess; the racks are typically well sifted through.

See map p. 210. 57 Spadina Ave. ☎ 416-585-2052. TTC: St. Andrew station, then King streetcar west to Spadina. Open: Mon–Wed 9:30 a.m.–7 p.m., Thurs–Fri 9:30 a.m.– 9 p.m., Sat 9:30 a.m.–6 p.m., Sun 11 a.m.–5 p.m.

Keeping it local: Toronto originals

Especially when shopping Toronto's neighborhoods, you'll likely stumble across a familiar name or two that still looks much like an independent store. The story is always the same: Open up in one neighborhood, achieve some measure of success, have a go at a neighborhood across town, and — kaboom! — a chain is born.

Book City
The Annex

Though it's been around since 1976 (or nearly 20 years longer than the Chapters superstores), this small chain of Toronto-only bookstores quickly became the city's anti-Chapters, complete with neo-activist customers willing to pay slightly more for a smaller selection of titles to support this locally owned independent chain (or perhaps more to protest the big-box concept of bookselling — it's hard to tell). Of course, Book City has good, nondefiant reasons to draw loyal customers. Its discounted titles are only slightly less discounted than those at Chapters and Indigo, the smaller selection of titles is balanced by a doggedness to track down special orders, you'll always find an interesting and eclectic collection of deep-discounted titles, and the Book City staffers really know — and love — their books. This store in The Annex is the chain's first, and four other stores are placed in the city's best neighborhood shopping areas, including The Beaches (1950 Queen St. E.; ☎ 416-698-1444), Greektown on the Danforth (348 Danforth Ave.; ☎ 416-469-9997), and Bloor West Village (2350 Bloor St. W.; ☎ 416-766-9412).

See map p. 210. 501 Bloor St. W. ☎ 416-961-4496. TTC: Bathurst station. Open: Mon–Thurs 9:30 a.m.–10 p.m., Fri–Sat 9:30 a.m.–11 p.m., Sun 11 a.m.–10 p.m.

Caban
Queen West

This seven-store Canadian housewares-and-more chain started in Toronto; four of the locations are here, including this flagship store in the diverse Queen Street West shopping district. Caban promises a stylish and crisp look in both its shopping environment and its product line, which ranges from bath products to kitchen essentials, from home furnishings to clothing. You won't find everything you need for the home here, but everything you find can find a place in your home. Caban is a division of Club Monaco, another local creation (see below); other Caban locations include the Queens Quay Market store near the Harbourfront (10 Lower Jarvis St.; ☎ 416-366-4222), and one just a few blocks south of St. Lawrence Market.

See map p. 210. 262 Queen St. W. ☎ 416-596-0386. TTC: Osgoode station. Open: Mon–Wed 10 a.m.–7 p.m., Thurs–Fri 10 a.m.–8 p.m., Sat 10 a.m.–7 p.m., Sun 11 a.m.–6 p.m.

Club Monaco
Bloor/Yorkville

With a range of casual clothing along the lines of a Gap or a Banana Republic, Club Monaco is a local creation, founded in 1985 and subsequently expanded throughout Canada and into the U.S. (catching the attention of Ralph Lauren, which scooped it up in 1999). Boasting more of an upscale casual look for men and women, as well as assorted accessories, this beautiful flagship store matches the elegance of its Bloor/Yorkville neighborhood. Other Club Monaco locations around Toronto include the Queen West store (403 Queen St. W.; ☎ 416-979-5633) and the Eaton Centre (☎ 416-977-2064).

See map p. 210. 157 Bloor St. W. ☎ 416-591-8837. TTC: Bay station. Open: Mon–Wed 10 a.m.–7 p.m., Thurs–Fri 10 a.m.–8 p.m., Sat 10 a.m.–7 p.m., Sun 11 a.m.–6 p.m.

Kitchen Stuff Plus
Bloor/Yorkville

For an inexpensive, if not overly upscale, selection of kitchen and home essentials, this Toronto chain offers a fairly wide assortment of brands and designs. In addition to the usual cookware, small appliances, and dishware (mostly scattered designs, not sets), the plus stuff includes a nice collection of photo frames and candles, as well as more kitchen gadgets than you can probably use.

See map p. 210. 703 Yonge St. ☎ 416-944-2718. TTC: Bloor–Yonge station. Open: Mon–Fri 10 a.m.–9 p.m., Sat 10 a.m.–7 p.m., Sun 11 a.m.–6 p.m.

Mastermind Educational
The Beaches

Not a university textbook store, not a store for brainiacs: Mastermind Educational is a store for *future* brainiacs. With ten stores in the Toronto area, Mastermind primarily carries toys, games, books, and music that encourage kids to explore their own creativity and challenge their imagination. In addition to, for example, popular children's book fare from such names as Ian Falconer and Robert Munsch, Mastermind carries an extensive reference collection, including children's dictionaries, atlases, and historical titles. The newborn, infant, and toddler product line is heavily skewed toward motor skills development, though you can also find your standard dress-up gowns and pirate outfits. Each location offers free gift wrapping if your purchase is for a young'un back home. This store lies in the heart of The Beaches neighborhood, and Mastermind also manages the gift shop at the Ontario Science Centre, another kid-friendly destination.

See map p. 210. 2134 Queen St. E. ☎ *416-699-3797. TTC: 501 Queen east streetcar. Open: Mon–Wed 9:30 a.m.–6 p.m., Thurs–Fri 9:30 a.m.–8 p.m., Sat 9:30 a.m.–6 p.m., Sun 11:30 a.m.–5 p.m.*

Nestings
Bloor West Village

If any home furnishings store can reflect a casual elegance, Nestings is the one. Items carried at Nestings' two Toronto locations (the other is in the Leaside neighborhood north of downtown at 1609 Bayview Ave.; ☎ 416-932-3704) range from the simple to the lavish, but none of it carries the aura that says, "Feel free to look, but you won't be taking me home." In addition to the sofas and ottomans (which locals wait weeks for via special order), lamps, decorating books, home accessories, and tasteful holiday trinkets await the curious visitor. Nestings also operates a store for kids, **Nestings Kids,** at 418 Eglinton Ave. W., with the same emphasis on classic and accessible design for the kids' rooms at home.

See map p. 210. 2274 Bloor St. W. ☎ *416-604-3366. TTC: Runnymede station. Open: Mon–Sat 10 a.m.–6 p.m., Sun noon to 5 p.m.*

Sugar Mountain
Queen West

Satisfy your sweet tooth at this sugary oasis in the Queen West shopping district. Fill a bulk bag with loose chocolates, candies, or gummy items (who're we kidding — loose chocolates, candies, *and* gummy items); choose from a rotating selection of packaged sweets; or down a bottle of soda, including one of their own private label bottles. Sugar Mountain has three stores in Toronto (and eight more across Canada), including a location north of downtown (2299 Yonge St.; ☎ 416-486-9321) and one in The Beaches (1920 Queen St. E.; ☎ 416-690-7998).

See map p. 210. 320 Richmond St. W. ☎ *416-204-9544. TTC: Osgoode station. Open: Daily 11 a.m.–10. p.m.*

Tilley Endurables
Harbourfront

This Toronto-based clothing and travel accessory mail-order company got its start in the early 1980s with a single hat — the famed Tilley Hat. Fashioned by founder Alex Tilley as a sailing hat, the Tilley Hat looks a bit like a soft-sided canvas version of a safari hat, and comes in a wide array of colors — from natural to khaki (well, you may also find a navy one around). The company made its name in mail order, expanding into other clothing lines and travel accessories; in fact, most of its product line is designed with travel in mind. Tilley's flagship store is in Toronto (900 Don Mills Rd.; ☎ 416-441-6141), but it's a bit outside the downtown core (it's just a few blocks north of the Ontario Science Centre, though). This second, and smaller, store is located in the Queen's Quay Terminal along the Lake Ontario waterfront.

See map p. 210. 207 Queens Quay W. ☎ 416-203-0463. TTC: Union station, and then the 509 Harbourfront W. streetcar. Open: Daily 10 a.m.–6 p.m.; open until 8 p.m. Mon–Fri during the summer.

William Ashley
Bloor/Yorkville

You won't find this exquisite shop in this book's attractions chapters, but visitors still flock here just to browse. The displays are uniformly elegant, you can enjoy a mineral water compliments of the store's Water Bar, and the sales staff seem to intuitively know their buyers from their browsers (so you'll likely be left alone to view the displays, if that's your wish). However, William Ashley does carry fine items for sale, including fine china (Wedgwood, of course, among other brands), elegant silver and tableware (singles and sets), eclectic gifts (in the store's "Eclectic Room," obviously), and kitchen essentials (including gourmet gadgets and small appliances). And, annually in November, the William Ashley Warehouse Sale draws teeming crowds of locals and visitors alike to its main warehouse in north Toronto (62 Railside Rd.; ☎ 416-515-7253).

See map p. 210. 55 Bloor St. W. ☎ 416-964-2900. TTC: Bay station. Open: Mon–Wed 10 a.m.–6 p.m., Thurs–Fri 10 a.m.–7:30 p.m., Sat 10 a.m.–6 p.m.

Importing style: Drawing the international players

Toronto lures all the heavy hitters: Wal-Mart has a half-dozen stores in town. I've included a few of the other international big names here, limiting the list to those stores that you can find in the shopping neighborhoods (and malls) discussed later in this chapter.

- ✔ **The Body Shop:** This U.K. brand of beauty products, including skin, hair, and body-care items, operates more than 20 stores in the Greater Toronto Area (GTA). Prominent locations include Bloor/Yorkville (138 Cumberland St.; ☎ 416-928-1180), Queen West (286 Queen St. W.; ☎ 416-599-4385), and Church & Wellesley (71 Wellesley St.; ☎ 416-323-1878).

✔ **Eddie Bauer:** This popular casual and outdoor clothing retailer has eight Toronto-area stores, two of which are downtown: Bloor/Yorkville (50 Bloor St. W.; ☎ 416-961-2525) and the Eaton Centre (☎ 416-586-0662).

✔ **Gap:** With a dozen stores in the GTA, this popular crossover clothing brand fits well with the city's younger urban set. Key locations include Bloor/Yorkville (60 Bloor St. W.; ☎ 416-921-2225), the Eaton Centre (☎ 416-599-8802), and the Entertainment District (100 King St. W., at First Canadian Place; ☎ 416-777-1332).

✔ **GapKids/babyGap:** Not to be outdone, you can find apparel for the miniature "Gappers" in your family at many of the same destinations: Bloor/Yorkville (80 Bloor St. W.; ☎ 416-515-0668), the Eaton Centre (☎ 416-591-0512), and the Entertainment District (100 King St. W., at First Canadian Place; ☎ 416-364-9200).

✔ **HMV:** This music store, an import from the U.K., also carries the latest videos and DVDs of hit theater releases. Look for an HMV "record store" — if, no longer, records — in Queen West (272–274 Queen St. W.; ☎ 416-595-2828) and Bloor/Yorkville (50 Bloor St. W.; ☎ 416-324-9979), among other locations.

✔ **Kiehl's:** Loyal customers of this high-end skin- and hair-care product line swear by its quality and effectiveness. You may find yourself swearing to yourself about the high-end prices at this new Queen West store (407 Queen St. W.; ☎ 416-977-3588).

✔ **Lush:** Not a badly named liquor store (LCBO has the market on the badly named liquor stores), Lush features handmade cosmetics, bath, and skin-care products in a store that's as funky as its product line. Prepare your nose for a scent invasion in Queen West (312 Queen St. W.; ☎ 416-599-5874), the Eaton Centre (☎ 416-646-5874), and Bloor/Yorkville (116 Cumberland St.; ☎ 416-960-5874).

✔ **New Balance Toronto:** New Balance, offering performance and casual shoes, is one of the few branded running shoe lines that pay at least lip service to the wider and narrower widths. This Bloor West Village location is one of three Toronto stores (2250 Bloor St. W.; ☎ 416-766-8882).

✔ **Old Navy:** The ever-popular little sister to Gap stores, Old Navy started expanding into Canada in 2001. Its Toronto flagship store is in the Eaton Centre (☎ 416-593-2551).

✔ **Pottery Barn:** For home furnishings, this U.S. retailer has few detractors (though its high prices, upgraded for the Canadian market, may draw some more). Among Toronto locations are Bloor/Yorkville (100 Bloor St. W.; ☎ 416-962-2276), with a Pottery Barn Kids upstairs (☎ 416-961-2276), and the Eaton Centre (☎ 416-597-0880).

✔ **Tiffany & Co.:** From the sad-but-true department, the Canadian jewelry institution Birks once turned down a chance to buy Tiffany. Regardless, this blue-box legend has made its way to Toronto's Bloor/Yorkville neighborhood (85 Bloor St. W.; ☎ 416-921-3900).

✔ **Whole Foods Market:** The first non–U.S. location of this organic and natural-foods grocer, this store includes *some* local product in its aisles (87 Avenue Rd., in Hazelton Lanes; ☎ 416-944-0500).

✔ **Williams-Sonoma:** You can find the familiar upscale kitchen essentials and gourmet cooking supplies in Bloor/Yorkville (100 Bloor St. W.; ☎ 416-962-9455) and the Eaton Centre (☎ 416-260-1255).

Taking It to the Street (Markets)

Toronto markets aren't limited to the streets; you can find the usual and the unusual both indoors and out at these popular (and sometimes overcrowded) locations.

Kensington Market: Toronto in a nutshell

Wander up and down the narrow streets of this neighborhood and you feel as though you're meandering through a mini version of multicultural Toronto itself. Less of a booth- and kiosk-oriented market and more of a storefront and open-air market district, Kensington reflects the diversity that is Toronto, especially in its collection of ethnic eateries offering Chilean, Middle Eastern, East Asian, and Caribbean cuisine, among others. And much of the area still acts as a market for many local restaurants, with produce and refrigerated trucks weaving in and out of traffic from the early morning hours, headed for the fruit and vegetable vendors that seem to occupy every street corner in the neighborhood. Finally, take a step back to a more Bohemian time, with old neighborhood homes now serving as storefronts for vintage-clothing shops that emphasize the hard-to-find, the retro, the funky, the camouflaged, the Dead (Grateful, that is) — the kind of area where a bookstore with the name **Uprising Books** fits right in and where you don't really mind the annoying-if-it-were-anywhere-else late-'70s and early-'80s music heard up and down the street.

✔ **Courage My Love** (14 Kensington Ave.; ☎ 416-979-1992) is one of those retro stores, and it's nearly always full of regulars and browsers in search of a bargain on vintage clothing of all styles, jewelry, stringed beads of seemingly every color and style, and more.

✔ Among the many produce markets in the area, **Oxford Fruit** (255 Augusta Ave.; ☎ 416-979-1796) stands out, both for its location (on the heavily trafficked corner of Augusta Avenue and Nassau Street in the heart of Kensington) and for its vast selection, all beautifully displayed in bins and baskets.

- ✔ Break for one of a half-dozen fresh-roasted coffee blends (or a bowl of soup and a wrap) at **Moonbean Coffee Company** (30 St. Andrew St.; ☎ 416-595-0327), where the coffee is roasted on-site four times a week and where you can find ample seating out front on an outdoor patio or in two indoor seating areas.

- ✔ Need a truffle to go with that coffee? **Chocolate Addict** (185 Baldwin St.; ☎ 416-979-5809) offers all things chocolate, including quite a diverse collection of flavors in its truffles case (chili pepper?!).

- ✔ And for the snackers, here's just a sampling of what you can find: tall walls of cheese (and plenty of samples) at **Global Cheese; Akram's** for a falafel or some tahini; **El Trompo** for authentic Mexican; **Jumbo Empanadas** for, well, empanadas; both meat and vegetable patties at, you guessed it, **Patty King.**

The neighborhood generally considered Kensington Market runs from Spadina Avenue to Bathurst Street, east to west, and from Dundas to College streets, south to north. But the core market area lies within those boundaries: Oxford, Nassau, Baldwin, and St. Andrew streets are the primary east–west shopping streets; Augusta and Kensington avenues handle the north–south traffic. A number of "Green P" parking areas are nearby, including designated Kensington Market parking on College Street, but you're better off to make your way by transit and foot: streetcars run on each of the four core boundary streets, but the 510 Spadina line gets you the closest.

St. Lawrence Market: A weekend getaway (for all of Toronto?)

For over 200 years, the oddly shaped block bounded by King and Front streets, north to south, and Market and Jarvis streets, west to east, has served as Toronto's primary public market. With two buildings dedicated to daily and weekend market activities, the St. Lawrence Market has been a fashionable shopping stop and meeting place for Torontonians for years. Have fun trying to make your way through the Saturday morning produce shoppers at the weekly Farmer's Market.

- ✔ **North Market:** This building is home to St. Lawrence Market's weekend festivities. On Saturday, the **Farmer's Market** comes to town, with over 60 vendors gathering from all over southern Ontario to set up and sell everything from produce to honey to flowers to meat to fish to even some non-food items. Don't expect to rush your way through, however, especially during the morning when the crowds are heaviest. And the market has (obviously) multiple vendors for the various wares, scattered in haphazard locations throughout the floor; so if you're looking for a great deal on Ontario apples, for example, take the time to browse the aisles before making your final purchase. Hours for the Farmer's Market are 5 a.m. to around 5 p.m. on Saturdays, though vendors tend to pack up and leave whenever their weekly supply of goods runs down.

On Sundays, the North Market, on the northwest corner of Jarvis and Market streets, loses the food vendors and gains the antiques vendors, as the floor fills with more than 80 antiques dealers for the **Sunday Antique Market.** Hours are 5 a.m. to 5 p.m.

✔ **South Market:** Across Front Street from the North Market, this building houses the more permanent vendors in St. Lawrence Market. The focus remains on typical market fare — fruits, vegetables, meat, and fish — but you can also pick up a sandwich and a coffee; gourmet gift items; crafts, candles, and other trinkets; handmade clothing; kitchen gadgets and housewares; and, of course, souvenirs. Hours are Tuesday through Thursday 8 a.m. to 6 p.m.; Friday 8 a.m. to 7 p.m., and Saturday 5 a.m. to 5 p.m.

For more information about the St. Lawrence Market, call ☎ **416-392-7120** or check out the market's Web site at www.stlawrencemarket.com.

Searching Out the Best Shopping Neighborhoods

From the bazaar-like atmosphere of Kensington Market (discussed in the preceding section, "Taking It to the Street [Markets]") to the chic trendiness of Bloor/Yorkville, Toronto neighborhoods draw shoppers from throughout the city to their blend of locally owned storefronts and brand-name retailers, cozy eateries and sidewalk-covered produce markets, and accessible and affordable parking options. This section covers a few of the best and the brightest, highlighting some can't-miss stops along the way.

The Beaches

Quaint and *quirky* are two apt words to describe this preciously protected local neighborhood; you won't find any Chapters or Gaps or other big brand-name retailers here. With one exception (a small "Green P" lot off Queen and Lee), you'll find only street parking here — all pay spaces on Queen, free (if you can find them) on the side streets. My advice: hop on the 501 Queen streetcar heading east, which runs 24 hours and gives you the flexibility to hop off for some antiques browsing along Queen before you get to The Beaches.

Bloor West Village

With bookstores and boutiques, housewares and High Park, Bloor West Village stretches from roughly High Park Road in the east to Jane Street in the west, with all the action centered around Bloor Street. A number of "Green P" parking areas are available north of Bloor, or you can access the district on the TTC's Bloor–Danforth line, with stations at High Park, Runnymede, and Jane.

Bloor/Yorkville

This area boasts the highest of the haute in Toronto, including upscale department stores, upscale clothiers, upscale shoe stores, and even upscale parking (you can have your car washed while you shop at the "Green P" garage between Yorkville and Cumberland). From Avenue Road to Yonge Street (west to east) and Scollard Street to Charles Street (north to south), you'll find your best shopping (and shopping-break choices) on Yorkville Avenue and Cumberland and Bloor streets.

On the Danforth

Toronto's Greektown has diversified. This area along Danforth Avenue thoroughfare runs roughly from Broadview Avenue in the west to Jones Avenue in the east, with four TTC stations along the way (Broadview, Chester, Pape, and Donlands). With a high density of housewares and home decor stores, as well as a number of eating and drinking choices that extend beyond the enduring Greek eateries, this neighborhood is best explored near mealtime.

Leaside

An underappreciated shopping district, Bayview Avenue features a couple of blocks of shopping and dining venues. You'll find plenty of storefronts that cater to the local residents, as well as both casual and upscale shops and bistros to attend to the curious visitor. TTC access is available via a transfer (subway to the Davisville station and then onto the 11+ bus route), but parking is not usually a problem — at least not until Leaside becomes *less* underappreciated as a shopping destination.

King Street West

You can find much more than just theater-specific shopping around this main thoroughfare in the Entertainment District. Start at Mountain Equipment Co-op (which has an overlooked public parking garage underneath, where spaces are usually available, even on the weekend), and head east, west, north, or south for a variety of shops and eateries to while away a day. Or ride the subway to the St. Andrew station at King and University and work your way west.

Queen West

The most eclectic shopping strip in Toronto, you can start at University Avenue and head west for blocks and blocks (in fact, the area west of Bathurst and on to Trinity Bellwoods Park has its own distinct neighborhood designation: West Queen West) and still not run out of unique and interesting shops to saunter through. From Bohemian to boutique, from counter-culture to high culture, this dynamic street has just about everything. Don't bother with a car (though parking isn't too hard to come by); start at the Osgoode station and go west, young shopper, go west.

Index of Stores by Merchandise

Antiques
Sunday Antique Market (St. Lawrence Market)

Bath and body-care products
The Body Shop (Bloor/Yorkville; Queen West; Church & Wellesley)
Kiehl's (Queen West)
Lush (Queen West; Eaton Centre; Bloor/Yorkville)

Books
Book City (The Annex; The Beaches; Bloor West Village; Greektown on the Danforth)
Chapters (Bloor/Yorkville; Bloor West Village)
Indigo (Bloor/Yorkville)
World's Biggest Bookstore (Downtown)

Candy/Chocolates
Chocolate Addict (Kensington Market)
Sugar Mountain (Downtown; The Beaches)

Clothing
Club Monaco (Bloor/Yorkville; Queen West; Eaton Centre)
Courage My Love (Kensington Market)
Eddie Bauer (Bloor/Yorkville; Eaton Centre)
Gap (Bloor/Yorkville; Eaton Centre; Entertainment District)
GapKids/babyGap (Bloor/Yorkville; Eaton Centre; Entertainment District)
Harry Rosen (Bloor/Yorkville)
Mountain Equipment Co-op (Entertainment District)
Old Navy (Eaton Centre)
Roots (Bloor/Yorkville)
Tilley Endurables (Harbourfront)
Winners (Entertainment District)

Drugstores
Shoppers Drug Mart (Downtown; Bloor/Yorkville)

Department stores
The Bay (Downtown)
Canadian Tire (Bloor/Yorkville)
Holt Renfrew (Bloor/Yorkville)

Housewares and china
Caban (Queen West; Harbourfront)
Kitchen Stuff Plus (Bloor/Yorkville)
Nestings (Bloor West Village; Leaside)
Pottery Barn (Bloor/Yorkville; Eaton Centre)
William Ashley (Bloor/Yorkville)
Williams-Sonoma (Bloor/Yorkville; Eaton Centre)

Jewelry
Birks (Bloor/Yorkville)
Tiffany & Co. (Bloor/Yorkville)

Markets
Farmer's Market (St. Lawrence Market)
Oxford Fruit (Kensington Market)
Sunday Antique Market (St. Lawrence Market)
Whole Foods Market (Bloor/Yorkville)

Miscellaneous
Moonbean Coffee Company (Kensington Market)

Music
HMV (Queen West; Bloor/Yorkville)

Shoes
New Balance Toronto (Bloor West Village)
Nike (Bloor/Yorkville)

Sporting goods
Mountain Equipment Co-op (Entertainment District)

Toys
Mastermind Educational (The Beaches)

Chapter 13

Four Great Toronto Itineraries

In This Chapter

▶ Planning a whirlwind tour of Toronto

▶ Exploring Toronto in a week

▶ Finding the best stops for families

▶ Sticking to the subway (and bus)

*P*lanning a vacation itinerary is a very personal task. Only you know what interests your family most. You know best how to spend the busiest days of your vacation and those occasional less-busy days. But a few good ideas certainly won't hurt. This chapter will help you get started with some suggested itineraries, each with its own clever theme. Of course, feel free to diverge from the planned themes here; I won't be hurt — too much.

Taking in the Town on a Long Weekend

Whether you're driving in for the long August weekend from Ottawa or flying in for the four-day American Thanksgiving holiday, this section helps you frame a Toronto visit on a whirlwind. When in Toronto for just a few days, you want to give yourself the best opportunity to hit the hottest of the hot spots and the chicest of the chic spots and still have time to wind down in the calmest spots.

Because you're limited to just a few days (say, three days for the sake of this section), you want to contain your Toronto discovery tour to the downtown core. That way, you'll be able to cram in as much stuff as possible. To further maximize your minimized time, you should probably avoid the CN Tower on this trip — unless you're traveling with kids, of course. The lineups during prime tourist season can be long, and the reward is not necessarily worth the time spent when your time to spend is so limited.

Instead, start out **Day One** by making your way to Union Station, preferably by subway (or just cross the street if you're staying at the Royal York). From here, you can head east on Front Street toward **St. Lawrence Market.** Because it's a long weekend, Saturday is the best day to visit this Farmer's Market — the earlier, the better. You can stock up on fresh fruits and cheeses for the day ahead, and also pick up a coffee and pastry for breakfast, either at the market itself or at one of the many coffee places nearby (**Lettieri** is a good bet for a nice espresso and a scone).

The St. Lawrence Market may take up a good part of your first day, especially if you get caught up in the buzz of locals picking up the week's produce. If you can get away, however, start heading back toward Union Station, stopping in for a tour of the **Hockey Hall of Fame** if you have any sports aficionados in your crowd. If not, and a leisurely margarita is more your cup of tequila, a late lunch at nearby **Hernando's Hideaway** will help you spoil a couple of hours.

With Union Station still serving as your landmark, the area has a few more options for exploring. On a nice day, you can head south toward the lake and explore the **Harbourfront,** or if you haven't satisfied your sports nut enough, the **Air Canada Centre** offers tours of the facility Wednesday through Saturday from 11 a.m. to 3 p.m.; admission is C$12 (US$9.85) adults, C$10 (US$8.20) students and seniors, C$8 (US$6.55) children 12 and under.

Your first day (especially if it's a Saturday) is also your best bet for some nice evening entertainment. You can make your way across downtown to the **Entertainment District** for a play or a concert, or you can stay around Union Station for an offering from CanStage at the **St. Lawrence Centre for the Arts.** Before the show, however, make sure to stop by the Royal York hotel's dark-toned **Library Bar** for an early evening drink — as well as a few bar snacks to tide you over until a light, late dinner at **C'est What?**

Even a short trip to Toronto needs a shopping day, so make **Day Two** yours. If it's Sunday, opening hours will necessitate a late start, so a good breakfast is in order. Head for the Bloor/Yorkville neighborhood and enjoy the fresh offerings at **Flo's.** After a leisurely breakfast, a browse of the Sunday *New York Times,* and an extra cup of coffee, you're ready to tackle the trends found in the upscale shops along Yorkville and Cumberland avenues and finally on Bloor Street.

If shopping is not your thing, you're close enough to a couple of Toronto museums to make this an art day instead of a shopping day. Both the **Royal Ontario Museum** and the **Gardiner Museum of Ceramic Art** are within easy walking distance from the Bloor/Yorkville neighborhood. Whether you spend your day shopping or admiring, don't leave the area without a pint and a burger at nearby **Bedford Academy** or a nice dinner at one of the area's trendy spots, including **Café Nervosa** or **Sassafraz.**

Finally, use **Day Three** to experience Toronto's multiculturalism. Whether it's the ethnically diverse vendors at **Kensington Market** or the many merchants in **Chinatown** or the Italian and Portuguese restaurants along **College Avenue,** the area northwest of the downtown core is your best bet.

Spending a Week in Toronto

If you're planning a weeklong stay in Toronto, you can fill three of your days with the suggestions offered in the preceding section, "Taking in the Town on a Long Weekend."

On **Day Four,** spend your time in Toronto's west end. You may end up doing a lot of walking as you browse the eclectic shopping options along **Queen Street West,** but you also have many choices for resting weary feet and quenching thirsts. And if you make it as far west as Bathurst Street, keep it moving just a few blocks farther for a greasy, to-go-only, but heavenly selection of fish and chips at **Chippy's.**

Head back east toward downtown along **King Street West,** just a few blocks south of Queen. You'll keep a brisker pace — you won't find as much to dawdle over on King — but you're in a better position to stop for extended visits at places such as **Mountain Equipment Co-op** or the **CN Tower** or to enjoy a tour of the **Rogers Centre** (formerly known as the SkyDome), **Steam Whistle Brewery,** or the **CBC's Canadian Broadcasting Centre.**

This is another day on which you can take in some art. Catch a play at either the **Royal Alexandra** or the **Princess of Wales** theaters. Hear the Toronto Symphony Orchestra at **Roy Thomson Hall.** Your proximity to King Street West allows you these options, as well as a pre- or post-show dinner at one of the many restaurants on King's restaurant row, such as **Dhaba** for Indian or **Reuben S.** for delectable sandwiches.

On **Day Five,** get out of town — or at least get out of the downtown core. You may need a rental car for this day, unless you don't mind the myriad transfers necessary via public transit to get to, say, the **Ontario Science Centre** or the **Toronto Zoo.** Other options away from the central city range from the kid-friendly (**Riverdale Farm**) to the inspirational (**McMichael Canadian Art Collection**) to the historical (**Black Creek Pioneer Village**).

With so much to do even farther outside of Toronto, reserve **Days Six and Seven** for a day trip or two. Depending on your interests, you can explore the natural wonders of the Niagara region, take in a repertory theater production or two, or just appreciate the Ontario countryside while partaking of a round of golf. And each of the day-trip destinations has plenty of enjoyable lodging options, in case you decide to stick around for another day. You can find out more about your day-trip options in Chapter 14.

Toronto for Families with Kids

With many of Toronto's attractions, it's sometimes tough to see the (enchanted) forest for the (full-foliaged) trees. Okay, even I don't quite get the metaphor, but the point is that most of Toronto's kid-friendly attractions will appeal to most adults as well. So when you're looking for something to help keep the kiddies occupied, remember that chances are good you'll find yourself enjoying the diversion as well.

To fill a full day in your itinerary, the Toronto area offers a number of fun-filled destinations to keep every member of your family happy and busy.

✔ **Fun in the sun, amusement-park style:** There's nothing like a good old-fashioned roller-coaster ride (and its accompanying waiting line) to help while away the day, in solid half-hour increments. Toronto has a number of choices to consider for hopping on rides, slurping back sodas, and even strolling the midway to play a few games of chance. **Paramount Canada's Wonderland, Ontario Place,** and **Centreville Amusement Park** are all worthwhile summer destinations for this type of activity. And the **Ex** (the Canadian National Exhibition, held each summer in late August through Labour Day) brings a carnival-like atmosphere to Toronto, complete with the aforementioned midway where you can spend a few hours (and loonies).

✔ **Fun-in-the-sun of the water variety:** Both Ontario Place and Paramount Canada's Wonderland have water parks, but your kids may also enjoy some of the natural water activities that the Toronto area has to offer. You can swim in **Lake Ontario,** though make sure to observe the city's flag system for determining the water quality. And, of course, just a couple of hours around Lake Ontario is **Niagara Falls,** where you may be able to find a drop or two of water that will interest the kid in all of you.

✔ **Talk to the animals:** The **Toronto Zoo** is a natural destination for families with kids. A less-known destination, but just as entertaining, especially for the younger ones, is **Riverdale Farm,** in the heart of the city.

✔ **Entertainment and education:** Your kids are sure to have fun, perhaps without even recognizing that they're also learning, at family-friendly attractions such as the **Ontario Science Centre** and **Black Creek Pioneer Village.** Outside town, in Stratford, even a rollicking interpretation of *As You Like It* or *Measure for Measure* may keep your kids interested in Shakespeare.

If you're looking for something that will captivate the kids but you only have a couple of hours to fill, a visit to the **CN Tower** or the **Hockey Hall of Fame** can do the trick — and you don't have to worry about getting back downtown to catch your parents' night-out special dinner.

Parents and kids — shopping together?

This phenomenon may not be something you see back home too often, but a couple of areas in Toronto are conducive to bringing the family together for a little bonding via the credit card — well, sort of.

The Eaton Centre in downtown Toronto offers classic North American mall shopping, complete with a couple of flagship department stores, a fast-food-laden food court, and enough trendy shops to keep even the fussiest of your family happy. And it's big enough that you and your teenagers can spend hours under the same high ceiling and never even see one another until you meet again at your designated rendezvous.

The mile-long stretch of shops and restaurants along Queen Street west of University Avenue features the funky and the stylish, the urban sophisticates and the pierced and tattooed, and just enough of each to keep the parents busy while the kids sample the big-city offerings — or vice versa.

Toronto by Public Transit

You've just arrived in Toronto with nothing but the clothes on your back and in your backpack. You have no intention of renting a car, and paying for a cab will throw your travel budget for a loop. Relax — getting around Toronto without a rental car or a cab is quite doable. In addition to using your own two feet, the Toronto mass transit system is set up perfectly to let you easily get to most of the destinations covered in this book.

The Toronto subway system has two main lines that either circumvent or pass through parts of the downtown core. While you'll need more than a day each to complete the itineraries in the upcoming two sections, you should be able to get an idea of what attractions and dining and/or snack opportunities you can select from when planning your subway tour.

Before you start, make sure to pick up one of the day passes or other special multi-fare passes discussed in Chapter 8. Getting on and off the subway all day at C$2.50 (US$2.05) a pop will dent your travel budget. The passes are cheaper and more convenient. Refer to the map of the TTC subway lines on the Cheat Sheet in the front of this book.

Riding the Yonge–University–Spadina loop

While technically more of a U shape than a loop, the Yonge–University–Spadina line does make a loop around the interior downtown core. The best stations from which to start your tour are Spadina, if museum-hopping is more your goal, or Bloor–Yonge, if you must get in some shopping on your tour. This section works from west to east, starting at Spadina.

About halfway between Spadina and St. George stations, the **Bata Shoe Museum** is the first of three museum options within the first three stations heading this way. The other two options — the **Royal Ontario Museum** and the **Gardiner Museum of Ceramic Art** — are just off the aptly named Museum station.

One block north of the St. George station — and just a couple more blocks north of the Museum station — Prince Arthur Avenue has several good places for lunch after you've spent the morning at one of the museums. You can sample Indian cuisine at **The Host,** or enjoy a pint and an upscale pub meal at **Bedford Academy.**

At the next stop, Queen's Park, hop off to visit the **Ontario Legislature** and perhaps observe the Ontario Parliament if they're in session (call ☎ 416-325-7500 or visit www.ontla.on.ca for details).

Get off at St. Patrick station for some more museum-hopping. The **Art Gallery of Ontario** and the **Textile Museum** are on either side of the station. You're also not far from Chinatown, if a meal at a restaurant such as **Happy Seven** is in the cards.

The Osgoode station is the destination for the eclectic offerings of Queen Street West, be it stylish shopping at places such as **Caban** or **Urban Mode,** book browsing at **Pages Books & Magazines,** or an outdoor pint at the **Black Bull Tavern.** You can head west on foot for a number of blocks before you run out of things to do, but if you end up on the west end of the district with sore feet, just catch the 501 Queen streetcar east to get back to Osgoode station.

If your travel plans include a play at the **Royal Alexandra** or the **Princess of Wales**, or a symphony concert at **Roy Thomson Hall,** St. Andrew station is where you get off. This stop at the corner of University and King is also near many restaurant options, including **Big Daddy's** for Cajun or **Dunn's** for deli.

The Yonge–University–Spadina line makes its turn north through Union station, a stop always busy with commuters (making transfers to the commuter GO Trains) and visitors enjoying the many activities nearby. This station is your best bet for heading to such attractions as **Rogers Centre, CN Tower,** and **The Harbourfront** (although with a healthy walk to each), as well as to the less distant **Hockey Hall of Fame, St. Lawrence Market,** and **Hummingbird Centre for the Performing Arts.** You may also want to save time for a meal and/or a drink in this area, with multiple options in every direction.

King station is a good alternative stop for the Hockey Hall of Fame and St. Lawrence Market if you're heading north. When you've finished at these attractions (or if you just want to skip them altogether), the **Irish Embassy Pub & Grill** is just around the corner.

The Queen station is your stop for festivals (in summer) and ice skating (in winter) at **Nathan Phillips Square.** One of two downtown locations of **The Bay** department store has an underground entrance from the station, and concert venue **Massey Hall** is just a couple of blocks north off Yonge Street.

Head for Dundas station for some serious shopping at the **Eaton Centre.** You're also just steps away from the **Canon Theatre** if you've been able to pick up tickets to a Broadway-caliber production.

Finally, you can skip a couple of stops on this line (College and Wellesley, which are mostly used by office and hospital workers) and head straight for Bloor–Yonge station and the trendy shopping and dining extravaganza that is **Bloor/Yorkville.**

Riding the Bloor–Danforth line

This subway line serves the western and eastern outlying Toronto neighborhoods, running through the northern strip of the downtown core. Several stations are shared with the Yonge–University–Spadina line (and serve as transfer points between the two lines), including Spadina, St. George, and Bloor–Yonge (you can find details about attractions around these stations in the preceding section). A fourth station in the downtown area, Bay, is an alternative destination to Bloor–Yonge for the Bloor/Yorkville neighborhood.

Three stations on this line west of downtown are of particular interest to Toronto visitors. The Jane and Runnymede stations let you off on either end of **Bloor West Village** with its myriad neighborhood shops, services, and restaurants. An extended browse through the Runnymede location of the Chapters book superstore chain is a lovely way to while away a couple of hours; the bookstore is in a renovated neighborhood theater.

The High Park station (just east of Runnymede) is the dropping-off point for a pleasant afternoon in this city park, complete with hiking and biking trails and even a park restaurant — **Grenadier** — for breakfast, lunch, or snack.

If a day on the **Danforth** (the home of **Greektown**) is in the offing, three stations east of downtown are your best bet: Broadview, Pape, and Chester. In addition to the many Greek restaurants in the neighborhood, just around the block from the Broadview station is **Allen's**, a fine place to stop for a pint from a large selection of beers and ales and one of the finest burgers in town.

Technically, you can get to **The Beaches** neighborhood via the subway, but it requires a transfer to a bus at the Main station east of downtown. A better option is to hop on the 501 Queen streetcar east anywhere along Queen Street in the downtown area. The ride can be a bit slow, but you're aboveground the whole way, so you can get in lots of interesting people-watching before you hit Woodbine Avenue, where The Beaches neighborhood really begins.

Chapter 14

Shakespeare and the Falls: Day Trips around Toronto

*Y*ou can find so much to do in Toronto that you may not need to look farther afield. However, getting away from the city — whether for a few hours or for a couple of days — presents a variety of wonderful options. This chapter directs you to the best of the best no more than a couple of hours' drive from Toronto.

Stratford and Shakespeare

A one-time industrial community in what's considered southwestern Ontario, Stratford now relies heavily on the revenue from tourists and theatergoers. Just two hours southwest of Toronto, Stratford is home to the highly respected Stratford Festival, a repertory theater company that produces 12 to 14 plays per year for a season that runs from May through November.

The Stratford Festival started in 1953 as a Shakespeare company, and has expanded over the years both physically and artistically. The festival now boasts four theaters around town and produces works by playwrights from most genres and eras, including four or five works by the Bard and at least one musical annually.

When you've had your fill of festival productions, the surrounding communities present alternative activities, from browsing for antiques (say, in nearby Shakespeare) to wandering through a farmer's market (see the sidebar on St. Jacobs later in this chapter) to exploring the quaint village of St. Marys (about 20 minutes west of Stratford).

Getting there

If your plan while in Stratford is to see the plays, eat in some of Stratford's finest restaurants, and wander around the city's core, consider taking the train from Toronto's Union station to Stratford. VIA Rail (☎ **888-842-7245;** www.viarail.ca) offers a couple of trains a day each way; the round-trip fare is around C$27 (US$22) for adults and the travel time is about the same as if you drive yourself (about $2^1/2$ hours).

You can easily spend a couple of days in Stratford without a car. Two of the festival's theaters (Avon and Studio) are right in the heart of the city. The two other theaters (Festival — the flagship theater — and Tom Patterson) are on the banks of the Avon River, less than a mile from downtown.

The drive to Stratford is an easy trip once you get away from the Toronto traffic. Make your way to Highway 401 north of Toronto, and head west. Take Highway 8 west through Kitchener before venturing into Stratford on Highway 7/8. If you're lucky enough to miss the heaviest traffic out of Toronto, the 150-km (93-mile) drive will take you a couple of hours.

Taking a tour

To introduce visitors to Stratford, the city offers free walking tours that focus on the town's history. A good way to get your bearings around town, the casual one-hour tours run Tuesday through Saturday during July and August, Saturdays only in May, June, and September. When operating, the tours begin at 9:30 a.m. and 11 a.m. and start from York Street in downtown Stratford.

The Stratford Festival offers a few specialized tours of its own. All run during the season only and cost C$7 (US$5.75) for adults and C$5 (US$4.10) for seniors and students.

- ✔ A **backstage tour** of the Festival Theatre is a fascinating look at the nuts and bolts of staging a play on this thrust stage. The one-hour tours run four times a day on Wednesdays and Sundays, all starting during the 9 a.m. hour.

- ✔ Four times a day, Wednesday through Saturday, the costume-making facilities of the festival are opened to the public for tours. The **costume warehouse tour** includes a look at how costumes are conceived, designed, and created, as well as a sneak peek at costumes of productions past. The 45-minute tours start at 9:30, 10, 10:30, and 11 a.m.

- ✔ The festival gardens — primarily outside and around the Festival Theatre — are well worth a look as well. Hour-long **tours of the Arthur Meighen Gardens**, as well as adjacent outdoor art displays, get under way Tuesday through Friday at 10 a.m.

Seeing the sights

Stratford offers more to do than just the festival, but reminders of the festival always seems to be lurking in the background — whether it's festival posters or festival postcards or festival T-shirts or festival tote bags. So when you want to "see the sights" in Stratford, you have to start with the festival, as I do in the next section. However, I also have a few ideas for passing the time either when the stages are dark . . . or when you've darkened too many stages.

Feasting on festival festivities

To be brutally honest, the Stratford Festival (☎ 800-567-1600; www.stratfordfestival.ca) drives this town. With more than 600,000 tickets sold each year for the festival's slate of plays, nothing else in the area draws as much attention or as many of the area's tourist dollars. So when in Rome . . .

The festival has four theaters to accomodate its slate of 12 to 14 plays per year:

- ✔ **Festival Theatre:** This flagship theater opened in 1957 at the location of the canvas tent that hosted the festival's plays for the first four years of its life. The thrust stage is surrounded on three sides by amphitheater-style seating that holds over 1,800 attendees. The Festival is where most of the biggest productions are held.

- ✔ **Avon Theatre:** The building opened as a vaudeville theater in 1901, but the festival began using the facility for its plays in the mid-1950s. A deep proscenium stage (the more traditional arch-style stage, complete with stage curtain) allows for stylish productions both large and small. The theater seats just under 1,100 patrons.

- ✔ **Tom Patterson Theatre:** This small, intimate space (maximum seating is 487) allows the festival to take on plays that are equally small and intimate in scale, if not in spectacle. But don't dismiss the opportunity to see the frenetic pace of a Shakespeare production in this seemingly confining space. The U-shaped seating arrangement is only six rows deep, so you're never far from the action.

   Studio Theatre: The newest venue (opened in 2002), this theater seats only 260 and was designed for experimental works and offerings from new playwrights. The Studio is just around the corner from the Avon, but has a thrust stage similar to the one at the Festival.

Through the years, the mostly Canadian-born company has included some well-known names, including Sir Alec Guinness, Maggie Smith, Christopher Plummer, Sarah Polley, William Shatner, Paul Gross, Brian Bedford, Jessica Tandy, Peter Ustinov, and many more. At press time, the 2005 season promises the first-time appearance of Tony Award–winner Amanda Plummer (daughter of Christopher) and the return of 38-year festival veteran William Hutt.

Ticket pricing requires a bit of translating, with price levels that are based on time of year (summer tickets are higher-priced than spring or fall tickets), type of production (expect to pay ten bucks more for a musical), and seat location. And that's before you consider discounts for seniors and students or for preview performances. That said, however, regular ticket prices for 2004 productions ranged from C$50 to C$112 (US$4–US$92); expect about the same for 2005 and beyond.

You can buy tickets online at www.stratfordfestival.ca or by calling the festival box office at ☎ 800-567-1600. Box office hours during the season are Monday to Saturday 9 a.m. to 8 p.m, and Sunday 9 a.m. to 2 p.m. (off-season hours are Monday to Saturday 9 a.m. to 5 p.m.).

After the festival

When you're done with the festival, you can otherwise occupy your time both inside and outside Stratford.

✔ Time spent at **Gallery Indigena,** 69 Ontario St. (☎ 519-271-7881; www.galleryindigena.com) is time well spent. Curator and shop owner Erla Boyer has devoted herself to a lifetime of interest in native arts and it shows in this renowned collection of indigenous paintings, sculptures, masks, jewelry, and more. The gallery's gift shop is in front and worth a long browse as well. Boyer has also converted three lofts above the gallery for overnight guests (see the listing in the upcoming "Where to stay" section).

✔ Take time out from the theater — and from the shopping, for that matter — and settle in for a good cup of coffee (and maybe a nice ice cream or pastry) at **Balzac's,** 149 Ontario St. (☎ 519-273-7909; www.balzacscoffee.com). The coffee is roasted on-site, and plenty of seating is available to allow for a leisurely hour or so of sipping and chilling. A second Balzac's location is open in Toronto's Distillery District (see Chapter 10).

✔ Just 23km (14 miles) west of Stratford, the town of **St. Marys** is a quaint diversion that will take you a couple of hours (and a couple of blocks) to see. The town's main street is a mix of small-town stores for the locals (hardware store, post office, and the like) and cutesy shops and eateries for those just passing through. St. Marys' claim to tourism fame is its limestone heritage (its town hall, library, and old water tower are all made of the stuff) and status as home of the **Canadian Baseball Hall of Fame and Museum** (☎ 877-250-2255 or 519-284-1838; www.baseballhalloffame.ca).

✔ Five minutes east of Stratford (you drive through it on Highway 7/8 on the way to Stratford from Toronto), the little, er, hamlet of **Shakespeare** is the place to go in this area for antiques shopping. With five shops within a two-block area, you can easily spend a morning or afternoon and come away with a find or two. The best of the lot is Land & Ross, with two locations and offering custom-made reproductions as well as antiques.

Shopping Stratford

It doesn't matter where you shop; if you're in need of some flowers for your hotel room or some tissues for your stuffy nose or a book for the ride back to Toronto, you're going to run into Stratford Festival paraphernalia. And this is never more true, of course, than at the Stratford Festival stores (there are two of them). But if you're looking for some non-festival-related knickknacks, here are a few suggestions.

✔ Not much of a high-fashion destination, Stratford nevertheless has a few passable shops for men's and women's clothing. **Bloomer's,** 19 Downie St. (☎ 519-271-6587), has women's apparel, lingerie, and a generous supply of pajamas from such names as Joe Boxer and Nick & Nora. With two locations, **Gordon's,** 77 Ontario St. for men (☎ 519-271-2181) and 10 Downie St. for women (☎ 519-271-4691), takes you back in time to the age of the local haberdasher who sets up shop on a small town's main street and offers fine, if conservative, dress at prices higher than you'd pay at the big-city department store.

✔ For kids, **The Pumpkin Patch,** 19 York St. (☎ 519-273-3336), has a great selection of infant and children's clothing (including a couple of Canadian brand names — Robeez and Kooshies), as well as a few toys and games from such manufacturers as Manhattan Toy. More kids' clothes are off Ontario Street a couple of blocks at **Daboo,** 10 George St. (☎ 519-271-5829). This local firm makes all of its own merchandise — some on-site that you can watch through a viewing window in the store, and some at a facility outside of Stratford.

✔ **Family & Company,** 6 Ontario St. (☎ 519-273-7060; www.family andcompany.com), is a little slice of fun and games that kids and parents alike love. And the proof is in a recent renovation that nearly doubled this fun store's floor space. Whatever your toy and novelty needs, this store has it — magic tricks, newborn and infant development toys, gag gifts, educational toys, and even the now-politically-incorrect candy cigarettes. You can sample just about anything, kids can fashion a quick bead necklace, and adults can enjoy an Italian soda in one of 20 flavors. The family-run operation encourages the "employees" to walk through the aisles demonstrating the merchandise — nice work if you can get it.

✔ If you're in need of a good read for the ride back to Toronto — or you want to pick up a copy of the play you just saw — you have a couple of options in downtown Stratford. **Callan Books,** 15 York St. (☎ 519-273-5767), has the most eclectic inventory around. It's a small store that's well worth a browse, perhaps while you're waiting for your sandwich order at York Street Kitchen. Up on the main drag, **Fanfare Books,** 92 Ontario St. (☎ 519-273-1010), has a fine collection of literary, theater-related, and kids books. Also for kids — but a great store for parents too — **Fundamentals Books and Toys,** 73 Albert St. (☎ 519-273-6440), has the best selection of children's books in town. Kids will appreciate the toys and games within easy reach while the parents browse the bookshelves.

✔ If you have a mind to pick up a few things for the house, start at **Bradshaws,** 129 Ontario St. (☎ **519-271-6283;** www.bradshaws canada.com). For kitchen accessories, china and crystal, and classic seasonal items, you can find brand names such as Wedgwood, Waterford, Denby, and Crabtree & Evelyn among others. **Kitchen Connaisseur,** 75 Ontario St. (☎ **519-271-3311;** www.kitchen connaisseur.com), is a great stop for chefs and chef wanna-bes in your family, offering all sorts of sauces, oils, herbs, and more for home-style gourmet cooking.

✔ Finally, when in Stratford for the festival, you'll need to save some time for one of two **Stratford Festival Theatre Stores** (☎ **519-271-0555;** www.stratfordfestival.ca). Of the two locations, the one in the Festival Theatre lobby (55 Queen St.) is the biggest and has the widest variety of merchandise — from the usual T-shirts, tote bags, pens, and notepads, to the not-as-usual umbrellas and jewelry and children's toys, to the expected theater-related lot including playbills, posters, and music related to each season's productions. The Avon Theatre (99 Downie St.) has a smaller store with similar souvenir-type merchandise — just not as much of it. And if you don't make it to the store before you leave town, you can purchase a limited supply of stuff (mostly playbills, posters, books, CDs, and videos) online.

Where to stay

With over two dozen hotels or motels and over 100 bed-and-breakfast choices, Stratford has no shortage of options when it comes to finding a place to stay. Yet with all those establishments, you still may find a shortage of rooms when you're looking for a place to sleep for the night — the town is *that* busy during the festival season. A few of my favorites are listed in this section (see the nearby "Stratford" map).

If the ones described here are full or don't suit your style, **Tourism Stratford,** at 47 Downie St. (☎ **800-561-7926** or 519-271-5140; www.city. stratford.on.ca), has a complete listing of all accommodations both in Stratford and in the surrounding communities. If you call, the tourism office can also direct you to the lodgings that are most likely to have availability, though they can't make the actual booking for you. The Stratford Festival Web site (www.stratfordfestival.ca) also has a complete accommodations listing for Stratford and surrounds.

Stratford

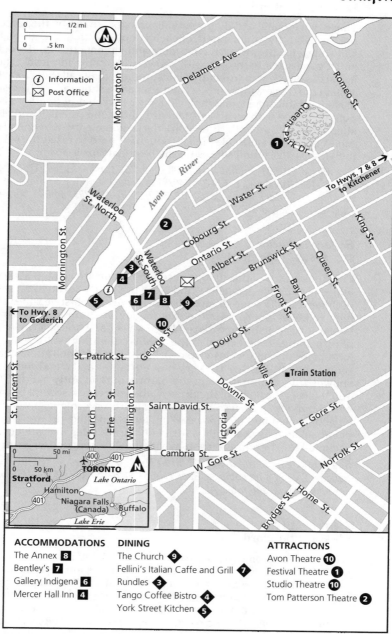

ACCOMMODATIONS
The Annex **8**
Bentley's **7**
Gallery Indigena **6**
Mercer Hall Inn **4**

DINING
The Church **9**
Fellini's Italian Caffe and Grill **7**
Rundles **3**
Tango Coffee Bistro **4**
York Street Kitchen **5**

ATTRACTIONS
Avon Theatre **10**
Festival Theatre **1**
Studio Theatre **10**
Tom Patterson Theatre **2**

Bentley's/The Annex Inn
$$–$$$ Stratford

These two lodging and dining establishments are run by the same owner-operator, but the atmosphere of each is quite distinct. Bentley's features 13 two-level suites, with the bedroom and kitchenettes on the main level and a good-sized bathroom with shower/tub on the loft level. The Annex has six luxury suites (executive guest rooms, they call them), each with a Jacuzzi tub (to go with a shower) and a separate sitting area. The restaurants at each establishment match the lodging's personality. Bentley's is a lively pub, complete with an above-standard pub menu (the fish and chips and shepherd's pie are both top-notch), darts, and plenty of beer and ale. The Annex has a more upscale menu (though it's hard to resist the selection of individual pizzas) and serves up the best martinis in town.

*See map p. 237. 99 Ontario St. and 38 Albert St. (respectively). ☎ **800-361-5322**, 519-271-1121 (Bentley's), or 519-271-1407 (The Annex). www.bentleys-annex.com. Parking: Free. Rack rates: C$160–C$250 (US$131–US$205) double May–mid-Nov; C$80–C$150 (US$66–US$123) double mid-Nov–Apr. AE, MC, V.*

Gallery Indigena
$$$–$$$$$ Stratford

The three suites of this unique accommodation are located above Gallery Indigena, a native art gallery and store in a prime location on the corner of Ontario and Downie streets. The open-concept loft-style suites all feature high ceilings, incorporate the existing architecture of the former warehouse space (including exposed-brick walls), and house an eclectic blend of furnishings (one example: the "Above the Alley" suite reuses school lockers for the suite's closet space). Each suite has a full kitchenette, living room and sitting areas, very comfortable beds and bedding, and shower/tub combinations in the bathroom. The aptly named "Over the Top" suite is the finest of the three, with two levels, a second bedroom and bathroom, and a Jacuzzi tub. Parking is free overnight, but located in a city-controlled and metered parking lot behind the gallery. The primary drawback here is availability, with only three suites that are occasionally occupied for the entire season by visiting directors and/or actors.

*See map p. 237. 69 Ontario St. ☎ **519-271-7881**. www.galleryindigena.com. Parking: Free, if a bit complex. Rack rates: C$175–C$450 (US$144–US$369) double; ask about off-season rates. AE, MC, V.*

Mercer Hall Inn
$$–$$$ Stratford

With ten rooms on two floors, the Mercer Hall Inn is a relatively new star on the Stratford hotel scene. Opened in 2001, the inn is in the restored old *Beacon-Herald* (the Stratford daily newspaper) building. Each room is individually designed, mostly with king beds (two rooms with queens), covered by down duvets and plush linens in muted tones. Four rooms feature flat-screen TVs and electric fireplaces, and all rooms include a DVD player (a DVD library is available in the lobby) and are amply sized with room for a sitting area and chaise longue. Bathrooms are adequate in size — though not extravagantly large — and most include a shower/tub combination. The inn's rooms are on two floors above the Tango Coffee Bistro (see listing in the upcoming "Where to dine" section), and there is no elevator, though the inn will make sure your luggage gets to your room without you lugging it up the carpeted stairs.

See map p. 237. 108 Ontario St. ☎ *888-816-4011 or 519-271-1888.* www.mercerhallinn.com. *Parking: Free. Rack rates: C$125–C$200 (US$103–US$164) double May–Oct; C$75–C$150 (US$62–US$123) double Nov–Apr. Rates include continental breakfast. AE, MC, V.*

Where to dine

Like the best theater towns (Toronto, New York, and London come to mind), Stratford has a great selection of restaurants to cater to out-of-town theatergoers. For a day trip, I'm assuming that you're more interested in spending your evenings at the theater rather than lingering over an extended gourmet meal (though all restaurants in town clearly know where their bread-and-butter comes from, making sure that all theatergoers finish their meals on time). So the restaurants reviewed in this section — as well as **Bentley's** and **The Annex** (mentioned in the preceding section) — are casual and easy on the budget, but you'll still enjoy a good meal.

If you want to include a fine dinner in your Stratford itinerary, two of the best options are Rundles and The Church, both of which offer a prix-fixe menu. Tables at **Rundles** (9 Cobourg St.; ☎ **519-271-6442**; www.rundlesrestaurant.com) overlook the Avon River, providing a tranquil setting for a menu that changes regularly but always includes entree selections from the vegetarian, seafood, poultry, and meat categories. If your perfect meal always ends with the perfect dessert, the Grand Dessert is a sampling tray of Rundles' desserts. Tables at **The Church** (70 Brunswick St.; ☎ **519-273-3424**; www.churchrestaurant.com) overlook the towering stained-glass front of a church nave — dare I say, a heavenly setting for dinner. In addition to the three- and four-course prix-fixe menus, The Church offers a changing à la carte menu that is just as likely to include ostrich or wild boar as it is seafood or steak.

Fellini's Italian Caffe and Grill
$–$$ Stratford   ITALIAN

This eatery is a good choice for both pre-theater and no-theater dining. If you're attending a play after dinner, the menu offers enough light choices, including salads, individual pizzas, and reasonably sized pastas that won't weigh you down (or leave you feeling drowsy) during the show. If you're planning to relax at your table while other patrons suck down dessert in time for the 8 p.m. curtain, Fellini's features a variety of traditional Italian entrees, including a nice but filling stuffed chicken marsala, as well as baked calzones that are highly recommended but take a little longer to prepare. The wine list is adequate with an emphasis on wines from Italy and Ontario.

See map p. 237. 107 Ontario St. ☎ **519-271-3333.** www.fellinisstratford.com.
Reservations accepted Dec–April; lunch reservations only May–Nov. Main courses:
C$7–C$18 (US$5.75–US$14.75). AE, MC, V. Open: Mon–Thurs 11:30 a.m.– 8 p.m.,
Fri–Sat 11 a.m.–9 p.m., Sun noon to 8 p.m.

Tango Coffee Bistro
$ Stratford   BISTRO

Funky, fresh, and not-quite-free are the best descriptors of this light-fare
eatery connected with the Mercer Hall Inn. Fellini's may be another F-word
for this place, operated by the same folks who run the popular Italian
eatery across Ontario Street (see listing earlier in this section). Breakfasts
feature a couple of choices of deep-dish quiche and deliciously crusty
baked strata (egg and toasted-bread casserole) to go along with the usual
pastries and coffee. Lunch and dinner options range from salads and wraps
to more quiche, lasagne, and even pizza. But go for the sandwiches — on
thick-sliced whole-wheat or flaxseed bread, with the freshest of toppings.
For under C$7 (US$5.75), add a bowl of homemade soup or a small platter
of three kinds of salads — a great deal. A licensed bar is on-site as well; try
the local Waterloo Dark on tap. Friday and Saturday nights, the bistro hosts
live Canadian-heritage music, ranging from blues to jazz to folk and more.

See map p. 237. 104 Ontario St. ☎ **519-271-9202** *or 519-271-1888.* www.tango
coffeebistro.com. *Reservations not accepted. Main courses: Breakfast under*
C$5 (US$4.10); lunch and dinner C$6–C$8 (US$4.90–US$6.55). AE, MC, V. Open: Mon
7:30 a.m.– 4 p.m., Tues– Sat 7:30 a.m.–7 p.m., Sun 8 a.m.–4 p.m.

York Street Kitchen
$ Stratford   ECLECTIC

Breakfasts are yummy and filling; the breakfast burrito can really get your
morning off to a kick, especially if you add a dash of one of the dozens of
hot, hot sauces available at the counter. Dinners are wholesome and also
filling, featuring meat loaf, ribs, and pastas. But the only reason that York
Street Kitchen is a must-stop on my Stratford trips is the sandwiches. No
more requests for mustard on the side or for leaving off the onions: here
you create your own sandwich. Start with your basic smoked turkey or
egg salad or liverwurst (on a choice of seven home-baked breads, of
course) and add just about anything your little deli heart desires. Like a
little horseradish with your roast beef? It's yours. A few black olives with
your peanut butter and jam? Go crazy. If you're decision-phobic, you can
choose from a handful of pre-designed sandwiches — but why hold back?
Seating is limited in a tiny and narrow eating area, but a take-out window
is open during the warm months so that you can pick up your sandwich
and head for the river or a nearby park bench for a makeshift picnic.

See map p. 237. 41 York St. ☎ **519-273-7041.** www.yorkstreetkitchen.com.
Reservations not accepted. Main courses: Breakfast C$4.75–C$5.95 (US$3.90–US$4.90);
sandwiches C$3.25–C$6.25 (US$2.65–US$5.15); dinner C$12–C$17 (US$9.85–US$14). AE,
MC, V. Open: Daily 8 a.m.– 8 p.m. (closes at 3 p.m. during off-season).

Don't fritter away St. Jacobs' shopping

On the way to Stratford (or on the way back to Toronto, for that matter), consider a detour to the tiny village of St. Jacobs, located just north of Kitchener. This community (population 1,400) can welcome as many visitors as it has residents — and more — on a busy summer weekend day. The draw? Shopping, shopping, and more shopping — and a bit of culture, if you're so inclined.

Founded as a Mennonite community in the mid-1800s, residents have worked the fertile land for over 200 years. Some of the earliest buildings are still standing — including the St. Jacobs Schoolhouse Theatre and The Steiner House — and are accessible to visitors. Okay, so much for the culture.

Remember the draw? Shopping, shopping, and more shopping. The village boasts over 100 shops and boutiques selling wares of all shapes and styles. The emphasis, however, is on crafty bits — especially traditional Canadian crafts, many with a Mennonite heritage. From beads to quilts, from candy to maple syrup, St. Jacobs is likely to have something you're looking for — or just can't pass up.

The village also is home to some significant outlet shopping, with many of the outlet standbys such as Liz Claiborne, Levi's, and Rockport. But you really want to schedule your visit to St. Jacobs for a Thursday or Saturday (or even a Tuesday between June and Labour Day). On those days from 7 a.m. to 3:30 p.m. (8 a.m. to 3 p.m. on summer Tuesdays), the St. Jacobs Farmers Market & Flea Market becomes the real attraction, packing in locals and visitors (from Ontario and beyond) for fresh treats and bargains galore. If you're uncomfortable in tight spaces and in the crush of humanity, you may want to stay outdoors on Saturdays, as the market's indoor hall is wall-to-wall and counter-to-counter people — but at least venture inside far enough to line up for a fresh apple fritter or six, made on the spot.

The Niagara Region: Wine, Theater, Casinos (and the Falls)

Navigate the so-called Golden Horseshoe (the communities around the western point of Lake Ontario) along the QEW for about 90 minutes or so, and you'll reach the Niagara region. You can easily spend a couple of days in and around this area and still not see everything of interest. So depending on your personal tastes — be they wine tasting, theater, recreational gambling, or the natural wonder that is Niagara Falls — you can create your own themed day trip.

Getting there

Taking the train or bus to Niagara Falls is a viable option. On the train, the two-hour journey will run you around C$60 (US$49) round-trip riding VIA Rail (☎ 888-842-7245; www.viarail.ca). The hour-and-a-half bus ride will cost about C$55 (US$45) round-trip riding via Greyhound (☎ 800-661-8747; www.greyhound.ca) and runs more frequently than the train. But you'll likely end up at a disadvantage without your own wheels to cruise around in.

Driving to the Niagara area is pretty easy in that it's six-lane provincial highway just about the whole way. However, those six lanes (three, I guess, since you can only travel one direction at a time) can fill up pretty quickly if you're anywhere near weekday rush-hour time in Toronto (generally 7 to 10 a.m. and 3 to 6 p.m., but often worse). So if your first stop is an 8 p.m. play at the Shaw Festival in Niagara-on-the-Lake, allot plenty of extra time to make the curtain.

To get to the Niagara region from downtown Toronto, get on the Gardiner Expressway heading west. The Gardiner becomes the Queen Elizabeth Way (QEW) just past Highway 427, and the QEW takes you all the way to Niagara Falls, with an exit for Niagara-on-the-Lake on the way. By avoiding rush hour in Toronto, the 130-km (81-mile) drive takes 90 minutes and a bit.

Planning your personal themed day trip

Niagara is more than just the falls — at least, it is on the prettier side of the falls. The Niagara region has developed some renown as a wine-growing region, and the Shaw Festival has been producing quality theater since the early 1960s. And even the prettier side of the falls — that would be the Canadian side, in case you had any doubts about my personal preference — has its tacky charms, with new casinos opening up in Niagara Falls.

Discovering the falls — and other Niagara natural bounty

There are plenty of reasons why Niagara Falls from the Ontario side is the best. Visitors have a better vantage point from which to view the falls, the public park area that lines Niagara Parkway alongside the falls is immaculately kept, and the first departure of one of the Maid of the Mist tours (the boat ride that takes you as close as you can get to the falls) is from the Canadian side. Don't limit yourself to the falls portion of the Niagara Parkway; the drive north of the falls is nearly all lovely parkland, with several worthwhile stops along the way (see the "Niagara Falls" map, later in this chapter).

✔ The most breathtaking way to see the falls is aboard one of the boats of the **Maid of the Mist** (☎ 905-358-5781; www.maidofthemist.com). You will get wet as you cruise past both American Falls and Horseshoe Falls, though the plastic ponchos provided offer some protection on a calm day. The boarding dock is at the foot of Clifton Hill just south of the Rainbow Bridge. Admission is C$13 (US$11.50) adults and C$8 (US$6.55) children ages 6 to 12; children under 5 are free.

✔ A couple of observation towers offer an above-the-falls view of the natural wonder, but you're better off sticking with the free ground-level view alongside Niagara Parkway and saving your bucks for the

Maid of the Mist. If you insist on a tower view, **Skylon Tower,** 5200 Robinson St. (☎ **905-356-2651;** www.skylon.com), offers the most to do, with both an indoor and outdoor observation area and a revolving restaurant. Admission to the observation deck is C$10.50 (US$8.40) adults, C$9.50 (US$7.60) seniors, and C$6 (US$4.90) children 12 and under.

✔ The **Niagara Parks Botanical Gardens,** 2565 Niagara Parkway (☎ **905-356-8554;** www.niagaraparks.com), makes up in beauty what it lacks in size. You won't need more than an hour to view the gardens that include an herb garden, a rock garden, and an arboretum. You can walk about on your own for free (parking is C$5/US$4.10), or join a guided tour for C$3 (US$2.45). Open year-round from dusk to dawn.

✔ Just up the road, the **Butterfly Conservatory,** 2405 Niagara Parkway (☎ **905-371-0254;** www.niagaraparks.com), is a climate-controlled conservatory that allows you to observe native and non-native butterflies in a rain-forest setting. Kids of all ages enjoy this little piece of the tropics in Ontario. Admission is C$10 (US$8.20) adults, C$6 (US$4.90) children ages 6 to 12; free for children 5 and under.

✔ The final must-see on the Niagara Parkway north of Niagara Falls is the **Floral Clock**, 14004 Niagara River Parkway (no phone; www.niagaraparks.com). This free attraction was built in 1950 and measures 12m (40 feet) in diameter, the clock face planted with a floral and greenery design that changes twice a year. It is at its most handsome during spring, when planted predominantly with violas; the summer and fall image features primarily colorful ground cover. Open April through September.

Gaming in Niagara

While it's certainly true that the Canadian side of Niagara Falls is the prettiest (I promise, this is the absolute last reference to the prettiest side of the falls), the city itself has had a bit of a seedy reputation — at least in appearance. That is changing, gradually, partially helped along by the opening of two casinos in town — Casino Niagara and Niagara Fallsview Casino Resort. Both casinos are open 24 hours a day, and both offer a variety of restaurants and lounges to sate the hungry and thirsty gambler.

✔ **Casino Niagara:** The first casino in town, Casino Niagara, 5705 Falls Ave. (☎ **888-946-3255;** http://discoverniagara.com/casino/main), opened in 1996. To keep even the heartiest gambler occupied, you can find 79 table games, including the standards such as blackjack, roulette, poker, and baccarat, as well as over 2,400 slot machines. The casino features both a Hard Rock Cafe and a Planet Hollywood, which seems a bit redundant if you ask me. Five other restaurants and cafes, as well as a number of bars and lounges, are scattered throughout the casino.

Niagara Falls

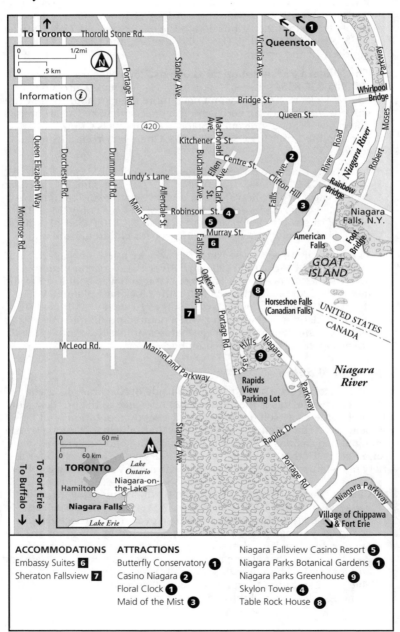

To Toronto   Thorold Stone Rd.

To Queenston

Information ⓘ

Victoria Ave.

Portage Rd.

Stanley Ave.

420

Queen Elizabeth Way

Dorchester Rd.

Drummond Rd.

Lundy's Lane

Main St.

Allendale St.

Kitchener St.

MacDonald Ave.

Buchanan Ave.

Ellen Ave.

Clark St.

Centre St.

Bridge St.

Queen St.

Falls Ave.

Clifton Hill

River Road

Robert

Mosson

Niagara River

Whirlpool Bridge

Rainbow Bridge

Niagara Falls, N.Y.

Robinson St. 4

5

Murray St.

6

Fallsview Dr.

Oakes Blvd.

American Falls

Foot Bridge

GOAT ISLAND

ⓘ

8

Horseshoe Falls (Canadian Falls)

UNITED STATES

CANADA

Montrose Rd.

McLeod Rd.

Marineland Parkway

Stanley Ave.

Portage Rd.

7

Upper Niagara River

Hills

9

Rapids View Parking Lot

Niagara River

Niagara Parkway

Rapids Dr.

Portage Rd.

Niagara Parkway

Village of Chippawa & Fort Erie

To Buffalo ↓   To Fort Erie ↓

TORONTO

Hamilton

Lake Ontario

Niagara-on-the-Lake

Niagara Falls

Lake Erie

ACCOMMODATIONS	ATTRACTIONS	
Embassy Suites **6**	Butterfly Conservatory **1**	Niagara Fallsview Casino Resort **5**
Sheraton Fallsview **7**	Casino Niagara **2**	Niagara Parks Botanical Gardens **1**
	Floral Clock **1**	Niagara Parks Greenhouse **9**
	Maid of the Mist **3**	Skylon Tower **4**
		Table Rock House **8**

✔ **Niagara Fallsview Casino Resort:** Opened in summer 2004, the newest casino in town has over 150 gaming tables and 3,000 slot machines on its floors. Fallsview, at 6380 Fallsview Blvd. (☎ **888-FALLSVUE;** http://discoverniagara.com/fallsviewcasino), offers more than just gambling and eating and drinking. Vegas-style entertainment takes place in the Avalon Ballroom; recent performers have included the Pointer Sisters, Canadian native Anne Murray, and even the Las Vegas icon himself, Wayne Newton. Local acts and lesser-known names have two other lounges to wow the crowd. A 368-unit hotel is also on-site, with rack rates ranging from C$149 to C$329 (US$122 to US$270) double.

Supporting the arts in Niagara-on-the-Lake

This town (see the nearby "Niagara-on-the-Lake" map) has a distinct Victorian feel to it, which is appropriate given the major attraction in town. The Shaw Festival is a repertory theater that started in homage to playwright George Bernard Shaw, whose early works were written during the peak of the Victorian Age. Just about all you can see and do in this small town is along Queen Street, the main drag. The shopping environment puts one in mind of a Thomas Kincaid painting, and if that's not your style, there's always the theater, which is top-notch.

✔ The original mandate of the **Shaw Festival** (☎ **800-511-7429** or 905-468-2172; www.shawfest.com) was to showcase plays by Shaw and his contemporaries. In 2000, the company expanded the mandate slightly to include plays that are set during Shaw's lifetime (which spanned 1856 to 1950). The Shaw has three theaters in Niagara-on-the Lake, running between 10 and 12 plays per season in repertory. A typical season may see works by Shaw as well as such known authors as Noël Coward, Anton Chekhov, George S. Kaufman, and Oscar Wilde. Ticket prices range from C$47 to C$77 (US$39–US$63) (C$42–C$50/US$34–US$41 for preview performances).

✔ The region's proximity to the U.S. made the area a prime battleground during the War of 1812. Just steps from downtown Niagara-on-the-Lake, **Fort George National Historic Site** (☎ **905-468-4257;** www.pc.gc.ca/fortgeorge) was one hard-fought-over location. The fort has been restored to replicate what the site would have looked like while a combination of British, Canadian, and native forces fought against U.S. soldiers to preserve Ontario for what was then Upper Canada. Site guides are dressed in period costume. Admission is C$8 (US$6.55) adults, C$7 (US$5.75) seniors, and C$5 (US$4.10) for kids ages 6 to 16; free for children under 6. Fort George is open daily, April to October, 10 a.m. to 5 p.m.

✔ With the exception of a few places such as Crabtree & Evelyn and Ten Thousand Villages, shopping in Niagara-on-the-Lake is almost exclusively made up of one-off shops. As such, you're likely to pay a bit more for a similar item than, say, at the Pen Centre in nearby St. Catharines, but the stroll along Queen Street, in and out of shops that interest you, makes for good browsing and even better people-watching.

Niagara-on-the-Lake

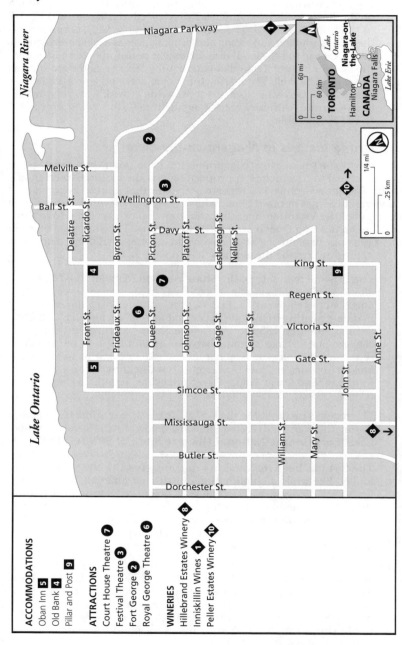

ACCOMMODATIONS
Oban Inn **5**
Old Bank **4**
Pillar and Post **9**

ATTRACTIONS
Court House Theatre **7**
Festival Theatre **3**
Fort George **2**
Royal George Theatre **6**

WINERIES
Hillebrand Estates Winery **8**
Inniskillin Wines **1**
Peller Estates Winery **10**

- Ever try to get one of those personalized license plates or personalized bracelets for someone whose name doesn't happen to be David or Susan? At **Just Christmas,** 34 Queen St. (☎ 905-468-4500), you can get a personalized Christmas ball ornament for anyone on your Christmas list — from Bridget to Harper to Samantha — in just ten minutes.

- For handmade fudge and other sweet goodies, **Maple Leaf Fudge,** 114 Queen St. (☎ 905-468-2211), has satisfied sweet tooths in Niagara-on-the-Lake since 1967. As is standard for these type of establishments, you can see the whole process of making the fudge right on-site — a handy diversion if you're visiting with kids.

- **Lakeshore Antiques & Treasures,** 855 Lakeshore Rd. (☎ 905-646-1965), crams over 600 sq. m (6,000 sq. ft.) of floor space with, ahem, antiques and treasures of all kinds. Not in the heart of Niagara-on-the-Lake, it's nevertheless worth the trip along the road to St. Catharines, both for the pleasant drive and for the large selection of merchandise to browse through.

Discovering Ontario wines

Ontario's Niagara region has quietly built a reputation for wine growing and, with the Okanagan Valley region of British Columbia, has to be considered among the premier wine regions in Canada. And many of the finest wineries are right around Niagara-on-the-Lake within just a few minutes' drive of each other. Most are open year-round for tours and tastings. With their proximity, you can easily take in two or three wineries in a single day; the tours are fairly standard, however, so you really only need to save time for one.

If you decide to take in a number of wineries in a day, be smart about designating a driver for the travel to, from, and among wineries. And remember that other drivers in the area may also have visited a winery or two and may not be driving as smartly as you. Even if you're a teetotaler, the two-lane roads around Niagara-on-the-Lake require cautious driving even for sober drivers, never mind for someone who has had a couple of tastings down the road.

- ✔ In the mid-1970s, **Inniskillin Wines,** off Niagara Parkway at Line 3 (☎ 905-468-3554; www.inniskillin.com), was the first modern winery to open up in this area. Inniskillin offers free guided tours year-round (twice a day daily from May through October, and twice a day weekends only from November through April). A wine store and tasting bar are also open year-round for purchases and samples.

- ✔ A year-round daily tour schedule is one of the draws of **Hillebrand Estates Winery,** 1249 Niagara Stone Rd. (☎ 905-468-7123; www.hillebrand.com). The free hourly tours (running from 10 a.m. to 6 p.m.) include an end-of-tour tasting. A tasting bar separate from the tour is also available four times a day for C$5 to C$8 (US$4.10–US$6.55) per guest.

✔ **Peller Estates Winery,** 290 John St. E. (☎ **905-468-4678;** www.peller.com), is on its third generation of family wine growers since the first Peller Winery opened in British Columbia in the 1960s. Peller celebrates that heritage and more during its hourly year-round tours offered daily 10:30 a.m. to 5:30 p.m. Samples in the tasting room range from C$1 to C$5 (US82¢–US$4.10).

Where to stay

If your day trip to the Niagara region keeps you there overnight, your best bet for finding the most availability is in either Niagara Falls or Niagara-on-the-Lake. But each destination offers some distinctive lodging choices.

For a healthy selection of chain hotels, it's tough to beat Niagara Falls. (Of course, it's also a great destination for small roadside motels and motor courts, for the Norman Bates fans among you.) Logically, you'll pay quite a bit more for a room with a view of the falls than for what most locations call a "cityview" room. You'll also want to make sure that your "fallsview" room doesn't actually have a landscape view of the hotel directly between you and the falls, with an obscured view of the falls just over the south corner of its roof. Ask when making your reservation about the quality of the "fallsview."

For an overnight in Niagara Falls, you can start with one of the familiar names listed here, or check with **Niagara Falls Tourism** (☎ **888-918-2888;** http://discoverniagara.com), which operates a 24-hour booking service. One of the newest additions to the crowded hotel scene is the **Embassy Suites,** 6700 Fallsview Blvd. (☎ **800-420-6980** or 905-356-3600; www.embassysuitesniagara.com). The hotel's triangular shape affords a greater percentage of its 42 stories of rooms with some kind of fallsview; rack rates range from C$115 to C$325 (US$94–US$267) double, depending on season and view. The **Sheraton Fallsview,** 6755 Fallsview Blvd. (☎ **800-618-9059** or 905-374-1077; www.fallsview.com), is one of the more established hotels battling for prime viewing acreage on the Canadian side of the falls; rack rates start at C$129 (US$106) for off-season cityview and go up to C$289 (US$237) for summer fallsview.

If you want something a little more quaint — well, quite a bit more quaint — consider bunking (luxurious bunking, that is) in Niagara-on-the-Lake. The town's Chamber of Commerce offers an accommodation booking service (☎ **905-468-4263;** www.niagaraonthelake.com) that can reserve accommodations at most of the establishments in Niagara-on-the Lake.

With over 400 units in four properties around town, **Vintage Inns** (☎ **888-669-5566;** www.vintageinns.com) is the most logical place to begin to find a room, though the rooms are also just about the most expensive in the area, starting at C$225 (US$185) double from May through October. Room rates are identical in each of the four properties, though the Oban Inn offers the most peace and quiet and the Pillar and Post is the most opulent.

For a less opulent lodging experience, the **Old Bank House,** 10 Front St. (☎ **905-468-7136;** www.oldbankhouse.com), was once the first home of the old Bank of Upper Canada, the house dating from before 1802. The nine units of this bed-and-breakfast are individually decorated, and all have private baths. Rates range from C$125 to C$225 (US$103–US$185) and include a full gourmet breakfast.

Where to dine

If one of your top criteria for selecting a destination is the quality of its restaurants, take Stratford over the Niagara region. Niagara Falls restaurants cater to the assembly-line tourists, shuttling busloads of diners in and out of their restaurants fast enough to allow the next busloads through. Niagara-on-the-Lake has a bit more selection, but not quite the diversity that you find in Stratford.

The Oban Inn
$$$–$$$$ Niagara-on-the-Lake   CONTINENTAL

A popular destination for locals celebrating family holidays over an elegant Sunday brunch spread, the Oban offers festive twists to standard-bearer entrees during other mealtimes as well. Specialties focus on the region's British heritage, tempting diners to sample a traditional beef with Yorkshire pudding or chicken marinated in stout ale. While an acquired taste, the classic meringue is a melt-in-your-mouth (literally!) knockout for dessert. Arrive early for a pre-dinner drink in the over-the-top mahogany-wood and tartan-carpeted lounge. Breakfast and lunch is also served.

See map p. 246. 160 Front St., Niagara-on-the-Lake. ☎ *905-468-2165.* www.vintageinns.com. *Reservations required. Main courses: C$22–C$43 (US$18–US$35). AE, MC, V. Open: Daily 7:30–10 a.m., 11:30 a.m.–2 p.m., 5–9 p.m.*

Queenston Heights Restaurant
$$ Queenston   CONTINENTAL

Though a dinner menu is available (and on average about ten bucks more expensive than the lunch menu), lunch is the best meal here. The food is solid, if not spectacular, with basics such as salads, sandwiches and wraps, and entrees that take advantage of the fresh local ingredients available to the kitchen. The service is adequate, about what you'd expect for a park-operated establishment. No, the real draw here is the setting and the view. Located along the Niagara Parkway, Queenston Heights sits at the edge of the Niagara Escarpment, and the panoramic view from the restaurant out the dining room's tall bank of windows is as stunning as that of any revolving tower restaurant.

14184 Niagara Parkway, Queenston. ☎ *905-262-4274.* www.niagaraparks.com. *Reservations recommended. Main courses: C$13–C$18 (US$11–US$15) lunch; C$21–C$30 (US$17–US$25) dinner. AE, MC, V. Open: Lunch daily noon to 3 p.m.; dinner Apr–Oct Mon–Sat from 5 p.m.; Sun brunch 11 a.m.–3 p.m.*

Part V
Living It Up after Dark: Toronto Nightlife

The 5th Wave   By Rich Tennant

"Toronto's a very sophisticated place, but it's also a hockey town. That's why Hamlet was holding a goalie mask when he said "Alas, poor Yorick..."

In this part...

If Part IV surveys Toronto's options for taking in the city during the day, then Part V clues you in to what's happening around town after the sun goes down. From world-class theater to improvisational comedy, from pubs and taverns to hotel bars and classy clubs, Toronto has many nightlife alternatives to consider.

Chapter 15

Toronto's Cultural Scene

*T*oronto tourism groups love to boast that Toronto is Broadway North when it comes to staging and promoting theater. (This is not to be confused with Toronto as Hollywood North, where the U.S. film industry comes to save money on production costs for movies, television shows, and commercials — which is also not to be confused with Vancouver, British Columbia's claim to be Hollywood North, but that's the subject of another debate.) The city's theater fans and visitors had grown used to the idea of hit productions running on for year after year after year. *The Phantom of the Opera,* for example, played Toronto for ten years. The year 2003, however, was not one of the best for Toronto theater.

A slump in theater admissions, which was widely blamed on extensive media following a SARS outbreak, precipitated the closing of long-running shows and the slow openings of new productions in Toronto. The Toronto production of *The Lion King* ended in November 2003 after nearly four years of stellar success. The musical *Mamma Mia* went on a three-month hiatus during the normally busy summer season. And *The Producers,* an instant and smash success when it opened on Broadway, stumbled out of the Toronto box-office gate with mediocre ticket sales, eventually closing after less than a year in production.

Toronto theater has since rebounded somewhat. *Mamma Mia* returned and has now entered its fifth year. The popular *Hairspray* ended a successful short run in late 2004. The quality and energy of the variety of local theater groups continued to rebound from their own SARS-related slumps.

And if the stage doesn't intrigue you, explore the other cultural options available in the city, including orchestra, opera, and concerts. The "Toronto Nightlife" map, later in this chapter, can help with your exploration.

Toronto Nightlife

NIGHTLIFE:

Amsterdam Brewing **25**
  Company
Avenue **2**
The Cameron House **6**
Canoe Bar **17**
Canon Theatre **12**
Club 22 **1**
Horseshoe Tavern **7**
Hummingbird Centre **16**
  for the Performing Arts
The Laugh Resort **23**
Library Bar **18**
Madison Avenue Pub **4**
Mahogany Lounge **23**
Massey Hall **11**
Molson Amphitheatre **26**
Montréal Bistro & **14**
  Jazz Club
Princess of Wales **21**
  Theatre
Rex Jazz and Blues Bar **9**
Roof Lounge **3**
Roy Thomson Hall **19**
Royal Alexandra **20**
  Theatre
Second City **24**
Shmooze **22**
The Silver Dollar Room **5**
St. Lawrence Centre **15**
  for the Arts
Top O' the Senator **13**
Winter Garden Theatre **10**
Yuk Yuk's **8**

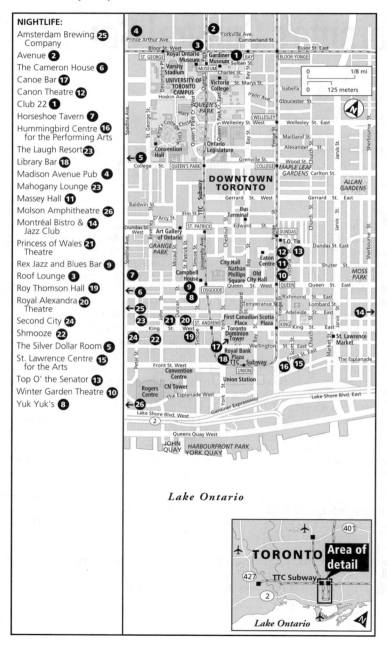

Getting the Inside Scoop

Wherever your performing arts interests lie, you'll find something to your liking while in Toronto. And the facilities that host the variety of performances are world class, many of them theaters that have been in operation for decades.

The so-called Entertainment District is only the beginning when it comes to outstanding theater and concert venues. Here's a rundown of some of the major facilities in and around town.

- ✔ **Entertainment District:** It may be only the beginning, but this area is still the main draw for high-profile performing arts in Toronto. The heart of this area is a four-block radius surrounding King Street West between John and Simcoe streets. With two theaters, the Princess of Wales and the Royal Alexandra (box office ☎ 416-872-1212; www.mirvish.com) and Roy Thomson Hall (the city's premier concert hall at 60 Simcoe St.; box office ☎ 416-872-4255; www.roythomson.com), as well as Canada's Walk of Fame, you can take in a lot of culture without ever having to hail a cab.

- ✔ **More Mirvish:** Mirvish is *the* theater production company in town when it comes to Broadway-type shows. In addition to the Princess of Wales and Royal Alexandra theaters, Mirvish produces plays at the Canon Theatre and the Winter Garden Theatre, both on Yonge Street between Dundas and Queen streets.

- ✔ **Historic Massey Hall:** Having presented theater and concerts since the 1890s, Massey Hall, 178 Victoria St. (box office ☎ 416-872-4255; www.masseyhall.com), is now primarily reserved for concerts and comedy shows, with a wide variety of acts ranging from Alison Krauss to Marilyn Manson.

- ✔ **Staging in St. Lawrence:** (The market, not the seaway.) A couple of performing arts venues are located in the St. Lawrence Market area. The St. Lawrence Centre for the Arts, 27 Front St. E. (box office ☎ 800-708-6754 or 416-366-7723; www.stlc.com), is home to a number of local performing arts troupes, including the CanStage theatre company and Music TORONTO for chamber music. The Hummingbird Centre for the Performing Arts, 1 Front St. E. (box office ☎ 416-393-7476; www.hummingbirdcentre.com), hosts a variety of touring shows (from concerts to plays to kids' programs) and is the home (for now) of both the Canadian Opera Company and the National Ballet of Canada.

The Four Seasons Centre for the Performing Arts is scheduled to open in 2006. The state-of-the-art entertainment facility at Queen Street and University Avenue will be the new home of the national opera and ballet companies.

✔ **Outdoor concert-going:** The Molson Amphitheatre, located in Ontario Place, 909 Lakeshore Blvd. W. (☎ **416-260-5600;** www.hob.com/venues/concerts/molsonamp), is the major outdoor concert facility in the Toronto area. Most acts are of the pop, rock, and hip-hop variety, but you can occasionally take in a more "cultured" show featuring performers such as the Three Tenors, B.B. King, or Pink.

Unless you've scammed some tickets to a gala premiere of some sort, don't worry too much about what to wear to a show or a concert. There's little in the way of dress code at Toronto's performing arts venues, so follow the masses and consider a business-casual look for your evening wear.

To be safe, try to get to your show or concert at least 20 minutes before performances begin. Companies generally like to get things going on time around here in staid Toronto, so if you arrive fashionably late, you may miss enough of a performance to be fashionably out of touch.

Finding Out What's Playing and Getting Tickets

The free Toronto arts weekly *NOW Magazine* is available in street newspaper boxes all over town. The tabloid features a weekly calendar of arts events from the major companies to the local troupes, as well as individual concert and comedy events. You can also access the calendar online at www.nowtoronto.com.

Another good online resource for discovering the goings-on around Toronto is the Web version of the local daily *Toronto Star* (www.thestar.com).

With the following two exceptions, all the major performing arts companies in Toronto operate their own booking facilities, both via phone and online. Check with the individual companies listed in the next section for details and contact information.

✔ **TicketKing** (☎ **800-461-3333** or 416-872-1212; www.ticketking.com) is the ticketing agent for performances at all the Mirvish theaters (Princess of Wales, Royal Alexandra, Canon, and Winter Garden). You can purchase tickets from them online or over the phone, and you can also get to the online ticketing site through the Mirvish site (www.mirvish.com).

✔ **Ticketmaster** (☎ **416-870-8000;** www.ticketmaster.ca) is your best bet for non-company events such as concerts and sporting events. Attending a Canadian Opera Company performance or a concert at the Molson Amphitheatre also requires a conversation (online or otherwise) with Ticketmaster.

For same-day half-price tickets, check out the T.O. TIX booth in Dundas Square (on the southeast corner of Dundas and Yonge). The vendor also has a limited number of advance discounted tickets. Tickets available include those for theater, dance, comedy club, and musical shows in Toronto, as well as some plays at the out-of-town Stratford Festival (Stratford) and Shaw Festival (Niagara-on-the-Lake), both within two hours' drive of Toronto. You can purchase these discounted tickets only in person, but you can find out which shows are being discounted daily by calling the T.O. TIX hotline at ☎ **416-536-6468,** ext. 40.

Raising the Curtain on the Performing Arts

A big city in so many ways, Toronto has a variety of big-city offerings on the performing arts front as well.

Taking in a show: Toronto theater

Mirvish Productions (☎ **416-593-0351;** www.mirvish.com) dominates the popular-theater community in Toronto, bringing in a host of Broadway and off-Broadway productions for their Canadian premieres. Past successful runs include *The Lion King, Mamma Mia,* and a ten-year run of *The Phantom of the Opera.* Single-ticket prices range from C$56 to C$94 (US$46–US$77). Mirvish Stages productions in four downtown theaters:

- ✔ Princess of Wales Theatre, 300 King St. W.
- ✔ Royal Alexandra Theatre, 260 King St. W.
- ✔ Canon Theatre, 244 Victoria St.
- ✔ Winter Garden Theatre, 189 Yonge St.

CanStage (the Canadian Stage Company; box office ☎ **416-368-3110;** www.canstage.com) showcases Canadian plays and playwrights, as well as international works, with an annual series of six to nine productions including new plays developed through its CanStage Play Development program. The company's primary venue is the Bluma Appel Theatre in the St. Lawrence Centre for the Arts. Single-ticket prices range from C$26 to C$77 (US$21–US$63).

With a season of five to six productions, **Soulpepper Theatre Company** (☎ **416-203-6264;** www.soulpepper.ca) may have moved from its current home at Harbourfront to a new facility in the Distillery District by the time you arrive in Toronto. The young company (founded in 1999) focuses on classic productions; recent seasons have featured works by Samuel Beckett, Brian Friel, and Anton Chekhov. Single-ticket prices range from C$30 to C$49 (US$25–US$40).

Theater alfresco

The Toronto cultural scene offers a couple of out-door theater opportunties during the summer. **CanStage** produces one Shakespeare play for performances at the Amphitheatre in High Park, the city's west-end park. The evening performances have become a Toronto summer tradition, now nearing 25 years of productions. Admission is free, but a C$15 (US$12) donation is encouraged. Performances are generally held Tuesday through Sunday starting at 8 p.m.

In 2004, a second outdoor Shakespeare tradition (at least its producers hope it will become one) began with the inaugural production by the **ShakespeareWorks Company** (☎ 416-463-4869; www.shakespeareworks.com). ShakespeareWorks by the Lake presented *Romeo and Juliet* at a new outdoor stage—well, large tent really—in Ashbridge's Bay Park near The Beaches.

Attending the symphony

Under the musical direction of Peter Oundjian, the **Toronto Symphony Orchestra** (box office ☎ 416-593-4828; www.tso.ca) performs a full season at Roy Thomson Hall. The season runs from September through June, and regularly welcomes such well-known guest artists as Yo-Yo Ma and Joshua Bell. Single-ticket prices range from C$27 to C$115 (US$22–US$94).

Music TORONTO (☎ 416-214-1660; www.music-toronto.com) performs chamber music with a variety of individual and ensemble performers. The company performs from October through April at the St. Lawrence Centre for the Arts. Single-ticket prices range from C$39 to C$43 (US$32–US$35) and are available only through the St. Lawrence box office (☎ 416-366-7723; www.stlc.com).

Following the surtitles: Toronto opera

Offering seven operas each season—between September and April—the **Canadian Opera Company (COS)** (☎ 416-363-6671; www.coc.ca) is the largest opera company in Canada. Founded in 1950, the COS currently performs at the Hummingbird Centre for the Performing Arts, but hopes to be in its new home—the Four Seasons Centre for the Performing Arts on the corner of University Avenue and Queen Street—in time for its 2006–07 season. The company is a technological pioneer in addition to an operatic leader, having invented surtitles, a translation of the opera's libretto that is projected onto a screen above the stage. The technology was first used in 1983.

Jazzing it up in Toronto

The **Toronto Downtown Jazz Festival** (www.tojazz.com) is 10 nights of jazz at nearly 40 venues in and around, appropriately enough, downtown Toronto. A main stage at Nathan Phillips Square is the focal point for the biggest names and bigger crowds, and is also one of a half-dozen venues that offer free daytime performances throughout the festival.

For three nights in late July, Queen Street East shuts down to all vehicular traffic and opens up to thousands of jazz lovers flooding to Toronto's east end for the **Beaches International Jazz Festival** (☎ 416-698-2152; www.beachesjazz.com). Dozens of ensembles set up stage on street corners and in front of storefronts on Queen between Woodbine and Beech avenues. This Streetfest takes place Thursday through Saturday nights of the festival from 7 to 11 p.m. A main stage is set up in Kew Gardens (west of Queen St. and Lee Ave.) for Saturday and Sunday afternoon performances by higher-profile groups.

The opening year of the Distillery District (2003) also included the first **Distillery Jazz Festival** (☎ 416-588-9094; www.distilleryjazz.com). Seven venues inside the Distillery District host a variety of individual performers and ensembles over eight nights in May.

Dancing to the beat

The **National Ballet of Canada** (☎ 416-345-9686; www.national.ballet.ca) presents eight productions in a season that runs from November to May. Home base for this company is the Hummingbird Centre for the Performing Arts, but the National Ballet plans to move to the Four Seasons Centre for the Performing Arts by 2006. Single-ticket prices range from C$36 to C$126 (US$30–US$103).

Chapter 16

Hitting the Clubs and Bars

• •

In This Chapter

▶ Clubbing it: Toronto's clubs and pubs
▶ Clubbing it in style — Toronto's best hotel bars
▶ Sounding out Toronto's music scene
▶ Seeking out laughs in the big city

• •

*W*hether you're in the mood to down a quick pint or linger over a long cocktail, this chapter suggests a few prime spots to consider, including the best hotel bars in the city.

If you need a little music, comedy, or dancing to go with your drink, this chapter also helps you find a fun nightspot. For a more complete listing of nightclub entertainment, the free Toronto arts weekly *NOW Magazine* is available in street paper boxes all over town. The tabloid features a weekly calendar of arts events that includes most of the local music and comedy venues. The calendar is also accessible online at www.now toronto.com. Another good online resource for discovering the goings-on around Toronto is the Web version of the local daily *Toronto Star* (www.thestar.com). To find the locales discussed in this chapter, refer to the " Toronto Nightlife" map in Chapter 15.

Yes, Toronto's restaurants are all smoke-free, and most Toronto hotels also prohibit smoking in public areas. And don't even think about the exhibition halls of Toronto's museums. If you're a smoker, you have only one option — find a bar, right? Wrong. As of summer 2004, bars are also no-smoking zones (though you will find locations scattered around the city that have created "designated smoking rooms"). Look on the bright side: Think of your Toronto visit as a forced smoking-cessation plan.

Doing the Bar Scene: Pubs and Clubs Style

For the young urban professional set, Toronto is a terrific after-hours schmoozing town (especially at Shmooze, one of the newer, currently hot locations). No matter which neighborhood you end up in at night, you can find plenty of choices for a snappy (or snooty) martini. If you prefer to sample the local brew, no need to settle for a Moosehead or

Labatt. Creemore Springs has a nice hefty lager, Steam Whistle is a good choice for a lighter lager, and Sleeman brews a variety of light and dark ales and lagers.

The recommendations in this section are so minimal, in comparison to the volume of drinking holes in Toronto, that it's hard to even say they're representative. For a few more ideas, consider also the following restaurant/bars reviewed in Chapter 10:

- ✔ Allen's (The Danforth)
- ✔ Bedford Academy (The Annex)
- ✔ The Black Bull (Queen West)
- ✔ C'est What? (St. Lawrence Market)
- ✔ Irish Embassy Pub & Grill (Financial District)
- ✔ The Pilot Tavern (Bloor/Yorkville)
- ✔ Quigley's (The Beaches)
- ✔ Rebel House (Rosedale)
- ✔ The Rivoli (Queen West)

You won't be able to drink through to breakfast in Toronto; bars and pubs generally close around 2 or 3 a.m. When heading home, remember that plenty of cabs roam the city streets during the late-night hours — at most locations, you'll only need to wait a few minutes, if at all, before seeing one drive by whatever bar you're at — so take one and leave the rental car in the hotel garage.

✔ For house-brewed beer (from both a bar and a retail store), the **Amsterdam Brewing Company,** 600 King St. W. (☎ **416-504-1040;** www.amsterdambeer.com), is a worthy stop for beer-lovers. Locals enjoy a couple of lagers and even a stout beer, as well as the specialty beers Amsterdam brews, including the Nut Brown and the Framboise (fermented with raspberries). Tours of the brewery are available Friday through Sunday for C$10 (US$8.20), which includes a half-dozen samples. Amsterdam has a second brewing location in the basement of The Strand, a new steakhouse at 75 Victoria St. (☎ **416-368-7771**).

✔ If you make it as far west as Spadina while on a walk along Queen Street, don't stop. Cross the street and admire the unavoidable exterior of **The Cameron House,** 408 Queen St. W. (☎ **416-703-0811;** www.thecameron.com). From the giant ants crawling above the muraled exterior, to the monthly exhibitions of local artists, to the artsy regulars that frequent the establishment, The Cameron is an eye-opening experience. Oh, and yes, these regulars gather for shots and beer in a great room or for regular local bands in a back room.

✔ At the **Canoe Bar,** TD Bank Tower, 66 Wellington St. (☎ **416-364-0054;** www.canoerestaurant.com), sip a S'Mores martini — vanilla vodka, crème de cacao, and toasted marshmallow — or one of the other martinis from a cocktail menu that changes monthly. The Canoe Restaurant is one of the premier dining spots in the city, with one of the best views of the waterfront from its 54th-floor perspective, and the bar menu reflects the sophistication of the restaurant's offerings.

✔ **Dora Keogh,** 141 Danforth Ave. (☎ **416-778-1804;** www.allens.to/dora), a traditional Irish pub, is right next door to Allen's (see Chapter 10) — they have the same owner — and is favored by locals as a stop for a pint or a shot. The dark décor even features a fireplace and a "snug."

✔ A British-style pub in the heart of The Beaches action, **Lion on the Beach,** 1958 Queen St. (☎ **416-690-1984**), is an informal pub that's popular with residents and non-residents alike. The pub has two patios — one on the corner of Queen and Kenilworth, the other quietly nestled between the pub and its neighboring retail buildings — and hosts live music on weekends.

✔ Encompassing three old Victorian homes in The Annex, **Madison Avenue Pub,** 14 Madison Ave. (☎ **416-927-1722;** www.madisonavenuepub.com), has the feel of the neighborhood pub gone production line. There's plenty to do here — and plenty of people to see, many drawn from the nearby University of Toronto — but very little intimacy. Granted, intimacy is hard to achieve when you can accommodate a couple of thousand patrons on any given night.

✔ With cathedral ceilings, dark cherry-wood tones, and, of course, a large open space for, er, schmoozing, **Shmooze,** 15 Mercer St., just across the street from the Hotel St. Germain (☎ **416-341-8777;** www.shmooze.ca), is a plush lounge in every sense of the word, with a large outdoor patio for summer partying. Expect to wait in a lineup at this spot, presently one of the hottest clubs in town, unless you splurge for the C$20 (US$16) "front-of-the-line access." Shmooze definitely caters to the up-and-coming, with a 25-year-old age threshold (for men — 23 for women). Open Friday and Saturday only until 2 a.m., cover is C$7 (US$5.75).

Doing the Bar Scene: Hotel Style

Some of the most stylish bars in Toronto are in the most stylish hotels in Toronto. This section previews a few of the best and the darkest.

✔ Perhaps the Four Seasons is paying a backhanded compliment to the Roof Lounge at the Park Hyatt across the street. The primary bar in this 32-story hotel is on the ground floor (the 32nd floor is reserved for meeting rooms). Nevertheless, **Avenue,** 21 Avenue Rd. (☎ **416-928-7332;** www.fourseasons.com/toronto), is a sophisticated venue — starting with its imposing onyx bar — for a casual glass of wine or a cocktail with a business associate.

✔ In the heart of the Bloor/Yorkville neighborhood, **Club 22**, in the Windsor Arms Hotel, 18 St. Thomas St. (☎ **416-971-9666;** www.windsorarmshotel.com), is small, but definitely has an updated old-school clubby feel to it (think leather and suede seating, cigars, and grand piano). The cigar lounge is separate, in keeping with Toronto's non-smoking bylaw, and thus convenient for non-smokers.

✔ With dark leather chairs accompanying two levels of seating, dark wood paneling, and bookshelves full of (mostly untouched) literature, the **Library Bar** in the Fairmont Royal York, 100 Front St. W. (☎ **416-368-2511;** www.fairmont.com), has the classic feel of a traditional hotel bar on the main floor of a massive old-style city hotel — which, of course, is what it is. Stop by for lunch (daily noon to 2:30 p.m.) when the atmosphere — if not the fare — is a little lighter. Stout-battered sole fish and chips headline the pub-style menu that includes sandwiches, soups, and salads.

✔ At **The Lounge,** in the Drake Hotel, 1150 Queen St. W. (☎ **416-531-5042;** www.thedrakehotel.ca), you could start hanging out at 11:30 a.m.; take advantage of a lunch menu that may include (as it did on one visit) both an all-day breakfast of bacon and eggs and grilled chili-rubbed lamb chops served with a creamy cucumber salad; watch Queen Street pass by outside its massive floor-to-ceiling windows; catch the occasional live nighttime act; and stay on through the evening for the sushi bar.

✔ On the Park Hyatt's 18th floor, the **Roof Lounge,** 4 Avenue Rd. (☎ **416-324-1568;** www.parktoronto.hyatt.com), bills itself as the only rooftop bar in Toronto, which is not quite true unless you're talking about rooftops higher than two or three floors above the street. Nevertheless, it's a vintage location for classic cocktail, complete with fireplace, leather furniture, and marble-top tables. Prepare to spend prettily, however, for the experience.

✔ In the heart of the Entertainment District, you can find one of those classic hotel scotch-and-cigar bars that you typically see on a Broadway stage or on a Hollywood (or Hollywood North) sound stage. The **Mahogany Lounge,** at the Holiday Inn on King, 370 King St. (☎ **416-599-4000;** www.hiok.com), is just that kind of place, tucked away in a fairly remote part of the hotel (a lower-level corner location). The lounge features a single-malt scotch bar, a separate cigar lounge, and pool tables to help pass the time.

Following the Music

Most of Toronto's big-venue shows take place at the Molson Amphitheatre, the Air Canada Centre, or even the Rogers Centre (formerly known as the SkyDome). If you prefer the intimacy of the smaller venues, check out some of the offerings here. Or, if you prefer to just follow the music, Toronto's unofficial "clubbing district" is along Richmond Street, west of University Avenue (just north of the slightly-more-official Entertainment District).

✔ Loud, louder, and loudest is a good way to describe the music and dance scene at **The Docks,** 11 Polson St. (☎ **416-469-5655;** www.thedocks.com). With a half-dozen clubs and party rooms, not counting rooms reserved for private events, this massive complex on the waterfront draws partiers in by the throng. In summer, much of the activity centers around the Patio, with an outdoor dance floor, bar, pool tables, and such. You can also work on your golf game, baseball swing, or even your rock climbing prowess at its year-round outdoor sporting complex. Cover ranges from C$10 to C$15 (US$8.20–US$12).

✔ Over the years, the classic **Horseshoe Tavern,** 370 Queen St. W. (☎ **416-598-4753;** www.horseshoetavern.com), has hosted the likes of The Police, Melissa Etheridge, The Rolling Stones, Bruce Cockburn, and The Ramones. Since its opening in 1947, the tavern has also triggered the rise of such Canadian bands as Blue Rodeo and The Tragically Hip. But most importantly, the Horseshoe is in a prime nightlife location (right in the heart of Queen Street West) and a great stop at which to hear Canadian bands of all genres, from rock to rockabilly, from blues to ska. Cover ranges from C$3 to C$5 (US$2.45–US$4.10) during the week and C$5 to C$10 (US$4.10–US$8.20) on weekends.

✔ Since 1979, the **Montréal Bistro & Jazz Club,** 65 Sherbourne St. (☎ **416-363-0179;** www.montrealbistro.com), has hosted the likes of Montreal native Oscar Peterson, Diana Krall, George Shearing, Marian McPartland, and more. Check the Web site to find out who's playing when you're in town; if an act interests you, you should have a good chance of catching them—most sign on for a weeklong gig. The bistro features an adequate selection of fairly standard meat, seafood, and poultry dishes (C$12–C$25/US$9.85–US$15).

✔ Just west of University Avenue, the **Rex Jazz and Blues Bar,** 194 Queen St. W. (☎ **416-598-2475;** www.jazzintoronto.com), offers at least two sets a day, seven days a week (up to 18 sets during any given week). The big names do occasionally show up (say, Diana Krall or Harry Connick Jr.), but the atmosphere at the Rex is decidedly local, with regular and semiregular combos and soloists appearing on stage. Cover ranges from free to C$10 (US$8.20).

✔ A steady stream of blues masters make their way through Toronto with a prerequisite stop at **The Silver Dollar Room,** 486 Spadina Ave. (☎ **416-763-9139;** www.silverdollarroom.com). Jazz, bluegrass, R&B, and more are also regulars on the musical menu. Covers range from C$8 to C$18 (US$6.55–US$15).

✔ At the **Top O' The Senator,** across from the Canon Theatre, 253 Victoria St. (☎ **416-364-7517;** www.jazzintoronto.com), the bar and front wall are lined with long, slick, leather seating and small round tables, not unlike something you might find in a Prohibition-era speakeasy. One floor above the Senator Diner (see Chapter 10), the jazz generally doesn't get going until at least 8 p.m., but it's well worth the wait. Occasionally, big names such as Branford Marsalis, Diana Krall, and Cyrus Chestnut schedule a set or two. Covers can be pricey (ranging from C$8–C$25/US$6.55–US$21).

Tracking the Laughs: Toronto's Comedy Clubs

With high-profile comics such as Jim Carrey, Dan Aykroyd, Eugene Levy, and Mike Myers hailing from Canada, it's not surprising that Toronto has a robust comedy-club profile. Many of these talents got their start at Second City, still going strong in Toronto after 30 years. You can catch stand-up acts at a few music clubs around town, but for a pure comedy experience, try one of these establishments.

✔ When it's not highlighting stand-up talent from Canada or from south of the border, **The Laugh Resort,** at the Holiday Inn on King, 370 King St. W. (☎ **416-364-5233;** www.laughresort.com), occasionally hosts some bigger names on the comedy circuit. Past guests have included Ray Romano, Ellen DeGeneres, and Adam Sandler. And Wednesday nights feature an open mike, perhaps introducing the next big name to a hopeful audience. With shows Wednesday through Saturday, covers range from C$7 to C$15 (US$5.75–US$12).

✔ Generally recognized as the top comedy club in the city, the **Second City** complex, 56 Blue Jays Way (☎ **800-263-4485** or 416-343-0011; www.secondcity.com), now includes a training center for up-and-coming comics (Tim Sims Playhouse), a restaurant (Leoni's Italian Kitchen), and a long-running production of the campy *Tony n' Tina's Wedding.* This comedy troupe mini-industry got its start in Chicago (home to such Second City alumni as Alan Arkin, Robert Klein, Bill Murray, and John Belushi) in 1959. Toronto's club was the troupe's first expansion, opening in 1973, and its stage has seen the likes of John Candy, Gilda Radner, Martin Short, Ryan Stiles, and Colin Mochrie, in addition to the stars listed at the beginning of this section (and dozens more from Canada and the U.S.). Shows — like live, extended *Saturday Night Live*–style sketches — run Tuesday through Sunday (closed Mondays); ticket prices range from C$20 to C$34 (US$16–US$28).

✔ If Second City is the place to be for comedy sketches, **Yuk Yuk's,** 224 Richmond St. W. (☎ **416-967-6425;** www.yukyuks.com), is the premier stand-up franchise. And *franchise* is the correct term, with 13 franchised clubs across Canada. But Toronto remains the headliner location, drawing such names as Jim Carrey and Jerry Seinfeld to the stage. Covers range from C$10 to C$17 (US$8.20–US$14) for the Wednesday through Sunday shows; Tuesday's Amateur Night show is C$2 (US$1.65); and the club is closed Mondays.

Part VI
The Part of Tens

The 5th Wave   By Rich Tennant

"Sure, there's room for one more. Everyone just
scrunch back a little."

In this part...

As if the rest of this book hasn't done enough to stoke
the fire of curiosity about visiting the city of Toronto,
this fun and slightly irreverent part — a standard feature of
every ...*For Dummies* book — may be just enough to put your
destination decision to bed. In this part, you'll find lists of tips
to help you maximize whatever time you have in Toronto. I
offer suggestions for what to do in Toronto when you have an
extra hour or two to kill, recommendations for specific weeks
to book your visit, and ideas about where to go to get the most
bang for your travel buck. Finally, the Quick Concierge appendix
includes some need-to-know facts about Toronto, as well as a
handy list of travel-related phone numbers and Web sites.

Chapter 17

Ten Things to Do to Fill a Free Hour

*I*t's a beautiful day and the lineup at the CN Tower wasn't nearly as long as you had expected, so you have a bit of time to waste. Or it's a rainy day and your plans for a trip to the Toronto Zoo are a washout. Or you simply have an hour to kill before or after dinner and on your way to a play. This chapter explores a few options if you find yourself in Toronto with a spare hour (or more) to while away.

Drinking Coffee or Beer at a Sidewalk Table

Choose your poison—caffeine or booze—but whatever you drink, all over Toronto you can find spots outdoors to drink it. Whether it's side-walk seating on the narrow sidewalks of Yorkville or patio seating along Queen Street (east and west) or even the plastic tables at a Tim Hortons (no beer, though), Torontonians love imbibing (and dining) alfresco. And, naturally, the nicest days draw the biggest crowds.

Sipping Afternoon Tea at a Toronto Hotel

For something a bit more cultured, cozy up to one of the city's more staid lodging establishments for a spot of afternoon tea and scones. The King Eddy, the Four Seasons, and the Windsor Arms all are fine choices. For the (clotted) cream of the crop, however, the Royal York is home to Canada's only tea sommelier. Never knew there was such a career path? Head over to the EPIC restaurant and find out what skill sets you need to pursue such a career—and to appreciate a carefully selected pot of tea.

Savoring Ice Cream

Just about anywhere in Toronto, you're only a few steps away from an ice cream place — or at least a place that includes ice cream among its offerings. But if you're yearning for something really special of the frozen variety, seek out Greg's Ice Cream (with its famous toasted marshmallow among the flavors to consider) in The Annex, Ed's Real Scoop in The Beaches (the Callebaut milk chocolate is a local favorite), La Paloma Gelateria in midtown at St. Clair and Dufferin (Ferrero Rocher gelato, anyone?), or Hollywood Gelato on Bayside Avenue in Leaside.

Walking the Boardwalk in The Beaches

It may be a little out of your way if you have to be downtown at the end of the hour you have to fill. But the boardwalk that follows the shore of Lake Ontario in The Beaches neighborhood offers one of the more pleasant walks in the city. Just a couple of blocks south of the neighborhood's hub street (Queen Street), the boardwalk is a popular draw for local residents and their kids and/or dogs. Enjoy the lake view. People-watch from one of the dozens of benches along the walk. Admire the Toronto skyline to the west (albeit over the unseemly stretch of lower-rise industrial facilities to the east of downtown). And, whatever you do, look both ways (twice) before you cross the parallel paved path used by cyclists and in-line skaters.

Checking Out the Antiques Stores on Queen

If you have time on your way back downtown from your walk on the boardwalk, the eight or ten blocks along Queen Street East between Carlaw Avenue and Leslie Street include eight or ten smallish antiques shops worth exploring. All Most Antiques, City Rooster, and Zig Zag Collectibles are among the best, but all are within easy walking distance of one another.

Strolling through Kensington Market

Not much more than half a kilometer square (about a fifth of a square mile), Kensington Market won't take long to cover, but it's an hour well spent. The vintage-clothing shops and fruit-and-vegetable markets and specialty and eclectic vendors of this culturally diverse district offer a world tour, all in a few blocks. The markets of the area serve clientele from surrounding Chinatown, Little Portugal, Little Italy, and beyond.

Browsing the Bookshelves of Toronto

Of course, you don't have to visit Toronto to shop in a bookstore. But browsing for books — either to buy or to pass the time — is part of just about everyone's vacation tradition. In Toronto, you can spend a solid hour (or more) at a number of smaller, independent establishments that offer a fascinating and eclectic collection of books and magazines. Consider Pages Books & Magazines if window-shopping along Queen Street West, or one of the five Book City outlets scattered around town. You can also lose yourself in one of Canada's two book superstores: Chapters or Indigo, both with downtown locations and elsewhere around Toronto.

Lacing Up for a Skate at Nathan Phillips Square

Join the crowds in downtown Toronto — just south of City Hall — for a leisurely skate around the outdoor ice rink at Nathan Phillips Square. (In summer, the rink is a nice little reflecting pool.) Skates are available for rent, but the skating is free. A snack concession stand is nearby, as are ubiquitous fry trucks and hot dog vendors (and a Starbucks across Queen Street).

Checking Out the St. Lawrence Market Vendors

While it's open any day of the week (except Mondays), try to reserve your visits to Toronto's St. Lawrence Market for the weekends. You'll likely spend more than an hour meandering through the Farmer's Market (on Saturdays) or the Antiques Market (on Sundays), but the weekend crowds create a more festive atmosphere and the number of vendors increases (and so too do the number of bargains — or at least, opportunities for bargains).

When in Doubt, Just Look Around

If worse comes to worse, and you have an hour or so to squander but you're not quite sure where to go, take a look around you. Toronto is bursting with vibrant neighborhoods and distinct yet also strangely assimilated cultural heritages. Chances are good that you're just steps away from a fascinating neighborhood that's worth a walkthrough. Chapter 8 previews many of Toronto's neighborhoods.

Chapter 18

Ten (or So) Weeks to Consider for Your Toronto Visit

In This Chapter

▶ Enjoying springtime in Toronto
▶ Savoring Toronto's summer festivals and more
▶ Moving back indoors for the fall
▶ Appreciating winter

*Y*es, you'll probably notice that some of the events suggested in this chapter are around for longer than a week (longer than a month, in a couple of cases). Or maybe you'll discover that a few of these are only weekend (or even day) events. I appreciate your meticulous reading of the material. I really do, but . . .

If you're looking to narrow down your visit to a particular time period — say, one week — this chapter draws your attention to a few time periods when exciting stuff is happening in and around Toronto. This whirlwind review of fun-filled weeks (give or take) begins in the spring.

Attending Previews at the Stratford or the Shaw

While still not a cheap date, taking in a preview at one of Ontario's two major repertory theater companies is significantly less expensive than paying full price when a play has officially "opened." The best times for previews are in April and May, when both festivals have the most number of preview performances available as they gear up for the beginning of a new season. Both the Stratford Festival in Stratford and the Shaw Festival in Niagara-on-the-Lake are within a couple of hours' drive of Toronto (see Chapter 14).

Following the Leafs in the Stanley Cup Playoffs

You won't find any particularly remarkable date or event on the calendar during the weeks (hopefully) that the Toronto Maple Leafs are participating in the Stanley Cup playoffs (which begin in mid-April and conclude in early June). And you surely won't be able to get any tickets, especially if the Leafs go deep in the playoffs. But sports fans will appreciate the atmosphere of a city that rabidly supports its home team. Marvel at the number of cars on city streets sporting blue-and-white Leafs flags. Smile at the blue-and-white "business" wear on game days. Cheer (and jeer) along with the locals at one of many sports bars around town.

However, if the Leafs make it to the Stanley Cup Finals, and you happen to be in Toronto on a night that the Leafs have even the possibility of winning the Cup, you may want to consider getting out of Dodge. The Leafs haven't won the Stanley Cup since 1967, so the celebration would be, er, festive.

Taking Pride in Pride Week

Covering 3km (nearly 2 miles) of downtown Toronto just west of the city's principal gay district (Church–Wellesley), the colorful Pride Parade is the highlight of **Pride Week.** The weeklong celebration in late June features concerts, speakers, and events that celebrate the diversity of Toronto's gay and lesbian community. Festivities range from beer gardens and arts events to music on several stages in and around Church Street. But the centerpiece is the parade. With nearly a million people lined up along the parade's route, "colorful" is a polite way to describe the parade participants. Extravagant, yes; over the top, perhaps to some; a sight to behold, most definitely.

Partying with the Caribana Crowd

Join the pageantry and color and energy of Toronto's biggest street festival, with more than a million people typically celebrating Caribbean heritage with song, dance, food, and the traditional Parade of Bands, featuring thousands of masqueraded revelers and dozens of bands playing everything from calypso to salsa. Falling over two weeks in the heat of summer (starting in late July), the fun and frivolity can get pretty hot too, including a festive King and Queen masquerade competition, and music and dance events at venues around Toronto. But the nearly 4-km (2.5-mile) Parade of Bands is the can't-miss event if you're visiting Toronto during late July (or some years during early August).

Jazzing Up the Streets of Toronto

Taking over Queen Street East in The Beaches neighborhood for one weekend every July, the Beaches International Jazz Festival is an outdoor celebration coming up on 20 years strong. Over 750,000 music lovers wander up and down Queen Street, which is closed to traffic for the duration, taking in the various styles of jazz emanating from street corners, storefronts, and even rooftops. Upwards of 50 combos participate in this three-night-long streetfest, with bigger-name groups performing at an outdoor stage in Kew Gardens, on Queen Street, on Saturday and Sunday.

Also taking place during summer is the Toronto Downtown Jazz Festival. This ten-day festival in late June and early July features hundreds of artists performing in clubs, theaters, and outdoor stages throughout downtown.

Tasting on the Streets of Toronto

Capitalizing on the multicultural dining atmosphere in the city, several neighborhoods around Toronto sponsor outdoor weekends highlighting the city's best food. Two of the best are the Taste of the Danforth, featuring the foods of Greektown and more along the heavily restaurant-populated thoroughfare east of downtown, and the Taste of Little Italy, with the best of College Street eateries taking part in the fun and festivities. The Taste of Little Italy takes place in mid-June, and the Danforth event occurs in mid-August.

Enjoying Excitement at the Ex

Officially known as the Canadian National Exhibition (CNE), locals call it simply "The Ex," and it's nearly three weeks of carnival rides, farm and animal exhibits, and, yes, a midway with all the usual games of chance. And of course, you can eat all kinds of standard carnival fare to your heart's content (or detriment). Several stages feature a variety of music and dance acts, though little in the way of internationally renowned acts (unless you count timeless groups such as the Village People). For a chance to join the fun at the CNE at Exhibition Place on the waterfront, follow the crowds during the two-and-a-half weeks leading up to Labour Day.

Screening the Toronto International Film Festival

During ten days in September, you can screen as many as 300 films from over 50 countries at multiple cinemas (and venues set up as temporary cinemas) around downtown Toronto. Well, really, you can't screen them all, given that many films play at conflicting times and you can't be in more than one theater at a time and . . . you get the idea. Nevertheless, the Toronto International Film Festival welcomes the Hollywood elite "home" to Toronto (many films, television shows, and commercials are produced on Toronto sound stages), as well as films and stars and producers and directors from countries around the world. The festival typically takes place in mid-September.

Browsing for Books on the Waterfront

Not at a bookstore, mind you, but at a book-reading series, featuring more than 100 authors reading their own work and sharing in panel discussions over ten days in October. The International Festival of Authors is the premier event of the Harbourfront Reading Series, which runs from September through June at the Harbourfront Centre on Toronto's waterfront. Check the festival schedule to find out if your favorite authors are scheduled to appear. You may just hear a snippet from something that you're dying to read.

Welcoming Santa Claus for the Season

Okay, so admittedly, November often may not be the best time of year to visit Toronto. It can be cold and snowy; it's often cold and rainy; it's just plain cold. But every year, on one Sunday in mid-November, Toronto launches the holiday season with a welcome for Santa Claus, the Santa Claus Parade. The parade has all the standard draws: floats, bands, and red-cheeked kids waiting anxiously for the main man himself.

Another draw in November? The Royal Agricultural Winter Fair, with livestock and agriculture exhibits, the annual Royal Horse Show, and a variety of special guests, sets up its tent for ten days in mid-November at the National Trade Centre.

Celebrating Winter at Its Peak

If you flee to cold weather during winter the way snowbirds flock to Florida, Toronto in February may be just your cup of hot, steaming tea. The City of Toronto sponsors two weeks of free entertainment (at both indoor and outdoor venues, to satisfy the warm- and cold-blooded in everyone) featuring performers and troupes from Toronto's arts community, as well as special culinary events (not free!) and dining packages from local restaurants, all to commemorate the winter season.

Chapter 19

Ten Toronto Bargains (No Matter Your Currency)

*B*argains are great; free is better. This chapter highlights both, recommending some great things to do in and around the city of Toronto that won't cost a lot. And remember, with the current rate of exchange, free in Canadian dollars still equals free in American dollars.

Spending a Day on Centre Island

Just C$6 (US$4.90) buys you a round-trip fare on the Centre Island Ferry that leaves Toronto's Harbourfront every half-hour in summer. You can still spend more money once you're on the Islands (for example, buying ride tickets at Centreville Amusement Park or picking up a couple of pizza slices at one of the concession stands that dot Centre Island), but it's all up to you. You can also take advantage of the many walkways and grassy areas and picnic spots just to enjoy the natural beauty of the Islands — and some prime people-watching.

Taking Time to Smell the Roses

In neighborhoods throughout Toronto you can find public gardens — both big and small — to wander through and appreciate. Gardens worth a special trip include Allan Gardens, with six greenhouses covering more than 1,500 sq. m (16,000 sq. ft.) in downtown Toronto, and the Toronto Music Garden on the waterfront, inspired by Bach's "Suites for Unaccompanied Cello."

Talking to the Animals at Riverdale Farm

From the working farm, complete with horses, cows, goats, sheep, pigs, and chickens, to the well-kept floral and herb gardens to the live demonstrations of a variety of farm life activities, Riverdale Farm is one of the best values in Toronto, especially for families with young kids. No feeding the animals, but your kids can interact with them under the helpful supervision of farm staff.

Browsing for Bargains at Honest Ed's

Is it shopping? Is it entertainment? What exactly is it? Since founded in 1948 by Ed Mirvish (patriarch of the Mirvish Productions family), Honest Ed's has been a bargain-basement tradition in Toronto. Head west from downtown on Bloor Street and look for the garish marquee surrounding the corner of Bloor and Bathurst. There you'll find 15,000 sq. m (160,000 sq. ft.) of merchandise, as they say, priced to sell! Even if you're not in the market for anything, a visit just for the experience is well worth the price of admission, which of course is free. Scattered throughout the store are Honest Ed's corny adages, guaranteed to elicit a chuckle or a groan ("Honest Ed attracts squirrels because at his prices, they think he's nuts."). Of course, part of the production are the store's promotions, though none as outrageous as the very first on the store's opening day: "Name your own price — no reasonable offer refused!"

Following the Crowds to ROM Friday Nights — It's Free!

For museum-goers on a budget, you can't beat Friday nights at the Royal Ontario Museum. Between 4:30 and 9:30 p.m. every Friday, admission is free, except for temporary exhibitions that carry an additional charge of C$10 (US$8.20) adults, C$5 (US$4.10) for seniors, students, and children.

Other museum bargains in Toronto include free Thursday nights (after 5 p.m.) at the Bata Shoe Museum and "Pay What You Can" Wednesday nights (after 5 p.m.) at the Textile Museum of Canada.

Spending an Evening with the Bard in High Park

A 1,000-seat amphitheater in High Park is the setting for a 20-plus-year tradition in Toronto theater. Evenings during July and August, CanStage (the Canadian Stage Company) presents a work by Shakespeare . Officially, admission is free, though the company suggests a C$15 (US$12) donation. For the quality of the production, the donation is a bargain; throw in a warm night under the stars and the donation becomes an outright steal.

Opening Doors to Toronto's Diverse Architecture

Doors Open Toronto is a free two-day event that opens more than 100 buildings of architectural or historic interest to the public. What's significant about the event (besides its admission charge — none!) is that many of the sites are either closed to the public the other 363 days of the year or are accessible only with a paid admission. To walk through these open doors, schedule your visit to Toronto during the last weekend of May.

Finding Fireworks — Not Just One Night a Year, but Two!

Canada celebrates its nation's birthday (Canada Day on July 1) with fireworks, just like its more populous neighbor to the south. But that's only the beginning. Another fireworks party takes place the weekend before Memorial Day. Victoria Day weekend (also known as the May two-four long weekend — so named to celebrate either the date of Queen Victoria's birth or the 24-packs of beer consumed by Canadians during the weekend, it's not quite clear), marks the beginning of summer, and Canadians use the long weekend to make sure the gardens are in shape, to open up summer cottages north of Toronto, and to consume those previously mentioned cases of beer.

You can see fireworks from locations around the city. The prime staging areas are at Ashbridge's Bay Park in The Beaches (the fireworks look great from the boardwalk), at Nathan Phillips Square in downtown next to City Hall, and at Mel Lastman Square in North York, north of Toronto proper.

Perusing the Galleries in the Distillery District

The opening of the Distillery District in 2003 did more than introduce a potentially thriving new arts scene to Toronto — for travelers on a budget, the Distillery District is a must-see stop on the Toronto bargain tour. Even if you just want to meander through the grounds, admiring the old distillery buildings or watching your step on the original brick paths, the Distillery District makes for a comfortable — and free — stroll. On the way, you can window-shop in the eclectic array of shops, browse several of the handsome galleries, and settle in for a cup of good coffee at Balzac's — all for only the price of the coffee and a minimal parking charge (if you drive).

Taking a Chance on Half-Price Theater Tickets

Have an itch to take in some quality theater but not sure whether your vacation budget can withstand the burden of a full-price ticket or two? Head for Dundas Square (on the southeast corner of Dundas and Yonge, just across from the Eaton Centre) to check out the daily offerings at the T.O. TIX booth. The ticket booth sells a limited number of same-day half-price tickets for theater productions in Toronto, as well as some plays at the out-of-town Stratford and Shaw festivals. You may also be able to pick up advance tickets for dance shows and comedy club revues. Call ahead (☎ **416-536-6468,** ext. 40) to find out which shows are available on that day.

Appendix

Quick Concierge

• •

This appendix is filled with handy alphabetical lists of phone numbers, Web sites, and other tidbits of information that you can turn to when planning your trip to Toronto.

Fast Facts

American Express

Toronto has two major American Express travel offices that handle such business as emergency card replacement, currency exchange, and traveler's check transactions. In the **Holt Renfrew Building** at 50 Bloor St. W. (☎ 416-967-3411), hours are Monday to Wednesday 10 a.m. to 6 p.m., Thursday and Friday 10 a.m. to 7 p.m., and Saturday 9 a.m. to 4 p.m. At the **Fairmont Royal York**, 100 Front St. W. (☎ 416-363-3883), hours are Monday to Friday 8:30 a.m. to 5:30 p.m.

To make inquiries or to locate other branch offices, call ☎ 800-297-2977 or visit www.americanexpress.com.

Area Codes

The Toronto metropolitan area has three area codes: **416** and **647** for most of Toronto proper and **905** for the surrounding communities.

ATMs

Automated teller machines (ATMs) are widely available throughout Toronto (you may also see them called ABMs). They're one of the best options for getting cash at a favorable exchange rate. The two most popular ATM networks are **Cirrus** (☎ 800-424-7787;

www.mastercard.com) and **Plus** (☎ 800-843-7587; www.visa.com). For more about ATMs in Toronto, see Chapter 4.

Baby-sitters

Check with your hotel to find out what baby-sitting services, if any, are available. A local and reputable service is **Christopher Robin** (☎ 416-483-4744; http://christopherrobin.homestead.com).

Business Hours

In Toronto, most public businesses are open by 10 a.m. (11 a.m. or noon on Sundays). Malls generally stay open until 9 p.m. during the week and 6 or 7 p.m. on weekends. Neighborhood businesses tend to close around 7 or 8 p.m. in order to provide service to local residents coming home from work. Bank hours vary, but if you count on similar hours as banks in the U.S., you'll be safe.

Credit Cards

For credit-card emergencies, call the following numbers: **American Express** ☎ 800-992-3404, **MasterCard** ☎ 800-307-7309, and **Visa** ☎ 800-847-2911.

Customs

For details about what you can take home with you from Toronto, see Chapter 12.

Doctors

Every consulate can recommend local doctors and dentists. See the list of embassies and consulates in the "Embassies/Consulates" section, later in this Appendix.

Electricity

Canada uses the same electrical-plug configuration and current as the United States: 110 to 115 volts, 60 cycles.

Embassies and Consulates

All embassies are in Ottawa, Canada's national capital. You can, however, find a number of consulates in Toronto:

The **U.S. consulate,** 360 University Ave. (☎ 416-595-1700; www.usconsulate toronto.ca; TTC: St. Patrick station), is open Monday to Friday 8:30 a.m. to 1 p.m. The **British consulate,** 777 Bay St., Suite 2800 (☎ 416-593-1290; www.britain incanada.org; TTC: College station), is open Monday to Friday 9 a.m. to 4:30 p.m. The **Australian consulate,** 175 Bloor St. E., Suite 1100 (☎ 416-323-1155; www.ahc-ottawa.org; TTC: (Bloor–Yonge station), is open Monday to Friday 9 a.m. to 1 p.m. and 2 to 4:30 p.m. The **New Zealand consulate,** 225 MacPherson Ave., Suite 2A West (☎ 416-947-9696; www.nzembassy.com; TTC: Dupont or Rosedale station), is open Monday to Friday 8:30 a.m. to 4:30 p.m.

Emergencies

Dial ☎ **911** for emergency.

Hospitals

For downtown Toronto hospitals, try **Toronto General Hospital,** 200 Elizabeth St.

(☎ 416-340-3111) or **Mount Sinai Hospital,** 600 University Ave. (☎ 416-596-4200).

Information

For specific travel information, check out the section "Where to Get More Information, " later in this appendix.

Internet Access and Cybercafes

Toronto has plenty of places where visitors can check their e-mail (or catch up on their favorite blog). You can find cybercafes around the city, and your hotel is likely to have Internet access (often high-speed Internet) available. Branches of the **Toronto Public Library** also have banks of computers set up for online use, including the branch at 789 Yonge St. (☎ 416-393-7131; TTC: Bloor–Yonge station).

Liquor Laws

All beer, wine, and liquor is sold in provincially run stores (**The Beer Store** for, well, beer only, and **LCBO** for beer, wine, and liquor). Most are open seven days a week, but the store hours vary. The minimum drinking age in Ontario is 19.

Mail

Canada Post (☎ 800-267-1177 within Canada, or 416-979-8822 from outside Canada; www.canadapost.ca) is the national mail carrier for Canada. To send a first-class letter or postcard costs C50¢ to Canadian addresses, C85¢ to U.S. addresses, C$1.40 to other international addresses. These rates are effective January 2005, but they tend to go up regularly.

Actual post offices are few and far between. Instead, look for one of many "Postal Outlets" around Toronto. Your best bets are pharmacies, travel agencies, or even general stores.

Maps

Contact **Tourism Toronto** (☎ 800-499-2514; www.torontotourism.com) to request a map before your visit. The Web site also has downloadable maps.

Newspapers/Magazines

In addition to the local dailies (the *Toronto Star* and the *Toronto Sun*), Canada's two national newspapers, the *Globe and Mail* and the *National Post,* are both based out of Toronto. *Maclean's* is a Canadian weekly newsmagazine similar to *Newsweek* or *Time.* You should also have no trouble finding newspapers from around the world in this metropolitan city. Check with your hotel to find the nearest newsstand.

Pharmacies

You can find drugstores and pharmacies throughout Toronto, including in the major grocery stores such as Loblaws or Dominion. As in the U.S., Canada has a number of national drugstore chains, but one dominates: **Shoppers Drug Mart**. Most Shoppers Drug Marts are open until midnight, but one downtown Toronto location is open 24 hours (700 Bay St., at Gerrard Street; ☎ 416-979-2424; TTC: College or Dundas station).

Police

In emergencies, dial ☎ **911**.

Restrooms

Truly public restrooms are hard to find in Toronto, but you should still have little trouble finding a clean, safe restroom that's available to the public (called "washrooms" here) in Toronto. Look for them in the lobbies of downtown hotels, in one of the hundreds of coffee shops in the city, or even at strategic locations in the PATH underground walkway.

Safety

For general safety issues, use your common sense, just as you would at home or in any large city. Avoid deserted and poorly lit areas, especially at night. Always lock the doors of your car and don't keep anything valuable inside. Be alert in hotels and don't let strangers into your room unless they are hotel staff that you've called or that you expect to see. Don't hesitate to call the front desk to verify an employee's identity. Store your valuables and cash in an in-room safe (if available) or in the front-desk safe; don't assume your valuables are safe in your hotel room just because it's always locked.

Run by the Toronto Transit Commission (TTC), the Toronto subway system is one of the safest in the world, but still use common sense when traveling at late hours. Also, when riding one of the city's streetcars, take care when disembarking, especially on a road with more than one lane. You don't want to step into the path of the occasional thoughtless driver who passes a stopped streetcar on the right.

Toronto is one of the most culturally diverse cities in the world, so your chances of encountering discrimination are lower here than just about anyplace else.

Smoking

The opportunity to smoke indoors is almost nonexistent in Toronto. With few exceptions, if you want to light up, you have to go outdoors. As of 2004, Toronto's smoking bylaws even prohibit smoking in bars and clubs. In some restaurants, bars, and coffee shops, you may find a "designated smoking area," essentially a fully enclosed, self-contained room with its own separate ventilation system.

Most hotels in Toronto still have designated smoking rooms, but their number is dwindling.

You must be 19 or older to buy tobacco products in Ontario.

Taxes

Throughout Canada, you will be charged a federal **goods and service tax (GST)**, a 7 percent tax on virtually all goods and services. In addition, Ontario has an 8 percent **provincial retail sales tax (PST)**, and Toronto adds a 5 percent **lodging tax.** The good news is that some of the GST you pay is eligible for rebate for non-Canadian residents. See Chapter 4 for details.

Taxis

When in downtown Toronto (or even some of the more heavily trafficked neighborhoods, such as The Beaches or Bloor West Village), you should have little trouble hailing a cab. If you need to call for a taxi, try one of these: **Beck Taxi** (☎ 416-751-5555; www.becktaxi.com), **Crown Taxi** (☎ 416-750-7878; www.crowntaxi.com), or **Royal Taxi** (☎ 416-777-9222; www.royaltaxi.ca).

Telephone

The Canadian phone system is the same as in the U.S. Canadian phone numbers have 10 digits: The first three numbers are the area code; the remainder is a seven-digit local number.

To call a number within Toronto, you have to dial the area code plus the seven-digit number. If you're making a long-distance call, you need to precede the local number with "1" plus the area code.

To make a call to an international destination outside Canada and the U.S., dial 011 and then the country code (U.K. 44, Ireland 353, Australia 61, New Zealand 64). Next you dial the area code and number.

For directory assistance in Toronto, dial ☎ **411**. For operator assistance, dial ☎ **0** (zero). Toll-free numbers in Canada begin with the 800, 888, 877, 866, and 855 prefixes.

Time Zone

Toronto lies in the Eastern time zone, which is the same time zone as New York City, Philadelphia, Miami, and all other cities up and down the eastern seaboard. The city observes daylight saving time from April to October.

Tipping

The rules for tipping in Canada parallel those in the United States. For good service in a restaurant, tip 15 to 20 percent. Tip hairdressers or taxi drivers 10 percent. Bellhops get C$1 per bag for luggage taken to your room; for valets who fetch your car, a C$2 tip should suffice.

Canada's one- and two-dollar coins are quite handy when it comes time to tip. Hang on to them for this purpose as you accumulate change during your trip.

Transit Info

The **Toronto Transit Commission (TTC)** operates all public transit in the city. For information, call ☎ 416-393-INFO or log on to www.ttc.ca.

Weather Updates

To check the weather forecasts online, log on to www.weather.ca, www.weather.com, or www.cnn.com/weather.

Toll-Free Numbers and Web Sites

Airlines

Air Canada
☎ 888-247-2262
www.aircanada.ca

Air New Zealand
☎ 800-262-1234 or -2468 in the U.S.
☎ 800-663-5494 in Canada
☎ 0800-737-767 in New Zealand
www.airnewzealand.com

American Airlines
☎ 800-433-7300
www.aa.com

America West Airlines
☎ 800-235-9292
www.americawest.com

British Airways
☎ 800-247-9297
☎ 0345-222-111 or 0845-77-333-77 in
Britain
www.british-airways.com

Continental Airlines
☎ 800-525-0280
www.continental.com

Delta Air Lines
☎ 800-221-1212
www.delta.com

Northwest Airlines
☎ 800-225-2525
www.nwa.com

Qantas
☎ 800-227-4500 in the U.S.
☎ 612-9691-3636 in Australia
www.qantas.com

United Airlines
☎ 800-241-6522
www.united.com

US Airways
☎ 800-428-4322
www.usairways.com

Car-rental agencies

Advantage
☎ 800-777-5500
www.advantagerentacar.com

Alamo
☎ 800-327-9633
www.goalamo.com

Avis
☎ 800-331-1212 in Continental U.S.
☎ 800-TRY-AVIS in Canada
www.avis.com

Budget
☎ 800-527-0700
www.budget.com

Dollar
☎ 800-800-4000
www.dollar.com

Enterprise
☎ 800-325-8007
www.enterprise.com

Hertz
☎ 800-654-3131
www.hertz.com

National
☎ 800-CAR-RENT
www.nationalcar.com

Payless
☎ 800-PAYLESS
www.paylesscarrental.com

Thrifty
☎ 800-367-2277
www.thrifty.com

Rent-A-Wreck
☎ 800-535-1391
www.rentawreck.com

Major hotel and motel chains

Best Western International
☎ 800-528-1234
www.bestwestern.com

Clarion Hotels
☎ 800-CLARION
www.hotelchoice.com

Comfort Inns
☎ 800-228-5150
www.hotelchoice.com

Courtyard by Marriott
☎ 800-321-2211
www.courtyard.com

Days Inn
☎ 800-325-2525
www.daysinn.com

Doubletree Hotels
☎ 800-222-TREE
www.doubletree.com

Fairfield Inn by Marriott
☎ 800-228-2800
www.marriott.com

Four Seasons
☎ 800-819-5053
www.fourseasons.com

Hampton Inn
☎ 800-HAMPTON
www.hampton-inn.com

Hilton Hotels
☎ 800-HILTONS
www.hilton.com

Holiday Inn
☎ 800-HOLIDAY
www.basshotels.com

Howard Johnson
☎ 800-654-2000
www.hojo.com

Hyatt Hotels & Resorts
☎ 800-228-9000
www.hyatt.com

Inter-Continental Hotels & Resorts
☎ 888-567-8725
www.interconti.com

Marriott Hotels
☎ 800-228-9290
www.marriott.com

Quality Inns
☎ 800-228-5151
www.hotelchoice.com

Radisson Hotels International
☎ 800-333-3333
www.radisson.com

Ramada Inns
☎ 800-2-RAMADA
www.ramada.com

Renaissance
☎ 800-228-9290
www.renaissancehotels.com

Sheraton Hotels & Resorts
☎ 800-325-3535
www.sheraton.com

Travelodge
☎ 800-255-3050
www.travelodge.com

Westin Hotels & Resorts
☎ 800-937-8461
www.westin.com

Wyndham Hotels and Resorts
☎ 800-822-4200 in Continental U.S.
and Canada
www.wyndham.com

Where to Get More Information

Tourism Toronto, 207 Queens Quay W. (☎ **800-499-2514;** www.toronto tourism.com), provides good information about traveling to and in Toronto. They can help you secure a hotel room for your stay, give you leads on what to see and where to dine, and even provide a few tips about what makes the city tick. Before you leave, make sure to check out the Web site, which is chock-full of advice and information, including a current calendar of events.

Find other valuable Toronto information at the following Web sites: the **City of Toronto** (www.toronto.ca); **Toronto.com** for lodging, restaurant, shopping guides, and more (www.toronto.com); **Eye Weekly,** a freely distributed weekly with entertainment listings and restaurant reviews (www.eye.net); *NOW,* another free weekly found throughout town (www.nowtoronto.com); and the Web site of the monthly magazine *Toronto Life,* which regularly features browsable "City Guides" to area restaurants, shops, and opportunities for kids and parents (www.torontolife.com).

For excursions in Ontario beyond Toronto, the **Ontario Tourism Marketing Partnership** (☎ **800-668-2746**) operates a helpful Web site at www.ontariotravel.net, including destination ideas and seasonal travel packages around the province.

Finally, check your local bookstore (or online book retailer) for one of the other books relating to travel in Canada published by Wiley Publishing, Inc., including *Frommer's Canada* and *Frommer's Toronto.* And don't forget the valuable Web site **Frommers.com** (www.frommers.com), for travel tips, reviews, online booking, bulletin boards, travel bargains, and travel secrets for hundreds of destinations.

Index

See also separate Accommodations and Restaurant indexes at the end of this index

General Index

• A •

• *V* •

• *W* •

walking tours, 20, 203–204
wallet lost or stolen, 45–46
War of 1812, 17, 18, 19
Wayport, 71
Web sites
accessible travel, 58–60
airlines, 47–48, 54–55
Airport Express, 79
ATMs, 43
attractions, 179
bed & breakfasts, 109
Canada Border Services Agency, 78
car rentals, 66
city tours, 202–205
clubs and bars, 260
consolidators, 49
credit cards, 68
credit-reporting bureaus, 46
cultural events, 28, 29, 31, 32, 33
customs, 209
exchange rates, 42
family-oriented vacations, 56–57
gay and lesbian travelers, 60–61
Greyhound, 242
health insurance, 69
hotel deals, 105–107, 108
interactive maps, 88
luggage, 73
music events, 30, 31, 256, 258, 259
online travel agencies, 49–50
package tours, 54–55
passport information, 63–64
public transit, 88
restaurant sources, 30, 131–132
senior travelers, 57–58
special events, 27–34
sports tickets, 29, 32, 33, 199–200
taxis, 92
theater tickets, 29, 31, 233, 245, 255, 256
tourism information, 87, 88, 98, 108
train tickets, 51, 232, 241
Transportation Security Administration, 73
travel insurance, 68
traveler's checks, 45
wireless connections, 70–72

wiring money, 46
West Nile Virus, 69
West Queen West, 87
Western Union, 46
Wheel-Trans, 58
White House, 18
Whole Foods Market, 219
Wi-fi, 71
William Ashley, 217
Williams-Sonoma, 219
Winners, 214
Winterfest, 27, 28
winter festivals, 275
Winter Garden Theatre, 255
wireless capabilities, 70, 72
The Word on the Street, 33

• *X* •

Xtra, 60

• *Y* •

Yahoo! Mail, 71
Yonge–University–Spadina subway, 228–230
York (Toronto), 17, 18
Yuk Yuk's, 265

Accommodations Index

Annex Guesthouse Bed and Breakfast, 126
Bentley's/The Annex Inn (Stratford), 238
Best Western Primrose Hotel, 126
Bond Place Hotel, 112
Cambridge Suites Hotel, 113
Clarion Selby Hotel and Suites, 113
Delta Chelsea, 11, 113–114
The Drake Hotel, 114
Embassy Suites (Niagara region), 248
Fairfield Inn & Suites Toronto Airport, 103
Fairmont Royal York, 11, 114–115

Restaurant Index

SPORTS, FITNESS, PARENTING, RELIGION & SPIRITUALITY

0-894413-49-0   0-7645-5418-2

Also available:
- The Bible For Dummies
  0-7645-5296-1
- Buddhism For Dummies
  0-7645-5359-3
- Catholicism For Dummies
  0-7645-5391-7
- Curling For Dummies
  1-894413-30-X
- Golf For Dummies
  0-7645-5146-9
- Hockey For Dummies
  0-7645-5228-7
- Judaism For Dummies
  0-7645-5299-6

- Martial Arts For Dummies
  0-7645-5358-5
- Pilates For Dummies
  0-7645-5397-6
- Religion For Dummies
  0-7645-5264-3
- Rugby For Dummies
  0-470-83405-6
- Teaching Kids to Read
  For Dummies
  0-7645-4043-2
- Weight Training For Dummies
  0-7645-5168-X
- Yoga For Dummies
  0-7645-5117-5

TRAVEL

0-470-83414-5   0-7645-5453-0

Also available:
- Montreal & Quebec City
  For Dummies
  0-7645-5624-x
- Vancouver & Victoria
  For Dummies
  0-7645-3874-8
- Cancún and the Yucatán
  For Dummies
  0-7645-2437-2
- Cruise Vacations For Dummies
  0-7645-6941-4
- Europe For Dummies
  0-7645-5456-5
- Hawaii For Dummies
  0-7645-5438-7

- Ireland For Dummies
  0-7645-5455-7
- Las Vegas For Dummies
  0-7645-5448-4
- London For Dummies
  0-7645-4277-X
- New York City For Dummies
  0-7645-6945-7
- Paris For Dummies
  0-7645-5494-8
- Walt Disney World & Orlando
  For Dummies
  0-7645-6943-0
- Nova Scotia, New Brunswick &
  Prince Edward Island For Dummies
  0-470-83399-8

GRAPHICS, DESIGN & WEB DEVELOPMENT

7645-4345-8   0-7645-5589-8

Also available:
- Adobe Acrobat 6 PDF
  For Dummies
  0-7645-3760-1
- Building a Web Site For Dummies
  0-7645-7144-3
- Dreamweaver MX 2004
  For Dummies
  0-7645-4342-3
- FrontPage 2003 For Dummies
  0-7645-3882-9
- HTML 4 For Dummies
  0-7645-1995-6
- Illustrator cs For Dummies
  0-7645-4084-X

- Macromedia Flash MX 2004
  For Dummies
  0-7645-4358-X
- Photoshop 7 All-in-One Desk
  Reference For Dummies
  0-7645-1667-1
- Photoshop cs Timesaving
  Techniques For Dummies
  0-7645-6782-9
- PHP 5 For Dummies
  0-7645-4166-8
- PowerPoint 2003 For Dummies
  0-7645-3908-6
- QuarkXPress 6 For Dummies
  0-7645-2593-X

NETWORKING, SECURITY, PROGRAMMING & DATABASES

645-6852-3   0-7645-5784-X

Also available:
- A+ Certification For Dummies
  0-7645-4187-0
- Access 2003 All-in-One Desk
  Reference For Dummies
  0-7645-3988-4
- Beginning Programming
  For Dummies
  0-7645-4997-9
- C For Dummies
  0-7645-7068-4
- Firewalls For Dummies
  0-7645-4048-3
- Home Networking For Dummies
  0-7645-42796

- Network Security For Dummies
  0-7645-1679-5
- Networking For Dummies
  0-7645-1677-9
- TCP/IP For Dummies
  0-7645-1760-0
- VBA For Dummies
  0-7645-3989-2
- Wireless All In-One Desk Reference
  For Dummies
  0-7645-7496-5
- Wireless Home Networking
  For Dummies
  0-7645-3910-8

HEALTH & SELF-HELP

0-470-83370-X

0-7645-2566-2

Also available:

- Alzheimer's For Dummies
  0-7645-3899-3
- Asthma For Dummies
  0-7645-4233-8
- Controlling Cholesterol For Dummies
  0-7645-5440-9
- Depression For Dummies
  0-7645-3900-0
- Dieting For Dummies
  0-7645-4149-8
- Fertility For Dummies
  0-7645-2549-2

- Fibromyalgia For Dummies
  0-7645-5441-7
- Improving Your Memory For Dummies
  0-7645-5435-2
- Pregnancy For Dummies †
  0-7645-4483-7
- Quitting Smoking For Dummies
  0-7645-2629-4
- Relationships For Dummies
  0-7645-5384-4
- Thyroid For Dummies
  0-7645-5385-2

EDUCATION, HISTORY, REFERENCE & TEST PR

0-7645-5194-9

0-470-83411-0

Also available:

- Algebra For Dummies
  0-7645-5325-9
- Canadian History
  1-894413-19-9
- Calculus For Dummies
  0-7645-2498-4
- English Grammar
  0-7645-5322-4
- Forensics For Dummies
  0-7645-5580-4
- The GMAT For Dummies
  0-7645-5251-1
- Inglés Para Dummies
  0-7645-5427-1

- ...mmies
- ...Dummies
- ...es
- ...For Dumm
  0-7645-5460-3
- U.S. History For Dummies
  0-7645-5249-X

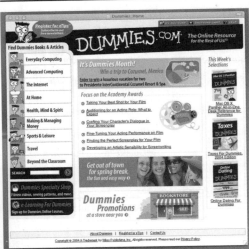

Get smart @ dummies.com

- Find a full list of Dummies titles
- Look into loads of FREE on-site articles
- Sign up for FREE eTips e-mailed to you weekly
- See what other products carry the Dummies name
- Shop directly from the Dummies bookst
- Enter to win new prizes every month!